By the Editors of Consumer Guide®

THE ALL NEW MEDICAL BOOK OF REMEDIES

FOR PEOPLE OVER 50

With Albert Einstein Medical Center
Premier Years Program

COORDINATING CONSULTANTS: SUSAN M. MOYER, M.D., AND DONNA B. FEDUS, M.A.
CONTRIBUTING WRITERS: CHARLES D. BANKHEAD, STEPHEN BREWER,
MARYAN BUCKNUM BRINLEY, EVAN HANSEN, KAREN SANDRICK

Publications International, Ltd.

Consultants:

Premier Years, Albert Einstein Medical Center's free health promotion program for people aged 55 and older, helps empower its more than 51,000 members by educating them about health care, health insurance, entitlements, and other health issues that affect them. Albert Einstein Healthcare Network is a 1,000-bed healthcare system offering a full array of services. With four hospitals and several outpatient centers, it is one of the busiest healthcare organizations in the Philadelphia region. Albert Einstein Healthcare Network, a private, not-for-profit healthcare system, includes Albert Einstein Medical Center; Willowcrest, a center for subacute care; MossRehab Hospital; and Belmont Center for Comprehensive Treatment.

Susan M. Moyer, M.D., is a staff physician in the Division of Geriatrics at Albert Einstein Medical Center in Philadelphia, Pennsylvania, and an Assistant Professor in the Department of Medicine at Temple University. A founding member of the Academy of Hospice Physicians, she served as Medical Director of the Hospice program at Albert Einstein Medical Center from 1984 to 1993.

Donna B. Fedus, M.A., is Director of Premier Years at Albert Einstein Medical Center in Philadelphia, Pennsylvania, a position she has held since 1990. She holds a master's degree in social gerontology and frequently speaks to groups about gerontological issues. As Director of Premier Years, Fedus plans and supervises 100 health promotion programs each year.

Contributing Writers:

Charles D. Bankhead is a freelance writer and editor who specializes in medicine and healthcare. His work appears regularly in a wide range of consumer and physician publications, including *Medical World News* and The University of Texas *Lifetime Health Letter*.

Stephen Brewer is contributing editor of *Longevity* and *Fitness* magazines. He writes on health for numerous publications, including *American Health*, *Family Weekly*, and *Good Housekeeping*.

Maryan Bucknum Brinley is a former editor at *Ladies' Home Journal*, *McCall's*, *Good Housekeeping*, *Family Health,* and *Woman's Day* who writes about health and family issues.

Evan Hansen is an editor and writer who has researched, written, and edited a variety of healthcare publications, including *Health After 50*. His work focuses on a wide range of health-related topics, including medical self-care and geriatrics.

Karen Sandrick is a freelance health and medicine writer who writes regularly for *Oncology News International* and *Diagnostic Imaging*. She also has contributed to *The New Book of Knowledge* and *The New Book of Popular Science*.

Editorial Assistance:
Ruthan Brodsky is a health and medical writer whose work has appeared in a variety of publications, including *Modern Maturity* and *Home Health Care*.

Illustrations: Yoshi Miyake

••

MEDICAL AND TECHNICAL ADVISORS

Harold Adams, M.D., Professor of Neurology, University of Iowa, Iowa City, Iowa

Max Ali, M.D., Hemorrhoid Clinics of America, Oak Park, Michigan

David Allison, M.D., St. Luke's-Roosevelt Hospital, Obesity Research Center, New York, New York

Gita Amini, B.S., Physical Therapist, Hutzel Hospital, Detroit Medical Center, Detroit, Michigan

H. Vernon Anderson, M.D., Associate Professor of Internal Medicine, Division of Cardiology, University of Texas-Houston School of Medicine, Houston, Texas

James Anderson, M.D., Professor of Medicine and Clinical Nutrition, University of Kentucky Medical School, Lexington, Kentucky; Chief of Endocrinology, VA Medical Center, Lexington, Kentucky

Philip Anderson, M.D., Chairman of Dermatology, University of Missouri-Columbia School of Medicine, Columbia, Missouri

Sinan Baran, M.D., Psychiatrist, Sleep Disorders Fellow, University of Michigan Medical Center, Ann Arbor, Michigan

Jeffrey Barnett, M.D., Professor of Internal Medicine, University of Michigan Medical Center, Ann Arbor, Michigan

Herbert Bez, D.O., Chief of Surgery, Botsford Hospital, Warren, Michigan

Henry Black, M.D., Charles J. and Margaret Roberts Professor of Preventive Medicine, Chairman, Department of Preventive Medicine, and Professor, Internal Medicine, Rush-Presbyterian-St. Luke's Medical Center, Chicago, Illinois

Kate Boron, B.A., Athletic Trainer, Assistant Physical Therapist, Health South, Van Nuys, California

Stephen Brinley, D.O., Private Practice, Florence, Alabama

Sheilah Brodsky, M.A., R.D., Chief Clinical Dietician, Michael Reese Hospital, Chicago, Illinois

Jackie Brown, M.A., Director, Mourning and Discipline for Hospice of Michigan, Southfield, Michigan

Felicia Busch, R.D., Spokesperson, American Dietetic Association; Nutrition Consultant, Minneapolis, Minnesota

Rosalind Cartwright, Ph.D., Director, Sleep Disorder Service and Research Center, Professor of Psychology and Chair, Department of Psychology and Social Services, Rush-Presbyterian-St. Luke's Medical Center, Chicago, Illinois

H. Dwight Cavanagh, M.D., Vice Chairman, Department of Ophthalmology, University of Texas Southwestern Medical Center, Dallas, Texas

Nancy Clark, M.S., R.D., Nutritional Counselor, SportsMedicine, Brookline, Boston, Massachusetts

Jerome Cooper, D.O., Surgeon, Oakland General Hospital, Madison Heights, Michigan

Thomas Corbridge, M.D., Pulmonary Specialist, Northwestern Memorial Hospital, Chicago, Illinois

Dennis Costa, Spokesperson, VZV Research Foundation, New York, New York

Peter Creticos, M.D., Respiratory Specialist, Johns Hopkins Asthma and Allergy Center, Johns Hopkins Bayview Medical Center, Baltimore, Maryland

Rubin Cuadrado, M.D., Gastroenterologist, Pinelake Medical Center, Mayfield, Kentucky

Michael Deenihan, D.D.S., Private Practice, Montclair, New Jersey

Seymour Diamond, M.D., Director, Diamond Headache Clinic, Chicago, Illinois

Anne Dougherty, M.D., Associate Professor of Internal Medicine, Division of Cardiology, University of Texas-Houston School of Medicine, Houston, Texas

Steven Edmundowicz, M.D., Professor of Gastroenterology, Thomas Jefferson University Medical School, Philadelphia, Pennsylvania

Walter Evans, M.D., Chief of General Surgery, Hutzel Hospital, Detroit Medical Center, Detroit, Michigan

Eugene Farber, M.D., President, Psoriasis Research Institute, Palo Alto, California

Mark Feinglos, M.D., Endocrinologist, Professor of Medicine, Duke University Medical School, Durham, North Carolina

William Fintel, M.D., Oncologist, Lewis-Gale Cancer Center, Roanoke, Virginia; co-author, *A Medical and Spiritual Guide to Living with Cancer*

Margaret Flaum, R.N., Manager of Lung Line, National Jewish Center for Immunology and Respiratory Medicine, Denver, Colorado

Janet Fogler, M.S.W., Turner Geriatric Services, University of Michigan Medical Center, Ann Arbor, Michigan

Elizabeth Fonpham, M.D., Associate Professor, Department of Pathology, Louisiana State University, New Orleans, Louisiana

Stephen Fortmann, M.D., Deputy Director, Center for Research in Disease Prevention, Palo Alto, California; Associate Professor of Medicine, Stanford University School of Medicine, Stanford, California

Grant Fowler, M.D., Associate Professor of Family Practice and Community Medicine, University of Texas-Houston School of Medicine, Houston, Texas

Barry A. Franklin, Ph.D., Director, Beaumont Cardiac Rehabilitation and Exercise Laboratories, Royal Oak, Michigan

Anne Munoz Furlong, The Food Allergy Network, Fairfax, Virginia

Kim Galeaz, R.D., Spokesperson, American Dietetic Association; Nutrition Consultant, Indianapolis, Indiana

Fae Garden, M.D., Assistant Professor, Physical Medicine and Rehabilitation, Baylor College of Medicine, Houston, Texas

Ray Gifford, M.D., Chairman, Joint National Committee on Detection, Evaluation and Treatment of High Blood Pressure; Cleveland Clinic, Cleveland, Ohio

Patricia Gillespie, R.N., Nebraska Burn Institute, Omaha, Nebraska

Ken Goldberg, Ph.D., Psychologist, Male Health Center, Dallas, Texas

Toni Goldfarb, Editor, *Medical Abstracts Newsletter,* Teaneck, New Jersey

Ken Goodrick, Ph.D., Assistant Professor of Medicine, Baylor College of Medicine, Houston, Texas

Philip Gormley, Wilderness Emergency Medical Technician; Operations Director, Wilderness Medical Associates, Bryant Pond, Maine

Jose Granda, M.D., Ph.D., Internist, Hutzel Hospital, Detroit Medical Center, Detroit, Michigan

David Gurevitch, M.D., Ph.D., Geriatric Psychiatrist, William Beaumont Hospital, Royal Oak, Michigan

Charles Hennekens, M.D., John Snow Professor of Medicine and Ambulatory Care and Prevention, Harvard Medical School, Boston, Massachusetts; Chief of Preventive Medicine, Brigham and Women's Hospital, Boston, Massachusetts

Susan Herdman, M.D., Associate Professor of Otolaryngology, Head, and Neck Surgery, Johns Hopkins School of Medicine, Baltimore, Maryland

Harry Herkowitz, M.D., Chairman, Department of Orthopedic Medicine, William Beaumont Hospital, Royal Oak, Michigan

Mindy Hermann, R.D., Spokesperson, American Dietetic Association, Mt. Kisko, New York

Bruce I. Kaczander, F.A.C.F.A.S., Podiatrist, Private Practice, Southfield, Michigan

Harold Koenig, M.D., Psychiatrist, Internal Medicine, Duke University, Durham, North Carolina

Claudia Kraus, M.S.W., A.C.S.W., Sex Therapist, University of Michigan Medical Center, Ann Arbor, Michigan

Manfred Kroger, Ph.D., Professor of Food Science, Pennsylvania State University, University Park, Pennsylvania; Spokesperson, Institute of Food Technologists, Chicago, Illinois

Audrey Kron, M.A., L.L.P., Center for Coping with Chronic Illness, Hutzel Hospital, Detroit Medical Center, Detroit, Michigan

Jerome Litt, M.D., Assistant Clinical Professor of Dermatology, Case Western Reserve University School of Medicine, Cleveland, Ohio

Richard Mabry, M.D., Professor, Department of Otorhinolaryngology, University of Texas Southwestern Medical Center, Dallas, Texas

Richard Rudick, M.D., Director, Mellen Center for Multiple Sclerosis Treatment and Research, Cleveland Clinic Foundation, Cleveland, Ohio

Sachiko St. Jeor, Ph.D., Director, Nutrition Education and Research Program, University of Nevada Medical Center, Reno, Nevada

Rahul Sangal, M.D., Director, Bloomfield Institute for Sleep Related Disorders, William Beaumont Hospital, Royal Oak, Michigan

Richard Scher, M.D., Professor of Dermatology, Columbia University School of Medicine, New York, New York

Ann Silverman, M.D., Director of Gastroenterology, William Beaumont Hospital, Royal Oak, Michigan; Clinical Associate Professor, Wayne State University School of Medicine, Detroit, Michigan

Lynn Stearn, M.S.W., Senior Social Worker, University of Michigan Medical Center, Ann Arbor, Michigan

Daniel Steptner, Ph.D., Director of Psychology, Department of Psychiatry, William Beaumont Hospital, Royal Oak, Michigan

Robert Stern, Ph.D., Professor of Psychology, Pennsylvania State University, University Park, Pennsylvania; advisor to NASA on motion sickness

Fred Sutton, M.D., Gastroenterologist, Associate Professor, College of Medicine, Baylor University, Houston, Texas

Elizabeth S. Tam, M.S., R.D., Nutritional Counselor, West Bloomfield, Michigan

David Techner, Funeral Director, Kaufman Funeral Home, Southfield, Michigan

Robert Teitge, M.D., Chief of Sports Medicine, Hutzel Hospital, Detroit Medical Center, Detroit, Michigan; Associate Professor of Orthopedic Medicine, Wayne State University School of Medicine, Detroit, Michigan

Peter Terry, M.D., Clinical Director, Johns Hopkins Asthma and Allergy Center, Johns Hopkins Bayview Medical Center, Baltimore, Maryland

J. Thistle, M.D., Gastroenterologist, Mayo Clinic Medical Center, Rochester, Minnesota

Kenneth Thomson, Optician, Private Practice, Upper Montclair, New Jersey

Alicia Tisdale, Ph.D., Clinical Psychologist, Private Practice, West Bloomfield, Michigan

Frank Vinicor, M.D., Director, Division of Diabetes, U.S. Centers for Disease Control and Prevention, Atlanta, Georgia; President, 1995-96, American Diabetes Association

Deborah Weiner, M.D., Rheumatologist, Duke University Medical Center, Division of Geriatrics, Durham, North Carolina

Roberta Wigle, Music Therapist; Co-chairman, 1995 Great Lakes Regional Conference, Ann Arbor, Michigan

Kevin Wildenhaus, Ph.D., Clinical Psychologist; Director of Behavioral Science, Henry Ford Hospital and Health Centers, Department of Family Practice, Detroit, Michigan

Philip Wolf, M.D., Professor of Neurology, Boston University, Boston, Massachusetts; Principal Investigator, Framingham Heart Study, Framingham, Massachusetts

David S. Zee, M.D., Professor of Neurology, Ophthalmology, and Neurosciences, Johns Hopkins School of Medicine, Baltimore, Maryland

CONTENTS

Contents

FOREWORD

SENSIBLE ADJUSTMENT TO CHANGE

Perhaps the discoverer of the mythical fountain of youth will receive an exemption, but for the rest of us, the aging process continues. That shouldn't be surprising. After all, it is a perfectly natural process that begins at birth and follows us forever.

We can't avoid aging, but we can take sensible steps to maintain good health and make adjustments for the medical problems that are likely to arise over time. That's where *The All New Medical Book of Remedies for People Over 50* comes in. It has been tailored specifically to address the health concerns of this growing segment of the population. And it does so by offering practical and medically sound advice on remedies that can be followed at home to prevent, cope with, or treat more than 100 disorders common to this age group. *The All New Medical Book of Remedies for People Over 50* also provides insight into maintaining good health, such as proper diet, exercise, and smoking cessation.

This book is not meant to replace your doctor. On the contrary, we have attempted to draw attention to symptoms that suggest the possibility of a serious problem requiring a doctor's evaluation. In fact, we encourage you to discuss any health concerns or questions—as well as the suggestions in this book—with your doctor.

We also urge you to become actively involved in your own health care. *The All New Medical Book of Remedies for People Over 50* is designed to help.

AGE SPOTS

---

10 SELF-CARE TECHNIQUES

There's nothing like an age spot to make you feel like the passage of time is leaving its mark on you. Well, if it's any consolation, age spots aren't really signs of age, though you're most likely to begin developing them after the age of 40 or so. They are simply the telltale signs of long-term exposure to the sun.

Over the years, the sun wreaks havoc on the skin in many ways. It causes wrinkles, dry skin, and skin cancer. And it is responsible for those round or irregularly shaped, brownish marks on the face, back of the hands, and other areas that are most commonly exposed to the sun.

Age spots aren't dangerous. They don't in themselves become cancerous, although the same sun-induced damage to the epidermal layers that promotes age spots also causes skin cancer. While they are sometimes called liver spots—maybe because of their color or perhaps because they were once thought to be caused by a disorder of that organ—they have nothing whatsoever to do with the liver.

Age spots can be a bit unsightly, though. If their presence bugs you, here are some things you can do to keep from getting them in the first place and to lighten up the ones you might already have.

Slather on the sunscreen.

It's the way to avoid getting age spots and to prevent the ones you have from getting darker. Keep the number 15 in mind: Use a sunscreen that has a sun-protection factor (SPF) of 15 or higher, and apply it at least 15 to 20 minutes before you go out in the sun for full absorption into the skin. Remember to rub sunscreen liberally into the backs of your hands—that's prime age-spot territory.

Wear a hat.

Choose one with a brim that will protect your face and the back of your neck. It's important to use the sunscreen-hat combo even on days that are mildly overcast because skin-damaging ultraviolet rays from the sun can penetrate the clouds.

Don't go out in the heat of the day.

The easiest way to avoid the sun—and age spots—is to stay indoors. Even a sunscreen can't give you thorough, consistent protection when the sun is at full strength, from about 10 A.M. until about 2:00 P.M. (times vary depending on your location relative to the equator).

Hide them.

Not that age spots are anything to be ashamed of, but there may be times when you don't feel like flashing them in front of the world. That's when you should reach for a coverup cream, available at any cosmetic counter. Oil-based creams will probably do a better job than water-based creams at covering up dark spots. Two things to remember when using these products: Make sure they are absorbed completely before you let them come into contact with clothing, because they can rub off and stain; and make sure the product is hypoallergenic, which means the manufacturer has taken care to remove as many potentially irritating ingredients as possible.

Lighten them up.

Hydroquinone cream is the most commonly used lightening agent. It is sold in lower strengths over the counter at most drugstores and is available in higher strengths by prescription. Patience is the rule with hydroquinone creams: It may take months before you see results. Your age spots may still be visible after treatment, but noticeably lighter.

Shed your old skin.

That's what creams containing synthetic lactic acid do, and they replace the old remedy of applying doses of sour milk (which contains lactic acid) to age spots. Lactic acid acts as an exfoliant to slough off the dead skin that builds up on age spots, revealing healthier skin underneath. Sometimes it is used in combination with bleaching agents for extra effectiveness. But lactic acid increases sun sensitivity, so it's important to use a sunscreen in addition to a lactic-acid product.

Go for a peel.

Tretinoin, a prescription-only vitamin-A derivative marketed as Retin-A, can also be used to peel off the dead skin layers atop age spots. The fading process can take a couple of months, with two or three applications a day. Retin-A is widely used for its ability to erase tiny wrinkles, and the same drawback applies to using it for age spots as for wrinkles—it can cause skin inflammation. It also makes the skin sensitive to sunlight, so be sure to use sunscreen to protect the area you are treating.

Localize your treatments.

Whatever method you use, it's important to treat only the age spot. Otherwise, you run the risk of bleaching healthy skin around the age spot, creating an unwanted dappled effect.

Get out some baby oil.

All age spots are not created equal. The ones known medically as solar lentigines are flat and feel no different from ordinary skin; seborrheic keratoses are raised and scaly, and they can feel scratchy to the touch or feel prickly beneath clothing. One way to reform seborrheic keratoses into smoother characters is to rub baby oil or another moisturizer into them regularly. The treatments won't change the appearance of these age spots, but they may make them a little easier to live with.

Look for changes.

Age spots in themselves are not precancerous. However, the long-term exposure to sunlight that causes age spots can also promote the growth of skin cancers. In addition, the same areas of your body that are susceptible to age spots—those that are most often exposed to the sun—are also susceptible to skin cancer. If you notice a change in an age spot—for instance, if it seems to be growing or if sores appear on top of it—see a physician. Most skin cancers are easily curable when treated early enough; left unattended, they can be deadly.●

WHAT A DERMATOLOGICAL SURGEON CAN DO

○ ○ ○

If you want to be rid of age spots once and for all, any number of procedures are available. Laser treatment zaps the area with a pulse of light that destroys the tissue, allowing new, unblemished skin to grow in its place; all you're likely to feel is a sensation like the snap of a rubber band against your skin, then the area will turn bluish-gray for a couple of weeks before healing, a process that takes two or three months to complete. Cryosurgery freezes off the tissue with a metal probe cooled to minus 256 degrees Fahrenheit. The procedure is painless because it freezes nerve endings, too; a blister will develop during the healing process. In electrosurgery, a surgeon burnishes the area with an electrical device that applies high-frequency currency to slough off the tissue. The procedure is done under local anesthesia, and the area will heal in a month or so. Raised age spots, in which the dead tissue forms a heap on top of your skin, can simply be cut away, again under local anesthesia.

Remember, though, the only reason to undergo any of these procedures is cosmetic—there's no need to have an age spot removed unless you just don't like the way it looks. Be sure you are informed about possible risks or complications before deciding to implement any of these treatments.

ALLERGIES AND ASTHMA

26 WAYS TO STAY OUT OF TROUBLE

Allergies can make you feel miserable. Symptoms vary from mild to severe, but if you are one of the 40 million Americans who is allergic, your heart sinks at the first sign of a full-blown reaction. Perhaps your nose starts running and your eyes become watery or red. You may be a sneezer. Some people have itching attacks, get hives, develop a rash or sinus headache and upset stomach. If your allergies trigger asthma, taking a deep breath can become a hurtful chore and feels a little like the shock of cold air in your lungs on a winter day. You may even be able to hear yourself wheeze as you breathe in and out.

Basically, an allergy is an overly exuberant immune-system response to an element or allergen in the environment that you have eaten, inhaled, injected, or simply touched. The real culprit is an allergy molecule called an IgE antibody that attaches itself to cells in your body and can make your life miserable whenever you are exposed to a particular allergen. Depending on where those IgE molecules have attached themselves, you could end up with exploding chemicals on the surface of your skin, up your nose, in your eyes or sinuses, or even in your stomach and bowels. If you have asthma, these tiny chemical explosions set up a chain reaction in your lungs. The lining of your airways swells up. There is an increase in mucous production and a tightening of the airway muscles, making it difficult to breathe.

You can become allergic to more than one allergen at any time in your life, even after your fiftieth birthday. Allergies can develop slowly, over a period of years. Some are season-sensitive, while others come on strong after a sudden change in lifestyle. Have you taken a new job? Moved to a distant state? Adopted a pet?

If your symptoms are mild, perhaps even seasonal, these tips may help to keep you out of serious allergic trouble.

Dodge those triggers.

Identify the things that irritate you, and keep a list of them, a "trigger diary." Examples include pollens, dust, molds, dander (small skin flakes from cats and dogs), dirt, cigarette smoke, woodburning fires, gases, feathers, odors, and rubber (latex) gloves. Also note when and where you experienced problems.

Get to know your asthma symptoms.

Everyone's early warning signs are different. If you have experienced an asthma episode, write down exactly how you felt beforehand. Simply knowing what to look for in the early stages of an asthma attack can be lifesaving. Here's a checklist of danger signals: sweating; unusual paleness; flared nostrils when breathing in; pursed lips when breathing out; lips, nail beds, or skin tone turning blue; anxious or scared expression; or hunched-over posture. If you can't sit or stand straight; if you are restless, especially at night (and unable to sleep), fidgety, or fatigued; if your throat tickles or your chest is tight; if you experience coughing, wheezing, or any other signs of breathing discomfort (rapid or irregular breathing, noisy or difficult breathing, no breathing sounds), see your doctor. Finally, if the pupils of your eyes look tiny, if you have a sunken-in look at the base of the throat or between the ribs, if your heart is beating rapidly, or if you're vomiting, get to your doctor without delay.

Unclog sinuses.

When sinus passages in your face are congested, place a warm, moist washcloth across your nose so it covers your cheeks and forehead.

Rinse with a saline solution.

If you have an upper respiratory reaction to an allergen, experts at the Lung Line suggest that you clear your nasal passages with a saline solution you can make yourself. (The Lung Line is a toll-free information service operated by the National Jewish Center for Immunology and Respiratory Medicine in Denver, which can be reached at 800-222-LUNG, or 800-222-5864.) Simply mix a teaspoon of salt in a pint of warm water, and add a pinch of baking soda. Make the solution fresh every day, and store it in a clean glass or plastic bottle. Don't use salt substitutes, which can cause irritation. Flush out your nose and sinuses by snuffing a little of the solution up one nostril at a time. Bend over the sink, spit it out, and then lightly blow your nose. Check with your doctor about how often to repeat this procedure—once a day may be enough. Though commercial products are available for this same kind of nose cleaning, this simple method should be just as effective.

Stay squeaky clean.

After spending time outside during your particular allergy season, take long, hot showers and wash your hair thoroughly. Bits of pollen or other allergens can stick to your clothes, your skin, and especially your hair. In fact, a bout of coughing or sneezing can frequently be stopped by merely stepping under a stream of running water.

Soothe itching eyes.

Some allergists recommend a splash of cool, clean water to soothe eyes that are irritated and itchy.

Post no-smoking signs.

Seriously, don't let anyone smoke in your presence, especially if you have allergic asthma. Cigarette smoke is a poisonous gas that dries the lining of your airways, makes them sore, and forces your lungs to make mucus that clogs them up. If you smoke, quit.

Take pollution precautions.

During pollen season, buy a pair of sunglasses with side shields, and wear them when out of doors. If it's windy, a surgical mask or scarf tied across your nose and mouth is a good idea. A breeze will clear the air, but it can also blow dirt and allergens right into your respiratory system. Pay attention to air-pollution alerts, and steer clear of automobile exhaust from traffic congestion.

Stay inside to sidestep airborne allergens.

If seasonal pollen or mold spores released by growing plants, trees, and grasses wreak havoc on your health, time your outside adventures carefully to avoid these airborne allergens. For example, pick a rainy day—when pollination is minimal—for appropriate outdoor activities. Keep windows closed, especially on hot, dry days, because pollen and molds pass right through screens. Turn on air conditioners, and get an air purifier that can remove particles from the air. Some experts worry that such purifiers stir up dust, but others believe that the benefit is worth the risk. The most ef-

fective air purifiers are the HEPA (high-energy particulate accumulator) cleaners, which remove tiny particles like dust, mold, pollen, and dander.

Control your mold.

Do your allergies act up right after a rainy period in the warm months of the year? Not all mold spores stay outside. Some fungi prefer the damp, musty areas of your home: They just love cellars, bathrooms, laundry areas, and the inside of home humidifiers. In the bathroom, change the shower curtain frequently, don't lay carpeting, and keep a mold and mildew cleaner handy for quick clean-ups. In the basement, use a dehumidifier. If the buildup is heavy, try a coat of mold-inhibiting paint.

Meet the tiny enemy.

Do you wake up sneezing or sniffling? Do you feel miserable after making the bed? Dust mites—which are microscopic, sightless, eight-legged insects—

could be the cause of your allergies. Mites just love to eat the little bits of skin that have flaked off your body. In order to get close to you, these critters will make themselves at home in your bedding, rugs, and stuffed furniture.

Mites are at their most prolific when the relative humidity is between 75 and 80 percent. Keep it under 40 percent and they die.

Clean out the mites.

Take a long, serious look at your cleaning techniques and the dust-catching furnishings in your home.

- Do you really need those overstuffed chairs? Knickknacks on every available surface? Rugs underfoot? Use a damp mop, and don't vacuum more than once a week, since vigorous cleaning stirs up trouble.

- Don't store lots of dusty paraphernalia near where you sleep. Put your clothes in a closet before you go to bed, and shut the door. Close bureau drawers.

- Heavy curtains or blinds can be terrific hiding places for these critters. Put up simple cotton drapes that can be washed in hot water.

Don't pet pets.

Some of man's best friends could be his worst enemies. Dander and pet saliva are known allergens. If you can't bear to part with a pet, at least minimize petting, and try to keep your face turned away. Don't allow your pet on the bed.

Watch weather forecasts.

In winter, sudden blasts of freezing air can shock your airways and tighten them up. In spring, some plants produce allergen particles less than ten microns in diameter (that's super small), which will bring on breathing problems. In summer, heavy, hot, still air holds lots of pollen and pollution. But fall may be the worst time of the year for people with either allergies or asthma, or both, because of ragweed pollen and mold spores.

Breathe deeply.

People with respiratory disorders often become sloppy breathers. Don't rely on upper-chest muscles only, which lets your diaphragm off too easily in the work of respiration. When you are out of breath, don't pant. The good air can't get into your lungs, and the bad air can't get out. There are at least three symptoms of too much air trapped in your lungs: 1) a tightness across your upper chest area, 2) an inability to take a deep breath, and 3) a problem with breathing too rapidly or panting. Deep, slow breathing will make your abdomen move in and out. By breathing deeply, your diaphragm will descend, letting your lungs fill up with oxygen. This technique will slow down the shortness of breath you experience in times of panic or physical exertion.

Exercise: Use it or lose it.

Doctors used to tell people with asthma not to exercise at all, but today it is understood that less than five percent of asthma sufferers need to worry about too much exercise. Still, this is very much an individual matter, one that should be discussed with your doctor. Together, the two of you can find a sport or type of exercise that is not likely to bring on breathing problems, then it's up to you to just do it. Be sure you always begin with a warm-up period, and don't exercise outdoors when air quality is poor.

Slowing down physically is a big mistake, because the more you sit still, the worse you will feel. Moreover, the older you get, the easier it is to lose muscle power. Researchers have discovered that adult Americans tend to lose 6.6 pounds of lean body mass with each decade of life. However, exercise undertaken at any age—whether you are 50 or 90—can build strength. When you don't use your muscles, they waste away; even breathing becomes more difficult.

Debate your diet.

Experts are not in agreement as to the connection between the foods you eat and possible reactions to them. A valid distinction exists between a genuine allergy, which is an immune system reaction, and a food intolerance. Some say that although an estimated 40 percent of Americans claim to have food allergies, in fact, only about one percent are truly allergic. The U.S. Department of Agriculture puts the number of people who may be allergic to some food ingredients at 15 percent of the population. No matter how it is described, one thing is clear: Certain foods have emerged as messengers of trouble in certain susceptible individuals, with effects that range from itchiness to hives to migraine headaches.

Avoid these culinary culprits.

Among the most common culprits are cheeses, fungi (mushrooms, for instance), molds, nuts, seafood, and spices.

WARNING!
• • •

Asthma should always be treated under the watchful eye of a doctor. It's life threatening. Make an appointment with a board-certified allergist (a doctor who specializes in treating allergies) or a pulmonary specialist (a doctor who specializes in lung disorders).

Other potential troublemakers include bologna, chili, corned beef, dressings (including ketchup, relishes, and shrimp sauces), hot dogs, mayonnaise, pickled or smoked meats, and sausage. The best advice is to keep a list of the foods that cause a reaction, then do your best to avoid them.

Ask before you eat.

Monosodium glutamate, commonly referred to as MSG and often used in Chinese restaurants, can cause facial flushing, tingling sensations, and wheezing. Sulfites have also been identified as troublemakers; these agents are used to maintain the crisp appearance of fresh vegetables and to control the growth of microbes in wine. Don't take chances; feel free to be assertive in asking about foods and methods of preparation when eating out. Ask before you order.

Drink lots of water.

You can thin any mucus produced by your body by drinking lots of water. Try downing eight to ten glasses of H_2O a day if allergies or asthma have been making your mucus thick and sticky. It'll be easier to expel the stuff with a cough.

Go on a drug alert.

Carefully note the medicines you take. Research has shown that aspirin or any pain-relieving drug containing aspirin can trigger asthmatic episodes. The initials ASA, APC, or PAC on a list of ingredients should warn you away. An expert report published by the National Asthma Education Program suggests that you stick with alternatives such as acetaminophen, sodium salicylate, or a salsalate such as Disalcid. You can also cross off some nonsteroidal anti-inflammatory drugs (NSAIDs), such as ibuprofen, from your list of acceptable medicines. When in doubt, check with your doctor.

INHALING ASTHMA MEDICINE

○ ○ ○

Inhaling your asthma medication is a very effective way to treat supersensitive or "twitchy" lungs. Some doctors prescribe nebulizers, which are portable air compressors that change liquid medicine into a mist. Other doctors recommend inhalers, which are small, hand-held canisters. By inhaling, you lower the risk of certain side effects associated with oral asthma medications, and you give the drug a clearer shot at clearing the airways in your lungs.

Bronchodilators, the category of medications designed to open airways in the lungs, are potent and can cause shakiness, headaches, nausea, anxiety, or increased heart rate. They are often referred to as adrenalinelike medications. Be sure to report any problems to your doctor immediately. And make certain that you carefully follow the directions on the package insert. Don't throw it away. Read it. In fact, ask your doctor to spend some time showing you how to administer the drug. Experts suspect that you need 10 to 28 minutes to learn the proper technique. Incorrect use of canisters is a common problem. You might want to try an accessory device, called a holding chamber, to get the most benefit from your inhaler.

Use antihistamines the right way.

If you delay taking an over-the-counter antihistamine until after your nose starts running and your eyes begin itching, you're already too late. When possible, start antihistamine allergy medications a week or two before you expect your problem period to begin. Remember, too, that as you age your body metabolizes medications more slowly. You may find that your body reacts differently than it once did to some medications, and antihistamines may not be effective for you.

Stay calm, cool, collected.

Asthma is not an emotional or psychological disease, although strong emotions can sometimes make asthma worse. If you have sensitive lungs, anxiety can make your airways tighten, swell, and fill with mucus. Learn some relaxation techniques. Close your eyes and visualize soothing scenes while you tighten and then relax each muscle in your body. Find a comfortable spot, put aside at least ten minutes, and start by consciously relaxing your feet, then work your way up to your neck.

Find a friendly pharmacist.

Get to know the pharmacists where you buy your allergy or asthma medications. They are trained to advise their customers about prescription and nonprescription medications.

Plan ahead.

If you are planning a trip, prepare for the worst. Pack medicines, call your place of lodging to reserve smoke-free rooms, and bring your own allergy-proof pillow. Also consider packing a small portable air cleaner, and have your regular doctor provide an emergency treatment plan.

Get plenty of rest.

Changes in routine, holiday hassles, staying up late at night, and overexposure to people, places, and things can make you more susceptible to asthma or allergy attacks. Get a good night's sleep, and minimize your risk.●

ANGINA

10 Tips for Dealing with Chest Pain

*A*ngina comes from the Latin word *angere,* which means to strangle. At one time *angina* was a general term for any type of choking, suffocating, or spasmodic pain. Today the term is used almost exclusively to describe the pain associated with coronary heart disease.

Angina is an apt term for the constricting pain that can result from coronary disease. However, keep in mind that angina, like pain of any type, is only a symptom, not a disease in itself.

The underlying problem is coronary atherosclerosis. Fatty plaque accumulates in the coronary arteries and restricts blood flow to the heart. When blood tries to surge through a narrowed opening in an artery (which occurs when you exert yourself physically), the restriction in the flow may cause pain that emanates from beneath the breastbone, or sternum.

Not all chest pain reflects heart disease. In fact, any number of conditions can cause pain in the chest: spasm of the esophagus, lung injuries or disease, infections, panic attacks (a type of anxiety disorder), heartburn, blood-vessel spasms, and bruised or broken bones, to name just a few.

True angina is a reflection of a serious underlying medical condition that requires regular and careful monitoring by a physician. The approach to treatment depends on the severity of the disease, the patient's overall health, and other factors.

Patients with angina can help minimize their discomfort and manage their coronary risk by paying attention to the following tips:

Don't ignore the symptoms.

Pain is the body's way of telling you that something is not right. It's easy to rationalize that what you experience is not heart disease or not important. Always let your physician know about any unexplained pain you have, especially if the pain is recurrent. Then let your doctor decide how to evaluate the problem.

Know women aren't immune.

Many women still may not realize that they do in fact develop coronary disease. Women tend to develop coronary atherosclerosis later in life than men do, about ten years later. But after menopause, a woman's risk of heart disease begins to increase rapidly. The bottom line: Don't ignore chest pain simply because you're a woman.

Look at your risk.

Do you have high blood pressure, high cholesterol, or diabetes? Do you smoke? Are you overweight? As you answer yes to more questions about coronary risk, the suspicion of angina increases. People with multiple risk factors are at especially high risk for heart disease and should be examined regularly by a physician. They should also make a concerted effort to reduce the risk.

Keep your cholesterol in check.

If you have angina as a result of coronary disease, you can help lower your risk by keeping cholesterol levels under control. People who have been diagnosed as having coronary heart disease should strive for even lower cholesterol levels than the 200 milligrams per deciliter (mg/dL) that is considered desirable for people without coronary disease.

Don't smoke.

Smoking contributes to the initial risk of atherosclerosis and to the progression of the disease once it develops.

Lose weight.

Excess weight is related to both high blood pressure and cholesterol abnormalities. Extra pounds that add fat to the stomach and abdomen tend to be more dangerous, as opposed to added fat in the hips and thighs. Being overweight also makes the heart work harder, which leads to more episodes of angina.

Watch your diet.

Follow your doctor's recommendations for cholesterol, fat, sodium, and total-calorie intake. If you have coronary atherosclerosis, your target levels should be lower than the recommendations for the population in general.

EVERYONE BENEFITS FROM PHYSICAL FITNESS

○ ○ ○

Angina and underlying heart disease do not pose an insurmountable barrier to improved physical fitness. In fact, improved fitness offers an especially effective means of coping with angina. Here are some points to consider when it comes to exercise.

- Get your doctor's OK. A person with angina should never begin a fitness program without discussing the matter with a physician who is knowledgeable about exercise.

- Get an aerobic workout. Anything that gives the heart a workout is fine. Many people choose walking because it's convenient and requires no instruction or special equipment other than good shoes.

- Choose an activity you enjoy. Make sure you choose an activity that's convenient and one that you will stick with for the long term.

- Aim low in the beginning. If you can comfortably walk two miles at a pace of 20 minutes per mile, start out by walking only one mile instead.

- Build gradually. Intensity and duration of physical activity are key factors, but they must be increased very gradually. To use walking as an example, you might start by walking one mile in 20 minutes every day for one week. The next week, try to walk the mile in 19 minutes, 50 seconds. Subtract another ten seconds the following week and so forth. Use the same approach with duration of activity.

- Work on strength. Strength training increases muscle mass and helps reduce fat mass. As an example, start with very light weights and do perhaps ten repetitions daily for a week. Increase repetitions by two per week until you reach 16. Then increase the weight slightly, go back to ten repetitions, and start over.

Learn to relax.

Several studies have indicated that emotional reactions, especially anger, hostility, and certain responses to stress, may increase the risk of abnormal heartbeats in people with coronary disease and may increase the risk that a heart attack could be fatal. Biofeedback, relaxation therapy, yoga, and other ways to cope with stress may be helpful for some people.

Do you take aspirin?

If not, you probably should. More and more physicians recommend that all patients over age 40 take at least a baby aspirin daily. People with angina (and, by extension, coronary disease) are at high risk for heart attack, and daily aspirin therapy significantly reduces the risk, especially in men. If you're not already taking aspirin, ask your doctor for a recommendation.

Know it's never too late.

Studies have clearly shown that people can benefit from risk-reducing behaviors at any point. If you have coronary atherosclerosis—even if you've had a heart attack—you can lower your future risk by making changes in your lifestyle. You don't need a calendar to find the best day to start; it's called today.●

ANXIETY

14 APPROACHES TO OVERCOMING ANXIETIES

You know what it feels like to be anxious. It's the sensation of pressure in the pit of your stomach when you see a truck in the next lane inching toward you. It's the rapid heartbeat that follows the news about your grandson's injury.

Anxiety is that edgy, uncomfortable feeling you get when you're worried about something or when you must face a situation that could be stressful. It's based on fear that arises from the perception of a threatening or dangerous situation. The body responds and prepares to protect itself: Adrenaline is released throughout the body, producing what has been called the "fight or flight" reaction. You experience a rise in heart rate, blood pressure, and blood sugar, along with an increase in perspiration rate and muscle tension.

Uncomfortable as it can be, anxiety is a perfectly normal response to many ordinary circumstances. In fact, anxiety is not only normal, it's also helpful. It alerts us to threats and dangers and helps us react to crises. Anxiety is, anthropologists believe, a built-in defense mechanism that has allowed our species to survive. This reaction gave early man a boost of energy to stand and fight or to escape, and it continues to protect us on the battlefield and in other high-danger situations. On a lesser level, mild anxiety can give us an extra edge when competing, whether in a friendly game of tennis or on the job.

Although often annoying, worries are a part of everyone's life, and we come to understand that they can usually be resolved. Such normal anxieties commonly go unnoticed and don't require treatment. Many are expected; some, such as a case of the jitters before getting married, are even welcomed.

You may, however, become overly anxious and display symptoms of too much adrenaline production: heavy sweating, difficulty breathing, heart palpitations, faintness, dizziness, trembling, numbness, physical instability, and fatigue. These conditions place heavy demands upon your mind and body, and you become mentally and physically exhausted. This is the stage at which anxiety stops being helpful, for not only can your edginess be overwhelming, leading to complete passiveness and extreme pessimism, but you can also experience unhealthy boosts in blood pressure and in other ways put undue strain on your cardiovascular system.

Continuing, hard-to-manage anxiety is regarded as an anxiety disorder. Symptoms can be so severe that an affected person may be almost totally disabled: too terrified to enter an elevator, to attend ordinary social events, or even to leave home.

The good news is that most anxiety disorders, including the most severe, can be successfully treated with therapy, antianxiety medication, or a combination of the two. Unfortunately, some people may not get the help they need because they don't realize that this disease requires treatment.

Anxiety disorders cover a wide range of symptoms but may be separated into just a few categories. Panic attacks come on quite suddenly and are accompanied by disturbing physical symptoms, some of which resemble those of a heart attack (nausea, perspiration, and chest pain).

Intense but short-lived, panic attacks lead victims to fear that they are dying, which of course only worsens their anxiety. Obsessive-compulsive disorders are characterized by the joining of an idea that locks into your mind with behavior that you are unable to control. A common example is an obsession with cleanliness and the compulsion to wash your hands repeatedly, even though doing so is not rational under the circumstances (you may have washed your hands ten minutes ago). When this behavior is repeated to the extent that it begins to disrupt your normal life, it is considered more than just a peculiarity, it becomes a disorder. Phobias, the third type of anxiety disorder, are the result of strong fears of certain things or situations, such as the dread of closed spaces, certain animals or insects (spiders are common objects of this phobia), heights, and speaking in front of a group. Lastly, there is generalized anxiety, which doesn't arise from a specific object or event but results from a broader range of concerns. Thus, while someone may have a phobia about grasshoppers but otherwise be perfectly normal, someone with generalized anxiety disorder is more likely to be worried about a great number of things seen as threatening or fearsome, with the result that normal life can be disrupted.

Anxieties in the broad sense tend to be slightly more prevalent among women than men. Younger and older people also seem to be more susceptible than the population as a whole. If you have been bothered by generalized anxiety disorder, the following recommendations may help.

Get a complete physical.

A thorough physical examination will ensure that your anxiety is not caused by an illness and not the result of some other physical problem. A visit with your doctor is a good time to bring in all the drugs you may be taking, including prescription as well as over-the-counter medications, so they can be evaluated as potentially contributing factors in your anxiety.

Learn to recognize anxiety.

Realizing that anxiety exists is the fundamental step in taking control of it. The next step is recognizing the source of your anxiety and determining how to deal with it. You may find that a solution is readily available (you may realize, for instance, that you'll feel less anxious once you've seen a doctor about that pain you're worrying about). Or you may find that you have a problem, such as a phobia, that is beyond your personal control and requires the attention of medical professionals.

Move forward.

Once you've separated the problems you can act upon from those you cannot influence, it is time to take action where it will do the most good.

Find a confidant.

Tell someone you can confide in about your anxiety. Sharing your concerns with a close friend or family member can make them weigh less heavily on your shoulders, may provide a fresh perspective, and could even lead to a resolution of the problem.

It is just plain sensible to evaluate your social support system from time to time. Do you have friends and family members you can count on for emotional support when the need arises? Are you able to offer the same empathy and understanding to others? Perhaps it's time to put together a support system now if you don't have one.

Distract yourself.

Relax. Choose an activity you particularly enjoy, one that will free your mind from unwelcome anxiety. A game of golf or a gardening session may be just the thing to help you feel less anxious.

Get plenty of rest.

Just as it helps you cope with physical and other mental health problems, being well rested helps you to tackle anxiety with a vigorous attitude. Rest in itself may have a calming effect, and you're bound to feel more anxious if you haven't been getting enough sleep. Perhaps a day off or a long weekend is just what you need to help recharge your batteries.

Get some exercise.

Like getting enough rest, exercise can be beneficial in itself by lifting your spirits. It also leads to longer-term effects by increasing your energy level. Even a brisk 15- to 20-minute walk is likely to lessen your anxiety. You are also more likely to sleep better at night once you get into a program of regular exercise.

SYMPTOMS OF ANXIETY

o o o

Anxieties manifest themselves in many ways. The more common signs include the following:

- Sensing that something unpleasant is about to happen
- Increased heart rate
- Difficulty concentrating
- Sweaty palms
- Inability to relax
- Shortness of breath
- Difficulty sleeping through the night

Learn to relax.

Researchers have shown that when surgery patients listen to soothing music before their operation they feel calmer and more in control. You can gain a similar benefit from other relaxation techniques. Deep breathing, for example, is an excellent way to release tension. Sit in a quiet place; place one hand on your chest, the other on your stomach. Inhale deeply through your nose and concentrate on making the hand on your stomach rise as the hand on your chest remains still. Breathe out slowly through your mouth. Develop the habit of practicing this relaxation technique for five or ten minutes per day, or take a few deep breaths whenever you start to feel anxious.

Get a massage.

Whether it's a simple shoulder rub by your spouse or a thorough session with a professional, a massage is another way to break away from your anxiety, relax, compose and refresh yourself, and simply enjoy the comforting sensation of warm fingers.

Eat well-balanced meals.

Good nutrition is a sound defense against anxiety. Alcohol in particular is sometimes mistakenly thought of as a solution for anxiety, but the contrary is true: Alcohol is a depressant; it can only contribute to your down moods.

Give up coffee and cigarettes.

While these familiar habits can be comforting, like all stimulants they are bound to make you feel more anxious. You'll be doing yourself a favor in terms of your overall health, too.

Use your time well.

Having too much or too little time on your hands can bring on anxiety. Plan your daily activities to insure that you keep busy, but not too busy. Make a list, attach priorities to the items noted, then get started and enjoy crossing off jobs as you accomplish them.

Take medication under a doctor's care.

While antianxiety drugs can be helpful, take them only under the supervision of a physician. Most medication affects the nervous system and can have adverse side effects. Your doctor should be able to discuss the effects of these drugs and how you can take them safely.

Consider psychotherapy.

Therapy can be a godsend in coping with anxiety—provided you are comfortable with your therapist, can work sessions into your schedule without causing undue stress, and are able to afford it. Your doctor can offer advice as to specific professionals and suggest whether group or individual therapy is best for you.●

ARTHRITIS

24 WAYS TO COMBAT STIFF JOINTS

Everyone experiences aches and pains from time to time, but they are usually nothing major and typically people recover on their own. If you have a serious case of arthritis, however, you know how persistent and progressive the disease can be, sometimes making it difficult to function effectively at home and at work.

Arthritis means inflammation of the joints and is the most common chronic health problem in the United States. Actually, it isn't one single disease but rather an entire group of diseases characterized by stiffness, chronic pain, and loss of movement. In fact, there are over 100 different forms of these rheumatic conditions, which are caused by soft-tissue problems, trauma, inflammation, and degeneration. The two forms that occur most frequently are osteoarthritis and rheumatoid arthritis, but associated conditions such as gout, bursitis, fibromyalgia, and systemic lupus erythematosus are also common.

Most rheumatic diseases occur at or near a joint, where two or more bones meet. Some, however, such as bursitis, affect the muscles and soft tissues around the joints. The joint itself is completely covered with and sealed by a tough capsule called the synovial membrane. This membrane bathes joint surfaces in a fluid that allows them to move against each other without friction.

Different types of joints work in different ways, but all joints operate with tendons, muscles, and ligaments. Tendons—which are not elastic—connect the joints to muscles, which are elastic and can therefore contract and expand. Ligaments, on the other hand, are cords that connect bones to each other. Osteoarthritis and rheumatoid arthritis both affect the joints, but they act on them in different ways.

Rheumatoid arthritis (RA) is an autoimmune disease, which means it stems from the body's unexplained attack on itself. The attack targets not only joints but tissues and organs as well. For reasons that are not understood, the immune system reacts to joints, tissues, and organs as if they were riddled with infection, and then the system sends enzymes to attack the imagined infection. Over time, these enzymes begin to eat away at the synovial membrane and cartilage of the joint and create inflammation. As the disease progresses, bones, tendons, and ligaments within the joints are worn away as well—so it's important to treat RA early and aggressively before serious damage occurs. RA and related rheumatic diseases tend to be chronic; over time, they can produce deformed joints that don't function as well as other joints.

RA may strike at any age, but it occurs most commonly among people in their 20s and 30s and is found three times more often among women than among men. In addition to pain and joint stiffness, symptoms may include a decreased appetite (with a resulting drop in weight), feelings of fatigue and weakness, and low-grade fever. The stiffness usually peaks in the morning and lessens as the day wears on. The fingers, wrists, knees, ankles, and toes are the joints most susceptible to the inflammation and swelling of RA.

RA is difficult to detect when it first starts, although there are lab tests to check for its presence. For a lucky 10 percent of all patients who get RA, the disease will go into total remission within a year. Almost all of the remaining 90 percent will get relief within two years.

Osteoarthritis (OA), the kind of arthritis that affects more people than any other, stems from the gradual erosion of joint cartilage. Because it develops gradually, it typically strikes after the age of 45. In fact, something like 90 percent of people in that age group have evidence of osteoarthritis in the knees, shoulders, or hips that can be seen on X rays, even though an affected person may be unaware of any symptoms. Once you reach age 45, OA can strike at any time; progress rapidly, slowly, or somewhere in between; and remain mild or become more severe. Your susceptibility to OA depends on both your genetic heritage and your environment.

No treatment is available currently that can stop or reverse the progress of arthritis. But affected individuals can diminish their pain and take care of themselves in other ways so their joints function as normally as possible.

It was once thought that arthritis was an unavoidable part of aging and there wasn't much anyone could do about it. Today, effective treatment options replace resignation. Here are a number of ways to help you live with arthritis.

Contact the Arthritis Foundation.

Call 800-283-7800. You'll reach the 24-hour hot line of the nonprofit Arthritis Foundation, a national group that backs research into the disease and helps educate the public about it. Available services include recorded information about the disease, brochures, and regional office locations.

Take the Arthritis Self-help Course.

Available locally through the Arthritis Foundation, this course teaches about the disease and strategies for coping with it. The course (which meets for two hours per week over a six-week period) also explains how to communicate more effectively with your physicians. Research shows that graduates of the course develop a higher level of confidence in their ability to cope, which is so important in dealing successfully with arthritis.

Take medication on schedule.

Stick to the timing your doctor prescribes to keep an effective amount of the drug in your body at all times. This way you will be less likely to be awakened in the middle of the night because of pain.

Handle pain carefully.

If you have osteoarthritis, start your drug treatment with acetaminophen (Tylenol) to relieve the pain. Acetaminophen has fewer side effects than nonsteroidal anti-

WARNING!
. . .
Know the risks of oral medication. Your doctor may prescribe NSAIDs to relieve pain and reduce inflammation. But these drugs can cause stomach problems and elevate your blood pressure, so use them with caution and only with your doctor's guidance. Long-term use of NSAIDs, even in moderate dosages, can cause stomachaches, bleeding, and ulcers. Large doses can cause kidney damage.

inflammatory drugs (NSAIDs). On the other hand, if you have rheumatoid arthritis, try NSAIDs (naproxen [Aleve], aspirin, or ibuprofen) for relieving pain and reducing inflammation.

Maintain a healthy weight.

Follow a balanced, low-fat diet, shedding excess pounds slowly, so joints are not burdened by too much weight.

Apply heat treatments.

Heating pads or hot packs relax muscles and reduce stiffness. Work out a schedule of heat treatments with your physician. A few times a day, take 20 or 30 minutes to give painful joints an application of moist heat. Heat lamps, electric mitts, and foot warmers all can help. Warm compresses may also soothe the discomfort.

Use cold treatments.

Cold acts as a local anesthetic and decreases muscle spasms. Try cold packs to relieve pain in muscles that have stayed too long in one position.

Keep moving.

If a joint isn't used, in time it loses some of its capability to function normally. Of all the treatments for arthritis, exercise is the most crucial and should be done regularly—every day of the week if possible. Ideally, an exercise program should be supervised by a physician or a physical therapist.

Get help with splints.

When inflammation is at its worst, you may want to use splints and supports for protection and pain reduction. Whether you have them custom made or simply purchase them over the counter, make sure they are light in weight, permit range-of-motion exercises, and can be removed easily. Otherwise, stiffness may actually increase. And do not be tempted to overdo simply because you're wearing such a device.

Use assistive devices.

Such products are designed to make life easier. Walkers, crutches, and canes are commonly used to help arthritis sufferers get around more easily and be more independent. It's easier to get up from a sitting position if you have a raised toilet seat in the bathroom and firm pillows on chairs. Other assistive devices help open doors or jars, turn faucets, give comb and brush handles more surface area for gripping, and make tools easier to hold. Hook-and-eye fasteners and zipper attachments can ease stress on arthritic hands and arms.

Rest inflamed joints.

Inflamed joints are easily damaged; rest can decrease inflammation. You often overuse specific muscles to avoid putting too much strain on a sore joint. Rest helps any muscles that have been used excessively and temporarily relieves the pressure on sore joints.

Take a hot bath or shower.

A warm soak or splash right after you arise in the morning will do wonders for stiff and painful limbs—which may actually make an exercise program more doable.

Avoid contractures.

After even one week of inactivity, the tendons, muscles, and ligaments of arthritis sufferers can begin to shorten— a complication known as contractures. The shortening makes it tougher than ever to straighten your joint completely. Joints should be moved through the maximum range of motion to prevent contractures, which means full extension as well as full bending, or flexion.

Rub on relief.

Topical preparations, creams, lotions, and gels can provide temporary relief by soothing nerve endings and masking pain. They are also a diversionary tactic, since they irritate the skin just enough to keep you from noticing joint pain. Common ingredients include camphor, menthol, and turpentine oil. If you use capsaicin, an ingredient in Zostrix and other ointments, it keeps some of the pain signals from ever reaching the brain. Most physicians use capsaicin cautiously because more research is needed to confirm its effectiveness.

- Precaution: Protect open cuts from these medications, and don't get any of them in your eyes, mouth, or nose.

- When skin is coated with one of these medications, never bind it tightly with a bandage or apply heat to the area.

- Wash your hands thoroughly after every application.

- If you develop a reaction, stop using the product immediately.

Tell the doctor exactly how you feel.

Your doctor will depend on you for facts and feedback that will aid in diagnosis and treatment. The more accurate and specific the information you provide, the better the outcome. Don't downplay your symptoms; that only makes it harder for the doctor to diagnose accurately.

Team up with pros.

Athletes need trainers and coaches; so do you. In addition to a sympathetic physician—perhaps one who specializes in rheumatology—you may need a physical therapist (PT) to customize an exercise program for you. PTs focus on increasing your mobility, decreasing your pain, and maintaining (or expanding) your level of physical functioning.

Modify your home.

Install grab bars next to the toilet and bathtub. In the kitchen, store appliances within easy reach, build up saucepan handles, and sit on a stool while cooking, cleaning, and washing dishes. Replace small, round faucet handles with easily-grasped lever-type handles, and simplify opening your refrigerator by attaching a cloth loop to the door.

Wear adaptive clothing.

For example, clothing with hook-and-eye fasteners rather than buttons, zippers, or snaps will reduce discomfort as well as the time it takes to get dressed.

Accept your limitations.

Despite some pain and difficulty getting around, you can live a rich and relatively normal life. If there are some things you can't do, simply accepting that fact rather than fretting about it will make your life easier.

Eat properly.

No one diet has ever been scientifically proven to cure arthritis, but eating properly—with a variety of nutrient-rich foods—will help by keeping joints, bones, and muscles healthy. Seek general dietary advice from your doctor or registered dietician.

Exercise.

Muscle weakness is a concern for nearly 80 percent of osteoarthritis and rheumatoid arthritis sufferers. Typically it results from too little exercise. You can improve your strength and enhance your ability to carry out everyday tasks by participat-

ing in an appropriate program to strengthen muscles. Stronger muscles provide better structural support for the joints. Isometric exercises—in which resistance is created by pushing or pulling without moving the joint—are also useful. Don't overlook the following considerations when it comes to strengthening programs:

- Check with your doctor before you begin.
- Use a variety of approaches for strength training: elastic bands, free weights, isometrics, exercise machines, resistive water exercises.
- Make sure you learn the correct techniques for lifting weights.
- Start with small weights and progress slowly.

Maintain flexibility.

Do exercises that require full range of motion from your muscles and bones. Move a joint as far as you can in every direction without feeling pain. When you start feeling pain, stop. You've gone far enough.

Swim.

Because it exercises muscles throughout the body, swimming will enhance your total shape in a way that walking can't. And because it doesn't make the joints bear weight, swimming creates minimal wear-and-tear on joints. When you proceed through the full range of motion in water, the water's resistance gives your limbs even more exercise. The water's warmth also promotes relaxation as it lessens stiffness. Indeed, few exercises are as good as water-based ones. Contact the Arthritis Foundation for guidance in finding pools and instructors that are certified for water exercise classes.

Walk.

Walking is one of the exercises least likely to cause or aggravate problems with muscles or joints. Walking will also contribute to your overall health by improving cardiovascular fitness, strengthening muscles, and maintaining joint flexibility—factors that are particularly important for people suffering from arthritis. ●

EXERCISES FOR ARTHRITIS

○ ○ ○

As part of your warm-up and cooldown before and after daily exercise, make sure you do range-of-motion and stretching exercises for 5 to 15 minutes. Be careful not to stretch so far (or exercise so strenuously) that your joints or muscles begin to ache or become more painful than they already were.

Range-of-motion exercises.

- Turning your head slowly from side to side will increase range of motion in your neck. Look at something directly in front of you. Without moving your head up or down, turn and look as far over your right shoulder as you can without straining. Keep your head in place for two to three seconds, then move your head to the forward position again. Repeat six to ten times to the right, then do the same to the left.

- Raise your arms for shoulder range of motion. Stand with your arms hanging at your sides with palms against your thighs. Raise both arms above your head and up toward your ears, bending your elbows only slightly. Hold for two to three seconds. Repeat six to ten times.

Stretching exercises.

- Stretch your back and shoulder. Bend your right arm and reach over your left shoulder, your right elbow toward the ceiling. Reach as far down the back as possible, between the shoulder blades. Using your left hand, gently pull your right elbow to the left until a stretch is felt on the back of the right arm and down the right side of the back. Hold. Repeat with the left arm. Stretch each arm six to ten times.

- Stretch your back and hamstrings. Sit on the floor with your legs straight out in front of you and your hands on your thighs. Bend forward slowly, reaching toward your toes. Keep your head and back aligned as you move into the stretch. Bend your knees slightly, if necessary. Hold for a count of four.

- Stretch your back. Sit erect on the floor with legs out straight and feet spread apart. Place fingertips on shoulders with elbows out to the sides. Gently bend over and twist so you move one elbow across and down to the opposite knee. Straighten up and bring both elbows back. Repeat to the other side.

BACK PAIN

21 WAYS TO LIVE WITHOUT BACK PAIN

You were only lifting that air conditioner for a few seconds when you twisted the wrong way and felt a twinge low down in your back, followed by a surge of agony. You popped an ibuprofen (Advil and Nuprin are examples), rested in bed for a day or two, and then had a rubdown at the local health club. By the weekend you felt much better and figured the problem was behind you. Two months later, however, your back went out of kilter again. This time you called a doctor.

Although you can't always identify the precise cause of chronic back pain, typically it results from one particular injury or evolves over time as a result of either wear and tear or frequent muscle tension. Fortunately, lower back pain usually improves within a week or two whether you do something about it or not. The more troublesome problem is that it can recur often if you don't manage it correctly.

When hoisting some ungainly object like an air conditioner or bending in the wrong way results in lower back pain, the pain may be a sign of muscle strain or sprain. It may even result from a spasm. You could be in agony, or you could simply feel a constant ache in the middle of your lower back. The pain may be localized or spread over a wide area. A few days of rest and some over-the-counter pain relievers should reduce the pain enough to get you back to normal.

The good news is that pain can be resolved altogether with light exercise and mild pain relievers. This is a big improvement over traditional treatments such as a longer period of bed rest and prescription medication. The problem is that about 20 percent of all adults will experience some lower back pain, and once you've been touched by it, there's a 50 percent chance it will recur.

The architecture of the spine is impressive: Its two dozen vertebrae are aligned in a column, cushioned from each other by disks of elastic cartilage. The column is fastened in place by muscles and ligaments. But disorders can arise when problems are caused by gravity, turning and pounding motions, or bone-and-joint diseases. The bottom part of the spine is particularly susceptible to disease and damage.

While there's no panacea for back pain, you can take precautions to speed your recovery and to prevent relapses. Here are some ideas to keep in mind.

Take your medicine.

Over-the-counter pain relievers that reduce inflammation—such as ibuprofen and aspirin—are particularly effective for lower back pain. Acetaminophens, such as Tylenol and Valadol, may not be as effective.

Know when to take your next dose.

Take your pain medication every four to six hours; if you wait for the pain to return before you remedicate, you'll have trouble keeping a pain-controlling level of medication in your bloodstream.

Ditch the high heels.

Heels move your center of gravity forward, adding to the stress on your back—whereas lower heels or flats will improve your stability.

Put together a fitness program.

Your exercise regimen should include an aerobic activity—such as biking, swimming, or walking—and it should be performed consistently, for half an hour every other day at the very least. This will help control your weight and make your muscles limber. But be sure to start slowly and build gradually.

Include stretching.

The most beneficial workout program goes beyond mere aerobic conditioning to include training for strength and flexibility. Stretching can lengthen muscles made short by inactivity and build up your tendons and ligaments. Before vigorous workouts, stretching also helps the muscles warm up.

Warm up before you play.

Heat up your muscles by engaging in gentle aerobic activity for 10 to 15 minutes. If you're short of time for exercise, warming up should be given top priority, even if it means there will be less time available for engaging in your primary form of exercise.

Keep your hamstrings unstrung.

When hamstring muscles (at the back of the thigh, between the back of the knee and the buttocks) are too tight, they place too much stress on the lower vertebrae because they hinder forward rotation of the upper body during stooping and stretching.

Shed some weight.

If you are above your ideal weight, cut down on calories and get more exercise. Extra weight adds unnecessary stress to your back.

Cross-train.

Keep your muscle groups in equilibrium by including strength training for both the upper and lower body. For instance, abdominal muscles must work with back muscles for lifting. Cross training also helps keep muscle and bone mass at healthy levels.

Look into hormone treatments.

Postmenopausal women who are at high risk for osteoporosis and weak backs should consider a health-risk management program that would include calcium supplements, hormone replacement therapy, and exercise to retard bone loss.

Exercise every day.

An inactive body deteriorates faster than an active one. Daily exercise enhances strength, helps to reduce stress on your back, and lessens the risk of an injury or a fall.

Try yoga.

Before you attempt yoga positions, it's a good idea to check with your physicians. With their approval, consider easing into a basic program that provides beneficial stretching and breathing techniques.

Bend your knees, not your back.

And be kind to your back by holding objects close to your chest rather than away from your body. Don't lift and twist at the same time.

Rest.

Rest may be necessary for any kind of extreme lower back pain. Simply standing can cause extreme discomfort, and walking may be next to impossible, thanks to painful spasms.

Limit bed rest.

Gone are the days when back-pain sufferers were told to lie flat in bed for two weeks or more. Today, doctors believe in two or three days of bed rest, interspersed with warm showers and short walks.

Watch out for radiating pain.

If pain is not localized but radiates outward from the lower back, it's time to consult your doctor. Something pressing on the sciatic nerve—such as a herniated disk—can send pain shooting into the buttocks and down the back of the leg.

Don't lie on your stomach.

Sleeping on your stomach stresses the back by arching it. It's far preferable to lie on your back with your feet slightly raised or your knees slightly bent. A pillow under your knees takes some strain away from your back.

Hit the water.

Water provides a cushion that lessens the stress on your back as you exercise.

Relax.

Do whatever it takes to ease the stress out of your back muscles—listen to relaxation tapes, sit quietly and read, put on some soothing music.

Put some support in the car seat.

Back supports are common features in new cars these days. If your car doesn't have them, they can be purchased at auto supply stores or drugstores.

Exercise to prevent back injury

These exercises, which are easy to do at home, help strengthen muscles throughout your body that lend support to the back:

- Warm up. Stand straight and press your palms against the small of your back. Very gently, bend backward a few times, but bend only as far as you can with comfort.

- Abdominal crunch. Lie on your back with your knees raised and feet flat on the floor. Cup your hands gently behind your neck. Very slowly, raise your shoulders a foot or so off the floor, then lower. Repeat ten to 20 times for one set. Do three sets.

- Pelvic tilt. From a lying position on your back, bend your knees and place your feet flat on the floor, hip-width apart. As you exhale, press the small of your back against the floor. You should be able to feel your buttocks tighten. Inhale, relaxing your muscles. Repeat six times.

- Knee to chest. Lying on your back, place your feet flat on the floor close to the buttocks, hip-width apart.

Hold the back of your thigh and exhale while bringing your right knee to your chest. Continue to hold your thigh and then extend your knee about eight inches away from your chest. Repeat six times, then switch legs. Repeat the exercise six more times, only this time hold both legs.●

WARNING!
...

Seek professional medical help when:

- Intense pain makes movement impossible. A tumor could be putting pressure on the spinal column and causing pain.

- Back pain is accompanied by fever, nausea, sweating, and general weakness.

- Pain is felt in both thighs when walking. This can be a symptom of spinal stenosis, the formation of bony growths on the vertebrae that cause the lower spinal canal to narrow.

- Acute back pain is accompanied by changes in bowel or bladder habits.

- Pain is worse at night, and there is a history of cancer in your family.

- You feel numbness or weakness in your legs or feet.

- Pain is making you feel anxious or depressed.

BELCHING

12 REMEDIES TO HELP BREAK THE HABIT

Belching after a meal may be a polite sign of appreciation in some societies, but listen up—in case you haven't noticed, ours isn't one of them. Of course, sometimes you belch because you just have to. After all, we all have to belch occasionally—it's just a natural way of releasing the gases that build up in the upper digestive tract. But if you belch a lot, you may be swallowing too much air when you eat, drink, talk, or even breathe. You're a veritable windbag; your intestinal tract just can't handle all the excess air you take in—and out it comes as belches.

Well, if you suffer from aerophagia—the medical term for swallowing too much air—and belch a lot as a result, you can take some comfort in the fact that there are certainly a lot of more serious problems to have. The only real consequence of belching is some social embarrassment. By learning how to take in a little less air, you should be able to squelch that belch. Here are some simple remedies that will help you control your belching.

Don't eat with your mouth open.

If you keep your mouth open while chewing—and a lot of people do, as you've probably had the unpleasant experience of noticing—you take in excess air with each mouthful. Sure, we were all supposed to learn to eat with our mouths closed when we were kids, but a lot of us forgot that rule of etiquette as the years passed by.

Don't talk while you're chewing.

If you've noticed that you're more likely to belch after a dinner party than when you eat alone, that's probably because you like to partake in the lively dinner-table conversation. It's great to enjoy the banter, but make a conscious effort to chew thoroughly before speaking—that's not only good manners, but you'll reduce the amount of air you ingest.

Don't wolf down your dinner.

Here's a simple rule to remember: The slower you eat, the less you'll belch. When you gulp food down quickly, you're swallowing a lot of air with it. Belchwise, you're setting yourself up for a double whammy: First, you're going to release the excess air as a belch, and second, you're going to swallow more food than your stomach can comfortably handle at one time. As a result, you're creating a lot of excess gas down there, which you're going to release as belches and in other unflattering ways, too.

Check your dentures.

Loose dentures not only clack, but they allow a lot of air to pass through the gaps between your teeth and gums when you talk and eat. By making sure your dentures fit tightly, you'll be helping your digestive tract in a couple of ways: You'll be able to chew your food more thoroughly, so it will be easier to digest. And you'll take in less air, so you'll be less likely to belch.

Use a glass.

There's nothing like enjoying a cold beer right out of the can. However, not only does beer count as one of those carbonated beverages that increases the urge to belch, but the can's a culprit, too. When you drink any beverage out of a can, you suck in a lot of air by your efforts to extract the liquid through the little opening. The same thing happens when you drink from a bottle or a drinking fountain or if you sip through a straw.

Break the belching habit.

Like any bad habit, once you start belching it's hard to stop—one belch just seems to lead to another and on and on it goes. You probably belch, then swallow a lot of extra air, then belch again. The fact is, most of those belches are unnecessary. Make an effort to stop swallowing excess air and nix this habit.

BREATHING LESSONS

○ ○ ○

The human body is designed to take in air through the nasal passages—something many of us tend to forget as we fall into the habit of chronically breathing through our mouths. If you breathe through your mouth, you're probably taking in a lot more air than you need, hence your tendency to belch.

If you belch a lot, think about your breathing habits. If you notice that you tend to gulp air through your mouth, take a few minutes a day to practice proper breathing. Sit quietly, keep your mouth closed, and breathe deeply through your nose. After a while, nose-breathing will come naturally, and you may notice that you belch less. There's also another big benefit to breathing through your nose: Membranes in the nose are designed to filter the oxygen you take in, so the air that reaches your lungs is cleaner than the air you take in through your mouth.

Say no to champagne.

And don't replace it with Perrier. Any carbonated beverage will increase the amount of gas in your intestinal tract.

Go on an antibelch diet.

Like carbonated drinks, certain other beverages and foods beget belching. An airy soufflé, a frothy cappuccino, a crunchy lemon meringue pie, or any other concoction that has a lot of air whipped into it may well bring on the urge to belch. Some fatty foods, such as salad oils or sour cream, create belch-producing gas in the upper intestinal tract. If belching's a problem, take note of which foods are most likely to set you off, and eat them sparingly, if at all.

Relax.

You may be gulping air and belching because you're stressed out. And while it's fine to say that the solution to any stress-related problem is simply to relax, that's easier said than done. But you can learn how to relax as you go about your day-to-day business without sailing off to a South Sea island or otherwise interfering with your routine. For instance, if you notice that you belch when you're under stress, slow down a bit. Sit quietly for a few minutes, take a few deep breaths (through your nose), then carry on, making an effort to remain calm and breathe normally without gulping for air.

Kick the smoking habit.

Sorry smokers, but your chronic belching is yet another reason to quit. As you puff away on that cigarette, pipe, or cigar, you are taking in a lot of excess air.

Chew less, belch less.

As far as habits go, chewing gum or sucking on hard candy is a lot better, healthwise, than smoking. Belchwise, however, you're still swallowing excess air and setting yourself up for trouble.

Try antacids.

But choose and use them wisely. An over-the-counter antacid containing simethicone (such as Mylanta or Maalox) will break down large bubbles in your intestinal tract and should reduce the urge to belch. An antacid that fizzes, though, is not going to help—like a carbonated beverage, it's going to add a lot of air to your digestive system. Easy does it with any antacid, though. Prolonged use can upset the acid balance in your stomach and lead to more digestive problems—some worse than belching.●

BOILS

12 WAYS TO FOIL THEM

Let's face it—a boil is pretty darn gross. It festers beneath the surface of the skin and shows up first as a painful red spot. Before long it swells, erupts as an inflamed pus-filled abscess, comes to a painful head, and begins to drain and ooze.

As we said, *grrooss*. Boils usually aren't particularly serious, however. They're simply the signs of infection with *Staphylococcus* (a common bacteria that often affect the skin) that has set in around an oil gland, most often near a hair follicle. Accordingly, boils tend to occur on hairy parts of the body (the back of the neck, thighs, and buttocks) and are more common among men than women.

If you get a boil, don't think that someone has put a hex on you. It just means that you've unwittingly opened the door to an unwelcome staph infection. Maybe you've been overdoing it with a greasy moisturizer and have clogged an oil gland, or your shirt collar is too tight and rubs against the hair follicles on the back of your neck. Some folks are just staph carriers and can look forward to fairly frequent boil eruptions. You become a little more prone to them as you get older because your immune function begins to wane and you're less able to fend off staph and other infections.

Just remember, though, if you get a boil, you're in good company. Remember your Scripture? "And Isaiah said, 'Bring a cake of figs. And let them take and lay it on the boil, that he may recover'" (2 Kings 20:7). We have been plagued with boils for ages.

Pack some heat.

A warm clean washcloth is your best weapon against a boil. Soak the cloth in very warm water—as warm as you can tolerate, but not scalding—and apply it to the boil for 20 minutes or so, three or four times a day. Change the compress frequently so it remains warm. The warmth will pump more blood to the area and bring the boil to a head more quickly. You can also use a heating pad, but you won't get the cleansing benefits you do with a washcloth.

Clean it up.

A clean boil is a short-lived boil. Wash the area thoroughly and frequently with soap and water to ward off further infection. This is especially important once the boil breaks open and is more infection prone.

Keep up the treatments.

Once a boil has burst, continue to apply compresses for a few days. This way you'll be sure to drain all the pus that forms beneath the surface of the skin.

Avoid over-the-counter boil cures.

These solutions claim to bring boils to a head faster, but they're risky: They can cause the infection to move deeper under the skin and infect the bloodstream. Washing frequently with soap and warm water will do just as much good as an ointment, without the risks.

Keep an eye on cysts.

Cysts, saclike swellings that can develop around hair follicles and elsewhere under the skin, are distant cousins to boils. Cysts come from the nicer side of the family, though: Unlike boils, they usually are not infected, and you can happily coexist with them for years. But

WHEN TO WORRY

○ ○ ○

Most boils will erupt, drain, and disappear—good riddance—on their own, maybe with a little help from you and the remedies you choose. However, there are times when a boil will require the care of your physician.

- See your doctor, for instance, if you notice red lines radiating from a boil, if you feel swelling in your lymph nodes, or if you have a fever—these are all signs that the staph infection is spreading.

- A boil that occurs under a thick patch of skin—such as the tough skin on the back of your neck—may not be able to make its way to the surface and drain naturally. If a boil like this lingers, it may be necessary to have it lanced and drained.

- You should also see a doctor if a boil is unusually large (larger than a quarter) or if you have an outbreak of several boils—in these cases, you probably have a doozy of a staph infection.

- The elderly, or anyone whose immune system is suppressed by illness or by certain immunosuppressant drugs, should also see a physician when a boil erupts because it may be difficult to control the infection.

if you pick at a cyst, or if a cyst is continually scraped by clothing, it can become infected and turn into a boil.

Give it the squeeze.

To squeeze or not to squeeze, that is the big question with boils. You'll certainly be tempted to squeeze the heck out of a boil, and that's probably OK if you wait for the right time. If you squeeze and pick at a boil before the infection comes to a head, though, you're only going to make it painfully inflamed. But once a boil forms a white pus-filled head, you may want to pop it with a needle you've sterilized with rubbing alcohol, then squeeze out as much pus as you can (make sure your hands are squeaky clean).

Beware of the hot zones.

Never—and that means never—squeeze a boil that's located near your nose, in your armpits, or in your groin area. Squeezing a boil near your nose can shoot the infection right up to your brain. Boils in the armpits and groin are prone to infect the lymph glands and bloodstream, and from there the infection can spread throughout the body. Just let boils in these areas come to a head naturally and take care to keep them clean and infection free.

Bandage it.

Once a boil comes to a head and starts oozing, you'll probably want to cover it with a bandage to protect your clothing from the pus that will continue to drain for a few days. A bandage will also help prevent the boil from becoming infected. But keep the bandage loose so the boil can drain freely.

SHOULD YOU GO WITH FOLK REMEDIES?

ο ο ο

Isaiah used figs on boils, and you'll probably get all sorts of homey advice on how to treat yours. Common folk remedies include treating a boil with tea bags, mashed garlic, and slices of heated tomato. They all serve the same purpose—to bring a boil to a head faster, and they may well help to do that. The problem is, you may also irritate the dickens out of the boil and infect it further. A clean warm washcloth works just as well.

Keep it to yourself.

The *Staphylococcus* infection that causes boils is very contagious. Wash your hands thoroughly after touching a boil, and separate washcloths and clothing that come in contact with a boil when doing laundry—don't toss them in with the family wash.

Hit the showers.

A warm bath can be a good and soothing way to treat a boil, but shower thoroughly with soap and warm water afterward. This way, you'll reduce the risk of spreading the staph infection to another part of your body.

Go on the defensive.

If you're prone to boils, you may want to wash daily with a special antibacterial soap—several varieties are available in drugstores.

Loosen your collar...

As well as your belt, and keep those tight pants in the back of the closet. Tight-fitting clothes are a boil's delight: They make it easier for the oil glands around hair follicles to clog, setting the stage for a boil to take up residence.●

BRONCHITIS

---

10 WAYS TO FEEL BETTER

You can't ignore the symptoms: a cough that won't go away, more thick, yellow-green mucus than you could imagine, a sore throat, pain and rattling in your chest, inability to breathe easily, a slight fever, chills, and a general achy feeling. But most of all, you feel a burning sensation just under your breastbone. Sure, these symptoms all fit the pattern of a bad chest cold or perhaps even a touch of the flu, but that's not what you have. These are the symptoms of bronchitis. Experts say that bronchitis is usually brought on by a viral infection that causes inflammation of the bronchi (the main tubes, or airways, that connect the windpipe to the lungs). This inflammation causes a narrowing of the bronchi that reduces the volume of air available for breathing. The mucous membranes that line the bronchi also become inflamed, so they are more easily irritated by pollutants like tobacco smoke.

If you have any chronic health conditions—such as coronary heart disease or asthma—or have a weakened immune system, see your doctor before attempting any self-care measures.

On the other hand, if you have been healthy in general, bronchitis is not nearly as serious as it may seem, based on the way your cough makes you sound to others. And while it should not be taken lightly, with a little tender, loving care, you will get well. Here are 10 ways to speed up your recovery.

Drink up.

The main reason for your shortness of breath is the buildup of sticky mucus. The consumption of two to four quarts of water each day will thin mucus and make it easier to cough it up and out. And that's the main objective in your get-well plan—to rid yourself of as much mucus as you can. Drinking water does not always bring instantaneous relief if you have chronic bronchitis. It may take several weeks to notice a change, but stick with your increased intake of water. If you have kidney disease, prostate trouble, or heart disease, it will be especially important to check with your physician before loading up on fluids, however.

Lots of nonalcoholic liquids, especially warm teas and soups, will soothe your sore throat and dilute thick phlegm. Avoid milk and dairy products, as they increase the thickness of mucus.

Stay away from cola, tea, or coffee that contains caffeine, however. Not only do these drinks make your body lose fluids, but they can make you anxious and shaky. Alcoholic beverages can slow your breathing. Definitely skip that cocktail if you are taking sedatives, because those drugs don't mix with alcohol.

Breathe in more moisture.

Take a long, hot shower and breathe in the steam. Put a pot of water on your stove and let it boil. Invest in a vaporizer with a cool mist. Ask your doctor for a recommendation.

Get in bed.

If you have an acute case of bronchitis, rest will help you recover. Don't walk around, go to work, do household chores, or worry about what you were unable to do. Pick up a good book, rent an old movie, and sleep as often and as long as you can. If your problem is chronic, see your doctor for guidance. Curtailing all activity may not be your doctor's choice of treatment.

Gargle with saltwater.

Put a teaspoon of salt into a large glass of warm water, stir, and gargle. Not only will the mixture soothe your sore throat, it will cut through phlegm. Gargle as often as you like, but be sure to stick to the basic formula: Too much salt can be irritating and too little won't help.

Don't stop coughing.

Most medicines that are designed to dampen your cough reflex are not going to help you get well. Some of the common ingredients in cough drops and remedies are decongestants, antihistamines, alcohol, and sugar. Coughing is your body's way of ridding itself of the mucus. If you eliminate the cough, it could take longer to recover.

Rely on medication.

Bronchodilators are used for opening your airways to let air move in and out more easily. They are available in several forms, including pills, liquids, and sprays. If you feel nervous, can't sleep at night, or have an upset stomach, be sure to tell your doctor. These symptoms may be side effects of your medication. Your doctor might order oxygen therapy if your chronic bronchitis has progressed to a more serious condition and you don't have enough oxygen in your blood. Antibiotics treat infections in your bronchial tubes. Diuretics, or water pills, may be used to rid your body of excess fluid. Expectorants help make mucus thin so you can cough easier and expel phlegm. Sedatives and tranquilizers can help you relax, but be careful because they can also slow down your respiratory system. Steroids reduce swelling in your airways, but they have side effects that can be dangerous. Stomach ulcers, weakened skin and bones, higher risk of infection, and a tendency to bruise easily should be on your warning list if you are taking a steroid medication. Finally, aspirin and ibuprofen reduce chest pain better than acetaminophen.

Watch your symptoms.

Bronchitis will probably go away on its own, but complications occasionally develop, especially in people over 50. You don't want to end up with pneumonia or a sinus infection. Contact the doctor if your fever is persistently high, you are extremely short of breath, or coughing spells are prolonged. Severe chest pain or blood in your mucus also demands the attention of a doctor, as does any distinct change in its color or consistency.

Shun gassers.

Avoid foods that give you gas because they can bloat your abdomen and make it harder to breathe. The American Lung Association lists the following foods as major culprits: apples, beans (except green beans), broccoli, brussels sprouts, cabbage, cauliflower, corn, cucumber, melons, onions, peas, and turnips.

Avoid smoke.

Cigarette smoke irritates the bronchial passageways leading to your lungs. In addition to the bronchial infection, any irritation from smoking is only going to make you feel worse. If you haven't already dropped this habit, do so right away. If you live with a smoker, ask him or her to smoke outside.

Cough correctly.

When you come down with a case of bronchitis, too much mucus is produced. This causes your respiratory tract to get clogged up. By learning how to cough correctly, you can get the mucus up and out more easily.

1. Sit down in a chair, put both feet on the floor, and lean forward.
2. Take in a deep breath through your nose—slowly. Sniff the air in. Breathe deeply, using your diaphragm and letting your stomach puff out. Your objective is to get enough air in behind the mucus to push it out.
3. Hold your breath for two seconds. Count silently: one, two.
4. Cough once to loosen the mucus.
5. Cough a second time to push the mucus out. Don't swallow the mucus; it can upset your stomach. Use tissues or a paper towel to catch it.
6. Rest and repeat each step.●

BURNS

11 WAYS TO TURN DOWN THE HEAT

Think of your burn as a lesson in physics. A hot run-in with one of nature's most potent elements, fire, teaches you that human skin just can't tolerate heat above 120 degrees Fahrenheit. Actually, it's better to know this before you learn it the hard way—most burns can be prevented with a little common sense (see sidebar, "How to Prevent Burns"). And once you are burned, before you start thinking about physics, get relief fast. Not only will you spare yourself a lot of pain, but the measures you take immediately after being burned can make all the difference in how well the burned area heals.

While many minor burns can be treated at home, seek medical assistance for any burn that appears serious—if the heat seems to have burned through the skin entirely, if a burn is extremely painful, if it covers an area larger than about an inch and a half across, or if it isn't painful but looks ferocious (the nerve endings may have been damaged). It is especially important to seek medical assistance for what may be serious burns if you are elderly, because your skin tissue and your heart are less able to withstand the trauma of a burn.

Let's hope you never have to use these measures, but here's what to do when you get too close to the fire.

Remove hot clothing.

If your clothing is on fire, drop to the ground and roll, pushing the flames away from your face. It is very important to remove any clothing that has been soaked in hot grease or boiling water, because it can continue to transmit thermal energy, making the burn more severe. It will also be harder to remove this clothing once the burn has started to blister and inflammation has set in.

Turn on the tap.

The first thing you should do to treat a burn is run it under cool tap water, apply a cool compress, or immerse the area in cool water. Treat a burn in this way for at least ten minutes—or longer if it makes you feel more comfortable. Water will put out the fire in your skin, so to speak, preventing thermal energy from spreading and destroying surrounding tissue. It will also help soothe the pain. If the burn is caused by contact with a corrosive chemical, it's extremely important to run it under water to flush the chemical out of the burn area.

Keep it cool and gentle.

It's possible to have too much of a good thing, though. Make sure the water is not too cold, and don't apply ice to a burn—extreme cold will stanch soothing, healing blood flow to the area. And don't turn on the tap full force, because too much water pressure can destroy the remaining tissue.

Avoid the greasy stuff.

Forget the old myth about rubbing butter into a burn. Give ointments a pass, too. Why? Any of these greasy substances is likely to hold heat in, causing further damage. Furthermore, they may not be sterile, and an infection can easily breed in the burn-damaged area.

Elevate the affected area.

This can help reduce the painful swelling that can immediately follow a burn. Don't lift the affected area too high, though—keep it level with the heart so blood can reach the burned skin.

Know when to call EMS.

Most minor burns will heal on their own without complications. More serious burns require prompt medical attention. If a minor burn covers an area no larger than an inch and a half or so, it will probably heal on its own. If a burn is larger than that, see your doctor. If you are burned seriously, call your physician or emergency medical services (EMS) immediately, lay down with your feet propped up, apply cool water or a cool compress to the area, and wait for help to arrive.

Know shock symptoms.

Someone who has been burned severely may go into shock. The symptoms include drowsiness or confusion, very pale or cold skin, unusual thirst, vomiting, and a weak but rapid pulse. If you are assisting a burn victim and suspect shock, call EMS, lay the victim flat, elevate their feet about 12 inches, and cover them with a blanket to prevent loss of body heat. Don't give someone who is in shock anything to eat or drink—that could trigger vomiting.

Forget the fluff.

Never cover a burn with fluffy cotton or similar materials. They can adhere to the burned surface.

Take an aspirin.

If you can't tolerate aspirin, take acetaminophen or ibuprofen. Even minor burns can be extremely painful, and these drugs will probably make you feel more comfortable. They will also help reduce the inflammation.

Don't pop the blister.

The blister that forms over a burn is a natural bandage. It's the body's way of protecting the area while skin begins to grow back. Not only should you not pop a blister, but you should take measures to protect it while the body goes about healing itself: Apply a clean, cotton bandage over a blister so clothing doesn't rub against it.

Exercise extreme caution with electrical burns.

The severity of these burns can be deceiving because much of the damage can occur beneath the surface of the skin, where you won't be able to see it. Seek medical assistance immediately if you are burned by electricity.●

HOW TO PREVENT BURNS

○ ○ ○

Prevention is your first line of defense against burns. In fact, many burns can be avoided by taking practical precautions around the house.

1. Make sure the stove and the surrounding area are clean to prevent grease fires.

2. Keep cooking drippings and grease well away from the stove.

3. Don't keep utensils at the back of the stove, where you must reach across hot surfaces to get them.

4. Don't use dish towels, paper towels, or other uninsulated materials to grab hot pots and pans. Use pot holders and oven mitts.

5. Make sure the stove area is well lighted, so you can see what you are doing at all times.

6. Never leave pans unattended while cooking. If you absolutely must leave the kitchen for some reason, be sure to take a wooden spoon or another implement with you to serve as a reminder that you have something cooking.

7. Avoid wearing flammable clothes or clothes with large or loose sleeves when cooking.

8. Be extremely careful when uncovering a container when you take it out of a microwave oven. Steam from foods cooked in a microwave oven is a major cause of burns.

9. Make sure your hot water heater is set no higher than 120 degrees Fahrenheit to avoid scalding.

10. Check electrical cords for fraying and replace them if necessary.

BURSITIS

11 WAYS TO MANAGE THE PAIN

If you regularly play golf or tennis, tend your garden, work at a computer, or crochet, you may well suffer from bouts of joint pain, sometimes referred to as "housemaid's knee" or "student elbow." When your joints flare up like this, you may think you are suffering from arthritis, but think again. The problem may not be in the joint itself, but in the soft tissue surrounding it, the ligaments, tendons, and muscles.

Of all the painful conditions affecting the soft tissues, one of the most common is bursitis, an inflammation of the bursae (the plural of *bursa*). These little fluid-filled sacs are located around joints throughout the body, and their job is to act as cushions, preventing muscles and tendons from coming into direct contact with bones. If the bursae become swollen, the result is dull, persistent joint pain that increases with movement. Common sites for bursitis are the hips, elbows, shoulders, and toes (a bunion, by the way, is just a chronic case of bursitis that afflicts the joint of the big toe). Swinging a tennis racket; continually resting your elbow on a desk; chronic, irregular posture that affects the hips— any of these actions can irritate the bursae and bring on bursitis.

Bursitis is not a chronic condition, however. Much of the time it clears up by itself within a week or two, and it rarely does any permanent damage. But bursitis can recur—unless you take preventive measures. Here are some ways to prevent the flare-ups and to find comfort when suffering through a bout of bursitis.

Stop what you're doing.

Any activity that requires repetitive use of the affected area is going to exacerbate inflammation and cause pain. Avoid such activities until it's clear that the bursitis flare-up is on the wane.

Rest.

Give the affected area a break. Using a sling or splint, for example, will prevent you from exposing your shoulder or elbow to unnecessary motion.

Take pain medications.

An over-the-counter nonsteroidal anti-inflammatory drug (NSAID), such as aspirin and ibuprofen, can help reduce inflammation and alleviate pain.

First administer the cold.

At the onset of bursitis, use ice to bring down swelling and ease the pain. Twenty minutes every hour or two can helpx. If you don't have an ice pack, wrap ice cubes or even a bag of frozen vegetables in a dish towel and apply it to the area.

Then heat it up.

After a couple of days, stop icing and turn on the heat. Apply a heating pad to the area frequently and leave it on for 20 minutes or so. The heat will stimulate healing blood flow to the area and should provide some relief from the pain.

Stretch gently.

Once the pain begins to subside, ease the area back into action gently. Do a few easy stretches several times a day, but don't resume normal activities until the pain and swelling are gone.

Use little helpers.

There's no need to strain bursitis-prone joints. In fact, you're just looking for trouble when you do so. Instead, take some simple precautions. Use a steplad-der, for instance, to avoid shoulder strains; wear a knee support when walking or jogging; and use a wrist support for computer work.

Warm up and cool down.

You're looking for trouble if you don't warm up before exercise. Do some stretches before exercise to get the blood flowing to your joint areas. To avoid stiffness, do some cooldown stretches afterward.

Plan an exercise regimen.

The rule for muscles and tendons is to use them or lose them. With lack of use, they become weak and more susceptible to bursitis and other strain-related ailments. There's no need to run a marathon; any kind of moderate, three-times-a-week exercise regimen, such as walking or swimming, will help keep you in shape. If you haven't been exercising, check with your doctor first.

Exercise for flexibility.

Inactivity, not necessarily age, makes joints and muscles become stiff. The secret is to keep flexible. Beginning slowly, work into a stretching and exercise regimen (many gyms offer stretching classes) that will help you regain full range of motion and slightly lengthen tendons and muscles for flexibility.

Work out in the water.

Water eliminates most of the weight-bearing pressure on your joints and ligaments. Doing aerobic, range-of-motion, and strengthening exercises in a pool is a great way to bounce back from a bout of bursitis.●

PREVENTING BURSITIS

○ ○ ○

- Bursitis in the shoulder is common among weekend athletes. Throwing a baseball, for example, or swinging a tennis racket are common triggers of bursitis in the shoulder area. To avoid the problem, use proper form when engaged in sports, and seek the assistance of a pro if necessary.

- Bursitis in the knee is usually brought on by kneeling on hard surfaces, standing for long periods of time, or other activities that put a lot of pressure on the kneecap. If you must kneel when you garden or do household chores, use a pad or cushion and shift positions frequently to minimize strain on the kneecap. If you must stand for long periods, shift your stance from time to time and take sitting breaks frequently.

- Bursitis in the heel can usually be traced to wearing high heels or shoes that are too tight in the back or across the top (a common problem with athletic shoes). Get fitted properly.

- Bursitis in the elbow is usually caused by banging or continually resting the joint on a hard surface. Use a little common sense: Try to break the habit of leaning on your elbows, but if you must lean (while reading or writing, for instance), use a cushion to relieve the pressure.

- Bursitis in the hips is usually the consequence of continual stress on the area—from lying on one side continually, getting out of a chair in such a way that you put a lot of pressure on the hips, incorrect posture when walking or climbing stairs, lifting heavy objects improperly, even wearing shoes with worn-out heels that throw the hips out of alignment. Check your posture to make sure you don't put all your weight on your hip area, and when lifting, use your legs, not your hips and spine.

- Bursitis in the groin area, between the abdomen and the thigh, is often the result of lifting heavy objects. Bursitis in this area can cause pain that radiates down the leg to the knee. Thigh stretches can help keep the area pliable and less prone to strains, and it's important not to twist, putting strain on groin muscles, when lifting heavy or cumbersome objects.

CANCER

17 TIPS ON PREVENTING AND DEALING WITH CANCER

Cancer occurs when normal cells divide and multiply out of control. This process results in the formation of tumors that invade the surrounding parts of the body and spread to distant areas. Cancerous tumors are considered life-threatening. Benign tumors usually are not dangerous because they do not invade local areas or spread to other organs.

Though cancer is obviously a serious disease, most people survive cancer treatment and many even thrive afterward. The National Coalition for Cancer Survivorship reports that more than eight million people have won their fight with cancer. In fact, far more people survive cancer than die from it. Breast cancer is the most common type of malignancy in women, yet more than 70 percent of women whose cancer has spread into the areas surrounding the breast live longer than five years after detection. Prostate cancer, the most common form of cancer in men, will be diagnosed in some 200,000 men this year, but only about 38,000 of them will die from the disease.

Exciting developments are occurring every day in cancer research. Tumors that only a few years ago were considered to be inoperable now can be removed easily without harming important blood vessels, nerves, and organs—often without affecting a person's appearance.

Devices and techniques are being used to kill tumor cells by freezing them or by focusing tiny beams of radiation directly on them. New drugs appear capable of stopping defective genes from making cancer cells, and complex gene therapy is making tumor cells more susceptible to potent cancer-killing drugs.

PREVENTION STRATEGIES

Although it is currently estimated that one in three Americans will acquire some form of cancer at one time or another during their lifetime, the survival rate is improving. By understanding risk factors, learning how to reduce the influence of those factors, learning the warning signs, and getting regular medical checkups, you can decrease your chances of getting cancer and minimize its impact if you do get it.

Understand the risk factors.

The following factors are believed to increase the risk of cancer:

- Smoking. The American Cancer Society estimates that cigarette smoking is the cause of about 87 percent of cases of lung cancer.
- Personal history. There is an increased likelihood of getting cancer a second time if you've already experienced the disease once.
- Age. As the years pass, the risk of cancer grows. This increase is particularly noticeable after age 40.
- Sun exposure. Worshipers of sunlight and a golden tan take note: If you spend a lot of time outdoors without proper protection from the sun, your chances of developing skin cancer increase considerably.
- Family history. A strong link exists between some types of cancer—

breast cancer and cancer of the female reproductive system, in particular—and a person's family history of these diseases. It is therefore important—especially if you're woman—to learn whether anyone in your family has ever had cancer.

- Overweight. If you exceed the weight recommendations for your height, gender, and age by 40 percent or more, you risk an increase in the likelihood of coming down with cancer of the breast, colon, ovaries, prostate, and uterus.
- Dietary habits. If your diet includes many foods that are low in fiber and high in fat or nitrates, your risk increases.
- Excessive drinking. An excessive amount of alcohol raises the danger of acquiring cancer of the esophagus, larynx, throat, and liver.

Reduce your risk.

Now that you have a clear understanding of what the risk factors are, here are some ideas on how to go about limiting them.

- Quit smoking.
- Maintain a healthy weight. Consult with your doctor to determine a weight that is appropriate for you, then adjust your balance of eating and exercise to achieve and maintain that weight.
- Watch your diet. Be sure to eat enough high-fiber foods. Limit your intake of foods containing a lot of fat. Also avoid foods that are smoked, salt cured, and nitrate cured.
- Schedule regular medical exams. You should see your doctor at least once every three years if you're in good health, more frequently if not. This is a matter to discuss with your doctor.

DIET AND THE RISK OF CANCER

○ ○ ○

The best current estimate is that 35 percent or more of all cancers are associated with diet. This does not mean that these types of cancer are caused entirely by diet, but that diet contributes to their development. These steps may help protect you:

- Eat five servings of vegetables a day. For example, try a glass of juice in the morning, a large mixed salad for lunch (which counts as two servings of vegetables), a fruit snack, and a vegetable with the evening meal. Hundreds of studies around the world have shown that people with a low intake of fruits and vegetables have a high risk of cancer. Individual nutrients, such as beta carotene, vitamin C, and fiber have had a protective effect with respect to lung, stomach, and colon cancer. However, if you eat lots of fruits and vegetables, you get not only these nutrients but other substances that may have a protective effect against cancer.

- Limit fat. The current recommendation is to hold dietary fat to no more than 30 percent of the total number of calories. You can work toward this goal by reducing the amount of red meat and dairy products you eat and replacing saturated and polyunsaturated fats with monounsaturated fat such as olive oil.

- Spice up your life. Potent cancer-protective compounds can be found in many spicy foods and seasonings, such as red and yellow onions, garlic, and turmeric. There are no specific recommendations regarding these foods right now, but it wouldn't hurt to include them in your diet. They can also replace some fatty sauces by enhancing flavor.

A yearly exam might be recommended for you, taking your individual risk factors into account.

- Minimize exposure to the sun. If possible, avoid direct sunlight when the sun's rays are strongest, from about 10 A.M. until about 2:00 P.M. (times vary depending on your location relative to the equator). When you are outside, wear sunblock with a sun protection factor (SPF) of at least 15, apply it 15 to 20 minutes before you go out in the sun, and wear a wide-brimmed hat that protects your face, ears, and neck.

- Perform regular exams on yourself. Women should carefully examine their breasts, men should examine their testicles, and members of both sexes should inspect their skin periodically. Check with your doctor for specific guidelines.

- Women, consider progesterone. Postmenopausal women who have an intact uterus and who are receiving estrogen therapy should also take progesterone.

Learn the warning signs.

You've heard and read them before, but they can never be repeated too often. People over 50 should be especially conscious of the warning signs of cancer and contact their physician immediately if they notice any of them:

1. Any unusual bleeding or discharge

2. Any obvious change (such as itching, enlargement, or bleeding) or a lack of symmetry in a mole or wart

3. The appearance of a lump or thickening in the breast or elsewhere beneath the skin

4. Nagging hoarseness or a cough that is persistent

5. A sore or scab that does not heal in a reasonable period of time (within three weeks)

6. Any marked change from normal bowel or bladder function

7. Difficulty swallowing or a stubborn case of indigestion

Recognize cancer without delay.

Survival and overall quality of life are far better when cancer is treated in its early stages. Regular checkups by your doctor and routine self-examinations can spot many types of cancer before they progress too far.

More than 90 percent of women survive longer than five years when breast cancer is found before it has spread beyond the breast itself. The American Cancer Society (ACS) therefore recommends that women examine their own breasts once a month. This examination should include visually studying the entire breast and armpit as well as checking up and down the breast using the finger pads to feel for lumps, thicknesses, or other abnormalities. The ACS also asks women to have a doctor examine their breasts once a year and to have a yearly mammogram if they are over age 50.

Women should also have regular gynecologic exams that include a Pap test. The Pap test is an examination of the cells swabbed or scraped from the surface of the cervix. It is highly accurate in detecting cancer of the cervix or uterus, which affects about 45,000 women each year. After three consecutive annual Pap smears and pelvic exams that are normal, women can then schedule these tests at least once every three years.

Men over 40 should have an annual prostate examination by a physician to check for prostate cancer, which affects approximately one of every ten males in the United States. Signs of possible prostate cancer include difficulty urinating, frequent urination (especially at night), blood in the urine, and pain in the hips or back. Men who have such symptoms should consult their doctor about the need for appropriate analysis, which might include a digital rectal exam, a prostate-specific antigen (PSA) blood test, and an ultrasound.

Both men and women over the age of 50 should have an annual stool test, which assesses a sample of the stool for signs of colon and rectal tumors.

COPING TIPS

People with cancer are discovering that they can do many things to feel better and to help their bodies combat cancer.

Expect change.

Cancer will change your life. It will change your relationships with friends and family, your appearance, your sexuality, your physical endurance and strength, and your finances. All these changes will affect how you feel as a person. But if you learn ahead of time what to expect, not only in terms of the physical changes that are inevitable but the social and emotional changes as well, these changes will not seem as strange when they do come. And you will be better prepared to handle them.

Prepare for "help" from your friends.

You need to be ready for the comments and suggestions well-meaning but often misguided friends will offer. According to experts, friends and relatives will come up with all kinds of suggestions and advice, including what helped their Uncle Fred or Granny Jones. Some of this information may be extremely helpful, but other remarks may be unintentionally hurtful.

You also need to be aware that some friends and family members will feel they can help you the most by constantly being upbeat and cheerful or by avoiding the topic of cancer altogether.

If you realize that your friends and family are themselves having difficulty accepting your disease, you may find it easier to deal with their advice. If your friends and family seem uncomfortable in your company, let them know they don't have to avoid using the word *cancer* when you are together. They should not be overly protective, nor should they fail to ask about your illness or stop including you in their activities.

Let go of your emotions.

At times, you will feel incredibly sad, angry, frightened, or disbelieving. These are normal, healthy reactions to your disease and represent the stages of grief every person goes through when confronted with a major loss. Understand that every cancer patient has a certain number of tears to shed. If you don't shed your tears, they will just bottle up inside and lead to depression. Go ahead and let the tears fall. Crying will help to cleanse your spirit and soothe your nerves; eventually the time for crying will pass.

You will also need to laugh to bring warmth and light into your life. Yell and scream if necessary when your anger rises to the surface or when your physical or emotional pain is particularly acute. Whenever you can, share your thoughts and fears with others—a family member, friend, member of the clergy, health care professional, or support group.

Don't accept blame.

The whole notion that it is somehow your fault that you have cancer is nonsense. Don't believe your cancer is due to your divorce or the fact that you lost your job. Placing blame is counterproductive and unhealthy. At one time or another you will be plagued by the question, "Why has this happened to me?" Get past this stage as quickly as you can by thinking about the next question: "What can I do now?"

Maintain a good self-image.

It is important to keep your body clean and well-groomed. Don't stay in your nightclothes and robe during the day. Wear a hairpiece after chemotherapy and go shopping for some new clothes. There are certain things we all need to do to feel good about ourselves, to feel that we are attractive. Take pride in your body. You will not only look better, you will feel better, and you will minimize the shock waves that occur when you lose your hair or have some other obvious reaction to surgery, chemotherapy, or radiation.

Think positively.

Doctors recognize that many people who live long, healthy lives and who overcome incredible afflictions have a characteristic called a positive attitude. Not everyone with a positive attitude survives and thrives after cancer, but a connection appears to exist that involves a person's mental attitude, the neurons in the brain, the immune system, and one's health.

You can strengthen this connection in a number of ways. One is by establishing a strong working relationship with your doctor and assuming an active role in your treatment and recovery. Another is by discovering the aspects of your life or treatment that cause fear, anger, trepidation, or dread and asking your doctor or a qualified therapist, or both, how you can approach these situations without evoking such negative emotions.

Join a support group.

If you feel you may have difficulty on your own dealing with the emotional or psychosocial effects of cancer and its treatment, consider joining a support group. There are several types of cancer support groups, but all operate according to the same basic principle: that people who face similar problems can draw knowledge, understanding, and strength from one another.

In a support group, newly diagnosed cancer patients can learn from long-term survivors about the details of treatment and recovery. New patients can talk about their most intimate concerns with individuals who have experienced the same problems. And they can learn an important lesson from people who have "been there," which is that you can have cancer and still relish life. Ask your doctor to order a consultation with a psychologist who can help you explore available options and choose the group that will be right for you.

Make a toll-free call.

Contact the Cancer Information Service at 800-4-CANCER (800-422-6237). Offered by the National Cancer Institute, this service can provide information about a support group in your state along with a wealth of other information on subjects that include cancer prevention, smoking cessation, lists of accredited hospitals, and general data on different types of cancers.

Look for spirituality or inner peace.

Physical health and well-being can be affected by spiritual health and the maintenance of a constant conversation with your inner self through prayer or meditation. There is no best way to pray, but one commonly held belief is that prayer should be a routine part of life, not a haphazard one.

Yoga (which combines limbering exercises with deep-breathing techniques) and meditation help you clear your mind of distractions and focus on your inner being and health. These practices should be done regularly to achieve the maximum effect. That means a daily routine at a set time and place. You can learn more about yoga and meditation through books, videotapes, television programs, or formal educational programs.

Start walking.

When you learn you have cancer, you may feel that your body has failed you; so you lose a little trust in it and worry that you may overly tax your body by doing too much. However, you need to keep active to improve the operation of your circulatory system, increase your energy and endurance, alleviate pain or stiffness in the joints, and reduce fatigue. Regular activity also enhances eating, sleeping, and your sense of well-being. People who remain moderately active do better in treatment, have a better quality of life and less depression, and just feel better all around.

One of the best exercises for people who are undergoing cancer therapy or recovering after remission is rhythmic walking. Rhythmic walking is not the rapid form of competitive walking known as racewalking. Nor is it a slow stroll through the park. It is a regular, once-a-day or once-every-other-day program of exercise that combines brisk walking with vigorous movement of the arms to stimulate the action of the circulatory system.

At first, you may be able to walk only five minutes a day, but you should gradually build up over time to reach the ideal schedule of 45-minutes per day or every other day. During every walking session, begin by walking slowly for about five minutes to warm up. Then walk briskly for 35 minutes. Finally, cool down by walking slowly again. Some mild upper-body weight training, consisting of raising and lowering one- to three-pound hand weights, is also recommended.

Join an exercise program.

You may wish to visit an exercise physiologist or join the local YMCA if you want to participate in a supervised exercise program. Water therapy, which involves repetitive body movements in a swimming pool, is another option.

Relax, relax, relax.

There are several methods of reducing discomfort you can try that do not involve the use of drugs. Relaxation is one of the best. Relaxation techniques help you cope with discomfort by eliminating tension from the muscles and reducing anxiety. You can perform relaxation

BE MELLOW

○ ○ ○

One relaxation technique involves lying on the floor with your eyes closed, your legs and feet apart slightly, your hands and arms flat on the floor next to your body. Once you are in this position, begin to breathe deeply. Inhale slowly, exhale slowly, making sure to release all the air from the lungs. Then, as you exhale, relax your muscles and try to release all the tension in your body from the tips of your fingers and toes. Continue for as long as ten minutes. When you wish to stop, count slowly from one to five, open your eyes, and slowly begin moving again.

Relaxation techniques work best when performed for five to ten minutes every day. Pick one technique you are comfortable with. Keep trying to follow the procedure even if you don't feel any results at first. It may take a few days or weeks to start getting the full effect.

techniques on your own or purchase tapes to help you along.

Imagery often accompanies relaxation. When you practice imagery, you create peaceful pictures or situations in your mind to help you sleep or reduce anxiety. You may also imagine a scheme for eliminating your discomfort.

Become preoccupied.

You might try to distract yourself from uncomfortable symptoms by performing a repetitive activity like knitting or painting, reading a good book, or watching a video tape.●

CANKER SORES

5 WAYS TO EASE THE DISCOMFORT

Do you occasionally have a pesky little sore in your mouth that makes it hard to eat and even talk? Chances are it's a canker sore, known in medical terms as an aphthous ulcer, which means fire sore—an apt description for this temporary nuisance.

How do you know if it's a canker sore? A canker sore occurs inside the mouth—on the gums, tongue, or interior linings of the cheeks. In contrast, a cold sore, that other common ailment of the mouth region, crops up on or around the outside of the lips. Usually, canker sores are only about an eighth of an inch in diameter—the size of a pencil eraser.

The first sign of a canker sore may be a tingling, burning sensation inside the mouth, followed shortly by the appearance of a white or yellowish spot edged by a red halo. Thankfully, canker sores usually travel solo (though they can appear in clusters), don't hang around for much more than a week, and unlike cold sores are not contagious. While medical science has yet to uncover the cause of canker sores, such factors as dealing with emotional stress and eating highly acidic foods (like citrus fruits and tomatoes) have been cited. An injury to the inside of the mouth, such as a scrape caused by the bristles of a toothbrush, is another culprit. And while there's no known cure for canker sores, over the years sufferers and their doctors have come up with some surefire ways to make them easier to live with.

Watch what you eat.

Acidic, sugary, or salty foods will irritate canker sores. On the list for canker-sore sufferers to avoid: chocolate, citrus fruits and citrus drinks, nuts, and tomatoes. Salty, sharp-edged snacks like potato chips are definitely to be avoided. Lay off hot foods, too—that means spice-wise and temperature-wise.

Brush with care.

Avoid the affected areas with your toothbrush. Otherwise, you might scrape off the protective membrane that forms over a canker sore during healing.

Take out a styptic pencil.

It's an old remedy, but it still works. Dab the sore with the medicated end of a styptic pencil (available in drugstores), just as you would to stem bleeding from a shaving nick. This will numb inflamed nerve endings. Be sure to use a new pencil to avoid infecting the sore with bacteria.

Dull the pain.

There are several easy ways to do it. Aspirin, acetaminophen, or ibuprofen may keep the pain at bay. Topical anesthetics may also help. These range from ice, ap-

---

CAUSE FOR ALARM?

○ ○ ○

If pain from your canker sore continues to get the best of you or if you develop a fever, call your doctor. A secondary bacterial infection (caused by touching the sore with a dirty finger, for example) may have set in. The infection can be treated with antibiotics. Sometimes a doctor will treat severe cases with cortisone.

Definitely see a doctor if the sore in your mouth doesn't heal after a couple of weeks. A mouth ulcer that sticks around, even if it's not causing pain, could be the sign of oral cancer or a number of other disorders, including vitamin deficiency, anemia, or Crohn disease.

---

plied to the sore to reduce swelling, to over-the-counter treatments. Those medications with xylocaine numb the area temporarily. Ointments like Orabase and benzocaine coat the sore, protecting it from being irritated by food and from becoming infected.

Pass the antacids, please.

Yes, those same tablets you munch on to ease your stomach after a big dinner can also soothe canker sores by reducing the acidity in your mouth that can irritate them. Consider this home-brewed antacid remedy: Combine equal parts of the liquid form of Kaopectate or Milk of Magnesia (both antacids) with Benylin or Benadryl (both mild anesthetics). Apply the mixture to the canker sore with a cotton swab. You'll cut down on painful acidity in your mouth and numb the sore, too.●

COLDS

14 TACTICS TO TAKE

Of course you've heard it before: There is no cure for the common cold. But that doesn't mean you must accept the runny nose, stuffy head, watery eyes, ticklish or sore throat, slight fever, and muscle aches without fighting back.

A cold is an upper respiratory infection caused by a virus. And there are hundreds of viruses out there to blame for your cold. Meanwhile, none of these microscopic invaders will fall down dead in response to drugs. As far as this fight goes, you are on your own. Luckily, your immune system comes to your defense as the viral particles enter the tissues of your nose or throat and begin to reproduce. In fact, the symptoms you love to hate simply indicate that your immune system is doing its job. Your body is releasing chemicals, triggering inflammation, and bringing white blood cells to your defense to fight infection. This makes your temperature shoot up. In the midst of this metabolic warfare, histamine is produced, making you sneeze and sniffle. Mucus production also speeds up as your respiratory system tries to trap the virus and get rid of it. Proteins such as interferon in your blood even join the fray, coating the virus as well as any infected cells so your own white blood cells can find these bad guys faster. Don't worry, most skirmishes with a cold last only about seven days, although it often seems longer.

Here are tactics to take you through this hard week of cold confrontation and make you more comfortable.

Drink, drink, drink.

Almost any kind of fluids will thin the mucus being produced by the membranes in your nose and throat and make it clearer. Fill up every two hours and aim for at least eight ounces each time. A cold will dehydrate you, so stay away from liquids containing caffeine and alcohol.

Make fresh lemonade. Lemon is an effective cleanser. If you are making a lot of mucus, find some ways to add lemons to your diet. Put honey in a warm lemony drink. Sip decaffeinated herb tea with one of these enhancers: cinnamon, peppermint, or licorice root. Any one of them will make your tea even more of a symptom-fighter.

Relax.

Don't schedule any high-pressure meetings, parties, or travel. If you can, take a day or two off from work. As you age, your immune system can become compromised by various factors, so it needs all the help you can give it to fight ordinary infections like the common cold. Don't feel guilty about unfinished work if you stay home. You aren't doing your coworkers any good when you sneeze, sniffle, blow your nose, or cough around them. Plan a nap each afternoon. If you must go to work, find a quiet spot to snooze for a brief period of time.

Dress in layers.

You want your body to remain comfortable and focused on its fight against the viral invasion. Cold weather won't cause a cold, but it won't make it any easier to recover either. Wear light layers, inside and out—as many as you need to stay cozy and warm. Peel off a layer if you feel too warm. Avoid going outside at all in severe or wet weather, especially if your head is wet.

Make chicken soup.

While doctors aren't quite certain just how or why chicken soup clears nasal passages, modern research has confirmed how effective this time-honored remedy can be: When chicken soup was tested along with hot and cold water, soup was far better able to clear mucus. Hot water came in second and cold water was a distant third.

Take Vitamin C.

Though a debate still rages over the value of vitamin C in fighting cold symptoms, many doctors now favor taking this mighty vitamin. Check with your own doctor before you try it, but for some people, taking 2,000 milligrams (mg) of vitamin C can lessen the severity of cold symptoms. Some reports indicate that you can shorten that long week of suffering to two or three days of mild sniffling. Vitamin C can also boost the body's resistance to other viruses while fighting off the cold. Though you will be relatively safe in doses up to 10,000 mg per day, don't overdo it. Too much can cause diarrhea. Spread your doses out during the day, taking 500 mg at four different times. Try eating foods high in vitamin C content, too. Oranges, lemons, grapefruits, as well as fresh juices made from oranges, grapefruits, and cranberries can supplement your vitamin C intake.

Gargle with salt water.

Put half a teaspoon of salt in an eight-ounce glass of warm water and gargle every two hours to soothe a sore throat. The saline solution will soothe inflammation and make the phlegm easier to cough up and out. Try snuffing some of the solution up one nostril at a time to clean out clogged nasal passages and reduce any swelling. The cause of the swelling is an overproduction of molecules called lymphokines. If you can get rid of these troublemakers, you'll feel better fast.

Steam yourself.

Use a vaporizer to loosen mucus, especially if you feel terribly stuffed with thick, yellow phlegm. Try making a steam tent by putting a towel over your head and leaning over a pot or pan of hot water. Be careful not to burn yourself. Since dry, cold air makes this infection hard for your body to fight, you want to put more humidity into your life. Put a pan of water near your heating vents or radiators. Watch out though: Inhaling steam isn't a good idea if you have asthma.

Follow doctor's orders as to medications.

Though your pharmacy may be filled with cold remedies that promise instant cures, be cautious about what you take. You may be on regular medication for some other disorder that will interact negatively with cold pills, pain-killers, cough syrups, sprays, or drops. Some multisymptom medications contain ingredients that work in counter-productive ways. For example, antihistamines do stop runny noses but they also irritate and dry out mucous membranes. This approach also thickens mucus, making it more difficult to cough out the stuff. Note any side effects or contraindications on the labels of any medication you buy, especially multisymptom cold cures. Some off-the-shelf remedies can cause nausea, sleepiness, or discomfort. Others contain alcohol. They may look or sound harmless in the advertising claims, but in actual use they can pack a powerfully dangerous punch. To be safe, ask the doctor first.

A decongestant ingredient called pseudoephedrine is great for unstuffing your nose, reducing any swelling, helping to drain your sinuses, and bringing excess fluids under control. However, it's not for everyone, and your doctor will probably warn you away from it if you have high blood pressure or heart disease.

Cough syrups with glyceryl guaiacolate—not dextromethorphan—will free up your phlegm and make the coughing less painful. Throat lozenges can combat a bad cough, too. Look for the kind with a topical anesthetic ingredient that will numb the pain for a short time.

THE GREAT GARLIC DEBATE

o o o

Medical researchers have taken garlic out of the kitchen and into the laboratory lately. Their findings: This common bulb, so great at enhancing the flavors of ordinary foods, may be good at fighting infection. Garlic, a member of the lily family and cousin to the onion, is in lots of old folk remedies now being examined under the microscopes at several research centers and reported in serious medical journals.

The powerful ingredient in that smelly clove of garlic is actually allicin. Tests show that the crushed raw garlic, loaded with allicin, is capable of killing lots of little microbes that can make your life miserable, including the viruses that cause colds. Eat it both cooked and raw. Its microbe-killing properties diminish when cooked, but some research indicates that even in a soup or stew, regular doses of garlic can help thin mucus. Make a salad of fresh garlic, tomatoes, and onions. Mash some and put it on your chicken tonight.

Try a menthol or vapor rub on your upper chest. The menthol vapor of a product like Vicks VapoRub may help to temporarily relieve your congestion at a time when you really need a good night's sleep. Rub some on, put on pajamas or a nightshirt, and cover up.

Don't eat too much.

Though there's an old saying, "Feed a cold and starve a fever," most doctors recommend that you stick to a light, low-fat diet when you are fighting a cold. Go easy on heavy meats, milk products, and fatty foods in general. Fill up on fresh fruits and vegetables.

Stop smoking.

A cold irritates your throat and upper respiratory system; cigarette smoke will just make it worse. If you are a smoker, stop at least until you get well. If you work or live with smokers, ask them to step outside or away from you when they want to light up.

Open a window.

Good ventilation is important to ensure that the air you breathe is clean. Though you should aim for a warm, mildly humid environment, an occasional breath of fresh, cool air is a good idea.

Use tissues.

Not only will they be softer on your sore nose, but you are less likely to spread your germs to others. Keep them handy for blowing your nose, catching that sneeze, or mopping up your dripping nostrils. You are most contagious during the first day or two of a cold, before your symptoms are full blown. The virus in your nose ends up on your handkerchief, which jumps right on over to your hands. The next time you touch something or someone, it can easily be passed on. Buy paper tissues and dispose of them quickly. Don't jam them in your pocket, where you are likely to touch them again.

Wash your hands.

A virus can spread easily through direct human contact, so don't give it a chance. Though viruses can also be spread through droplets in the air, you can limit their chances for living simply by using warm, soapy water and using it often.

Avoid crowds.

Stay home and be a couch potato the first day or two of your cold. That's when you are most contagious. Rest will help your immune system fight off the virus.●

COLD SORES

7 WAYS TO TREAT AND PREVENT THEM

You might have thought you said goodbye to unsightly facial eruptions long ago with the passage of your teenage years. Then, well into your adulthood, along come those annoying cold sores, a.k.a. fever blisters. Well, if it's any consolation, you're not alone. Cold sores are caused by herpes simplex, a virus like chickenpox, that infects most people on earth and usually lies dormant in nerve cells. But in many people, the virus is occasionally reactivated, causing unsightly and painful outbreaks around the lips.

Many different events seem to trigger cold sores. You might have an outbreak when you have a high fever, suffer from a cold, spend time in the sun, or experience a lot of stress at work. An outbreak usually begins with one or a few little blisters on or around your lips. They swell up, rupture, and scab over as they heal—the whole ugly process usually takes a week or two.

Many people confuse cold sores with canker sores. They're different beasts entirely and require different treatment. Unlike a cold sore, a canker sore is a small, round lesion inside the mouth.

The bad news is, once you contract the herpes simplex virus you have it for life. And it's easy to catch—all it takes is being in close contact with someone who has it. So, chances are the cold-sore outbreak you're suffering now probably won't be your last. The good news? There are many things to do to make it easier to weather the storm of an outbreak and some measures to take to keep the next outbreak at bay.

Don't be vain.

Tempted as you may be to cover cold sores with makeup, don't do it. Covering the sore with cosmetics may retard healing. It's better just to grin and bear it, at least until a protective scab has begun to form over the sore.

Keep the area clean.

To prevent the sore from becoming infected, wash it frequently with soap and water and blot the area dry with a towel.

Don't pick.

It's hard not to pick away at these annoying little devils, but the sore will take longer to heal if you pick at it, and you'll run the risk of developing a bacterial infection.

Visit the drugstore.

While over-the-counter medications will not cure a cold sore, several preparations will soothe the pain and prevent the sore from becoming infected. Any anesthetic lotion containing benzocaine may provide temporary relief. Once the blister ruptures, apply a lip balm to provide a protective coating that will keep out bacteria and minimize scabbing.

Beware of the sun.

Many a sun worshiper has returned from a day at the beach with a cold-sore outbreak to go along with the tan. If you're prone to cold sores, remember that exposure to the sun may well activate a recurrence. So, any time you go out in the sun, coat your lips and the surrounding area with sunscreen that has a sun protection factor (SPF) of 15 or higher.

Don't pass it along.

Herpes simplex, the virus that causes cold sores, is contagious, so you can easily pass it along with only a peck on the cheek. Keep oral contact to a minimum when you have an outbreak. It's also a good idea to avoid sharing towels, cups, dishes, and other objects that come into contact with your mouth during an outbreak.

Wash your hands frequently.

Why? Two reasons. One, even if you try not to pick at your sores, you probably will give in to the urge from time to time. And the cleaner your hands, the less likely you will be to infect the sores with bacteria. Two, you can spread the virus that causes cold sores just by touching something else after picking at a sore.●

IF YOU HAVE FREQUENT OUTBREAKS . . .

○ ○ ○

See a doctor, who may recommend that you take the antiviral drug acyclovir (several tablets a day on an ongoing basis) to suppress recurrences. Your doctor may also prescribe an ointment form of acyclovir to shorten the duration of outbreaks.

CONJUNCTIVITIS

8 REMEDIES FOR RECOVERY

You woke up this morning with your eyelids stuck shut because of a gluey, yellow discharge. When you were able to pry the lids open, you discovered that both eyes, including the whites, were distinctly pink. Uh oh. Your eyes are swollen, itchy, watery, and burning a bit. Bright light makes you want to blink, and the mucus may be blurring your vision. In fact, it feels a little bit like someone threw sand in your eyes. What you have is conjunctivitis, or pinkeye, a general term given to any inflammation of the membrane that lines the conjunctiva, the inner surfaces of your eyes.

Pinkeye probably won't affect your ability to see, but it's going to take a few days for you to recover. You could have picked it up anywhere. It might be bacterial or viral in origin or due to an injury. It could even be an allergic reaction to smog, smoke, airborne chemicals, or chlorine in a swimming pool. Most of the time your body's natural reflex to blink and tear keeps invaders washed right out. Sometimes your defense department isn't as diligent as it could be, however. When that happens and aggressive agents get stuck in your eyes, your immune system will try to wage war on them. The blood vessels in your eyes dilate, turning the whites of your eyes red or pink, and your eyes try to discharge the infection, producing the ugly yellow pus.

Seeing a doctor should be your first step because you may need a prescription antibiotic to speed your recovery. In the meantime, these steps might help.

HELLO, DOCTOR?

○ ○ ○

Conjunctivitis can become so severe that swelling forces the whites of the eye to protrude between the lids. Any worrisome eye condition calls for professional guidance, especially if 1) your problem has persisted for more than two or three days, 2) you are experiencing significant pain in the eyes, 3) your vision is not just a bit blurry but seriously affected, or 4) the amount of discharge increases and looks green as well as yellow.

Don't rub.

The urge to itch your eyes can be almost irresistible, but don't do it. As you age, the skin around your eyes becomes more susceptible to injury. Keep those hands off and wash them immediately after you apply any medication.

Wear sunglasses.

If your eyes are sensitive to light, put on a pair of sunglasses to give them a rest. If you choose to go swimming, wear goggles that fit tightly.

Take a tea-bag break.

Soak tea bags in warm water and place one on each closed eye. Rest for a few minutes. Any type of tea will do, but chamomile feels great on puffy eyes.

Try heat.

On the other hand, if your doctor said that you have a bacterial infection, a hot compress applied to the closed eyelids will dilate blood vessels, speeding the healing process. Heat will also relax your eye muscles. But first test the temperature of the cloth on the back of your hand.

Keep your eyes clean.

Dip a sterile cotton ball into warm water and gently swab across each eyelid to clean off any mucus or discharge.

Use cold compresses.

For soothing the itch of allergic conjunctivitis, take a clean washcloth, dip it in cold water, and press it against your closed eyes for several minutes. To reduce any swelling, put ice packs on your eyes.

Change your sheets.

Some types of conjunctivitis are very contagious. You may have deposited some gooey mucus on your bedclothes. Wash them in hot water. Don't share towels, handkerchiefs, or pillowcases with anyone. In fact, don't reuse your own towel. Toss it in the laundry every time you dry off.

Ask about eyedrops.

Over-the-counter antihistamine eyedrops are available for allergic conjunctivitis. But be sure to get a professional opinion before self-medicating.●

CONSTIPATION

23 WAYS TO GET YOUR BOWELS MOVING

You may have noticed that you've slowed down a little bit as you've gotten older. It's nothing serious, but you might not be able to walk quite as briskly as you once could or your reflexes may have slowed a bit. Well, the same thing happens with your bowels.

With age, the muscles that control bowel function, like all muscles, become a little lax. Add in some other factors—such as getting too little exercise, not eating enough fiber, taking certain medications—and what do you get? Nothing! You just don't feel the urge, even though you haven't had a bowel movement for days and days. Or you have to strain to get things moving down there. You're constipated.

Constipation is usually not serious, but it can be uncomfortable. Here are some ways to get your bowels moving.

Make sure it's really constipation.

If you believe commercials, you might think you're odd if you don't have a bowel movement every day. Well, listen up—it's quite normal to have only a few bowel movements a week or, for that matter, to have a few a day. You shouldn't be concerned unless you feel bloated, can't move your bowels without discomfort, or notice a change in your usual bowel habits.

Know when to call the doctor.

Ordinarily, constipation isn't serious, just one of the little nuisances of getting older or the consequence of not eating enough of the right foods. Cause for alarm, though, is constipation that lasts and lasts; a distended stomach accompanied by pain; or blood in the stool you finally manage to pass. If you experience any of these symptoms, be sure to contact your physician.

When you gotta go, go.

Sometimes we all get so busy we can't even find a few minutes to go to the bathroom. Well, make time—holding back when the urge strikes is going to make you constipated.

Don't strain.

If you gotta go, you gotta go, but if you don't, you don't. There's nothing wrong with going into the bathroom and trying, gently, but if your face is turning red and you're sweating, you're trying way too hard. No amount of huffing and puffing is going to produce the desired effect, and your efforts may wreak havoc on your innards. Straining on the toilet is a major cause of hemorrhoids and anal fissures; it can even be bad for your heart.

Get into training.

Maybe you've toilet trained a child, plopping the toddler on the toilet after meals in accordance with a set schedule. The same sort of training may work for you. Retire to the bathroom at a regular time once a day, within half an hour after a meal, and sooner or later your colon will get the idea.

Move around a bit.

When you're sedentary, so are your bowels. Any kind of regular exercise, like a good 20-minute walk every day, will help keep your bowels moving and avoid constipation.

Take it easy.

Stress has a way of making its presence known by influencing your bowels. You might react to tension with a bout of diarrhea, or stress might have the opposite effect on you. In either case, learning to take life a little easier will do some good things for your digestive tract.

Fill up on fiber.

Getting plenty of dietary fiber—and it's readily available in grains, fruits, vegetables, and legumes—is the easiest, safest way to prevent and treat constipation. What it comes down to is this: When you eat fiber, you produce large, soft stools that pass through your digestive system easily and quickly; when you don't, you produce hard stools that take longer to expel (see sidebar, "Where the Fiber Is").

Drink plenty of water.

Think of water as motor oil: It lubricates the system. If you don't drink enough of it, your stool is going to be dry and harder to pass. Water, and many other liquids, also bulk up the fiber you eat, producing softer, easier-to-pass stools. Eight glasses a day, even more in hot weather, is the recommended dose—provided you don't have kidney problems, glaucoma, or other conditions that make it necessary to limit your fluid intake. In such cases, stick to your doctor's recommendations.

Don't rely on just any other liquid.

Sorry, but a cup of coffee, a glass of beer, or a cold cola aren't going to do much to relieve your constipation. Caffeine and alcohol tend to go right through your system, drying you out. You don't have to avoid these drinks, but accompany them with a glass of water.

Go for grains.

Eat a high-fiber cereal at breakfast (*high-fiber* means it provides five or six grams of fiber per serving), nosh on high-fiber bread at lunch and snack time (two grams of fiber a slice), and eat long-grain brown rice with your afternoon and evening meals. Include any of these grains in your daily diet and you'll be adding some healthy fiber.

Get your five a day.

Servings of fruits and vegetables, that is. That's the amount recommended by the government to meet fiber requirements and for all-around good health.

Spread out your fiber.

If you try to cram all your fiber for the day into a single meal, you'll conquer constipation, all right—and may trade it in for a big bout of gas and diarrhea. Spread out your fiber intake and add fibery foods to every meal. But don't leap directly from a no-fiber diet to a high-fiber diet. Introduce high-fiber foods to the table on a gradual basis.

Put some prunes on your plate.

Or some juice in your glass. This age-old remedy really does work, in large part because prunes contain fiber. In addition, prunes contain a natural irritant that triggers the bowel muscles into action. A few words of warning, however—don't overdo it with prunes. A regular diet of them will probably cause diarrhea and you can become dependent on them to move your bowels.

Bulk up with beans.

They're the best source of dietary fiber. If you've been steering clear of them because they give you gas, try this bean degasser: Soak the beans overnight, drain them, then cook them for an hour and a half, replacing the water every half hour.

Limit refined foods.

The more refined the food, the less fiber it's likely to have in it. An orange has more fiber than a glass of orange juice, whole-grain bread has more fiber than white bread, and so on, right down your shopping list.

Go for fibery foods, not fiber pills.

It might seem a lot easier to pop a fiber pill than it is to worry about adding fiber-rich foods to your diet. But here's something to make you reconsider: Fiber pills don't contain that much fiber. In fact, you'll probably have to swallow five pills to get the same amount of fiber that is available from a single apple. Besides, an apple is less expensive.

Find the foods that are right for you.

Everyone's digestive tract reacts differently to different foods. Some people notice that milk and cheese, for instance, tend to constipate. For other people, dairy products cause diarrhea. If you notice that you become constipated after eating certain foods, eat a little less of them.

Lay off the laxatives.

Have you ever noticed how crowded the laxative section of your drugstore is? That's because a lot of people suffer from constipation, or think they do, and a lot of them grab some over-the-counter relief. These chemical laxatives work, but at a price: Your bowels become used to them, and pretty soon they won't empty until you've supplied them with a laxative. And that's the least of the woes you might experience with laxatives. They can damage the intestines, making it even more difficult to defecate. They can also inhibit absorption of prescription drugs and vitamins in your diet.

Choose a natural alternative.

If you feel you must take a laxative, look for a "natural" or "vegetable" product, such as Metamucil, in which the main ingredient is usually a highly concentrated form of fiber. These bulking agents are safe alternatives to chemical laxatives. Best yet, get plenty of exercise, eat fibery foods, and drink lots of water—and chances are you won't need laxatives anymore.

Read the labels on your prescription drugs.

Constipation is a common side effect of many prescription drugs. The list includes beta-blockers, which are prescribed for a number of heart disorders; some other blood-pressure medications; certain antidepressants and pain relievers; and some drugs prescribed for Parkinson disease. If you're suffering from constipation as a result of one of these medications, do *not* simply stop taking it—that can have serious consequences. Instead, ask your doctor to prescribe an alternative or to suggest some other treatment.

Watch out for over-the-counter medications, too.

Many of the remedies you take—for everything from a stuffy nose to an acidy tummy—may also cause constipation. For example, many decongestants and antihistamines do more than dry up your nasal passages. And keep this in mind the next time you grab an antacid: Those containing calcium or aluminum may make you constipated; those containing magnesium won't—in fact, they may give you diarrhea. The best choice may be an antacid that contains either calcium or aluminum as well as magnesium—the bowel-related side effects may balance each other out.

Bring in the heavy artillery.

You might want to resort to a suppository or an enema—but only as a last-ditch effort—when constipation is uncomfortable and nothing else seems to move your bowels. Choose nonirritating products, such as a saline or clear-water enema solution and a glycerin suppository. As with laxatives, *do not* get in the habit of using these products regularly because you may end up relying on them to move your bowels.●

WHERE THE FIBER IS

○ ○ ○

It's easier than you probably think it is to get the recommended 20 to 30 grams (g) of fiber a day. Some good sources, and the amounts of fiber they supply, are as follows:

one slice whole-wheat bread	1.5 g
⅓ cup oat bran	4.0 g
½ cup cooked brown rice	2.4 g
one apple with skin	2.8 g
one pear with skin	5.4 g
½ cup cooked broccoli	2.4 g
½ cup cooked frozen peas	4.3 g
½ cup cooked kidney beans	6.9 g
½ cup cooked pinto beans	5.9 g
½ cup cooked lentils	5.2 g

Don't forget high-fiber breakfast cereals. They provide 5 or more grams of fiber.

73

DANDRUFF

8 WAYS TO FOIL THE FLAKES

Do people ask you if its snowing outside . . . in July? Do people start brushing their shoulders when you walk into a room? Well, let us be the first to break the news—maybe you have dandruff.

All of us do, to some degree. Dandruff is simply the dead skin that your scalp continually sloughs off. These skin flakes mix with hair oils to produce those characteristic white deposits that, if you want to believe television commercials, keep you from getting dates and being popular. Your skin tends to be a little drier as you get older, so with each passing year you might notice more and more of these little flakes.

In most cases, dandruff is nothing to worry about medically. And it's not a sign of uncleanliness or hair loss. But if you're worried about what other people might think about your flakiness, here's what to do about it.

Wash out dead skin.

Frequent shampooing may be enough to do the trick for dandruff. Every other day should be enough, but sometimes a daily lather may be necessary. Frequent washing may make your hair dry and brittle, however, which is going to give you bad hair days in other ways. So be sure to use a gentle moisturizing conditioner in addition to your usual shampoo.

Bring out the big guns.

If your regular shampoo isn't doing the job of getting rid of your flakes, it's time to switch to a dandruff shampoo that has special ingredients. Look for one containing pyrithione zinc, sulfosalicylic compounds, selenium sulfide, zinc, or sulfur—all are powerful antidandruff agents that penetrate the skin layers and remove dead skin.

WHEN DANDRUFF IS SERIOUS

○ ○ ○

Severe flaking, itching, and crusting can be signs of more serious scalp conditions, such as seborrheic dermatitis, which can be treated with prescription drugs. Severe itching and flaking, accompanied by raised red patches, are symptoms of psoriasis, for which many treatments are available. Ask your doctor to help you decide the best way to treat your case.

Use them the right way.

To get the most out of these products, lather twice. First, to remove the dandruff that has mixed with oils and is clinging to your hair; second, to let the lather penetrate the scalp for at least five minutes.

Bring out the bigger gun.

If other shampoos aren't working, it may be time to move on to a shampoo containing coal tar. There are several drawbacks to using a coal-tar shampoo, so study the label carefully. The good news is that coal tar is quite effective at controlling dandruff.

Bring out the biggest guns.

If you've tried a number of over-the-counter dandruff shampoos and are still flaky (scalpwise), it may be time to talk to your physician. A prescription-only lotion containing any of the active ingredients in antidandruff shampoos can work very well in combination with these products. The lotion loosens the dead skin so the shampoo can really go to work. Corticosteroid creams are also sometimes prescribed.

Keep your hands out of your hair.

It's hard to resist the urge to scratch an itchy scalp, but don't do it. The itch of dandruff is just like any other itch: Once you start scratching, it's hard to stop. And pretty soon you'll start digging holes in your scalp. These cuts and scrapes will hurt like heck when you apply an antidandruff shampoo—and they can become infected.

Don't be a sweat head.

Sweat speeds up the skin flaking that causes dandruff. So hit the showers after exercising or otherwise exerting yourself, and bring the shampoo with you.

Give up the big hair look.

The style's not the problem—it's the mousse, hairspray, and gel you have to apply to keep it in place. These products contribute to the oily buildup that can worsen dandruff.●

DENTURE DISCOMFORT

9 STEPS TO STOP IT

Dentures can certainly become uncomfortable and perhaps downright painful. Emotionally, you may be worried about them looking false or changing the sound of your voice. Physically, they could be hurting your mouth, making it impossible to enjoy food the way you once did. Whether you have a full or partial set of removable dentures, experts explain that there are two times in your life when denture discomfort is likely to occur: when the dentures are first introduced to your mouth, and after you've worn them for several years.

At first, any dentures may feel foreign or create sore spots, and getting accustomed to them takes time. Work with your dentist to make sure the fit is accurate. After several years of wearing them, you may sense that the fit feels wrong. This is because your natural teeth aren't there to stimulate growth, and the bone structure in your mouth has changed. Bone is actually being reabsorbed by your body. Tissue may be growing in your mouth where it never was before. The underside of the denture remains the same, but your body has changed. The end result: Dentures slip, move around, make you sore, and prevent you from chewing thoroughly. Your taste buds can even be affected. You knew your dentures would never be quite as reliable as the real thing, but you certainly didn't expect them to be quite this contrary. Here's what you can do.

Brush thoroughly.

Excess bacteria can slow up the healing process for your gums and cause bad breath. Remove and clean your teeth at least twice a day. Use regular toothpaste or a special denture cleaner. Some dentists even suggest that you rely on plain old soap and water with a hand brush.

Clean your gums.

Even though your teeth may be gone, your gums continue to build up plaque daily. Take a soft brush and clean your tongue and the roof of your mouth as well. Brushing stimulates the membranes in your mouth and increases circulation, and that makes for a healthier mouth all around. But don't scrub; a gentle swishing will do the job.

Pop a pain pill.

An over-the-counter pain reliever can smooth over that initial period of discomfort. Aspirin, ibuprofen, or acetaminophen can help. But be careful about taking anything that might interfere with your regular medications.

Be kind to your mouth.

Dentures can create pressure, and readjustment takes patience. Avoid hard foods, which can pull on dentures and cause pain. Corn on the cob and hard apples may never be as easy to handle as they were before you got dentures. The trick is to remove the corn from the cob and cut the apple into bite-size pieces.

Use a dental adhesive.

An over-the-counter adhesive designed for dentures can help improve the function, retention, and contact of your teeth. Ask your dentist for advice about what to use and how to use it. But don't put an adhesive between your dentures to fill in spaces, since loading on this sticky stuff can affect the membranes and make them even sorer. Remember: A little adhesive goes a long way.

Take out your teeth.

The soft tissues in your mouth need time off. Pull out those dentures for eight hours of every day. Wearing dentures reduces the flow of blood to the gums. Give them a rest to keep them healthy.

Rinse.

Put half a teaspoon of salt in warm water and swish it around in your mouth every few hours whenever you develop a sore. Salty water will kill bacteria, toughen membranes, and promote healing.

Try hydrogen peroxide.

Mix a three percent hydrogen peroxide solution with water in equal amounts and use it as a rinse for 30 seconds once a day. Don't swallow it.

Don't tamper.

You may be tempted to make your own adjustments. Resist this urge. A kitchen knife can wreck your expensive investment, ruining the bite badly. Don't use tape or denture pads either.●

DEPRESSION

---

17 WAYS TO ALLEVIATE DEPRESSION

Everyone has their share of aches and pains during a lifetime. But what about that different kind of feeling, when a strong case of the blues hangs on and really slows you down? What happens when you become so overwhelmed that you find it difficult to function? What happens when, instead of lasting only a few days or weeks, your feeling of sadness drags on and on. Unlike a broken leg that requires immediate medical attention, however, you don't think of getting help for this feeling until its influence is severely disruptive.

That's too bad, because you may be suffering from clinical depression, an illness that can be treated effectively. Most people think of depression only as sadness, but in medical terms clinical depression is more than an ordinary "down" mood and more than the natural feeling of sadness after losing someone you love. When a depressed mood continues for some time, whether it follows a specific event or arises for no apparent reason, it can become a serious illness capable of disrupting the lives of entire families. It affects the mind and body alike, interfering with normal functions and daily activities.

Many people suffering from depression don't seek help because of the misperception that mental illness is in some way a sign of weakness. That couldn't be less true. Depression is a common disease that can afflict anyone at any stage and in any walk of life.

While it's known that twice as many women as men suffer from clinical depression, men are not immune—in fact, women may simply be more willing to seek help for the condition.

There are many forms of depressive illnesses, ranging from a single episode to a chronic condition. Clinical depression is a type of depression so severe as to cause major disruptions in your ability to live a normal life. It's well established that there are both psychological and physical causes of depression. The loss of a loved one, a disappointing relationship, a long illness or chronic condition such as heart disease, and prolonged periods of unemployment are all common triggers of depression. A bout of depression may be linked to a single traumatic event, such as divorce, or to a combination of events resulting in a feeling of being overwhelmed by the stress of life.

Depression is also known to be linked, in some cases, to complex interactions among brain chemicals, such as serotonin and norepinephrine, and to hormones. As a result, some of us may inherit a predisposition to depression. The chemical link also provides a key to treating depression—an ever-growing battery of medications that help restore the chemical balance in the brain are becoming available to relieve symptoms.

It may be more difficult to identify depression among older patients than among younger ones. For one thing, doctors and patients may be more concerned about purely physical conditions, so mental problems such as depression could be overlooked. In addition, there is a greater tendency for doctors to confuse genuine clinical depression with the aftereffects of life experiences that tend to affect older patients more, such as major surgery and the death of loved ones. And some doctors, unable to find a physical cause to explain the symptoms of depression, may conclude that no problem exists or that the patient should somehow "snap out of it." Finally, many older patients wrongly assume that depression automatically accompanies old age, so they don't seek treatment when they feel depressed.

In fact, depression is highly treatable. The following suggestions will help you get the care you may need.

Get a comprehensive evaluation.

See your doctor for a complete physical examination to uncover any physical basis for depression. Then get a referral to a mental-health specialist for his or her evaluation.

Consider your symptoms.

Most people don't appear at the doctor's office with a note declaring the reason for their sad moods. Cooperation is needed from the patient to describe symptoms clearly and from the doctor to listen carefully and make the correct diagnosis.

Find the right therapist.

Depression is highly treatable, and one of the best things you can do to cope with the symptoms is to seek out the help of a psychiatrist, psychologist, or social worker (your family doctor can help you locate one). The course of treatment may include medication, but much of the work is done through psychotherapy (treatment that relies principally on verbal methods rather than physical or chemical means). In fact, in about half of all cases psychotherapy alone is highly effective in treating depression.

Psychotherapy can lead to the recognition of underlying interpersonal problems, bring about appropriate ways of dealing with conflicts, and encourage a more positive overall attitude. While psychotherapy can continue for a long time, substantial relief from symptoms can be achieved after only a few months of therapy.

Shop around.

It's important to choose a therapist with whom you feel comfortable. After all, you will be confiding your most private thoughts and vulnerabilities to this person. Feel free to ask questions at your first appointment: What kind of people do you normally work with? What sort of treatment do you use? How much experience do you have in working with people of my age and background? If you don't think you can work with one therapist, look for another one. Remember, it's essential that you function with a therapist whom you will trust to help you do the necessary work to understand and overcome your depression.

Take medication as prescribed.

Some 70 percent of older adults who have been prescribed antidepressant medications fail to take them as directed, according to the National Institutes of Mental Health. Common reasons for stopping medications are concern about side effects, failure to see the expected benefit, and, conversely, a feeling of well-being that falsely indicates the medication is no longer necessary. It's important to remember that among older patients, it takes 6 to 12 weeks for medications to have an effect (this is more than twice the length of time needed by younger people), and they should be taken for at least 6 months after symptoms have subsided. When taking medication, work closely with your doctor to monitor dosage and keep an eye on your progress.

Understand your medication.

Discuss with your doctor how the medication works, how much time is needed before it begins to work, and what side effects you can anticipate. Medication prescribed for some conditions unrelated to depression can actually cause depression as a side effect. Certain medications—including some drugs used to treat high blood pressure and arthritis, for example—may cause symptoms like those of depression. Thus it is vitally important for depressed patients to make a complete inventory of all their medication—what is obtained both by prescription and over the counter—and have it reviewed by their doctor periodically.

Join a patient support group.

A support group may be very helpful for general encouragement during recovery and for learning how other people with depression have learned to cope.

Understand depression.

A little knowledge about the nature of depression and its treatment goes a long way in combating the illness. There are many prevailing myths about depression (one of the most common is, "We all feel sad sometimes, so why worry about it?"), and, fortunately, ongoing research is continually expanding our knowledge of depression and making new treatments available. By keeping yourself informed, you will more completely understand your depression and be in a better position to manage if it threatens in the future.

MEDICATION FOR DEPRESSION

○ ○ ○

For some people suffering from depression, lifestyle changes will not bring about relief: A change in body chemistry is needed. That's where medication comes in. Various medications play an important role in the treatment of depression. But don't expect antidepressant medications to relieve symptoms overnight: Most must be administered for weeks before they become effective.

Several types of medications are available to alleviate depression. They act by altering the chemicals in the brain. Such medications can be an effective temporary aid to overcoming depression.

Tricyclic antidepressants (TCAs) constitute one widely used class of antidepressant prescription drugs and are most often prescribed for patients who have the classic symptoms of depression: insomnia, loss of appetite, and feelings of hopelessness. They are available under a number of names, such as imipramine (Tofranil), nortriptyline (Aventyl and Pamelor), desipramine (Norpramin), and doxepin (Sinequan).

TCAs have a strong sedative action, so they are usually taken at night when that side effect is less disruptive. Since it can be hard to regulate dosage and to gauge side effects—which can include heartbeat irregularities, confusion, and general weakness—they are initially prescribed in small dosages that are increased after careful monitoring. In fact, it's important to monitor dosage of TCAs with extreme care, since large doses can be toxic and even life threatening. Of the many types of TCAs available, desipramine seems to produce fewer side effects among older adults.

The most commonly prescribed antidepressants are selective serotonin reuptake inhibitors (SSRIs). They are highly effective in treating depression and have fewer side effects than other antidepressants. Commonly prescribed SSRIs include fluoxetine (Prozac), paroxetine (Paxil), sertraline (Zoloft), and trazodone (Desyrel). While traditional antidepressants affect the activity of two or more neurotransmitter pathways in the brain, SSRIs increase circulating levels of a single neurotransmitter, serotonin, which controls moods. Prozac, the most widely prescribed SSRI—in fact, the most widely prescribed of all antidepressants—blocks the removal of serotonin from its site of action on neurons. This blockage allows serotonin to remain working for a longer period of time, resulting in a mood improvement for many depressed people.

SSRIs can trigger adverse side effects, including insomnia, anxiety, dry mouth, loss of appetite, nausea, and headaches. Studies in older adults with clinical depression show Prozac to be effective. But due to the fact that it metabolizes slowly, it remains in the body for several weeks after treatment ends.

Exercise.

With your doctor's approval and under his or her direction, make regular exercise part of your routine. Walking is a good activity for most people.

Do your homework.

Homework is a vital part of therapy. Talking with a professional lays the foundation and gives you the motivation and direction for learning how to help yourself. Read what you can about depression, assertiveness, and self-esteem.

Prepare for setbacks.

People over 50 are often confronted by a greater share of life's problems than are their more youthful counterparts. Physical illness, caring for aging parents, financial pressures, and the loss of friends all provide a perfectly legitimate basis for feelings of sadness and depression. Thus it is useful to anticipate and prepare for such circumstances and to try to lead a full and active life so when problems do arise—as they inevitably will—they will not be so devastating as to lead to clinical depression.

Limit alcohol.

Alcohol does not cause depression, but it can make depression worse by extending its duration and increasing its intensity.

Shun tranquilizers.

Like alcohol, tranquilizers do not cause depression, but they are known to worsen it.

Maintain a journal.

Keeping a journal is an excellent self-help tool. If you write down your feelings in a journal, then, at the end of the day, review how you reacted to certain situations, you often gain a fresh perspective on your behavior. You may notice, for example, that you are now confronting situations you haven't experienced in the past—knowledge that may help you to anticipate and prepare for similar situations in the future.

Seek informal support.

To deal fully with your depression, you're going to need help—perhaps a different kind of help than even medical professionals can provide. Let your friends and family members know what is happening in your life and what you are doing to resolve your problems. This is in addition to the more formal assistance available from an organized support group.

Look to religion for solace.

Studies indicate that depressed people who become actively involved in religious organizations show a better ability to cope with depression compared to those who are not so involved.

Eat a balanced diet.

If you're not getting the essential nutrients in your diet, you aren't going to have sufficient energy to deal with your depression. Ask your physician for help in setting up guidelines for a balanced diet and in recommending supplements if required.●

DERMATITIS AND ECZEMA

22 SOOTHING STRATEGIES

Call it dermatitis, call it eczema, call it whatever you want—all you really need to know is that your life can be miserable when your skin becomes inflamed and breaks out. Sometimes these eruptions are caused by contact with a strong detergent, a cosmetic, or a piece of jewelry. They may be triggered by a run-in with poison ivy or the neighbor's cat. They may be the symptoms of a full-blown allergy, so even a brief encounter will trigger a reaction, or they may be signs of irritation that comes with long-term exposure to a harsh substance. Sometimes you may have no idea what is triggering the reaction. Whatever the cause, though, often the result is the same—redness, itching, blistering, and swelling.

You might notice that these uncomfortable eruptions are becoming more frequent as you get older. That's because the skin loses some of its oil over time, leaving you more sensitive to many substances. That's all the more reason to keep in mind that when it comes to dermatitis and eczema, the best policy is to avoid anything that's likely to trigger a flare-up. Barring that, there's plenty that can be done when a rash has you wishing you could just crawl out of your skin.

PREVENTING A BREAKOUT

Here are some ideas on heading off a problem before it arises.

Rinse twice.

That's a good laundry-room rule, because a double rinse will help ensure that you get all the potentially irritating detergent out of the clothes. Also avoid those commercial fabric-softening strips that are intended to be put in the dryer with your clothes—they contain ingredients that may irritate your skin.

Wash before wearing.

Brand new clothes, that is. They're often treated with starches, formaldehyde, and other chemicals you don't want next to your skin.

Beware of strong ingredients.

While most manufacturers take great care to remove known irritants, any product that comes in contact with your skin has the potential of being an irritant—and the stronger it is, the more likely it is to irritate.

Try new cosmetics one at a time.

This way, you'll know immediately what's causing a reaction. If you suddenly get a reaction from the cosmetics you normally use but don't know what's causing it, stop using them altogether for a few days and reintroduce them one at a time until you isolate the offending substance.

Take it easy with soap.

Many soaps can irritate skin, so *gentle* is the word when choosing a skin cleanser. Try an extra-gentle soap, such as Dove; a nonsoap cleanser, such as Aveeno; or a liquid cleanser, such as Neutrogena. The trick is to find the cleanser that works best for you—if you notice that a product seems to irritate your skin, stop using it immediately and try another brand.

Put your products through the patch test.

Any time you are trying a new cosmetic, check it out first. Dab a little on your forearm and cover the area with an adhesive bandage. Repeat this testing for a few days, then wait a couple more days before actually using the product to make sure you don't have a reaction. Many products include patch-test instructions on the label.

Don't take labels as the gospel truth.

Oh, manufacturers aren't dishonest, it's just a question of interpretation. *Hypoallergenic,* for instance, simply means a product has been tested for possible allergens, but probably not all allergens. Likewise, *allergy-tested* or *dermatologist tested* simply means some testing has been done, but there are no laws regulating how extensive this testing must be. Unfortunately, the only surefire way to know how a product is going to affect you is the old trial-and-error method.

Fret about fragrance.

It's a major irritant for many people, and a $200-an-ounce perfume can be just as irritating to your skin as a cheap cologne. Besides, one product may contain many different fragrances, so it's often hard to know what's getting under your skin.

Sweat a little, but don't itch.

Antiperspirants contain some pretty strong drying ingredients—that's why they work, and that's also why they can trigger a reaction in sensitive skin. A deodorant soap and a little dab of absorbent baking soda under each arm may be a safer way to keep dry, or use a plain deodorant, without antiperspirants.

Be careful when stopping to smell the flowers.

Poison oak and poison ivy are common causes of dermatitis. If you've been exposed, be careful not to touch other parts of your body until you rinse your hands thoroughly in cool water (don't use soap, which can spread the toxic oil). Wash your clothing separately, and if a rash develops, treat it with cold compresses.

Think twice about hot tubs and pools.

Bacteria, cleaning solvents, and chlorine can all trigger skin reactions among hot tub users, as well as swimmers who use pools. Likewise, algae, fertilizers, and other contaminants in rivers and lakes can cause dermatitis. The best way to avoid the problem is to shower thoroughly when you get out of the water.

TREATING A BREAKOUT

When it's too late to avoid the problem, try these tips for relief.

Cool it.

There's nothing like a little cooling to ease the itching and swelling of a rash. Follow this old recipe for almost instant relief: Take a clean cloth and dip it in cold water or wrap it around some ice cubes, then apply it to the rash for about 10 minutes. Repeat as often as you like.

Try some milk.

Soak a piece of gauze in cool milk and apply to an oozing rash for 10 to 15 minutes. Resoak the gauze every few minutes because the skin will quickly absorb the milk. Rinse well with cool water after each treatment—but don't use soap, which will irritate the rash.

Don't scratch.

Unfortunately, scratching is only going to aggravate a skin rash; it can also break the skin and open the door to bacterial infections. Try to keep your hands occupied—stick them under your thighs, knit, or curl and uncurl your fingers.

Try an antihistamine.

Over-the-counter antihistamines may well relieve itching. They will also make you drowsy, so don't drive or do anything else that requires your full attention when using them.

Rub on some hydrocortisone cream.

These preparations, available over the counter, are especially helpful in treating the inflammation that accompanies allergy-induced skin reactions—such as the rash you develop after a romp through a patch of poison ivy. A few words of warning on hydrocortisone creams, though—they, too, can cause a

TOP OFFENDERS

○ ○ ○

Skin is fickle. Contact with just about any foreign substance—even cold air—may trigger an itchy rash and swelling in certain people. Here are some particularly infamous culprits from the annals of dermatitis.

- Pets. Your four-legged friend may be a walking disaster zone if you're allergic to dander. Keep Felix and Fido out of the bedroom (and out of the house, if necessary), have someone who's not allergic brush and bathe them regularly, and resist the urge to pet them.

- Pillows. Feather or synthetic, they may trigger a skin rash. It's important to find one that doesn't, because you spend so much time with your face pressed against it.

- Household cleansers. An allergy to these common substances is another reason to hire household help. Wear vinyl gloves if you do the scrubbing.

- Formaldehyde. It lurks in places you probably don't suspect—in insulation, wood paneling, carpeting, dry-cleaned fabrics, even in colored facial tissue and toilet paper. Avoid direct contact, and keep a window open to lower household levels. A philodendron plant, which absorbs formaldehyde, may be a good investment in cleaner air.

rash if you are allergic to them, and if you use them for long periods of time (several months), they can cause thinning of the skin.

Calm with calamine.

This old-fashioned remedy might take the itch out—but it is so drying that it can also promote itching. Try a little dab on an itchy patch, leave it on for an hour or so, and see how it affects you before applying it over a wide area of skin.

Don't linger in the tub.

And make it snappy in the shower, too. Lolling in the water can dry out your skin, making the itch and inflammation worse. Limit your bathing sessions to three to five minutes, and keep the water on the cool side because hot water is especially drying.

Add some oats.

Look no further for relief than oatmeal, which will sooth the skin. You can buy oatmeal-based bath products, or you can simply add a couple of cups of the breakfast staple or a cup of baking soda to your bathwater.

Leave the loofah in the cabinet.

Even a washcloth can be irritating to skin. To make your cleansing sessions as noninflammatory as possible, don't use anything but your fingertips—and use them gently.

Moisturize damp skin.

It's important to moisturize within a few minutes after washing up or bathing. Dab yourself dry, then apply a moisturizer to your still-damp skin—damp is the key word here, because a moisturizer does not add moisture, it seals moisture into your skin.

Moisturize all day long, too.

The moister your skin, the less you will itch. Find a moisturizer that works well for you and apply it every few hours.

DIABETES

---

11 APPROACHES TO MANAGING YOUR CONDITION

You have diabetes, but you're munching on a small candy bar and don't feel guilty. Times have changed. During the last ten years there has been much evidence to indicate that rigid diets for diabetes are no longer the way to go to manage blood-sugar levels. So much is different, in fact, that the American Diabetes Association (ADA) has modified its standards for diet and changed some of its approaches to managing this disorder.

Diabetes is a disruption in metabolism (the way your body uses food). It can strike suddenly or—more often—remain undiagnosed, silently attacking your body's blood vessels and nerves. It is estimated that the disease has not been diagnosed in about half of those who have it. Yet as a group, people with diabetes are more often afflicted with blindness, heart disease, stroke, kidney disease, hearing loss, and impotence than the general population.

Diabetes comes in two forms, one of which typically begins before age 30 (type I, or the juvenile-onset kind) and one of which is more common after your fortieth birthday (type II, or the adult-onset kind). What distinguishes them is that type I is an autoimmune disease—one in which the body inexplicably launches an attack on parts of itself. In this case, the attack strikes at insulin-producing cells in the pancreas. As these cells die off, the body loses its ability to produce insulin, and patients must compensate by taking insulin every day, with no end in sight. For this reason, type I is known medically as insulin-dependent diabetes mellitus (IDDM).

Type II—which is not an autoimmune disease—typically occurs in an overweight person whose pancreas still provides a limited amount of insulin, even though the body cannot utilize the insulin properly. For that reason, it's called noninsulin-dependent diabetes mellitus (NIDDM). Fortunately, a combined effort involving increased exercise, a healthy diet, and the shedding of some weight can often keep type II diabetes in check. If those steps don't keep the diabetes under control, the next step may be taking pills, which aid the insulin-producing process, or administering insulin by injection.

In the absence of diabetes, the body performs a number of vital functions spontaneously. When food is digested in the stomach and small intestine, portions are converted to glucose (a sugar), which courses through the bloodstream delivering energy throughout the body. As sugar is released into the bloodstream, the pancreas is alerted to send out a hormone called insulin, whose function is to help get the glucose into the cells. Without it, the energy-delivering sugar cannot enter the cells adequately. With it, blood glucose remains in delicate balance, and a natural control of sugar metabolism prevails.

For those who have diabetes—both type I and type II—an insufficient amount of glucose reaches the body's cells. When there is too little insulin or the insulin can't work properly, sugar levels in the blood soar—and you have something called hyperglycemia.

This affects many organs of the body. When there is a buildup of glucose, the surplus finds its way into your urine—which makes for frequent urination and increased thirst. Meanwhile, because of too little insulin, you lose energy-rich sugar through urination, and your body begins to tap its fat stores as an energy al-

ternative. Consequently, your weight might start to drop and you might experience hunger pangs more often. But it's also possible to be symptom-free. In any case, your system goes out of control and you should contact your doctor.

The suggestions that follow will help people with diabetes make better decisions on matters regarding their health.

See your doctor regularly.

Even if everything seems to be going well, keep all appointments with your doctor—and remember periodic checkups with specialists in diabetic complications, such as podiatrists and ophthalmologists. Doctors are your first line of defense against potential problems in their earliest, symptom-free stages.

Don't smoke.

Smoking increases your risk of cardiovascular disease, and people with diabetes have a high cardiovascular risk already.

If you're overweight, drop some pounds.

Keeping your weight down helps you curb blood-sugar levels. Excess body fat contributes to the inability of the insulin to reach the cells. In contrast, weight loss often improves insulin's effectiveness. Weight loss of 10 to 20 pounds has been shown to help keep blood-sugar levels down and may even allow you to curtail diabetes medication. The most effective way to lose weight is to combine a healthful diet with regular exercise.

Care for your health.

Doctors, nurses, dietitians, and diabetes educators can't make choices for you. You are the one who must integrate prescriptions, recommendations, and external events and pressures into your life. It is ultimately up to you to take responsibility for coordinating all the elements of your health care.

Moderate alcohol intake.

Contrary to past practice, recent studies have found that moderate alcohol intake with dinner has no adverse affect on blood-sugar levels. But don't take a drink on an empty stomach: That might result in blood sugar dropping too low.

Learn to self-monitor.

Simple and accurate tests are available to monitor blood-sugar levels so appropriate adjustments can be made in diet, exercise level, and insulin dose to maintain the best level of control possible. The only way to know if you are controlling your diabetes successfully is through frequent self-monitoring, which makes testing the backbone of diabetic management. Some tips follow:

1. Learn the right way to monitor your blood from a health care professional. Discuss the type of blood-glucose meter you need along with timing and frequency of tests. Review your testing technique during regular checkups.

2. Make sure your test strips and other supplies have not reached their expiration date, and clean your meter according to the manufacturer's instructions.

3. Keep careful records of your test results. This will help your doctor confirm appropriate treatment or make changes in your diabetes regimen.

Exercise

Regular exercise can help control your blood sugar, may prevent type II diabetes, and will enhance your sense of well-being. Although any activity helps you become more fit, you'll receive the greatest benefit from aerobic activities such as jogging, walking, and swimming.

The goal for type I is to gain access to the benefits of exercise in a safe way. Those who take insulin have to plan carefully for extensive exercise sessions because vigorous physical activity causes blood sugar to fall. By carefully timing exercise, meals, and insulin, you can ensure that the body has enough glucose available in the blood to fuel a workout.

- Check pre- and post-workout glucose levels. If most of the available blood sugar is used up during the activity and isn't replenished with food, blood sugar can drop too low.

- Exercise regularly, preferably at the same time each day, to first determine your insulin and food requirements and then to stabilize them. A regular schedule is very important for optimal blood sugar control.

- Don't inject insulin into the muscle you'll be exercising. The insulin will be mobilized faster and you may experience hypoglycemia (a condition of abnormally low glucose in the blood).

- Use your knowledge of changing diet and insulin dosage to ready yourself for increased physical activity.
- Prevent dehydration when exercising: Drink water before, during, and after exercise.

Know the warning signs of possible problems. You've gone beyond your limit if:

1. You become faint, dizzy, or nauseated; experience severe shortness of breath or pain in your chest; or lose control of your muscles, which indicates you should stop exercising immediately.

2. Your pulse or breathing rate doesn't return to its resting level within three minutes of the end of your activity, which means you're probably pushing too hard.

3. You're fatigued by moderate activity, which would be the case if you're still worn out several hours after you stop exercising.

WATCH YOUR DIET

The American Diabetes Association (ADA) released a new set of nutrition guidelines in 1994 for people with diabetes. The goal is to avoid high blood sugar and gain the long-term benefits of keeping blood sugar close to normal.

The ADA defines the normal range of blood glucose in the blood as between 80 and 120 milligrams per deciliter (mg/dL) before meals and from 100 to 140 mg/dL at bedtime. The exact proportions of carbohydrates, protein, and fat intake depend on your weight, cholesterol levels, and other factors.

The importance of proper diet is repeated, but the new guidelines now say that no one set of rules applies to everyone. You don't need special foods or unusual diet strategies to keep blood sugar on an even keel. The ADA encourages

you to work with a registered dietitian to develop a meal plan based on your food preferences, insulin therapy, and other health concerns, such as weight control. Also consider the following guidelines:

Control fat intake.

Keep fat intake to no more than 30 percent of total calories. To lose weight, lower this number to 20 to 25 percent of total calories.

On occasion, treat yourself.

Sugar is no longer forbidden. Simple carbohydrates like sugar do not affect blood sugar any more than complex carbohydrates like rice or potatoes. The total amount of carbohydrate in the diet is the critical factor affecting blood-sugar levels. Using modest amounts of sugar may not interfere with blood-sugar control if you substitute a sugary food for a starchy food that contains an equal amount of carbohydrate.

Control salt.

Follow a low-fat diet with a controlled salt intake. In some people, reduced salt helps to keep high blood pressure in check.

Don't worry about high fiber.

According to the new guidelines, you don't need to self-prescribe an excessive high-fiber diet; simply follow the same formula as everyone else: 20 to 35 grams of fiber a day, taken from vegetables, fruits, whole-grain breads, and legumes.

COMPLICATIONS OF DIABETES

Be on the alert for warning signs of complications. Since diabetes is a metabolic disorder affecting the entire body, it can lead to many different chronic, or long-

New Standards of Medical Care

o o o

Standards released in 1994 are based on extensive research. They show that people with type I (insulin dependent) diabetes who followed intensive treatment regimens to reduce blood-glucose levels reduced their risk of development or progression of retinopathy, nephropathy, and neuropathy by 50 to 75 percent. These new standards recommend treatment for lowering blood glucose levels, and, depending on the individual, include the following:

- Frequent monitoring of blood glucose
- Meticulous attention to meal planning
- Regular exercise
- Intensive insulin therapy, such as multiple daily injections of short- and longer-acting insulin or use of an insulin pump
- Less complex insulin regimens or oral-glucose lowering agents in some people with type II disease.

term, complications that have an impact upon a number of organs. These complications generally involve abnormalities of small and large blood vessels. The nerves, skin, heart, feet, teeth, and gums are also affected. The rule of thumb is that good control of blood glucose can prevent or at least postpone the complications and reduce their severity. Some of the major complications are noted below.

Blood pressure.

Learn to control your tendency toward high blood pressure (hypertension). Anticipate and manage the stresses that contribute to high blood pressure and that are a normal part of living. Blood glucose tends to rise immediately when you're stressed. In fact, diabetes and emotions are so interrelated that the disease can be exacerbated by even trivial upsets. In turn, these upsets can hinder diabetes control.

People with diabetes are twice as likely to have high blood pressure, or hypertension, as those who do not have diabetes, and high blood pressure is the cause of an estimated 30 to 75 percent of complications of diabetes. The ADA recommends a blood pressure reading of 130/85 millimeters of mercury (mm Hg) as an appropriate goal in hypertension management. Weight loss, aerobic exercise, and a reduction in salt intake are recommended to achieve this level.

Eyes.

Diabetes is the leading cause of adult blindness in the United States. Indeed, after five to ten years of living with the disease, most people have at least some evidence of eye damage. Some precautions to take include:

- Get diabetic cataracts removed. Although these cataracts don't differ significantly from cataracts in people free of diabetes, they occur more often and at younger ages. Keeping tight control of blood sugar can help prevent cataracts from forming.

- Be alert for diabetic retinopathy. In this complication of diabetes, leaking blood vessels on the retina at the back of the eye cause a reduction in vision. Retinopathy usually develops ten or more years after the onset of diabetes. An ophthalmologist will know when to begin treatment with a laser to seal damaged vessels and prevent further bleeding.

- Visit your ophthalmologist regularly, at least once a year, so complications can be identified at an early stage.

Cardiovascular system.

People with diabetes have a higher incidence of cardiovascular problems than the general population. They are more likely to experience heart attacks and strokes as well as circulatory disorders, especially in the hands and feet. The reduced blood flow and progressive blockage of arteries may result in a condition called intermittent claudication—a disorder that produces pain and disability and that may seriously limit one's ability to walk and use one's legs.

People with diabetes also tend to have high blood pressure and elevated blood lipids (cholesterol and triglycerides). Arteriosclerosis, or hardening of the arteries, begins at an earlier age and advances more rapidly. Disease of the heart muscle itself is also more common, leading to an increased risk of heart failure.

Kidneys.

Between 30 and 40 percent of people with type I diabetes will also be affected by kidney disease; add to that between 5 and 10 percent of type II sufferers, and you have a sizable group of people at risk. To prevent or lessen the effects of kidney disease, keep your blood pressure under control and get prompt treatment for urinary tract infections. It is also important to avoid the regular use of certain drugs, such as pain medications containing phenacetin, which can damage your kidneys.

Feet and skin.

Arteries tend to become obstructed as people age, and with that obstruction comes a reduction in blood circulation. Because poor circulation impairs healing, pressure sores or cuts can become real problems. Nerve damage makes the situation even worse. If you can't feel the pain, you may not even notice the injury, and breaks in the skin can lead to ulcers that don't heal properly. Infection may result. Some ways to avoid foot problems include:

- Give your feet a daily going-over to check for problems—sores, cuts, abrasions, etc.
- Bathe your feet each day in warm water with soap, taking care that the feet are fully dried.
- Cut toenails in a straight line, never in a curve.
- Wear shoes that aren't too tight or too loose and are designed to cushion impact.
- Keep circulation flowing to your feet by not placing anything tight around your ankles. Never sit with your legs crossed.
- Let your doctor know immediately if you spot any alterations in the way your feet look—including changes in color.●

WARNING SIGNS

○ ○ ○

All adults should have their blood-sugar levels tested at least once every three years. Get tested every year, however, if you are at a higher risk due to a family history of diabetes, are overweight, or are 50 years of age or older. If you have any of the symptoms listed below, see your doctor immediately.

- A need to urinate often
- Severe hunger or thirst
- Weight loss that can't be linked to dietary change
- Overwhelming fatigue
- Blurred vision
- Frequent infections, especially of the urinary tract, vagina, skin, or gums
- Slow healing of any cuts or abrasions

DIARRHEA

---

18 WAYS TO GO WITH THE FLOW

Granted, it's pretty hard to find much good to say on behalf of diarrhea. In fact, this common intestinal disorder is right up near the top of the list of life's major inconveniences. Well, diarrhea does have two things going for it—efficiency and thoroughness. Diarrhea is nature's way of purging your system of something it doesn't want—whether it's tainted food or a viral bug. And diarrhea works like a well-oiled machine: It just keeps on going and going until your system is clear of whatever has been troubling it.

Normally this cleansing process takes a day or two, then your bowels are churning away again with regularity. It's normal, too, if you notice that bouts of diarrhea become a little more frequent as you get older. There are at least two reasons for this: The first is that your system may not be able to handle certain foods. Second, people tend to take more medication as they grow older, and your diarrhea may arise as a side effect. If so, your doctor can help you find a way to take medications without suffering from diarrhea.

What's not normal is diarrhea that lasts and lasts or is accompanied by extreme pain or bleeding. And for someone who is frail or suffering from a chronic illness, diarrhea and the dehydration that accompanies it can quickly bring on severe complications. In these cases, it is important to seek medical attention promptly.

Usually, though, the best thing to do when diarrhea strikes is just to make yourself as comfortable as possible and let nature run its course. Here are some suggestions to help you cope.

Go with the flow.

Chances are, your case of diarrhea will run its course in a day or two. Unless you are at increased risk of dehydration (for instance, if you are frail or rundown from another illness), the best treatment is often just to let your bowels expunge whatever is causing your diarrhea.

Beware of dehydration.

The biggest danger diarrhea poses to anyone, of any age, is dehydration. You are at a greater risk of becoming dehydrated if you are elderly because you may have a harder time absorbing fluids. And for you, dehydration can trigger such severe complications as heart attack and kidney failure. If you live alone and don't have anyone to look after you, it may be difficult to keep your body supplied with the liquids you need to take in when you have diarrhea. Look for these signs of dehydration: inability to keep liquids down, cracked lips or dry tongue, or a feeling of soreness in your eyeballs. If you notice any of these symptoms, contact a doctor without delay.

Lap up liquids.

Water, fruit juice, warm salted broth, weak tea with sugar or honey, sugary soda drinks, and sports drinks are just the ticket when diarrhea lays you low. They help replace all the water you lose, and, depending on the beverage, can replenish lost body sugars and salts, too. Drink only liquids that are easy on the stomach: That leaves out citrus juices, tomato juice, alcohol, and coffee, all of which can irritate your innards and bring on diarrhea.

Sweeten up your liquids.

By adding a spoonful of sugar to water, tea, or fruit juice, you'll be supplying your gut with the glucose it needs to absorb water. Slurping on a soda drink is a good way to keep hydrated and get some extra sugar, but take off the top and let it defizz for a while before you drink up—those gaseous bubbles can irritate your stomach. Products without caffeine will also be gentler on the tummy. Easy does it with sweets, though. Too much sugar can cause diarrhea.

Hold the ice and sip.

Ice-cold liquids can send your stomach into a diarrhea-producing spasm. Handling liquids will be easier for the stomach if you sip them slowly.

Eat light.

Hold off on the fatty, greasy fare until you're feeling better. What you need now is kinder, gentler food, and that means bland. Stick to foods like toast, soda crackers, chicken soup, gelatin desserts, and rice—anything you can digest easily. A piece of chicken breast with the skin removed is about as fancy as you should get. Cooked carrots, by the way, are easy to digest and help replace the electrolytes and minerals your system is losing.

Say yes to yogurt.

Not only is it fairly easy on the stomach, but it also contains live bacteria cultures that may help wipe out the bugs that are causing your diarrhea and restore the natural bacterial balance in your system. Acidophilus milk (available in health food stores) and other fermented dairy products help as well.

Say no to other dairy.

You'll have a hard time digesting most dairy products, and the result will be just what you don't need—more diarrhea. In fact, diarrhea is often caused by an intolerance to lactose, the sugar found in milk products.

Try ORT.

Oral-rehydration therapy, often used by travelers to help replace electrolytes and minerals lost through diarrhea, can be a big help at home, too. Solutions for oral-rehydration are widely available at drugstores. Ask your pharmacist.

Don't feast after the famine.

Even after the diarrhea subsides, your insides will remain sensitive for a while. Reintroduce solid foods into your diet on a gradual basis. Stick with defatted chicken, rice, applesauce, broth and soup, toast, and other comfort foods for a day or two.

But know when to get back to normal.

The best way to ensure overall health is to eat a well-balanced, nutritious diet. While a regimen of liquids and bland foods may help you bounce back from a bout of diarrhea, chances are it's not going to provide you with the daily nutrients you need. As soon as you feel up to it, reintroduce protein, vegetables, grains, and other nourishing foods to your diet.

Go easy on the anti-diarrheal medication.

Your first instinct may be to grab an over-the-counter remedy. Be careful, though, because diarrhea is usually a sign that your system is eagerly trying to rid itself of a bug. Tamper with nature, and you'll be inadvertently keeping the bacteria in your system. If you feel you must take a diarrhea medication, your

THE ELDERLY AND DIARRHEA

○ ○ ○

Among the elderly, even a run-of-the-mill case of diarrhea can be life threatening. Diarrhea can be especially dangerous if you're suffering from any number of age-related diseases. In someone with hardening of the arteries (arteriosclerosis), for instance, the lowering of blood pressure that occurs with diarrhea-related fluid loss raises the risk of stroke and heart attack.

Even among the healthy elderly, bowel function often slows down with age, making it more difficult to absorb nutrients properly. As a result, diarrhea can more quickly deplete necessary fluids and nutrients than it might among younger folk. The elderly also often suffer from decreased kidney function, and in those cases fluid loss can lead to kidney failure.

When diarrhea strikes, watch for warning signs such as fever, dehydration, dizziness, or severe abdominal pain. Even if you don't notice any of these indications, play it safe and call your doctor any time diarrhea persists for more than a day or two. Those taking medication for a chronic disease should be especially careful.

best bet may be Pepto-Bismol. It is gentle on your stomach and has an antibacterial effect that can help kill the bug that's ailing you.

Remember, though, that you should avoid taking Pepto-Bismol or any medication that slows bowel action if you have an ulcer or other digestive problem. In addition, the water retention that results from taking an antidiarrheal medicine can pose a risk to anyone suffering from heart disease, glaucoma, and many other disorders. If you think an antidiarrheal could put you at risk, talk to your doctor before you self-medicate.

Check your other medications.

Some of the medications you take regularly may be causing or contributing to your diarrhea. Antibiotics, for instance, often bring on loose stools. Other causes include antacids and laxatives.

Forget the fiber.

What's the main advantage of fibery foods like bran and whole-grain breads? Your intestines don't absorb them, so they add bulk to your stool and stimulate movement of the bowels. Normally that's great. But if you have diarrhea, you already have more than enough movement.

Take it easy.

Diarrhea can weaken you, and so can the bug that's causing it. So give your body a chance to mend and fight off this unwanted visitor. Lay low, get plenty of rest, try not to tax yourself physically, and take a break from stress.

Don't pass it on.

Your diarrhea could be caused by a parasite that will be only too happy to find someone else in your household to visit.

Play it safe. Leave the cooking and washing up to someone else for the duration, wash your hands thoroughly after your visits to the bathroom, and make sure that no one else uses your towels.

When it's not just a bug.

Chances are, your case of diarrhea is caused by a short-lived bug or the food you ate in that out-of-the-way restaurant last night. But if it persists for more than a few days or so, or if it comes on only after eating certain foods, then your diarrhea may be a symptom of another condition.

If you notice that you have a bout of diarrhea after drinking milk or eating dairy products, you may be lactose intolerant, which means you are unable to digest lactose, the sugar in milk products (see LACTOSE INTOLERANCE). If your diarrhea seems to accompany your intake of bread, pasta, or other wheat products, you may be unable to digest gluten.

Alternating bouts of constipation and diarrhea can be a sign of irritable bowel syndrome, caused largely by stress. Chronic diarrhea accompanied by abdominal pain can also be a sign of ulcerative colitis or, especially if there's blood in the stool, bowel cancer. If you suspect your diarrhea is more than a bug, see a physician.

Take your temperature.

If you run a sustained fever of more than 101 degrees Fahrenheit, you may have a serious infection. See your doctor.●

DIVERTICULAR DISEASE

---

12 WAYS TO DIVERT ITS EFFECTS

When was the last time you thought about how well your colon is aging? Not recently, huh? Well, that's okay. There's not much reason to give a lot of thought to the matter except that you may have a condition called diverticulosis. About half of all Americans over sixty develop this condition, which occurs when small pouches known as diverticula form along the walls of the colon. Diverticula are telltale marks of age because they come about as the colon walls thicken over time, and the resulting pressure forms these little protrusions.

Normally, diverticulosis is nothing to worry about. In fact, most people aren't even aware that they have the condition—some occasional cramping and bouts of diarrhea are about the only symptoms you're likely to notice. What you should worry about, though, is diverticulitis, which can flare up when food and waste material become trapped in the diverticula. The resulting inflammation can be painful, and infection can set in. Unlike plain old diverticulosis, diverticulitis requires prompt medical attention (see sidebar, "Call the Doctor if...").

Now that you have all the medical terms straight, here's what to do about diverticulosis—and there's plenty you can do about it in terms of diet and lifestyle—and how to keep diverticulosis from becoming diverticulitis.

Feed on fiber.

Adding fiber to your diet is probably the single most helpful thing you can do for diverticulosis. Here's why: A fibery diet helps produce stools that are bulky and easy to pass, relieving the pressure in your colon that causes diverticulosis. The easiest way to ensure that you are getting enough fiber is to add fiber-rich foods to your daily diet and follow the U.S. government's recommendations for 20 to 30 grams of fiber a day. Top sources of fiber are: grains (one slice of whole-wheat bread has 1.5 grams of fiber, and a serving of high-fiber cereal has at least 5 grams); fruits (a pear supplies about 5.4 grams); vegetables (a serving of peas contains about 4.3 grams of fiber); and legumes (there are almost 7 grams of fiber in a serving of kidney beans). Make it a habit to check food labels for fiber.

Drink some fiber, too.

Another way to ensure that you are getting adequate amounts of fiber is to drink a daily supplement, such as Metamucil, that contains psyllium, a highly concentrated form of fiber. It's a lot easier to get your fiber through diet or a liquid supplement than it is with fiber pills—you have to swallow handfuls of them to get enough fiber.

Don't let a little gas blow you off fiber.

A little gas is a natural side effect of adding fiber to your diet. Gassiness, sometimes accompanied by bloating and diarrhea, usually subsides within a week or two after adding fiber to your diet, as your system gets used to handling the increased bulk. You'll have fewer side effects if you add fiber to your diet gradually, maybe adding one fiber-rich dish to each meal, and spread your fiber out over several meals instead of trying to cram it all in at one sitting.

Keep the water coming.

You should drink six to eight glasses a day for overall health, advice that is especially important if you have diverticulosis. Water aids digestion by keeping stools moist and easier to pass, and it adds bulk to the fiber you should be eating to produce softer stools.

Get moving.

A little exercise keeps your digestive tract in shape, too, by stimulating activity and keeping things moving down there. Even a regular walk around the neighborhood can do a lot to promote regularity and prevent diverticulosis flareups.

Go seedless.

Figs, popcorn, tomatoes, strawberries— any foods that contain little seeds can spell trouble if you suffer from diverticulosis. The seeds become trapped in the diverticula, causing painful inflammation and cramping. Wastes and bits of food form around them, and pretty soon an infection can develop.

CALL THE DOCTOR IF...

○ ○ ○

Usually, diverticulosis is nothing much to be concerned about. You may have this common condition and not even know it. But it can become serious, even life threatening, when complications such as bleeding or severe infection arise. The most common risk associated with diverticulosis is developing diverticulitis, a far more serious condition in which the diverticula become infected and can perforate.

Symptoms of an infection linked with diverticulitis include blood in the stool, a fever and chills, pain in the lower abdomen that tends to become more intense when you have a bowel movement, nausea, and a dramatic change in regular bowel habits. Call your doctor immediately if you notice these symptoms. A course of antibiotics may clear up such an infection or, depending on the severity, it may be necessary to go on a liquid diet accompanied by intravenous antibiotics. Surgery to remove an abscess may be needed in some cases.

Don't be too refined.

It's not your manners that are of concern, but your eating habits. One of the major reasons Americans are more prone to diverticulosis than people living in less-developed nations is that we rely so heavily on highly processed foods that contain little fiber. These foods contribute to the formation of dry, hard stools that cause pressure to build up in the colon and trigger diverticulosis.

Go ahead, have a drink.

A little alcohol can be a good digestive aid for diverticulosis because it relaxes the colon and relieves some of the pressure. Don't overdo it, though, because alcohol is also dehydrating.

Go easy on the coffee and cigarettes.

Nicotine and caffeine may both be wreaking havoc on your digestive tract because each of them helps promote the cramping to which diverticulosis sufferers are prone.

Don't strain.

The huffing and puffing that may accompany your bowel movements are probably a sign that your digestive tract needs some help. Straining during bowel movements puts extra pressure on your colon and causes diverticula to form. Adding fiber to your diet will help a lot.

Avoid constipation.

Easier said than done, but one of the best things you can do for diverticulosis is to keep your bowels on the move. That way, waste matter doesn't have a chance to become trapped in the diverticula, which can lead to bacterial infection and a full-scale bout of diverticulitis. Eating fibery foods and drinking plenty of water will help prevent constipation.

Pass on the laxatives.

Most laxatives, the chemical-based ones, work by irritating the walls of the colon—which can be damaging in the long run, especially if you have diverticulosis. It's also easy to become reliant on laxatives, with the result that you won't be able to move your bowels without them. A fiber-based stool-bulking substance like Metamucil is a safe choice, but it, too, can create dependency, which occurs because your body gets used to the large volume of fiber Metamucil provides. It's much healthier to rely on sound dietary sources for regularity.●

DIZZINESS

11 WAYS TO REMAIN STEADY ON YOUR FEET

Most of us probably have childhood memories of whirling around like a dervish in one spot and then stopping suddenly—for the sheer amusement of making ourselves so dizzy that it was hard to keep standing up. Or maybe you recall feeling lightheaded, disoriented, or queasy after taking a raucous roller-coaster ride, stepping off a merry-go-round, or looking down from the top of a tall building. Such reactions are completely normal, occurring when the systems that maintain the body's equilibrium are all working properly but become momentarily disrupted or overwhelmed by out-of-the-ordinary circumstances. Even hearty, well-trained astronauts can get violently nauseated when their world is turned topsy-turvy in zero gravity.

Maintaining balance is a very complicated thing, dependent upon the coordination of signals sent to the brain from the eyes, the skin, the muscles, and—in particular—the inner ear. Deep within each ear, beyond the eardrum, are tiny sacs and canals filled with a gel-like fluid. Head movements cause the fluid to circulate through these structures, which then relay information to the brain about the position of the head. But sometimes, when the inner ear either sends incorrect signals to the brain or sends signals that conflict with the information coming from the eyes and body, our normal sense of balance is disrupted—and we get dizzy.

Older people seem especially prone to dizziness. In fact, it is the number one complaint that prompts people over 70 to make an appointment with a doctor. More alarmingly, over half of all accidental deaths among the elderly are attributed to losing balance and falling down. In addition to the risk of falls, recurrent dizziness can profoundly interfere with the quality of life of those suffering from it. They may find themselves afraid to drive, unable to go to work, and wary about merely venturing outside of the house.

So while occasional episodes of dizziness are to be expected and are rarely anything to worry about, you should see a doctor as soon as possible if you experience severe, prolonged, or repeated episodes. A myriad of different—and possibly serious—medical conditions may be to blame (see sidebar, "The Many Causes of Dizziness"). The underlying cause of dizziness can be identified and treated in well over 90 percent of cases. Meanwhile, here are some easy-to-follow tips that can help to prevent or at least minimize your bouts of dizziness, whatever the cause.

Don't get up with too much get-up-and-go.

Whether sitting up from a horizontal position or standing up from a chair, take your time and rise gradually. Getting up too quickly can result in a brief but sudden drop in blood pressure (known as orthostatic hypotension) in the brain, leading to faintness and feelings of blacking out—which could precipitate a nasty fall. Orthostatic hypotension is especially prevalent in people over 50 as aging blood vessels respond more slowly to the body's immediate demands. In addition, some of the medications taken by older people to control hypertension (high blood pressure) actually increase the risk of hypotension. Be especially cautious when you first get out of bed in the morning: Give yourself plenty of time to adjust to an upright sitting position before standing.

No sudden moves!

One of the most common and highly treatable causes of unexplained dizziness—a disorder known as benign positional vertigo (BPV)—occurs when sudden movements cause malfunctioning structures in the inner ear to send a cavalcade of contradictory messages to the brain, producing the sensation that you're spinning wildly out of control. These episodes are often triggered by activities such as turning when you hear your name called or tilting your head back while shampooing or looking up at a high shelf. Such head motions should be executed gradually, not quickly. Likewise, avoid rapid changes in body position, particularly sudden turns.

Watch what you eat.

A low-sodium diet is strongly advised, since in certain people too much salt can affect normal blood circulation to all parts of the body, including the brain, resulting in dizziness. Similarly, cut down on foods that are high in saturated fat and cholesterol (meat, cheese, dairy products, and fried or greasy foods). These foods may eventually lead to atherosclerosis (so-called hardening of the arteries), which can restrict blood supply to the brain. Instead, try to get the bulk of your calories from fresh fruits, vegetables, and whole-grain foods, along with small to moderate servings of fish, skinless poultry, or lean meat.

Watch what you drink, too.

Obviously, alcohol can make you feel "tipsy," and older people are especially sensitive to its effects. But did you know that stimulants like caffeine (found in coffee, tea, and many carbonated colas and other drinks) can cause blood vessels to constrict, limiting the supply of blood to the brain? Therefore, if you are prone to dizziness, you should stick with non-alcoholic and decaffeinated drinks.

Stamp out the cigarettes.

Like caffeine, the nicotine in cigarettes and other tobacco products can temporarily decrease blood flow to the brain, causing dizziness. Over a period of time, habitual smoking also contributes to the development of atherosclerosis, a major cause of dizziness.

Catch up on your reading some other time.

Reading while traveling in a car or other moving vehicle is a notorious cause of motion sickness—a nauseating type of dizziness brought on when the body and inner ear sense movement, but the eyes are focused on a stationary object, like a book in your hands. The best advice is to keep your eyes fixed on distant scenery so they will sense the same motion as the rest of your balance system.

Seek out "sea-sick" medicine.

If you're prone to motion sickness, you can ward it off ahead of time by taking one of a number of preventive medications just prior to your trip. Over-the-counter drugs include brands like Dramamine, Bonine, and Marezine. More potent drugs, including tranquilizers, can be obtained by prescription.

Prudently procrastinate.

When you sense symptoms coming on, avoid risky activities—like driving a car or climbing a stepladder—that might make dizziness worse.

Exercise your equilibrium.

A program of regular physical exercise can help you maintain quick reflexes, strong muscles, and a sure sense of balance. Moreover, a brisk 20-minute workout several times a week can, over a lifetime, help to prevent atherosclerosis in the blood vessels to the brain. Beyond these general good health benefits, a doctor or physical therapist might be able to custom-design a set of exercises to help you relieve or even cure your dizziness problem. Exercises may include jumping, sitting up and lying down rapidly, or turning quickly from side to side. Eye exercises and balance retraining maneuvers (such as standing on one foot) may also be part of the program. Careful monitoring by your doctor is essential, but results can be astounding.

Take your medicine chest in for a check-up.

Various drugs can cause dizziness, especially if you take two or more in combination. This is of particular concern to people over 50, since the majority of people in this age group take more than one type of medication every day. Possi-

THE MANY CAUSES OF DIZZINESS

○ ○ ○

Dozens of medical conditions can produce repeated or severe bouts of dizziness. Your doctor will ask you a battery of questions and then run a number of diagnostic tests to determine what underlying conditions are to blame. The good news is that all are treatable. Here is a list of some of the common culprits.

- Anemia: an insufficient number of red blood cells, which can limit the amount of oxygen available to the body's tissues

- Atherosclerosis: the build-up and hardening of fatty plaque in the walls of the arteries, interfering with good blood circulation

- Cardiac arrhythmias: irregularities in the rhythm of the heartbeat, momentarily disrupting normal blood circulation

- Emphysema: progressive lung damage, leading to a decreased oxygen supply to the body's tissues

- High blood pressure: may lead to circulatory problems

- Hyperventilation syndrome: overly deep or rapid breathing, usually brought on by psychological distress.

- Hypoglycemia: low blood sugar, common when those being treated for diabetes have trouble controlling their blood-sugar levels

- Labyrinthitis: inflammation of the inner-ear structures that maintain balance

- Mastoiditis: infection of the inner ear and surrounding tissues

- Ménière disease: a poorly understood inner-ear problem, yet a common cause of dizziness

- Orthostatic hypotension: a drop in blood pressure in brain arteries

- Transient ischemic attack: a so-called mini-stroke, in which blood flow to a portion of the brain is momentarily blocked

- Trauma: forceful injury, often causing dizziness when involving the head, especially the jaw or ear regions

ble dizziness-inducing over-the-counter drugs include: antihistamines, sleeping aids, cough suppressants, and certain pain relievers. Medications for high blood pressure are among the most common types of prescription drugs to cause lightheadedness, as are tranquilizers, sedatives, and antidepressants. So be sure your doctor is aware of the drugs you take—especially those obtained without a prescription and those prescribed by a specialist or a doctor other than your primary care physician. It's best to bring all of your medicines to your doctor's office for a careful review to determine if, alone or in combination, they might be responsible for the development of your symptoms.

Wait it out.

When a bout of dizziness does strike, stay calm and still until symptoms pass. If possible, try to lie down in a dark room. You may want to keep your eyes open since many people with dizziness due to inner-ear disturbances find that closing their eyes only makes symptoms worse.●

DRY EYES

10 SOOTHING SUGGESTIONS

Your eyes feel as if they are burning or filled with gritty sand. The white parts could be inflamed, bloodshot, or perhaps even swollen. When you blink, the eyelids seems to scrape across your eyeballs. Could this be the result of merely reading too much or staring at the ball game on television for too many hours? Yes and no. Dry eyes are more common in middle-aged women than men and occur when the lacrimal glands—responsible for making tears—are not working properly. Tears arc not just for showing emotion. They also keep your eyes lubricated and make movements like blinking thoughtlessly simple. When your tears don't flow, every wink or blink of your eyes can be painful.

You can blame your age for dry eyes. Lacrimal glands produce fewer tears the older you get. But there may be other reasons for your condition. Lack of sleep can dry eyes. Other causes include rheumatoid arthritis, allergies, skin conditions, vitamin deficiencies, reactions to medication, overexposure to sun and wind, or hormonal imbalances. Even too much intense reading, TV watching, or computer work can dry eyes, especially if you are focusing so intently that your blink rate drops . You really need to see a specialist who may want to prescribe the regular use of artificial teardrops. Dry eyes could also be a sign of more severe problems. In the meantime, here are ten soothing suggestions.

Close your eyes.

By closing your eyes for the eight hours of a good night's sleep, you help to rehydrate them. Closing them for just a minute or two also helps.

Wear sunglasses.

Bright light can strain your eyes. Use sunglasses in sunny weather.

Pay attention to indoor lighting.

Working or reading in harsh overhead light can be tiring. Aim for soft lighting that won't put a glare on your work area—whether you are sitting at the computer, sewing, reading, or watching television. Indirect lamps, which throw their light up to the ceiling, provide more soothing reflected illumination.

Use a humidifier.

If dry air in your environment is aggravating your dry eyes, install a humidifier to add moisture to the air around you at work and at home. Keep your machine meticulously clean, however. Follow the manufacturer's cleaning directions to inhibit the growth of molds and microbes.

Stop cleaning.

Harsh chemicals in some soaps, sprays, and cleaning supplies, especially oven cleaners, can irritate the eyes. If possible, delegate such housecleaning duties, or ask your doctor to recommend products that won't irritate.

Tell your doctor.

Besides calling your eye specialist, make sure you describe your dry eyes to your family physician and any other medical professional treating you for ongoing health problems. Some prescription medications cause dry eyes or make the condition worse.

Check your lenses.

You may need a new prescription. And if you've purchased inexpensive reading glasses without a prescription at a drugstore, they could be part of your problem. Be sure to take your store-bought bargains with you to your next eye examination so the eye doctor can check both you and your "good deal."

Blink.

Remember to blink frequently. This simple act will help lubricate dry eyes.

Cool eyes off.

Moisten a small towel in cool water and lay it across your closed eyes for a few moments. It may help relieve eyestrain only a bit, but it will certainly offer your eyes a much-needed break.

Stop smoking.

Cigarette smoke irritates the eyes. If you smoke, give it up. If you must live or work with smokers, ask them for help in clearing the air around you. Secondhand smoke can be just as harmful as smoke you would create yourself. ●

DRY MOUTH

8 STEPS TO START THE FLOW

Up until recently you probably took the saliva in your mouth completely for granted, rarely giving these juices a second thought. Lately, however, your mouth is so dry that you want to cry. This is not the kind of dry mouth that results from sleeping with your mouth open. A continuously dry mouth is marked by chapped lips; difficulty swallowing or speaking; an increase in dental cavities; and a tongue that's sore, has changed texture, or keeps trying to stick to the roof of your mouth. If you wear dentures, this condition could make you even more uncomfortable.

You have three saliva-producing glands on each side of your mouth. The saliva supplied by these glands is important for your ability to eat and for your dental health. Saliva moistens food in your mouth, making it easier to swallow. It also contains an enzyme that begins the breakdown of nutrients, turning starches into digestible sugars, for instance. Saliva coats your teeth with calcium and minerals and has numerous proteins which kill the kind of bacteria that can cause tooth decay. When your body isn't producing enough saliva, you and your teeth will suffer. Call your doctor and your dentist so these medical professionals can coordinate their treatment.

Dry mouth is not a normal stage of aging. Though you may have to learn to live with it, you should never accept this condition without lots of investigation and professional input. Get a complete checkup. Some serious diseases, including glandular disorders and rheumatoid arthritis, can show up in the form of a dry mouth. If you've recently had radiation for your head or neck, the dryness could be directly related. In the meantime, read these tips on what could be causing your dry mouth as well as what to do about it.

Check your medicine cabinet.

A dry mouth can be a side effect of medication you take for another disorder. Hundreds of medicines can be at fault, including antidepressants, certain blood-pressure and heart medicines, as well as cold and allergy capsules. Even though your medicine may not have made your mouth dry at first, it could have built up in your body, bringing on this symptom gradually. Write down every medication you have taken in recent weeks and take this list to your checkup. Your doctor may be able to change your medication or alter the dosage to reduce dryness.

Drink lots of fluids.

Sip water or other liquids nonstop, especially with meals. When you don't want to swallow another drop, simply rinsing your mouth with warm water can help.

Take good care of your teeth.

Become especially conscientious about brushing and flossing. Schedule visits to the dentist often and ask for fluoride treatments to help protect your teeth from cavities. The decay brought on by a change in saliva chemistry and production can be devastating.

Cut your alcohol consumption.

Beer, wine, and hard liquor can dehydrate you.

Chew sugarless gum.

The act of chewing can help stimulate the saliva glands. Don't switch to sugared chewing gums, however. Sugar can be particularly dangerous in your malfunctioning mouth because you don't have enough saliva to fight off the cavities sugared gum can cause.

Suck lemon drops.

Be sure they are sugarless. The act of sucking can stimulate the saliva glands.

Stop smoking.

Cigarette smoke can dry membranes, even the ones in your mouth.

Investigate saliva substitutes.

With your doctor's or dentist's advice, try one of the over-the-counter artificial saliva products on the market. They don't usually contain any of the protective elements of natural saliva, but they do help keep mouth tissues lubricated.●

DRY SKIN

20 DRYNESS-DEFYING ACTS

You certainly don't look like a withered prune. But that might be just how you feel when your skin dries out like the floor of Death Valley and becomes flakier than a blizzard in Maine.

You can blame your dry, scratchy skin on a lot of things: exposure to the sun, sitting around a dry heated house, soaking in the bathtub. In fact, there is no end of factors that contribute to dry skin. Your skin has taken a heck of a beating over the years, and the result is dryness that may be driving you nuts.

Add to this regular wear and tear the fact that your skin tends to become drier as you get older. It also becomes thinner, therefore more susceptible to the effects of drying, and it produces fewer natural oils. What this means is that it is all the more important to keep as much moisture as you can in your skin and to work a little harder at putting lost moisture back in. Here's how.

Moisturize.

It's the best thing you can do to relieve the flaking, itching, and tightness of dry skin. There's no need to get fancy about it—in fact, basic oil-based products like petroleum jelly and baby oil provide the most protection by sealing moisture into the skin. Keep in mind, too, that the more ingredients a moisturizer contains, such as fragrance, the more likely it is to trigger a skin reaction.

Keep hand cream handy.

Your hands dry out quickly, and little wonder. You're forever washing them, dipping them into harsh household cleansers, exposing them to the elements, and drying them out in other ways. To counteract these ills, use a heavy-duty hand cream liberally—keep a tube near the sinks in the kitchen and bathrooms, and apply some every time you wash your hands.

Consider convenience.

You might like that special moisture cream you picked up on your vacation in Europe, but if it's hard to find, you're less likely to use it. Use a moisturizer that's easy to find—many highly effective brands are available at supermarkets and drugstores—so you can always have a supply on hand. Also make sure your moisturizer is affordable so you can use it liberally without worrying about the toll it's taking on your pocketbook. Remember, when it comes to moisturizers, effectiveness doesn't increase with price: Inexpensive, no-frills baby oil does a fine job.

Get damp to stay moist.

A moisturizer works best when it's applied to damp skin because the oils you're applying help trap moisture in the skin. When you get out of the tub or shower, pat yourself dry and apply moisturizer immediately.

Start early.

It's important to begin moisturizing at the onset of dry weather. This way, your hands will never have a chance to become chapped and cracked, effects that can take weeks and months of moisture therapy to overcome. (See FISSURES.)

Don't apply soap directly to your skin.

You'll be applying more than you need and heighten the risk of drying out your skin. You only need a little soap to get clean—mix soap with generous portions of water in your hand, and apply it with your fingertips.

Choose the right soap, every time.

A mild, moisturizing bar is going to be much less drying than a heavy-duty deodorant soap or an abrasive hand cleanser, and a super-mild, nonsoap cleanser is going to be gentler still. You can probably figure that one out for yourself, but the hitch is to use gentle soaps *every time* you wash up—if you step into the shower, notice you're out of soap, and grab an extra heavy-duty hand bar, it may take days to replace the moisture that could be lost.

Don't go batty about bathing.

It's almost unthinkable in our hygiene-hyped society not to bathe or shower at least once a day. Well, break with convention. Frequent bathing robs your skin

---

CHOOSING THE RIGHT MOISTURIZER

○ ○ ○

As you probably noticed the last time you walked into a drugstore, there are so many moisturizers available these days that it's hard to know which one is best. As a rule of thumb, water-based or oil-free moisturizers are not going to keep your skin as moist or provide as much protection as oil-based moisturizers. On the other hand, if you have adult acne or other chronic skin irritations, water-based or oil-free moisturizers are less likely to aggravate your skin. You'll also be confronted with a choice between creams and lotions. A lotion is just a cream to which water has been added to make it easier to apply; a heavier cream is probably the best choice for dry, flaky skin.

Some ingredients that are commonly found in moisturizers can trigger allergic reactions in certain users. These include lanolin and fragrances. If you've experienced reactions to these ingredients in the past or if you're not sure how you might react to them, try to avoid them: The last thing you want in addition to a dry skin condition is a rash.

of oils and dries it out. Consider bathing every other day or even less frequently. In between baths, you can probably keep yourself perfectly clean by cleansing your neck, armpits, and groin area without immersing yourself in a tub or standing under a shower.

Soak in short spurts.

A long soak in a hot tub may be your idea of heaven, but it can be hellishly drying for your skin. Limit your baths to ten minutes and showers to five (the pressure of a shower is especially drying), and keep the water in the cool-to-tepid range.

Pour in some bath oil.

But do so after you've stepped into the tub. Otherwise, the oil will keep moisture from saturating your skin thoroughly. Any sort of simple mineral oil—even a little corn oil from the kitchen cabinet—should do the trick. Scented oils may provide a sensual experience, but at a price—the perfumed additives may contribute to the skin-drying process. You are going to rub off most of the moisture when you dry yourself, so even if you've been soaking in oil, it's still important to moisturize when you get out of the tub. Exercise extreme caution when doing so because bath oils make enamel surfaces extra slippery.

Leave the washcloth on the towel rack.

And keep body sponges and loofahs in dry dock, too. To rub is to rob your skin of precious oils. It's safest to wash gently with your fingertips.

Be a savvy shaver.

Shaving is a little like putting meat tenderizer on a roast—it softens and sensitizes the skin. This might leave you feeling tingly, refreshed, and scruffy clean, but it leaves you prey to the drying effects of the elements.

Stay out of the sauna.

Sorry, Scandinavians, but saunas and steam rooms have a drying effect on the skin. Both of them promote perspiration, so you're losing moisture, not gaining it.

Turn down the thermostat.

Forced-air heating can suck every drop of moisture right out of your skin. Keeping the house warm but not too hot will help, as will using a humidifier to counteract the dryness.

Don't curl up next to the hearth.

A wood-burning fire dries out the air. Avoid sitting too close to a blaze, and use a humidifier to counteract its effects.

Don't chill out.

The harsh chill of winter is especially drying. Moisturize before you go outdoors, and cover up—gloves to keep your hands from drying out and a scarf or ski mask to protect your face.

Don't plug in the electric blanket.

The heat it generates will have a drying effect on your skin. It's better to use a comforter or to throw an extra blanket onto the bed.

Be wary of wool.

It's a great insulator, but wool can irritate dry skin. Don wool as outerwear, but when it comes time to put something next to your skin, make it cotton. It's less irritating, and it gently wicks perspiration from the skin: On the other hand, wool and synthetics tend to trap perspiration next to the skin and cause a damaging, drying effect. In general, clothes that fit loosely and that don't chafe are going to feel better next to dry skin.

Don't get dishpan hands.

Your hands take a real beating around the house and as a result can dry up like prunes. Take some steps to protect them: Wear rubber gloves any time you work with water and harsh cleansers (don a pair of cotton gloves underneath to prevent moisture loss through sweating); try to find kinder, gentler alternatives to harsh household cleaning agents (baking soda is an excellent cleanser that won't irritate your skin, and gentle vinegar can often do the job of harsh ammonia). Use long-handled brushes when you do the dishes or scrub a surface so you don't have to immerse your hands in hot, sudsy water.

Crack open a window.

Sometimes maintaining acceptable humidity levels is that easy. Obviously, it's not going to help very much when the air outside is so dry you can hear it snap. But in autumn and spring, when the weather tends to be cool and damp, an open window can effectively counteract the drying effects of the furnace.

Avoid alcohol.

Whether you apply it to your skin or drink it, alcohol can have a drying effect. The "avoid" list includes alcohol-based skin products such as aftershaves, astringents, bracers, toners, and cleansers. As to the other kind of alcohol, it tends to lower water concentrations in the blood, forcing the blood to draw water out of the skin and other cells as a replacement.

Shun the sun.

In case you haven't noticed (and if you haven't, just look in the mirror), the sun dries out your skin. That is one of many reasons—including wrinkling, age spots, and skin cancer—why it's so important to take measures to avoid the sun's harmful rays. Wear a sunscreen with a sun protection factor of 15 or greater any time you go out in the sun; apply it at least 15 minutes before you go out so it has time to sink in. Cover your skin with lightweight, cotton clothing; wear a hat; wear sun-protectant lip balm; and try to stay in the shade between 10:00 A.M. and 4:00 P.M., when the sun's damaging rays are strongest. Now that you're properly protected, go out and enjoy that sunny weather.●

EARACHE

8 ANSWERS TO THE PAIN

An earache should probably send you straight to the doctor. No matter how old you are, an untreated ear infection can lead to hearing loss, so you'll want to eliminate that possibility right away. Antibiotics can clear up infections. Wax could be blocking the outer ear channel, or ear pain could be a symptom of a medical problem somewhere else in your body, such as your throat, tongue, or jaw. You have an outer, middle, and inner ear to worry about, so a physician is the best judge of where the pain is coming from.

Some earaches are caused by blocked eustachian tubes. Have you had a cold or the flu? This could be an important clue to your pain. A eustachian tube is the thin, membrane-lined canal connecting the back of your nose to each middle ear, a small cavity between the eardrum and the inner ear. When your eustachian tubes are open, they perform several critical duties. For one thing, mucus can drain down the back of your throat from a stuffed nose. So if you wake up with throbbing ear pain in the middle of the night, it is likely the result of your eustachian tubes being unable to drain into your throat.

Air enters your middle ear, where it's absorbed. You can swallow and chew easily when the tubes are open. But if either of these passages get blocked, you end up with an ache, because the airless middle ear then acts like a vacuum, tugging at your eardrum and pulling it inward.

Frequent air travelers probably know exactly what it feels like to have blocked eustachian tubes. Just as a plane takes off, air pressure in the cabin drops rapidly, and upon landing, when the pressure changes rapidly back, the middle ear struggles to equalize. Similarly, when you have a cold or stuffy nose from respiratory congestion, the air isn't always able to get through the eustachian tube to equalize pressure. Even elevator rides in tall buildings can cause this kind of ear pain.

Here are some hints for stopping common earaches until you are able to see a doctor.

Force a swallow.

Swallowing causes the muscles that open the eustachian tubes to operate. Move your mouth even if it hurts. Wiggle your chin around. It helps to just open your mouth fully. Drink a little water and swallow hard. If your pain comes from flying in an airplane, start swallowing on takeoff and especially as the plane descends on landing. In fact, pressure in your ears is more of a concern when landing than when taking off.

Don't lie down.

If you've been sleeping or reclining on the sofa, sit up. Prop yourself up with pillows to keep your head up so the eustachian tubes can drain and diminish any swelling.

Oil it.

Put a bit of warm baby or mineral oil in the ear that hurts. If you suspect that your eardrum has been ruptured, however, don't try this pain-killing tip. How do you recognize a ruptured eardrum? If your earache was sudden and sharp, and if it followed a trauma such as an explosion, it could be a broken eardrum. Scuba divers are susceptible to this type of accident when they descend too rapidly into very deep water. Small perforations heal naturally within a few weeks. A large tear might require surgery.

Pinch your nose.

When your ears hurt on a plane, try this trick. Hold your nose tightly with your thumb and forefinger. Try to blow through your nose as forcefully as you can, but keep your mouth closed. Don't stop pinching. Repeat the blowing as hard as you can. What you are trying to do is reach the point where your ears pop. You might hear a crackling sound, but the pain should be eliminated. The pop tells you that pressure has been equalized. Your eardrum isn't being injured. This is not a remedy to use when you have a sore throat or fever, however, because you could end up sending infectious bacteria into your ears. And it should not be attempted if you have a heart or circulatory problem.

Yawn.

Like swallowing, yawning is one of the best ways to open your eustachian tubes. Yawn as much as you can, but don't go to sleep if you are on a descending airplane. Sleeping passengers won't swallow often enough to keep their ears open. Ask the flight attendant to wake you if it's a long flight and you are concerned about earaches.

Chew gum.

While you may have known this is a good trick for air traveling, you may not know that it's also helpful for midnight earaches. Keep gum in your medicine cabinet.

Take a decongestant.

When your sinuses are troubling you or your nose is clogged, rely on an over-the-counter decongestant to clear things up. To head off trouble, take your medicine before going to bed or before flying. If you have heart disease, high blood pressure, an irregular heartbeat, or thyroid disease, talk to your doctor before taking any decongestants.

Use a painkiller.

Aspirin, acetaminophen, or ibuprofen can kill your pain. Make sure that the medication you choose doesn't interfere with any other prescription drug or pre-existing medical condition.●

GET RID OF WAXY BUILDUP

○ ○ ○

The wax inside your ears won't put a shine on your dining room table, but it could block your outer ear canal enough to make you uncomfortable. Small glands in your ear produce wax to protect the ear canal, and though some people generate hardly any wax at all, others make lots of it. If a hard plug of wax forms, it can lead to an earache. But don't try to remove it with any kind of pointed object because you could puncture your eardrum Ordinarily, physicians soften the wax with drops before removing it. In stubborn situations, they pump warm water into the outer ear or use an electrical suction appliance.

EMPHYSEMA

---

11 WAYS TO BREATHE EASIER

Nature has blessed us with a generous surplus of lung tissue: If you were to unfold all the little nooks and crannies within the lungs and spread them out flat, there would be enough surface area to cover two entire tennis courts. That's six times the amount of lung tissue needed to breathe while at rest. Ironically, because this reserve is so plentiful, emphysema often damages 50 to 70 percent of lung tissue before most patients even experience their first symptoms.

To understand emphysema, picture the inner structure of the lungs as resembling an upside-down stalk of broccoli. There is the main stem at the top (the trachea, or windpipe), two major offshoots into each lung (the bronchi), and then branches of many smaller offshoots (bronchioles). At the ends of the bronchioles are clusters of tiny round air sacs called alveoli, where molecules of freshly inhaled oxygen enter the bloodstream in exchange for the carbon dioxide "exhaust" that's expelled when we exhale.

Each year emphysema is responsible for the deaths of some 13,000 of the 2.5 million Americans suffering from it. Fortunately, the disease is highly preventable: Approximately 90 percent of all cases can be directly attributed to cigarette smoking. The vast majority of patients are people over 50 who have smoked heavily (a pack or more per day) for at least two decades. Another 3 to 5 percent of cases are linked to a rare genetic deficiency. Air pollution or other irritants may also play a role in causing or aggravating the condition.

In emphysema, persistent inflammation deep in the lungs (caused by repeated irritation, usually due to cigarette smoke) eventually robs the delicate walls of the alveoli of their elasticity, causing them to burst. They may then fuse together with other burst alveoli, forming larger but far less functional air sacs. As the disease progresses, it becomes increasingly difficult for the lungs to meet the body's demand for oxygen. Another result of this process of deterioration is that more of the body's energy supply is required for breathing, so that many people with emphysema begin to lose weight unintentionally. In addition, poorly functioning lungs may lead to the narrowing or even the collapse of the small bronchioles, trapping carbon dioxide in the lungs rather than allowing it to be exhaled. This trapped air can give the torso a rounded or barrel-chested appearance. Meanwhile, muscles in the neck and shoulders may become overdeveloped as they work harder to aid breathing—producing a deceptively robust appearance. Emphysema may ultimately prove fatal. Breathing may become so severely impaired that respiratory failure occurs, or else the heart—pumping harder and faster in an effort to compensate for the low blood levels of oxygen—may ultimately give out.

While it's true that no methods have yet been discovered to reverse lung damage once it has occurred, it's a widespread misconception that nothing can be done about emphysema and that the disease must follow a hopeless downhill course. In recent years, many advances have made it possible to slow or halt the progress of the disease, and there are things patients can do to preserve—or in some cases even improve—existing lung function. Here are a number of ways that might make it easier to breathe.

Catch it early.

The sooner emphysema is detected, the better the outlook. That's why most experts in the field of lung disease think that a quick, simple, painless test called spirometry should be included as part of the routine physical examinations of all adults. The test, which measures the force of your breath as you inhale and exhale, can detect changes in lung function much earlier than other tests, and even before symptoms develop. If the test indicates airway obstruction, the next step will probably be to have a chest X ray to help determine the cause. The X ray is done to rule out other problems like lung cancer and to help confirm the diagnosis of emphysema. The bottom line: You should undergo a spirometric test at least once a year if you smoke or if you have any breathing difficulties, including wheezing, coughing, shortness of breath, or excessive production of phlegm.

Kick the habit!

If you are diagnosed with emphysema, smoking is the single worst thing you can do to aggravate your condition. In fact all smokers—whether they have any respiratory problems or not—should do whatever it takes to quit before trouble does start or becomes more serious. Likewise, try to avoid secondhand smoke, even if it means having to ask someone in your presence to please stop smoking (see SMOKING AND TOBACCO USE).

Protect your lungs from infection.

Emphysema sufferers are at increased risk of developing respiratory infections, and even a mild one can rapidly become serious, leading to further destruction of lung tissue. To protect yourself against such infections, be sure to get a flu shot

GETTING THE MOST FROM YOUR INHALER

○ ○ ○

Almost all people suffering from emphysema are required to take some type of inhaled medication using an inhaler device. How you operate your inhaler can have a significant effect on how well the medication works. For example, if you close your lips around the mouthpiece, you will be inclined to breathe through your nose, so most of the droplets of the drug end up in your mouth, the back of your throat, or on the mouthpiece—but not down in your lungs where it needs to go to be effective. To get the maximum therapeutic benefit from your inhaled medications, follow these simple steps:

- After shaking the canister well, invert the inhaler and position the nozzle about an inch to an inch and a half in front of your mouth.

- Open your mouth wide and exhale. Be sure the nozzle of the inhaler is angled to point toward the opening of your throat and not at your tongue or the roof of your mouth.

- Start spraying as you slowly inhale over a five- to ten-second period, drawing as much mist as you can as deeply into your lungs as possible. (If you discover you have difficulty coordinating your breaths with the release of the medication, ask your doctor about getting a spacer—a device that fits onto the end of the inhaler and holds the cloud of vaporized medicine in a chamber until you are ready to inhale.)

- Hold your breath five to ten seconds.

- Exhale slowly.

- If you normally take two puffs, wait a minute or two after the first one to take the second. After the first dose has had a chance to start working, it's that much easier for the second dose to reach deeper into your lungs.

- If you are required to take both an inhaled corticosteroid and a bronchodilator, use the bronchodilator first to open up your lungs, then administer the corticosteroid.

- If you use a corticosteroid, rinse your mouth afterward to prevent oral fungal infections, or take your corticosteroid just before mealtime.

in the fall of every year and a pneumonia vaccine (a single vaccination generally provides lifetime protection). Avoid large crowds in poorly ventilated rooms, especially during the winter months when flu epidemics are prevalent. Wash your hands after close contact with others, and be careful to avoid touching your face, since cold viruses and other germs commonly enter through the eyes, nose, and mouth after being transmitted by the fingers. Antibiotics should be administered at the first signs of respiratory infection, which may include fever, chills, cough, and an increase in phlegm production (especially phlegm that changes color or becomes thicker). Your doctor can give you a prescription for an antibiotic to keep on hand so no time is lost before starting treatment.

Learn to breathe better.

It's actually possible to learn to breathe in a more efficient manner and thus reduce the demands on your lungs. By doing so, you can be more physically active, minimize symptoms, and improve your overall health. For ten minutes a day, try this exercise: Lie on your back with your head on a pillow and breathe in through your nose. Tighten your abdominal muscles so your upper chest expands, then exhale through your mouth, pursing your lips. You should hear a hissing sound and feel pressure in your upper chest. This pressure keeps the airways open so the maximum amount of air can be exhaled. Take twice as much time to exhale as you take to inhale. After you've become accustomed to breathing this way, try it sitting up, then while walking (inhale on your first step, then exhale during the next two), and finally while climbing stairs or a hill. Your doctor or physical therapist can recommend additional breathing exercises.

Rehabilitate your lungs with exercise.

Even though shortness of breath understandably scares many emphysema patients away from exercising, dramatic strides have been made by those who participate in pulmonary rehabilitation programs. Under the close supervision of a specialist trained in pulmonary medicine, you can learn to make better use of respiratory muscles and steadily increase the amount of exercise you can tolerate. The doctor may prescribe supplemental oxygen to ease shortness of breath during exercise, but many patients improve to the point where their need for extra oxygen is reduced or eliminated. Those who were unable to climb a single flight of stairs before entering a pulmonary rehabilitation program commonly discover they can comfortably climb several flights afterward. A few even find themselves able to go out and play golf or take bicycle rides again. Ask your doctor for more information if you are interested in such a program.

Eat right.

Although it is often underemphasized, good nutrition can play a significant role in treatment. Foods containing too many simple carbohydrates (sugars) can actually promote breathing difficulty in some patients. On the other hand, complex carbohydrates—such as those found in fruits, vegetables, and whole grains—pose no such risks and are beneficial to overall good health. Nutritionists specializing in the treatment of lung disorders sometimes recommend a high-protein diet, with the protein coming preferably from low-fat sources, such as legumes (including peas, lentils, and kidney beans) and lean meats. Vitamin supplements may be recommended as well. If your treatment includes taking corticosteroids (which can increase the risk of the bone-weakening disease, osteoporosis), you maybe advised to take vitamin D and calcium.

Tip the scales in your favor.

While being overweight only makes the difficulty in breathing (and possible heart problems) worse for those with emphysema, a low-calorie diet is not necessarily a good idea. Since emphysema typically demands more and more of the body's energy just for breathing, it can be very difficult to regain weight in the event that you lose too much. So if you need to lose weight, don't start dieting without a doctor's close supervision.

Practice good lung hygiene.

It's very important to regularly clear mucus and other secretions from the bronchial passages to keep them open and functioning at maximum efficiency. Your doctor or physical therapist can show you a technique known as postural drainage, in which you assume various positions whereby your chest is higher than your head so gravity can help clear mucus from your lungs.

Listen to the weather report.

Lung diseases are easily aggravated by air pollution. So on days when the weather forecaster announces a poor-air-quality alert, try to stay indoors, preferably in a climate-controlled environment.

Pace yourself.

There are a number of ways you can learn to budget your time and energy to make living with a chronic disease like emphysema significantly less strenuous. For example, when you go to the grocery store, take an over-the-shoulder satchel, knapsack, or portable light-weight push-cart to help you carry your purchases home. Ask that your groceries be bagged in many light bundles rather than a few heavy ones, making it easier to carry

them from car to kitchen. Or ask that perishables all be bagged together so you can get them to the refrigerator without delay when you get home. Then you can rest before you put away nonperishable items. Perhaps find someone willing to do heavy shopping for you on a regular basis. Do household chores as if in an assembly line: For example, prepare meals by bringing all necessary items to the sink or counter area first, then progress to the stove, and then to the table. Sit on a stool to perform tasks such as ironing or preparing food. Take frequent breaks when engaged in potentially fatiguing work.

Don't go it alone.

People with emphysema and their family members must cope with constant day-to-day stress. Psychological counseling and group therapy with an emphysema self-help group can be extremely helpful. Such groups, which usually meet at least once a week, can provide ongoing motivation to keep exercising and may even schedule times for members to work out together. Your primary care physician or rehabilitation therapist can most likely refer you to a nearby group. For further information on support groups or other matters pertaining to emphysema, the National Jewish Center for Immunology and Respiratory Medicine provides an excellent service called the Lung Line. It is staffed by specially trained nurses and can be reached at 800-222-LUNG between the hours of 8 A.M. and 5 P.M. MST on weekdays.●

ENLARGED PROSTATE

15 WAYS TO LIVE WITH IT

Aside from fretting about your graying, thinning hair, you may never worry about the toll the years are taking on your body. Then you run smack dab into the symptoms of a problem that's every bit as common among men over 50 as gray and thinning hair—an enlarged prostate, known medically as benign prostatic hyperplasia (BPH). The harsh fact is, most men over 50 begin to develop this condition and experience its effects to varying degrees.

The prostate is the cluster of glands just beneath the bladder, surrounding the urethra. And this positioning is what is most likely to cause you problems: As the prostate enlarges, it presses against the urethra and can make it difficult to urinate. You may feel the urge to urinate more frequently but find it difficult to do so, and you may find it harder to sleep through the night without having to get up a couple of times and make a trip to the bathroom. In the worst-case scenario, it can become impossible to urinate, triggering serious medical problems that require emergency attention.

Sort of makes your concerns about your hair seem trivial, doesn't it? Well, you'll be happy to know that an enlarged prostate in itself is not likely to cause you any pain or affect sexual performance. And in many cases it's possible to live quite comfortably with the urination problems an enlarged prostate causes—and in the event it isn't, new drugs and new surgical techniques are at hand. In the meantime, here are some tips to make life with your peevish prostate more bearable.

Cut back on fluids before bedtime.

It may help you get a better night's sleep, because if the bladder is empty you probably won't feel the need to get up and urinate as often. So cut yourself off from beverages several hours before you go to bed, and try to urinate as often as you can during the evening so you can retire with an empty bladder—and peace of mind.

Sit to urinate.

This position puts a little extra pressure on the abdominal wall, helping the bladder empty its contents more thoroughly. Try this trick: Once you've urinated, stand up, then sit back down, lean forward, and try again. This extra exertion may help force remaining urine out of the bladder.

Make the men's room a regular stop.

Frequent urination is the only way to relieve the pressure that builds up in the bladder as a result of an enlarged prostate. You'll be more comfortable if you try to urinate every couple of hours.

Take your time.

No matter how strong the urge, it may be difficult to urinate. That's because as the prostate gland enlarges, it constricts the urethra, the duct that connects the bladder with the penis. It may not be possible to produce anything more than a dribble, and at times an attempt may be totally nonproductive. Any amount of urination, though, will take some of the pressure off the bladder. Be patient, and try to empty the bladder as completely as possible.

Don't let BPH put a crimp in your sex life.

An enlarged prostate does not affect the ability to have an erection, nor does it necessarily lessen the pleasurable sensation of orgasm. In fact, frequent ejaculation can help ease the effects of an enlarged prostate by facilitating urination—ejaculation helps expel the secretions that build up around the prostate gland and further block the urethra. The most likely way an enlarged prostate might affect your sex life is by raising your concerns about your ability to perform. Well, it shouldn't, so relax. If your concerns linger you might consider talking to a counselor (see IMPOTENCE).

Take a chilly view toward cold medications.

Decongestants and antihistamines not only stop the flow in the nasal passages, but they also slow down the action of the bladder. If you're already having trouble urinating, these cold remedies can complicate matters severely: Urine retention can lead to a serious bladder or kidney infection and may even be life threatening. If you must take a decongestant or antihistamine, start out with half the recommended dose and see how it affects urination. Don't increase the dosage until you're sure the medication isn't creating a problem. And stop taking it immediately any time you notice that it's becoming more difficult than usual to urinate.

Find an alternative remedy for your allergies.

If you suffer from hay fever and other allergies and take medications regularly, talk to your doctor about antihistamines you can use comfortably. Some antihistamines, such as terfenadine (Seldane), provide relief from allergy symptoms without affecting urination.

Give up caffeine.

Caffeine is not just an innocent vice if you suffer from an enlarged prostate. It not only increases the production of urine in the kidneys, but it also tightens the neck of the bladder and can cause prostate tissue to constrict. As a result, caffeine can increase the urge to urinate but make it even more difficult to do so. You will probably be more comfortable if you cut back on caffeine in all its forms.

Avoid alcohol.

Alcohol delivers the same kind of double whammy that caffeine does—it is a diuretic, so it increases the production of urine, but it also affects the bladder and makes it more difficult to urinate. If you're not ready to go on the wagon, drink in moderation.

Don't be a couch potato.

Sitting or lying for long periods allows urine to build up in the bladder behind the obstruction caused by the enlarged prostate gland. If it's necessary to sit for hours at a time, get up frequently and walk around the room. Taking an evening walk can make it easier to empty the bladder before turning in.

Fret about bladder failure.

Suddenly or gradually, as a result of an enlarged prostate, the bladder may lose its ability to empty its contents. Sudden bladder failure, known as acute urinary retention, is a serious condition that requires immediate medical treatment. Usually, a catheter is inserted in the bladder to drain the accumulated urine. Aside from the inability to urinate, the telltale sign of acute urinary retention is extreme pain in the abdomen. The most common symptom of gradual bladder failure is a tendency for urine to dribble out when you cough, sneeze, or exert yourself. Don't let these symptoms persist—seek medical help at the first signs.

Be on the lookout for infection.

Many men with an enlarged prostate experience few problems. Over time, however, urine retention and the strain on

---

WARNING!
. . .
Prostate Cancer Alert

An enlarged prostate does not in itself signal the onset of prostate cancer. Nonetheless, prostate cancer is one of the most common cancers in men—it's estimated that 13 out of every 100 American men will develop the disease during their lifetimes, usually after age 65, and 3 out of 100 men die from it. All men over 50, whether or not they have an enlarged prostate, should have a prostate examination as part of an annual checkup. Many hospitals sponsor prostate cancer screenings. Check with your local hospital for more information.

WHEN IT'S TIME FOR MEDICAL TREATMENT

○ ○ ○

Many men live comfortably for years with an enlarged prostate gland—without the need for any kind of medical treatment. In fact, over time the symptoms may clear up on their own. It's necessary, though, to have frequent checkups to keep a lookout for problems.

If problems persist or worsen—for instance, if the urine flow becomes severely blocked—surgery may be necessary to remove the enlarged tissue that is pressing against the urethra. This is often done with a procedure called transurethral resection of the prostate (TURP), in which an instrument is inserted through the urethra to cut tissue and seal blood vessels. TURP and other kinds of prostate surgery don't affect sexual performance, though they frequently render a man sterile by causing a condition called retrograde ejaculation (instead of flowing through the urethra to the penis, semen enters the bladder and is eventually expelled with urine).

the bladder can lead to serious complications. If the bladder does not empty completely, for instance, pools of urine that collect in it can become infected. The kidneys can become infected, as can the prostate gland itself (a condition known as prostatitis). Keep an eye out for signs that something is amiss. A change in urination habits, fever, chills, pain and swelling in the lower abdomen, blood in the urine, nausea, and painful urination are common signs of bladder and kidney infections. If you notice these symptoms, see a physician, who will probably prescribe a course of antibiotics.

Watch what you eat.

An enlarged prostate needn't put a crimp in your eating style. But since urination can be difficult, you may find that you are more comfortable if you avoid foods that might irritate the bladder. Topping the list of suspected bladder irritants are spicy foods, such as curry; tomatoes and tomato sauces; and sugary foods and drinks.

Modify your weight-loss regimen.

While keeping weight to desirable levels is one of the best things you can do for general good health, your efforts could have an undesired side effect if you have an enlarged prostate. That's because many weight-loss regimens call for increased fluid intake, which can be hard to handle if you have difficulty urinating. Go ahead and eat less, but modify your regimen so you don't compensate by drinking substantially more.

Keep drinking water.

Limiting fluid intake can reduce the need to urinate, but it also leads to dehydration. For good digestion and all-around good health, continue to drink at least six to eight glasses of water a day. Space out your trips to the water cooler, though, so your bladder doesn't become uncomfortably full. And taper off on water consumption in the evening to avoid going to bed with a full bladder.●

EXCESSIVE PERSPIRATION

13 WAYS TO STAY DRIER

Hey, did you just take a shower with your clothes on? Do you give out towels with your handshakes, sweaty palms? Yeah, you've probably heard all the jokes. In fact, sometimes it seems like one of the grossest things you can do in our society is sweat.

That's a shame, because sweating is a perfectly natural function of body mechanics and a pretty nifty one at that. When your body overheats, sweat glands draw fluid from the blood and bring it to the skin, where it cools things down as it evaporates. In short, sweat glands function as the body's air-conditioning system. Sometimes, though, you can sweat too much—it may be your genetic makeup or a sign of stress or sometimes the symptom of a serious illness.

In most cases, sweating is nothing to, well, get in a sweat over. Taking these precautions can help keep you drier.

Cut back on caffeine.

The caffeine in coffee, tea, and cola drinks is bad news for heavy sweaters in two ways: It stimulates the heart, making you sweat more, and it acts as a diuretic, causing you to pass water. In combination, these effects can cause you to become dehydrated quickly.

Avoid alcohol.

A gin and tonic may seem like just the thing on a hot summer's day, but if you're worried about sweating, a glass of cool water is a better choice. Here's why: Among alcohol's other effects on the body, it stimulates blood flow to the skin and as a result can cause you to sweat.

Watch your weight.

When you're overweight, even during mild exertion your heart strains to pump blood. As a result, you are likely to sweat more. If nothing else is going to motivate you to bring your weight down to a healthy range, perhaps the prospect of remaining drier will.

Drink plenty of water.

Depending on how much you sweat, how hot it is, and how active you are, you can lose as much as ten quarts of

---

WHEN SWEATING IS SOMETHING TO SWEAT OVER

○ ○ ○

If you notice that you are sweating more than usual, or if you begin to sweat even when it's cool outdoors and you're not exercising, there could be an underlying medical condition. Increased sweating is a perfectly normal symptom of menopause, for instance, and it will cease once you pass through this stage. In the meantime, cotton nightclothes may help you cope comfortably with the night sweats that are associated with menopause. Remember, too, that many women sweat more than normal during their periods.

Sweating can also be a sign of illness. Excessive perspiration may be one of the first signs that you have the flu or another bug. If sweating is associated with increased appetite, a rapid heartbeat, and weight loss, it could be the sign of an overactive thyroid gland. Likewise, sweating accompanied by a fever can be a symptom of a chronic infectious disease, such as tuberculosis or Hodgkin disease. If you're sweating more than usual and feel weak or just not yourself, see your physician.

---

water a day through sweating. It's important to replace that fluid, especially when it's very hot or if you've been exerting yourself. Try to drink at least eight glasses of water a day, more if you're sweating a lot, and plenty before, during, and after exercise. Boosting your intake of fluids neither increases nor decreases what is lost through sweating, but taking in more fluid prevents a cosmetic problem from becoming a health problem.

Stay away from "sweaty" foods.

Pepper and spices taste hot going down, and they raise your internal thermometer, too. In reaction to the heat they generate in your digestive tract, you'll probably sweat for a while.

Change your socks.

Sweaty feet are a common problem, exacerbated by the fact that all that moisture becomes trapped in the closed environment of your shoes and socks. Most footwear provides a hothouse in which athlete's foot and other fungi can thrive. Especially in warm weather, avoid nylon socks and pantyhose, which will only make your feet sweat more. Change into clean, dry socks or hose frequently. Consider going without socks and wearing open-toed shoes and sandals whenever possible. And ask your physician to recommend or prescribe a powder to sprinkle on your feet periodically.

Ask your doctor about aspirin.

If you take aspirin regularly—as a daily blood thinner, for instance—you may notice that you sweat more than usual. If this poses a problem, ask your doctor if there is another medication that may provide similar benefits without the same drenching consequences. Some other medications may also cause you to perspire more than usual—ask your physician about alternatives.

Get a grip.

Antiperspirants work on the hands as well as under the arms. If sweaty palms are a problem, dab on your antiperspirant or swab them with witch hazel, which can temporarily shrink pores.

Stay calm.

You might notice it every time your mechanic hands you a bill for fixing your car: Your palms begin to sweat and beads of perspiration form on your forehead. Yes, stress causes you to sweat. The next time you are in a stressful situation, try taking a couple of deep breaths and imagine yourself blowing away your cares with each exhalation. You'll bring down your heart rate a few notches, make yourself feel more relaxed, and stay a little drier in the bargain.

Turn down the electric blanket.

While night sweats can be a symptom of serious illness, happily they are often simply the consequence of sleeping in an environment that is too hot. Electric blankets are major culprits because they provide more heat than you probably need as you sleep. Synthetic blankets aren't much better: They don't breathe, thus they trap in body heat and raise your temperature to sweat levels. Blankets and comforters made from cotton and wool may be better choices—they provide a more comfortable and drier night's rest.

Know the difference between antiperspirants and deodorants.

Antiperspirants are classified as drugs because they affect a body function—they inhibit your sweat glands. Deodorants don't keep you from sweating; instead, they inhibit the odor-causing bacteria that grow on clammy skin, and some just mask the smell. If you perspire a lot, an antiperspirant is probably in order. Better yet, a combination antiperspirant and deodorant will do double duty by keeping you drier and smelling nicer.

Don't let an antiperspirant or deodorant irritate you.

Almost all antiperspirants contain aluminum compounds, which may or may not irritate your skin. Likewise, deodorants contain various ingredients that may cause skin irritation in some users. If you develop a rash in the area where you apply these products, hold off on using any product until the skin calms down, then try a brand that contains different ingredients.

Avoid aerosol sprays.

They're easy to use, but the mist tends to linger in the air and may irritate your eyes, nasal passages, and lungs. Besides, by not using such sprays, you'll be doing the ozone layer a favor. Use a roll-on or cream instead.●

EYESTRAIN

9 SECRETS TO SAVE YOUR EYES

Reading in poor light, watching television nonstop, driving for long distances at night, putting in full days at a computer terminal, or spending a lot of time crunching numbers can put tremendous pressure on your eyes, especially as you grow older. At around age 40, your lenses start to lose their elasticity and can't change shape or focus as quickly as they once did. This puts your eyes and eye muscles under stress. Tension in your neck and back after intense concentration on a project can also bring on eye pain. Did you finish up your income tax return for the IRS recently? Have you been reading without consideration of the proper lighting? If your eyes are aching, red, tired, dry, and giving you a headache to boot, then you are suffering from eyestrain.

Any number of medical factors could also be to blame for eyestrain. You might have astigmatism, which is a visual distortion caused by a defect in the cornea or lens of the eye. If so, you need glasses or contact lenses to correct the problem. If you've been experiencing pain in your eyes, don't delay seeking medical attention from an eye specialist. Several serious eye conditions can first appear as eyestrain. A doctor will want to rule out glaucoma, macular degeneration, diabetic retinopathy, and cataracts, as well as less serious situations such as dry eyes, floaters, and presbyopia. (See sidebar, "What Else Could Be Wrong with Your Eyes?") If you are over 50, have your eyes examined at least once a year. In the meantime, here are some basic tips to help ease eyestrain.

WHAT ELSE COULD BE WRONG WITH YOUR EYES?

○ ○ ○

Glaucoma. When fluid pressure builds up in your eyes and presses on the optic nerve, the condition is referred to as glaucoma. A doctor will prescribe eyedrops or pills to lower the pressure and prevent damage. Surgery can also release fluid from the eyeball. If you are over 50, don't put off having a checkup for glaucoma. Are you finding it difficult to adjust to lighting in dark places? Do you sometimes see a rainbow halo around lights? Aching eyes, dimming vision, and nausea can signal this serious condition. Or you may have no warning symptoms at all.

Macular degeneration. This disease affects millions of people over 50 and can lead to blindness. The macula is the central portion of your retina, located at the back of the eye. Is your central vision going wacky even though your peripheral vision is OK? Get an eye specialist to examine you right away.

Diabetic retinopathy. Long-term diabetes may result in diabetic retinopathy, which means the blood vessels in your retina are leaking. Lasers can seal these vessels, preventing further damage. Medication is available for diabetes that can prevent this kind of complication. Is your vision dimming? Do you see a hole in your field of sight? Does diabetes run in your family? Sometimes, sight problems are the first symptom of diabetes. Speak with your doctor if you are concerned.

Cataracts. Common with increasing age, cataracts occur when the lenses in your eyes cloud up, and you may need surgery to clear them. Does your eyeglass prescription need updating frequently? Do you find it difficult to drive in bright light or at night? Have you noticed a color change in the pupil of your eye? Cataracts can often be corrected quickly with surgery.

Floaters. Common among adults, floaters are bits of opaque tissue in the transparent part of your eyeball. You may see dark spots but they are considered harmless and won't affect your vision. However, if you notice a sudden increase in floaters or if they are accompanied by any other symptoms, such as blindspots, see your eye doctor.

Presbyopia. Have you noticed newspaper stories becoming more difficult to read? Can you see better if you hold the paper at arm's length? If so, you probably have presbyopia—the inability of the eye's lens to change shape and focus quickly on a close image—which affects almost everyone after age 40.

Check your lighting.

Don't work or read in dim light. You aren't going to do irreparable harm to your vision by working in poor light, but you are placing unnecessary stress on your eyes. Lights that are too bright can also make it tough to see clearly. Aim for a happy medium by using soft lighting that won't reflect straight back into your eyes. Lamps or fixtures that force their light upward create a glow that won't strain your eyes.

Go for glasses.

Schedule an eye checkup with an optometrist or ophthalmologist. If you've been holding your newspaper at arm's length lately, you probably need reading glasses. Be careful if you choose to buy the ready-made glasses now available in stores without a prescription. They may be all right if the level of magnification is appropriate for both of your eyes and if they fit properly. The best advice is to have such glasses checked by an eye specialist. These glasses are not necessarily fitted to your specific needs; they could end up increasing eyestrain rather than relieving it.

Buy glare-proof lenses.

Ask your eye specialist about lenses that reduce glare with ultraviolet filters, which block out certain wavelengths of light. They are especially useful if you work at a computer for long hours.

Blink.

When you blink, your eyelids help to cleanse your eyes, spread lubricating moisture over the eyeballs, and give them a bit of a massage.

Rest your eyes.

When you are doing visually demanding work, your eyes need frequent breaks. Every hour, spend a few minutes doing something else. Close your eyes and think of something pleasant. Relax. Take a deep breath. Move your head gently from side to side. Scrunch your shoulders up toward your ears, then let them relax. Repeat these movements slowly.

Go green.

Houseplants increase the humidity in your working or reading environment. If your eyes have been dry or strained, the moisture will help.

Take your vitamins.

Eat nutritious foods. When you can't, consider a multi-vitamin and mineral supplement. Vitamin A is essential for sight. So is zinc. Make sure you are getting enough B complex. Studies indicate that a day after increasing your vitamin B_2 intake, your eyes will feel less fatigue.

Stop smoking.

Cigarette smoke in the air can irritate your eyes. If you smoke, give it up. If you work with smokers, ask them to take their smoke outside.

Use a document holder.

Such paper holders can attach directly to a computer monitor. Shifting your focus between two different lighting environments—as you must do when you switch from the horizontal surface of your desktop to the vertical surface of your computer screen—can strain your eyes.●

FEVER

13 WAYS TO COPE

Y ou're hot one minute and shaking with chills the next. Your skin is flushed and warm to the touch. Your head hurts and you certainly can't concentrate. Sweating, feeling light-headed, aching, you are uncomfortable and restless. What is it? you wonder. What am I coming down with? Though a hand to your forehead may or may not confirm that you are running a fever, an elevated temperature is a symptom of something else happening in your body. A battle has begun.

Between 96 and 100 degrees Fahrenheit, body temperature is considered normal. From 100 to 102, you are in the slight-fever category. Higher than 102 and you have something to take a bit more seriously. In fact, high or persistent fever should send you straight to the doctor, especially now that you are over 50. Your body is using its temperature control system to fight off an invasion. It could be an infection caused by bacteria, fungi, viruses, or parasites. Perhaps you are having an allergic reaction. No matter what started the action, your metabolism has speeded up and heated up. White blood cells are attacking the invaders.

What's normal for you may not be normal for your next door neighbor, but 98.6 degrees Fahrenheit is considered a good average. When you are healthy, your own normal temperature may fluctuate by as much as two degrees during a single day. The lowest point is ordinarily in the morning and the highest in the evening. If you get a fever, try these ways to cope.

Take your temperature.

Don't guess about a fever. Find out for sure so you can decide how to treat it. Some doctors believe that a mild temperature should be left alone, in fact. (See sidebar, "To Treat or Not to Treat.") Fevers can actually kill bacteria, and antibiotics work better when you have a fever. However, a high fever—above 103 degrees Fahrenheit—needs attention. Moreover, if you are feeling exhausted and heading toward dehydration because of fluid loss, then you definitely need to bring your fever down. But don't try measuring your temperature with an oral mercury thermometer just after eating, drinking, or smoking: Your mouth won't offer an accurate reading under those circumstances.

Appease your appetite.

If you feel like eating, go ahead—satisfy your cravings. The old adage, "Feed a cold and starve a fever," is not necessarily good advice. Don't force yourself to eat if you aren't hungry, but let your body lead you and eat if you are. As your fever begins to break, you may become ravenous. Don't overdo it at the dinner table at first, especially if you've been eating very little during your illness. Your stomach may have shrunk in size, and your digestive system may not react well to heavy foods. Choose a variety of fruits, vegetables, and soups at first. Later, when your system regains strength, grains, carbohydrates, and low-fat meat, fish, or poultry will taste better. Splurge on fresh raspberries and strawberries. Some nutritionists believe that when you have a fever, your body burns up protein and tissues at a faster rate than when you are healthy. So it's important to make sure your diet is ample during a period of recovery: This is not the time to be concerned about a reducing diet.

TIPS FOR TAKING YOUR TEMPERATURE

○ ○ ○

Having someone feel your forehead the way your mother used to may be comforting psychologically, but it is not an accurate way to measure your temperature.

Use a glass mercury thermometer, preferably one with large, easy-to-read numbers. Don't eat or drink anything for at least half an hour before taking your temperature. Hold the thermometer firmly and shake it sharply several times with a flick of the wrist to force the mercury to the end of the bulb. Put the thermometer under the tongue so it's nestled deeply in the mouth and not right at the tip. (You want to measure the temperature of blood vessels in your body, not your gums.) Close your lips and wait at least three minutes in order to get an accurate reading. Try to be calm and still. Put on your reading glasses if necessary before you try to read the numbers—this is no time to guess at numbers that cannot be seen clearly.

Or use a digital thermometer, which can register temperatures accurately and almost instantaneously. What's inside the tip of a digital thermometer is a thermistor, a tiny piece of ceramic. Thermistor thermometers have revolutionized temperature taking, especially in many hospital settings. Some of them beep when the correct reading has registered; some light up. It's easy to read the temperature. Don't forget that digital thermometers do require batteries.

Avoid alcohol.

Stay away from wine, beer, or your nightly cocktail with hard liquor. Alcohol in such drinks dries you out and can add to the dehydration that accompanies high temperatures.

Consider other conditions.

Do you have a heart ailment, diabetes, or a breathing problem such as chronic obstructive lung disease? Have you undergone surgery recently? Carefully evaluate your recent medical history and do some detective work. You will be helping the doctor with his or her diagnosis if you've done your homework. In someone with a serious ongoing medical condition, a fever, however mild, should be a warning sign that something's amiss in their system. Take your elevated temperature seriously and call the doctor to get expert advice.

Take a pill.

Aspirin and acetaminophen can fight a fever, but check with your doctor if you are taking medication regularly. A physician will be alert to the possibility, for example, that you should avoid aspirin because of an allergy to it or because of an ulcer or liver problem.

Limit your pills.

A survey of 3,000 people over age 65 showed that many use more than one nonprescription pain reliever in the belief that more medicine or different kinds of pain relievers will be more effective than a single medication. This just isn't true. Taking more than one type of analgesic when you are sick or feverish isn't a good idea. You could end up with an adverse drug reaction. Always follow the pharmaceutical manufacturer's package directions, especially as to the quantity to be taken and the timing. Older people are also more likely than the general population to be taking multiple prescription medications. Be certain to check with your doctor or pharmacist about posssible interactions between two or more medications.

Stay cool.

Run some lukewarm water into your bathtub. Don't fill it to the top. Immerse yourself partially. Sponge off and let the water evaporate from your skin. Make sure the water isn't too cold. An icy bath could cause you to start shaking and actually make your temperature rise.

Use compresses.

Wet clean washcloths or hand towels in cool water and apply them to your forehead, neck, wrists, calves, or anywhere else that feels uncomfortably hot.

Reset the thermostat.

Many people are under the impression that the way to treat a fever is to go to bed and pile on the blankets. The goal was to "sweat out" whatever was making them sick. Since a fever indicates that your body is trying to rid itself of heat, adding more heat not only doesn't make sense, it's counterproductive. Doctors recommend that you keep cool. Sleep covered only with a light blanket or sheet. Turn the heat down or crank the air conditioning up. If you often wear pajamas or a long flannel nightgown, choose something lighter before you head for bed.

Dress lightly.

Take off your sweater. Don't sit under an afghan. Expose your skin to the air to release moisture from your body. If you start to feel chilled, however, shift gears and add a light layer. You don't want to get too cool—that could lead to shivering, which generates heat by setting muscles in motion. You'll end up hotter than ever if you catch a chill when you have a fever.

Drink fluids.

Even if you don't feel thirsty, force yourself to drink plain cold water, fruit and vegetable juices, and soups, especially chicken broth. When you are feverish you perspire and lose fluids. The perspiration cools you down, but if you don't have enough fluid in your system, sweat ducts won't work well. Then they shut down, and your fever won't be as manageable. If you are nauseated, vomiting, or have diarrhea, it is even more important to keep drinking to make up for the lost fluids. Try herbal teas. Or opt for homemade lemonade and sweeten with honey. Lemon has long been used to fight fevers.

Take your vitamins and minerals.

If your doctor has recommended a multivitamin with minerals, it's even more important to continue this supplement when you are sick.

Sleep.

A fever can exhaust your energy. Stay in bed and sleep as much as you can. Read an engrossing book or rent a good video,

TO TREAT OR NOT TO TREAT

○ ○ ○

A fever can be good for you under certain circumstances. Temperatures up to 103 degrees Fahrenheit aren't normally dangerous in healthy adults but should be monitored. That elevated number and the internal heat it represents could be helping to destroy an invasion of viruses or bacteria. Some doctors believe that by lowering your temperature, you lower your body's ability to fight off an infection. In this view, fever is seen as a way of marshaling your immune system to do battle.

If your fever hovers around 102 degrees Fahrenheit, your best bet may be to make yourself as comfortable as you can under the circumstances and ride out the heat. On the other hand, if you have an underlying disease, letting a fever hang on is not such a good idea. In people with respiratory ailments or heart conditions and for older patients, fever should be treated right away because the high temperature could cause other medical problems. If your temperature climbs as high as 103 to 104 degrees Fahrenheit or higher, refusing to come down even when you do treat it with medication, call your primary care physician to let him or her know about your symptoms. A fever above 104.1 should be brought down immediately under any conditions. Any fever that troubles you for more than a couple of days, no matter how low, also needs a professional's attention. Call your doctor.

and don't feel guilty about being a couch potato. It's important that you get all the rest you need in order to recover. If the weather is nice, open your window just a crack for a little fresh air.●

FINGERNAIL AND TOENAIL PROBLEMS

16 WAYS TO CARE FOR THEM

Horses have hooves, cats have claws, and we humans have those deposits of keratin known as nails at the ends of our digits. We might spend a lifetime trimming them, filing them, and polishing them, but, all things considered, we tend to take our fingernails—and toenails—for granted. Aside from fussing over a bad manicure, most of us don't spend a lot of time worrying about our nails, say, the same way we might worry about our weight or heart health.

That is, aside from worrying about their appearance, our nails usually don't give us much cause for concern until something goes wrong with them. Whether that involves breaking a nail, slamming a nail with a hammer, or developing a pesky fungus infection under a nail, sooner or later you may well develop problems with nails that require a little extra care or even, in such cases as a serious infection, a doctor's attention. The fact is, with age you're more prone to some nail problems, such as brittle nails or fungus infections. Because you can't always take them for granted, here are some ways to keep your nails healthy and some suggestions about how to deal with common problems.

Use nail products with care.

We all react to substances differently, and any nail product, while perfectly safe for most people, may trigger a reaction in you. The first rule when using nail products is to avoid any polish or hardener that contains formaldehyde, which can dry nails and cause them to crack. Nail-polish remover can also dry out nails, so use it sparingly—once a week at the most. Glues used to affix artificial nails can cause allergylike reactions that damage the nail and the nail bed. Nail strengtheners should be used with caution because, for one thing, they don't really strengthen the nail, but form a tough shell that only camouflages the underlying problem. For another, they may contain harsh ingredients that actually damage the nail. In general, a little common sense is required when using any nail product—if it seems to be harming the nail, refrain from using it.

Keep your nails out of the way of harm.

Certain otherwise harmless activities may well damage your nails. Immersing your hands in hot dishwater, working with strong household detergents, and any other activity that exposes your nails to hot water and chemicals is going to hurt your nails. That's why it's a good idea to wear vinyl gloves for wet work. For extra protection, wear a pair of cotton gloves inside the vinyl ones to absorb sweat.

Care for your cuticles.

Nail cuticles—the soft tissue that forms a lip between the nail and your finger—act as a natural barrier against infectious agents that might otherwise infiltrate the nail bed. The better you care for them, the better you'll be at fending off infections. And when it comes to cuticle care, simple, natural methods are best. Don't, for instance, hack away at cuticles with files and scissors—if you do, you run the risk of tearing them and opening the door to bacteria and fungi. Cuticle solutions, designed to prevent excess cuticle growth, often contain chemicals that can also damage cuticles if not used properly. The safest way to tame unruly cuticles is to soak your fingers in warm water with some gentle bath oil or dishwashing detergent, then to gently push back the cuticles with a moist towel.

Keep them short.

One of the best ways to ensure overall nail health is to keep your nails short and well-trimmed. You'll be less likely to snag, bang, break, and otherwise injure them. If you're a nail biter, you'll have less material to chomp down on. And if your nails are brittle, they'll be less likely to crack if they're short. The best time to trim your nails is after a bath, when your nails are soft and less likely to break. Use clean, well-sharpened instruments, and when it comes time to file, don't use a metal file, which can crack nails, but opt for a gentler, kinder emery board.

Beware of brittle nails.

It's just another sign of age—as we get older our fingernails and toenails become more brittle, which makes them more prone to splitting, cracking, and ripping. This natural process is helped along a bit by the dry environment of heated homes and the simple acts that get nails wet on a day-to-day basis.

Keep them dry.

Every time your nails get wet—and think of all the times during a day that they do—they absorb water. As they dry, they contract, causing them to become brittle. That's one of the reasons why it is a good idea to wear gloves when doing dishes and engaging in other activities in which you immerse your nails in water for prolonged periods of time.

Keep them moist.

This isn't a contradiction, just a question of what kind of moisture you expose your nails to. Replacing the moisture your brittle nails lose through normal activities is a good idea, and there are several ways to do it. One way is simply to brush some olive oil or other vegetable oil onto brittle nails a couple of times a day and after bathing. Another is to use an over-the-counter nail moisturizer, preferably one that contains lactic, urea, or phospholipid acids—all of which help the nails retain moisture.

Eschew nail biting.

As bad habits go, nail biting is pretty convenient: Those delicious munchies are readily available at the tips of your fingers, they grow back when you deplete them, and they don't cost a thing. Appealing as nail biting may seem, however, there are plenty of good reasons to drop the habit. For instance, not only do you turn the ends of your hands into ugly-looking claws, but you also create tears and nicks that act as welcome signs to bacteria.

Fight nail fungus.

You might notice that a nail is looking thick and a bit discolored, perhaps even a sickly yellowish color. Pretty soon, the toenail you used to have is an ugly, ragged-looking talon that's turning black and separating from the nail bed. Don't worry—you're not turning into a werewolf. You've probably contracted a nail fungus, a fairly common malady among people with immune systems that are weakened by a chronic illness or that are slowing down a bit with age.

WHEN NAILS BECOME INFECTED

○ ○ ○

Hangnails, brittle nails, broken nails, and just about any other nail problem can open the door to infection. The signs of an infection are redness, irritation, and pain. And while the symptoms and underlying infection will probably clear up with time, aggressive treatment may be in order. If the whole nail is affected, it may turn white or brown and lift off the nail bed. (The nail plate is the hard, visible part of the nail, and the nail bed is the tissue beneath it.) In this case, the nail is probably damaged beyond repair, and you will shed it as a new nail grows in.

The first thing to do in case of infection is to keep the area clean—this may mean covering it with a bandage or gauze when you are cooking, working, or engaging in any other activity that's likely to bring the infected nail in contact with dirt. For a little extra home care, spread an over-the-counter antibacterial ointment over the infected area.

It's important to see a doctor if you have diabetes or circulatory problems and pick up an infection. Even if you don't have such problems but an infection doesn't clear up in a week or seems to be getting worse, you would be wise to see a doctor: What seems to be a minor infection around the nail can lead to very serious complications. In people with diabetes, for instance, a simple nail infection can lead to gangrene and the loss of a toe or finger. In an otherwise healthy person, a nail infection can spread to the blood and throughout the system. So don't take chances. Keep a close eye on that infected nail.

Get out the hair dryer.

Fungi thrive in warm, moist climates—just like the environment inside your shoes and socks, in fact. You may want to change your socks several times a day and apply an antifungal powder with each change. For added protection, dry your feet thoroughly with a hair dryer on a cool setting after you shower. This will be much more effective than towel drying because the drying air will reach spaces around and under the nails. When it comes time to get dressed, choose your shoes with care. Vinyl, plastic, rubber, and patent-leather footwear don't breathe, which allows moisture to build up around your toes. You'll be better able to keep moisture around your toes to a minimum if you wear canvas, natural leather, or open-toed shoes like sandals.

Launch an antifungal counterattack.

There are plenty of antifungal ointments, sprays, and oral medications on the market, some available over the counter and others only by prescription. Follow directions for use to the letter, and if the infection seems to be getting worse, see a doctor immediately—fungal infections can be pesky invaders that require strong prescription drugs and months or even years to heal. Keep in mind that a fungal infection that's left unattended can get into the root of the nail, at which point about the only thing you can do is have the nail removed. And if you suffer from diabetes or other circulatory ailments, see a doctor immediately if you notice a fungal infection—even a minor infection can lead to the loss of a toe or finger and other serious problems.

Clean your hands after touching.

Fungi are always eager to branch out and move on to new places, so be sure to wash your hands after touching a fungus-infected toenail. You'll avoid spreading the infection to other toenails, fingernails, and other parts of your body.

Harass hangnails

You may have noticed that your skin has tended to become drier as you have grown older. Dry skin may be a special problem around your fingernails, creating hangnails—little flaps of dead skin that get caught on clothing, paper, and anything else your fingers contact.

Moisturize liberally. The softer and moister the skin around your nails, the less likely you'll be to develop hangnails. Don't forget your fingertips when you rub moisturizer into your hands, and take an extra minute or two to apply moisturizer to your cuticles.

Put them under wraps. After a bedtime application of moisturizer, swath your fingertips in plastic wrap. You'll wake up to softer fingertips that are less prone to developing hangnails.

Don't pick. Your reward for picking and tearing at hangnails may be a major infection. Why? The resulting rips in the skin are an open gateway to all the bacteria your fingertips come into contact with day to day. Instead of picking when you notice a hangnail, trim away the dead skin carefully with nail scissors sterilized in alcohol, and, for a dose of prevention, rub some antibiotic ointment into the area.

Avoid trauma.

Sooner or later it's going to happen— you'll bang a fingernail with a hammer, slam it in a door, or damage the nail, often seriously, in another way. Avoiding pain is a good enough reason to sidestep accidents like these, but disfiguring a nail permanently, damaging the nail bed, and opening the door to infections are other reasons to exercise caution.

Don't use your nails as tools.

Your fingernails may seem like the perfect portable tool kit. After all, you can use them as screwdrivers, picks, shovels, staple removers, knives, scoops, you name it. They're pretty darn handy. But listen up—resist the urge to use your nails for such utilitarian purposes. Any time you do, you are leaving them prone to breaking, splitting, tearing, and other injuries. Not only will you turn your nails into ugly-looking claws, but you run the risk of serious damage and infection.

SIGNS OF TROUBLE

○ ○ ○

Sometimes a discolored or disfigured fingernail is more than an indication that the time has come to have a manicure—it may be a sign of a serious health problem. Here are some signs of ailments that may show up in your nails: See a doctor if you notice any of them.

Bluish nails. Unusually pale nails that have a bluish hue are one of the signs of anemia.

Clubbed nails. Nails that grow in a noticeably curved shape, so they resemble the backside of a spoon, may be the sign of cardiovascular disease or lung problems.

Dark spots under the nails. These may be melanoma growths that crop up on the nail bed like the dark, molelike growths that appear on other parts of the body and can signal melanoma. Such growths may also appear on the skin surrounding the nail. Wherever they manifest themselves, melanoma growths require immediate medical attention.

Pitted Nails. These ugly-looking depressions on the nail can be a sign of psoriasis.

Treat your nails with respect.

Coming down on a thumbnail with a hammer, immersing your nails in a bucket of harsh detergent, or stubbing your toe against the legs of a chair are definitely not signs of respect. Nails are tough, but not that tough. Treat them well, and they will remain healthy and attractive.●

FISSURES

6 WAYS TO BRIDGE THE GAP

It can be a little upsetting to see the Grand Canyon forming at the side of your mouth, between your fingers and toes, or on your heels and hands. That's just what a skin fissure is, though. It's the dermatological equivalent of a long, deep canyon. Fissures aren't dangerous unless infection sets in, but, needless to say, it can be painful to have a big crack in your skin.

Usually, these cracks open because your skin is excessively dry. As skin loses moisture, it shrinks and stretches out, causing these gaps to form. It follows that the best way to keep from getting fissures is to keep your skin moist, and the best way to repair fissures is to replace moisture in the skin. Here's how to go about doing just that.

Soak, slather, and bandage.

It's the best combo for relief and healing. Soak the fissured area for five to ten minutes in lukewarm water (apply a lukewarm compress to fissures around the mouth and other areas you can't comfortably immerse). Then apply petroleum jelly or a petroleum-based moisturizer and seal the area with a bandage. In this moist environment, the skin will soften and grow back together.

Keep infections at bay.

A crack in your skin is an open door for any bacteria or fungi that happen to be crawling by. You may want to consider moisturizing with a petroleum-based antibiotic ointment or, if the fissure is near such fungus-prone areas as the corners of your mouth or between your toes, an antifungal cream. These ointments may help clear up existing infection and zap any infectious agent that tries to climb in and set up housekeeping.

Keep the hand cream handy.

Hand cream or petroleum jelly should always be available in your kitchen. Rub some into your hands liberally after working with water.

Take infections seriously.

Don't let an infection linger. If a fissure doesn't heal after a week or so and you notice signs of infection—swelling at the site or in the surrounding glands, redness, pain, pussy seepage, or an accompanying fever—talk to your physician. It's also important to get medical treatment if a fissure appears near your anus—it may not heal easily and can lead to serious infection and other complications.

If you have diabetes or circulatory problems, you are especially prone to infection at the site of a fissure because the flow of blood, and the infection fighters it carries, may be sluggish. Even a minor infection can flare up into big-time trouble. At the first sign of infection, talk to your physician about the best ways to bring it under control.

Protect your hands.

Immersing your hands in hot dishwater or plunging them into a pail of sudsy water is bound to take its toll, and one of the effects may be fissures. That's one reason why it's a good idea to slip on some vinyl gloves when you are working with water or harsh household cleansers.

Bathe gently.

There's nothing like a hot soak in the tub to dry out your skin. A few dos and don'ts, however, can prevent fissures from erupting as a result of your daily bathing. Don't bathe more than once a day, don't make the water too hot, and don't stay in the tub or shower longer than five or ten minutes. Don't use harsh soaps. For best results, blot yourself dry (don't rub), then be generous in the application of moisturizers.●

PROTECT YOURSELF FROM OLD MAN WINTER.

○ ○ ○

That dry winter chill can drain every ounce of moisture from your skin and crack it wide open. You'll be a lot more comfortable if you winterize your skin against dryness and fissuring. Wear gloves (apply some hand cream before you slip them on); coat your lips and mouth with lip balm; wear a scarf or muffler over your mouth area to protect it from harsh winds; and crank up the humidifier to counteract the drying effects of the furnace.

FLATULENCE

8 WAYS TO FOIL IT

Here's a subject that's hard to address in a dignified manner. Though seldom a truly serious problem, gas can be not only embarrassing, but at times downright painful. Still, gas is a normal part of the digestive process. It's caused both by swallowed air that works its way into the intestines and by the fermentation that occurs when bacteria in the intestines break down food.

Even if you never had a problem with gas in the past, as you get older you might notice that it's become more of a nuisance. That's because the bowels move slower, making it harder to digest some foods. The situation is compounded by the likelihood that you are more sedentary than you once were, causing food to stay in your digestive tract longer and ferment.

While gas is just a part of life, these degassing techniques may make it easier to live with.

Go easy on the gassers.

A lot of healthy foods, especially those that contain fiber, can cause gas. But don't stop eating them, because that would be like cutting off your nose to spite your face. Instead, try eating a little less of them to find out how much you can tolerate without feeling like a gas bag. Then, as your intake gradually increases, your intestines should be able to handle them better.

Some of the biggest offenders in the gas department include apples, apricots, bananas, beans, beer, bran and bran products, bread, broccoli, brussels sprouts, and cabbage. Add carbonated beverages, carrots, cauliflower, celery, citrus fruits, coffee, corn, cucumbers, and ice cream to the list. And watch out for lettuce, lima beans, oats, onions, milk, peaches, potatoes, pretzels, raisins, soybeans, spinach, and tomatoes.

Lay off the lactose.

If you notice that you feel a little gassy after your morning bowl of cereal, it's probably because you're lactose intolerant. That means your body doesn't produce enough lactase, the enzyme that breaks down lactose, the sugar in milk products. Instead of milk, try pouring apple juice over your cereal, and see if that doesn't make you less flatulent.

Brandish some Beano.

Available in many grocery, drug-, and health-food stores, this liquid product takes the wind out of beans and legumes.

Check your posture.

Remember when mom and dad used to tell you to sit up straight at the dinner table? Well, they had a point: If you slouch (or lie on the couch) when you eat, you're making it harder for your stomach to digest food properly, and you can get gas as a result.

Don't be a windbag.

You might have gas for the same reason you belch: You swallow too much air. All that air has to come out one end or the other. Here are some tips that may help. Don't eat with your mouth open and don't chat when you chew—in both cases you will swallow a lot of air. Don't gulp down your meals either, because when you take in food quickly, you're also swallowing air with it—and you're not chewing properly.

Calm down.

You probably know that stress affects your stomach, and one of the major symptoms of a tense stomach is gas. That's because muscles throughout your abdomen tighten when you're tense. Try taking a few deep breaths to relax your abdominal muscles.

Get moving.

A little exercise (it doesn't have to be strenuous) will help stimulate the passage of gas through your digestive tract, preventing bloating and uncomfortable gassy buildup. Exercise also aids digestion by encouraging the movement of food through the digestive tract.

Skip antigas products.

Over-the-counter preparations containing simethicone and activated charcoal may help relieve bloating and discomfort, but they only break down large gas bubbles into smaller ones. You'll still have gas. Remember, once gas builds up in the intestine there's only one way to get rid of it.●

FLU

10 HINTS TO HELP YOU FEEL BETTER

The flu doesn't feel like an ordinary cold, that's for sure. Your high fever, sore throat, dry cough, fatigue, pounding headache, chills, severe muscle aches, and pains-all-over came on within a few hours. What happened? You picked up a virus. It came from a tiny droplet of mucus in the air, or it was on something or someone you touched. This virus spent a day or two incubating, and your body's immune system wasn't able to fight it off. Be careful. Influenza epidemics often start each year between October and April among school children, and adults can end up with serious complications. The flu is quite capable of putting you in the hospital with pneumonia if you are over 50. Do you have an underlying heart or lung condition? Are you taking medication for any ongoing disability? Call your doctor if you suspect the flu. (See sidebar, "Get a Flu Shot.")

Influenza is caused by one of two major flu strains that show up annually. Researchers call them influenza A and influenza B, but these viral culprits are highly unstable and change their very natures from year to year. Since preventive vaccines are made using antibodies from the influenza epidemics of the year before, it's difficult to develop a vaccine that is 100 percent effective.

Whatever strain of flu you may have picked up, here are some hints to help you feel better.

Go to bed.

Fatigue and high fever will make this step easy. Don't feel guilty about remaining horizontal. You may end up feeling tired for weeks after the acute stage of your flu is gone. Become a couch potato.

Don't socialize.

Friends and relatives may want to cheer you up, but the last thing you need is to pick up a secondary bacterial infection or another virus from someone else. Moreover, you don't want to spread your disease to others, and the flu is highly contagious. Avoid stress and people for as much as a full day after your temperature has gone back down to normal.

Watch your fever.

The flu will push your temperature up to a range of 102 degrees Fahrenheit and above—high for a mature adult. To drop that fever, check with your doctor about which medication to use. For example, if you have any kind of gastrointestinal disorder or an ulcer, you won't want to take aspirin or ibuprofen. Nor would aspirin be recommended for anyone with asthma. Acetaminophen, on the other hand, will cut down on the aches, shakes, or chills that accompany high fevers. A physician may even suggest that you let the fever run its course without medication because fever is your body's own method of fighting the flu.

Drink up.

Dehydration is a serious concern. Drinking liquids—water, soups, fruit and vegetable juices—replaces fluids lost because of the fever. Sweetened drinks and sodas aren't recommended because they can upset your stomach. However, if you haven't been eating very much, a little

GET A FLU SHOT

○ ○ ○

A flu vaccine won't guarantee that you'll stay healthy throughout the winter, but these shots are up to 80 percent effective, and those are pretty good odds, especially when you consider the alternative. If you are in a high-risk category (see below), then you really ought to make an appointment for your shot in September or October before the flu season begins. Do you fall into one of these groups?

- People over age 65, especially those in nursing homes or health facilities where viruses spread rapidly
- People with chronic heart or lung disease, asthma, diabetes, kidney problems, or cancer
- Health-care providers

sugar will boost your body's glucose levels. Try diluted ginger ale that has gone flat. Make sure it's flat because carbonation could lead to nausea. Drinking fluids will also help keep your mucus moist. Phlegm that is thin and clear is easier to cough up and expel from your body.

Eat light.

Your appetite may be nonexistent when you are at your sickest. Bland, starchy foods—toast and cereal, for instance—will go down more easily as you try to re-build your strength.

Make your home cozy and warm.

This virus is happiest in cool, dry air. That's why it shows up in winter. Cold air will make you want to cough more, too. Turn up the heat and the humidity in your home. Let in some fresh air each day. Ventilation will keep unwelcome bacteria or viruses from making themselves at home while you recover.

Think twice about over-the-counter medicines.

Cold and flu medications that line the shelves of your local pharmacy can bring you temporary relief. But these drugs can also suppress symptoms to the point that you resume normal life and end up with a relapse.

Hold down a dry cough.

Cough medicines that contain dextromethorphan are the best at suppressing a dry, hacking cough, the kind that interferes with normal sleep patterns and prevents you from getting the rest your body needs. Your best bet is to ask your doctor for a specific recommendation.

Stimulate a "productive" cough.

In contrast to a dry cough, a cough that brings up mucus is considered productive and should be encouraged, not suppressed with cough medicines. Taking in lots of fluids will make it easier to achieve a productive cough that will ease the mucus out of your body.

Call the doctor.

If you develop chest pain, experience breathing difficulties, or begin coughing up thick, green or yellow mucus, see your physician. If your voice becomes hoarse, you have abdominal pain, or you can't keep any nourishment in your body because of prolonged or frequent vomiting, you need medical treatment.

FOOD POISONING

10 WAYS TO RIDE IT OUT

Maybe you've already had the misfortune of experiencing it. The turkey and stuffing were great, the picnic was a delight, or you never thought sushi could taste that good. Then, Wham! Bam! Slam! Suddenly, you feel like you've just been hit by a freight train. More specifically, you feel like a freight train has just roared into your gut. You've been poisoned—that is, the food on which you've been feasting was tainted with any of a number of bacteria and viruses that cause a reaction commonly known as food poisoning (though *food-borne illness* is a more accurate way to describe the problem).

Well, as anyone afflicted with food poisoning soon finds out, what toxins go down must come up or go out the other way. And as painful as the situation can be, the best thing to do when food poisoning lays you low (except, as we will see, among the elderly or ill) is just hang in there until the diarrhea and vomiting end. In most cases, your body will do a pretty good job of cleansing itself within a day or so, and there's quite a bit you can do in the meantime to make yourself comfortable and to ensure a speedy rebound.

Let it flow.

The diarrhea and vomiting you experience after eating tainted food may be inconvenient, to say the least, but they serve a purpose: They are ridding your body of toxins. Don't fight the urge to vomit—just make yourself as comfortable as possible while your body cleanses itself.

Look for the danger signs.

Food poisoning can be serious, even life threatening, in the elderly, chronically ill, or anyone whose immune system is impaired. In these people it's imperative not to let nature run its course, because the vomiting and diarrhea can cause severe dehydration, put a strain on the heart, and have other very serious consequences. A doctor should be contacted as soon as symptoms appear. An otherwise healthy person should also seek medical help at the onset of any of these symptoms: high fever; extreme thirst, decrease in urination, and other signs of extreme dehydration; difficulty swallowing or breathing; change in vision; severe diarrhea or vomiting that lasts more than a day; or bloody diarrhea.

Leave antidiarrheal medication in the medicine cabinet.

Antidiarrheals will interfere with the purging process, so the toxins will remain in your system that much longer. Antacids may make you more susceptible to the ill effects of bacteria because they reduce stomach acids that help ward off bacteria. If you feel you must take something for your aches, cramps, and fever, make it acetaminophen, which, unlike aspirin and ibuprofen, will not irritate your stomach and intestinal tract.

Talk to your doctor about your other medications.

A bout of food poisoning can put a real dent in the effectiveness of the medications you take regularly. The fact is, you'll probably be expelling them along with everything else, and you may not even be able to get them down without vomiting. This can pose a real problem if you depend on oral insulin, blood thinners, blood-pressure regulators, and other medications that must be taken frequently. Keep in touch with your doctor so your condition can be monitored.

Drink plenty of water.

As your body rids itself of toxins, you will lose a lot of fluids. That's why it's very important to rehydrate by drinking fluids. Begin by sipping water—as much as you feel comfortable drinking. And don't be alarmed if you experience a little watery diarrhea at first—that's only natural.

Sweeten it up.

When you feel you can tolerate them, try sipping sugary drinks, which are easy for your stomach to absorb and will boost your energy level. You might want to begin with fruit juice and weak herbal tea, adding a little sugar or honey. Soda may help settle your stomach, but choose drinks that are decaffeinated, and let them defizz for five minutes or so before drinking them.

Go for the bland.

After 24 hours or so, you'll probably be feeling like eating again. Reintroduce solids slowly. Start with toast, chicken soup, gelatin dessert, bananas, mashed potatoes, maybe a piece of skinless chicken breast—mild is the word. Build up to your regular diet slowly.

Sip, don't slurp.

Easy does it with any liquid you drink. If you take in too much, you may be making a beeline for the bathroom again.

Take it easy.

One of the best things you can do to help your body weather this crisis is to get plenty of rest. So cancel any appointments, make yourself comfortable, and try to get as much sleep as you can.

Contact your health department.

If you think your food poisoning came from a restaurant or some other public place, let your local health officials know about it. ●

How to Prevent Food Poisoning

○ ○ ○

Once you've weathered the effects of food poisoning, you'll be eager to avoid a repeat performance. Some tips to follow:

1. It's important to thaw food completely before cooking, or certain spots will remain cold and uncooked. Avoid raw foods, which are notorious hotbeds of bacteria. This means cooking meat and fish thoroughly. Check the internal temperature of meat and poultry with a meat thermometer.

2. Replace your wooden cutting board with a plastic one, which is less likely to harbor bacteria.

3. Don't let raw or cooked food stand unrefrigerated. Bacteria can't survive in the cold environment of the fridge, but they can multiply like crazy at room temperature. Thaw meat in the refrigerator rather than on the countertop.

4. Clean kitchen surfaces and utensils thoroughly with hot, soapy water. Since bacteria can lodge and multiply in sponges, use paper towels.

5. Be careful with foods that perish easily. These include creamy concoctions like coleslaw and potato salad.

6. Wash your hands thoroughly in warm, soapy water before and after handling food. It is particularly important to wash your hands after handling raw fish and meat, especially poultry.

FOOT PROBLEMS

---

19 REMEDIES FOR ACHING FEET

Your feet can be thought of as the foundation of your body. They are your shock absorbers, they support your entire weight, and they give you balance. However your feet feel, that's how the rest of your body probably feels, too. If and when they start to give out, other parts of your body—such as your back and knees—will feel the effect.

Your feet are strong, flexible structures made up of joints, tendons, muscles, bones, and ligaments. The lifelong punishment you've given to the 28 bones and 35 joints of the feet can cause many disabling foot problems, however.

It's hard to reach the age of 50 without facing at least one serious foot problem. And the news isn't likely to get better in the future because as you age, your feet physically change, making you more susceptible to other foot problems. For example, over time the fatty cushion beneath your heel diminishes in size and loses some of its springy, spongy quality—a condition known as plantar pad atrophy. As the fatty cushion declines, walking may become uncomfortable. A secondary effect is that whenever you walk or stand, stress on the the foot's bones and muscles increases, which makes irritation, swelling, and pain more likely. In addition, foot flexibility will decline if you suffer from a degenerative joint disease such as arthritis or osteoporosis. That decreased flexibility makes it harder for the bones in your feet to move normally and may result in poor posture.

Foot problems can also result from arteriosclerosis, or hardening of the arteries, since that disorder reduces circulation in the feet. Narrowed arteries supplying the feet and legs means there may not be an adequate supply of oxygenated blood—which makes it harder for any wound to heal.

Moreover, the changes that come with age are compounded by such factors as obesity and ill-fitting shoes that increase friction. In addition, after age 40, toenails become more susceptible to fungal infections as they thicken and grow more slowly.

Most foot problems, however, are the end product of wear and tear—the gradual deterioration of joints, supporting ligaments, and bony parts—after years of use and abuse. If you have flat feet with low arches, for example, you'll probably develop bunions and calf pain. If your arches are high, you're susceptible to arch pain and hammertoes. In either case you will be vulnerable to corns and calluses as well. Foot problems can also arise from gout, osteoarthritis, or a toe fracture.

Since you tend to accumulate foot problems over a lifetime, the older you get, the more likely you are to have some trouble. The skin on the sole of your foot is already 40 times denser than skin elsewhere, but calluses—which often grace the heel or ball of the foot—can make the skin 80 times thicker. At some point the callus gets too large, too thick, or too hard, and it drags on the skin underneath, causing painful tears.

The primary goals of good foot care are to manage any foot abnormalities you have, such as flat feet, and to prevent the complications of pain, deformity, and disability. Whatever the case, getting rapid relief is what's needed. Check out the following remedies for aching feet.

Consult your doctor.

If you have foot pain along with any change in color or a breakdown of skin in any part of the foot, talk to your doctor.

Inspect your feet daily.

Look for possible problems such as discoloration, ulcers, swelling or tenderness, early corns or calluses, cracking of the skin between the toes, and redness or infection around or under the toenails.

Keep 'em clean.

Wash your feet daily in lukewarm soapy water, then rinse. Gently pat your feet dry—don't rub. It is especially important to dry between the toes.

Soften corns and calluses.

Treat corns and calluses at home after a bath or by soaking the foot in warm water until the thickened skin softens. Then gently use a pumice stone to remove layers of dead skin, but be careful to not rub the area raw.

Wear clean socks.

Change them daily because bacteria, which thrive in warm moist places, can cause athlete's foot.

Make room.

Stretch the toes of your shoes if they're rubbing on your toes. Corns are like calluses: They're thick growths of skin caused by abnormal pressure and friction, but the difference is that they appear only on or between the toes.

Get used to new shoes gradually.

Resist the temptation to wear your new shoes for a long stretch of time until they're comfortable. Limit the first wearing to a few hours, and don't take them on vacation.

Soak 'em.

Soaking not only cleanses your feet and softens rough, dead tissue, it's also a good tension reliever. Adding Epsom salts to water that's slightly warmer than body temperature will help draw out an infection or inflammation. But don't use Epsom salts if you have diabetes or peripheral vascular disease unless you clear it with your doctor first.

Trim those nails.

Keep toenails trimmed straight across, not curved, and no longer than the tip of the toes. Use an emery board to file sharp edges. Don't dig under the nail or around the cuticle.

Don't go shoeless.

Bare feet are vulnerable to harm, so make sure you wear slippers at home and sandals at the beach.

Lubricate.

Keep your skin soft by lubricating your feet daily with lanolin cream to avoid calluses and corns. Feet appreciate rich moisturizers, since their skin is more rough-and-ready than hand skin.

Try orthotics.

Your feet get a jarring experience as you walk or run. This can cause pain in the hips, knees, ankles, and feet, especially if it happens repeatedly, as during exercise sessions. Orthotics, or foot supports for the inside of your shoe, can help make the movement smoother or modify pain-causing imbalances in your foot's structure. Made of materials as diverse as leather, foam, and plastic, orthotics also move pressure away from painful bunions or other foot problems. Orthotics should be prescribed and fitted by a podiatrist.

Check your gait and stance.

Get your feet checked by a podiatrist, physical therapist, or other expert in body mechanics. For instance, if your feet pronate, or turn inward, excessively, an expert can prescribe an orthotic device such as a heel cup or shoe insert to prevent heel pain.

Reduce inflammation.

Take an anti-inflammatory drug to reduce the swelling around the irritated area. Your doctor may prescribe a nonsteroidal anti-inflammatory drug (NSAID) for pain. If that doesn't work, it may indicate that something else is wrong and further investigation is needed.

Select the Right Shoe

○ ○ ○

Crunch time! A good term to keep in mind when you're purchasing that next pair of shoes. Few people have good-looking feet by the time they reach age 50. Conditions such as hammertoes or claw toes—besides your standard corns, calluses, and bunions—usually result when toes are cramped inside shoes that lack the necessary length and width for comfort.

- As your primary defense against foot problems, purchase shoes that fit. Keep in mind that your foot size may change with age, weight fluctuations, and lifestyle changes such as increased amounts of exercise.

- Always get a precise measurement of your foot. Remember that shoe sizes vary from brand to brand. To complicate matters further, for most people, one foot is slightly larger than the other. So measure both feet carefully and stand up while measuring. Then choose a shoe in the size of the larger foot. Allow a minimum half inch of space between the tip of your big toe and the very end of the shoe.

- Buy shoes that fit properly and are appropriately cushioned to relieve soreness from bunions. Adequate cushioning also prevents calluses.

- Use the appropriate athletic shoes for each sport. Don't compromise your foot's need for support by wearing broken-down shoes instead of buying new ones. You particularly need support if you're involved in sports such as basketball, racquetball, or tennis.

- Cushion your shoes' midsole with a foam pad.

- Purchase a custom-made orthotic device to redistribute weight and pressure away from the balls of your feet.

- Don't buy shoes that don't seem to fit in the hope that they will stretch as you wear them. Shoes should be comfortable from the first day.

- Buy the right shoe for your lifestyle. If you stand for hours at a time on the job, you need shoes with a thick sole and a soft upper. The needs of letter carriers differ from those of secretaries.

- Buy shoes in the afternoon or evening. Your feet are smaller in the morning. After several hours of walking, standing, and being generally active, your feet will be a bit swollen and will have reached their maximum size. That's the time to get a good fit.

- Buy a shoe with a slight heel for added arch support. Avoid shoes with soles that are higher in the front than in the back.

- Select shoes made of soft leather with lots of flexibility; synthetic leather is stiffer and doesn't breathe as well. You can justify the extra amount you spend for high-quality shoes when you don't have to pay to fix foot problems.

- Have a variety of comfortable shoes available, rather than risk foot problems if one special pair gets lost. It also helps to alternate shoes to allow each pair to air out.

- Throw out all the shoes in your closet that don't fit properly. They are not worth keeping.

Treat aches with cold.

Rub your aching heels repeatedly with a small, ice-filled plastic jar. Or do foot-rollers: Sit down and roll your heel over the ice-filled jar. Afterward, pull your toes upward with your fingers to stretch them.

Head off ingrown toenails.

Ingrown toenails can result from improper trimming, too-tight shoes, or stockings that press the nail into the tissue. The problem usually occurs when the big toe's nail edge bites into soft toe tissue, causing inflammation and swelling. Apart from the pain it causes, this condition can lead to infection. Avoid ingrown toenails by using heavy scissors to cut the nail neatly. And always be careful to trim the nail straight across, not in a curve.

Sidestep bunions.

If you're seeing signs of developing bunions, switch to shoes with a low heel and an ample toe box. Wearing open-toed shoes and soaking your feet in warm water will also help to keep bunions at bay.

Prevent heel pain.

Wear shock-absorbing shoes or heel cushions to avoid pain in the heel. Heel pain is felt most often either directly under the heel bone or just in front of the bone in the direction of the arch. The pain may make its presence known after a long run or walk, but many times no direct cause can be discovered, and the problem may linger for months.

Keep your weight down.

Being overweight adds to the strain on the tissues in your arch, aggravating conditions such as heel spurs.●

HIGH HEELS ARE A HAZARD

○ ○ ○

1. Don't wear heels that are very high and narrow, no matter what fashion urges. Stiletto heels don't encourage balance and are particularly dangerous on slippery surfaces. They can only cause trouble for your feet.

2. Choose a heel height—perhaps one inch, perhaps two—that suits you, is comfortable, and allows stability when you walk.

3. Avoid wearing high heels for long stretches on your feet. Instead, save them for sit-down dinners. Wear more sensible shoes to events where you'll be standing, such as cocktail parties. Especially avoid shoes that are pointed in the toe area: They will pinch your toes and may lead to difficulties.

FROSTBITE

19 WAYS TO NIP JACK FROST

Frostbite is the painful and often dangerous result of an encounter with Old Man Winter. Jack Frost isn't just nipping at you—he's attacking with fangs bared.

Unfortunately, he has the upper hand. The chill of winter is a dangerous foe and can easily catch you unaware and unprotected. When it comes to frostbite, even your own body works against you. In the extreme cold, your heart pumps extra blood to your vital organs in a heroic effort to keep them warm, and your skin pays the price—less blood reaches the surface of your hands, feet, ears, face, and other extremities. Without enough blood to keep it warm, the skin covering these areas begins to freeze, ice crystals form, and frostbite sets in. The result can range from temporary discomfort to damage so severe it may be necessary to amputate a deeply frozen body part.

There are plenty of measures you can take to keep the nip in the air away from your skin, however, and others to take if Jack Frost succeeds in sinking his teeth into you.

Act quickly.

That's the number one rule with frostbite, because the earlier you catch it, the less damage will be inflicted on skin tissue. At the first tinges of extreme cold and numbness, cover the area as best you can and get to shelter fast.

Refrain from rubbing.

You've probably seen the adventure movies where the frostbitten hero rubs himself with snow to get the blood flowing again. Well, don't do it: Your skin cells have been traumatized enough, and rubbing frostbitten tissue—with or without snow—will only damage it further.

Take a soak.

The best way to thaw frostbite is to soak in a tub of tepid water, about 105 degrees Fahrenheit. If no bathtub is handy, soak the afflicted area in a basin or apply warm compresses. Continue the treatment until the frostbitten area becomes red, which should take approximately 45 minutes.

Don't be drawn to the flame.

Don't huddle over the campfire or next to the kitchen stove to thaw out, don't use a heating pad, and don't sit down in front of a space heater. You'll warm yourself, of course, but with all these methods you run the risk of burning yourself as well. Remember: Your frostbitten nerve endings aren't going to know when your skin is getting too hot.

Do not apply ointments.

While some over-the-counter ointments make your skin feel warm, they won't do any good for damaged, frostbitten tissue. In fact, they may do some harm: They can prevent warm air from reaching the area, and they may interfere with the tissue regeneration that is part of the healing process.

Stay put or stay frozen.

Once you've found a warm place in which to thaw out, it's very important to stay put. Exposing frostbitten tissue to the cold a second time is only going to damage it further. In fact, if you must head out into the cold again—and it's a very dangerous thing to do—in the long run it's better if your skin remains frozen than if it thaws and then refreezes.

Use your own hot zones.

Your body has enough warmth to thaw frostbitten skin. For example, you can thaw your hands by putting them under your armpits or between your thighs—even blowing on them can help. One of

OLD MAN WINTER MEETS FATHER TIME

○ ○ ○

People are susceptible to frostbite at any age, but we are especially at risk as we grow older. As we age, we become less able to maintain a steady body temperature when exposed to extreme cold, and we may also be less able to detect the effects the cold is having on the body. Our circulation decreases, so less blood reaches the skin and extremities. We also become a bit thin-skinned with age—our skin simply isn't as resilient as it once was.

Many drugs, including the beta-blockers that are widely prescribed to treat heart disorders, can also affect circulation, reducing the amount of blood that reaches the skin. The upshot of these risks comes down to this: Stay indoors when it's cold outside, and take precautions when it's absolutely necessary to venture out.

the best ways to treat mildly frostbitten ears, nose, and cheeks is to cup your hands over them (assuming your hands are not frostbitten).

Shed wet clothes immediately.

As soon as you are able, get out of wet clothing. Body heat will be depleted quickly by wet clothes, and you need every degree of warmth you have to overcome frostbite.

Drink warm liquids.

When you've been frostbitten, it's important to drink something because a lack of fluids can lead to dehydration, and dehydration will make frostbite worse. So slurp down some hot broth, cider, or even warm water. Avoid alcoholic or caffeinated beverages: They constrict your blood vessels and lead to a reduction in the amount of warm, healing blood that reaches your frozen extremities.

Stay off your feet.

If your feet or toes are frostbitten, it's very important to stay off them. The pressure created by the weight of your body can inflict severe damage to tissue that has been frostbitten.

Elevate a frostbitten limb.

Swelling can interfere with proper circulation to the frostbitten area. To minimize swelling, elevate the affected limb. The trick is to lift the limb just high enough to cut down on swelling but not so high as to cut off circulation (when you're frostbitten, you want to keep blood flowing to the damaged tissue). Prop up frostbitten feet on a couple of pillows or the equivalent, and raise an arm touched with frostbite so it is no higher than the level of the heart.

HYPOTHERMIA: THE BIGGEST CHILL

○ ○ ○

Hypothermia is the medical term for a drop in body temperature to 95 degrees Fahrenheit or lower. Someone experiencing this kind of drop is literally freezing to death. Numbness, extreme fatigue, and disorientation are clues that body temperature is dropping. If someone's hands or feet are cold to the touch, or if the skin over the abdomen feels cold, hypothermia may well have set in. Cover the victim with some extra blankets; administer warm, nonalcoholic beverages; and get medical help immediately.

Find any port in a storm.

If you're frostbitten, it's very important to get out of the elements as soon as possible. Getting yourself into a heated room may be the only treatment you need for less severe cases of frostbite. If you are far from civilization, at least try to find a spot that is sheltered from the wind.

PREVENTION
Stay indoors.

Those days when you had to brave the elements and walk through the driving snow to school are far behind you. If it's too cold for comfort outdoors, stay indoors—it's the easiest, surest way to prevent frostbite. If you must go out or are itching to pursue a winter sport, prepare yourself by taking precautions.

Stay out of the wind.

Windchill factor can pack a potent punch, increasing the likelihood of frostbite many fold. Be particularly cautious during windy winter weather. Try to avoid going out of doors at all, but if you must, choose a route for your winter rambles that is as protected from the wind as possible.

Cover up.

Your first line of defense against frostbite is to stay warm and keep your skin covered. Outerwear made of high-tech synthetic fabrics provides a better barrier against the elements than natural fabrics do. Several layers of clothing are usually more protective than a single heavy garment because warm air is trapped between the layers.

Exercise caution with the extremities.

Fingers, toes, and the tips of your ears are especially prone to frostbite, so protect them well. Wear mittens instead of gloves because the single large pocket for your fingers in a mitten provides a toastier environment than the four small pockets in a glove. Wear a couple of pairs of socks, and wrap your feet in a boot liner or sandwich bags to keep them dry in case your boots get wet.

Drink water, not booze.

Alcohol leaves you vulnerable to frostbite in two ways: It constricts blood vessels, leaving skin more susceptible to freezing, and it impairs your judgment, so you may not have the sense to retreat from the cold. Instead, drink plenty of water before you set out and bring a thermos of water along. You dehydrate very quickly in cold environments, and that leaves you more susceptible to frostbite.

Yes, wear a hat.

You lose a lot of heat through the top of your head because so much blood circulates up there. Think of an unadorned head as a radiator that's casting your valuable body heat to the four winds. Be-

cause a warm hat limits heat loss, it not only keeps your head toasty, it helps prevent frostbite all over your body.

Stock the car.

If you plan on driving through wintry landscapes, prepare the car so it can provide temporary shelter if necessary. Put some extra blankets or sleeping bags in the trunk; bring along water and food; and consider investing in a car phone if you know your route will take you through cold, lonely territory. If stranded, stay in the car as long as possible—you'll retain energy longer, you won't run the risk of becoming lost, and it's easier for rescue crews to spot an automobile than a lone figure.●

GALLBLADDER DISEASE

13 WAYS TO CONTROL IT

The gallbladder is one of those organs we never think about. It's just there, dutifully performing its task of emptying bile into the intestines, day in and day out. Most of us are oblivious to the fact that the bile supplied to the intestine by the gallbladder helps break down fat in the food we eat.

Then, all of a sudden, pow! The gallbladder acts up. You might get gallstones, or an inflammation known as cholecystitis, or your gallbladder may even burst. It's at painful times like these when you are abruptly but emphatically reminded that you have a gallbladder.

There are some things you should know about your gallbladder: For one thing, you can live without it, and there are plenty of healthy people walking around whose gallbladders have been removed, usually because of chronic, painful inflammation or recurring gallstones. Second, you may have gallstones but not even know it. But if gallstones become trapped in the bile duct, the resulting pain, nausea, and vomiting are pretty good clues that something is seriously amiss.

If your gallbladder acts up, it's time to see a doctor, because the only way to treat a seriously ailing gallbladder is with drugs, surgery, or other medical procedures. Before it comes to that, though, there are measures you can take to keep your gallbladder functioning normally and painlessly.

Watch your weight.

Being overweight is one of the major risk factors for gallstones and gallbladder disease, especially for women. Studies show that being even moderately overweight increases a woman's risk almost twofold, while being obese increases the risk sixfold. That may be because your liver produces more cholesterol when you are overweight, and a buildup of cholesterol in the gallbladder triggers the formation of gallstones.

Lose weight gradually.

Start an exercise program, go on a diet, cut back on fatty foods—do what you need to do to lose weight. You'll not only be lowering your risk of gallbladder disease but providing a measure of protec-

THE GALLBLADDER AND GALLSTONES

○ ○ ○

The gallbladder is a small, pear-shaped organ underneath the liver. Bile, a liquid that helps break down fats during the digestion process, is produced in the liver and collects in the gallbladder. As food passes from the stomach into the intestines, the gallbladder contracts and empties bile into the upper intestine, where it helps disperse dietary fat into smaller droplets that are more easily digested.

Gallstones are round or oval deposits of matter, usually cholesterol, that is present in bile. You may have one or as many as ten or more gallstones at one time, and they can be minute or as large as an inch in diameter. It is possible to pass a gallstone into the intestine unnoticed. However, if gallstones become lodged in the cystic duct, which connects the liver and gallbladder to the intestine, you can develop severe pain and discomfort.

tion for yourself against heart disease, stroke, diabetes, and many other serious health problems as well. However, it is important to lose weight gradually, at the rate of no more than a pound a week. This pace is necessary because rapid weight loss can trigger the formation of gallstones, possibly as a result of altering the chemistry of the bile.

Watch your diet.

While the link between gallstones and diet is not fully understood, it is known that diet plays a major role in gallstone formation. Any number of dietary factors can upset the delicate balance of the chemistry in the gallbladder, and that's another reason why it's important to follow the dietary guidelines for overall good health: Keep your total fat intake to between 20 to 30 percent of your total daily calories; limit saturated fat to less than 10 percent of total calories; limit cholesterol intake to less than 300 milligrams a day; ensure that complex carbohydrates contribute about 55 percent of your daily calories; and ensure that low-fat sources of protein contribute approximately 12 percent of your total daily calories.

Cut back on cholesterol.

We all know how cholesterol can clog arteries in the cardiovascular system and cause heart disease. Well, this thick, waxy substance also accumulates in other tissues throughout the body, where it can have the same clogging effect. If there is too much cholesterol in bile that collects in the gallbladder, it can form clumps that grow into gallstones. A safe rule is to limit intake of cholesterol to no more than 300 milligrams per day—that's the amount recommended to keep blood levels of cholesterol within healthy limits, and it may also help maintain safe levels of the cholesterol that builds up elsewhere in the body, including the gallbladder.

Remember that cholesterol is found only in animal products, such as eggs, milk, cheese, meat, fish, and poultry. It is not present in plant products such as fruits, grains, and vegetables. But a single egg packs a whopping 213 milligrams (mg) of cholesterol. Other cholesterol-laden foods include butter (31 mg per tablespoon), cooked shrimp (160 mg in three ounces), and fried liver (410 mg in three ounces).

Avoid fatty foods.

Foods high in saturated fats are most likely to raise cholesterol levels. The major sources of saturated fat are meat, dairy products, and tropical vegetable oils, such as coconut and palm oil. For a healthier gallbladder and for overall health, limit your intake of saturated fat to less than 10 percent of your total fat intake.

Don't fast.

If you don't eat for long periods of time—a day or more—it only follows that your digestive system will slow to a crawl. This, too, may cause bile to back up in the gallbladder and promote the formation of gallstones.

Play it safe with starches.

Studies show that heavy consumption of starchy foods like breads, pasta, rice, and potatoes increases the risk of gallstones. But the connection is not a clear one. It may be that people who are overweight tend to eat a lot of these filling foods—so the risk actually lies in being overweight, not necessarily with eating these types of foods. Or it might be that since starches and other carbohydrates have a very low fat content, when you eat them to the exclusion of fattier foods the gallbladder

may not be stimulated to empty and, as a result, gallstones may form in the bile that backs up. Or there may be something in the chemical concentration of starches that affects the chemistry of bile and makes it more prone to the creation of gallstones.

This doesn't mean you should cut back entirely on these important foods—a diet that's low in fat and high in complex carbohydrates like starches can reduce the risk of coronary heart disease, stroke, diabetes, atherosclerosis, and certain forms of cancer. Try to get about 55 percent of the calories you eat each day from carbohydrates—and no more than that.

Eat your vegetables.

Studies also show that people who consume a lot of vegetables are less likely to develop gallbladder disease. That's probably because vegetables are an excellent source of fiber. The body does not digest fiber; instead, fiber passes through the digestive tract without breaking down and helps the intestines eliminate body waste. When the intestines are functioning efficiently, the gallbladder contracts regularly to empty its contents of bile to help break down dietary fat. As a result, bile is less likely to stagnate in the gallbladder and form gallstones. The United States government's dietary guidelines recommend three to five servings of vegetables a day for overall good health.

Eat more fiber.

In addition to vegetables, other fiber-rich foods seem to provide protection from gallbladder disease. Besides, they will also help keep your weight and cholesterol count down. Grains, fruits, and legumes are all excellent sources of fiber. The recommended intake is 20 to 35 grams a day. This recommendation contrasts sharply with the typical American diet, which includes only 11 to 15 grams of fiber per day. Specifically, some excellent sources are kidney beans (9.7 grams per half cup), frozen peas (4.3 grams per half cup), and bran cereals (between 5 and 8.5 grams per ounce). Not only will daily fiber help prevent gallbladder disease, but it also ensures overall digestive health.

Check your medications.

Cholesterol-lowering medications, such as niacin, increase your risk of developing gallstones. Although these medications lower your serum cholesterol, they increase the gallstone-triggering cholesterol in your bile. Estrogen replacement therapy (ERT), often prescribed to lessen the effects of menopause, may also increase the risk of gallbladder disease. That's because estrogen itself plays a part in gallstone formation. Talk to your doctor about the benefits versus the risks of these treatments and ask about alternative therapies that do not affect the gallbladder.

Know the symptoms.

As many as half the people with gallstones do not know they have them, though they might experience indigestion after eating. Chronic indigestion and abdominal pain may be the sign of cholecystitis; consult a doctor if you experience these symptoms for prolonged periods. Sometimes a gallstone will become stuck in the tube, or duct, that connects the gallbladder and liver to the intestine. When this happens, it causes acute pain accompanied by nausea, vomiting, and fever. The pain can radiate to the shoulder and breastbone, resembling the discomfort associated with a heart attack. While the gallstone may work its way out of the duct unassisted, it's important to seek medical help if the pain continues, because the blockage

can cause bile to back up, the gallbladder to burst, and severe abdominal infection to set in. It may be necessary to undergo surgery immediately.

Know the risk factors.

Some people are more likely than others to develop gallbladder problems. Women run twice the risk of men, probably because the female hormone estrogen slows the action of the gallbladder, giving gallstones more of a chance to form.

Obesity is also a factor. By age 60, about one-third of obese women can expect to develop gallbladder problems.

Get a complete diagnosis.

There are several tests to determine if you have gallstones. Blood tests, for example, can suggest the possibility of the presence of stones in the common bile duct. Ultrasound uses painless, high-frequency sound waves to scan your abdomen for gallstones. The echoes from the sound waves form an image on a video screen. Another diagnostic tool is a computed tomography (CT) scan, which provides a cross-sectional view of your organs.●

TREATING GALLSTONES

○ ○ ○

Gallstones are sometimes treated with drug therapy. It is necessary to take the drugs for as long as two years to dissolve the stones completely. The drugs are not always effective, however. Gallstones may recur, and the drugs may have side effects, including chronic diarrhea. Gallstones are also sometimes treated with a technique called lithotripsy, in which shock waves are beamed through the skin to pulverize the stones. But lithotripsy can be performed only if your gallbladder is functioning and you have only a few stones, none larger than one inch in diameter. In addition, you may feel abdominal pain for several weeks following the procedure, because you will continue to pass fragmented stones.

If you suffer from cholecystitis, or inflammation of the gallbladder, your physician may suggest you have your gallbladder removed. Though gallbladders are still removed through open abdominal surgery—a common operation called cholecystectomy—it is becoming more and more common to use a technique called laparoscopic cholecystectomy, in which several tiny incisions are made in the abdomen. A miniature optical camera is inserted through one incision to provide a video image of the gallbladder area; precision instruments are inserted through other incisions to remove the gallbladder. This technique is often called Band-Aid surgery because scarring is minimal. It can be performed in an outpatient surgery clinic, and you are often back on your feet within a few days. In fact, there are so many advantages to this procedure compared to traditional gallbladder surgery that 85 percent of gallbladder procedures are now done with laparoscopy. When talking to your surgeon about this technique, here's what to ask: what special training he or she has had in laparoscopy; how many gallbladder laparoscopies he or she performs a year; what complications might be anticipated; and if there would be any advantage to having traditional open abdominal surgery instead of laparoscopy.

GINGIVITIS

---

12 STEPS TO HEALTHIER GUMS

If you are over 50, the biggest problem area in your mouth probably isn't your teeth at all, but your gums. And the symptoms are hard to ignore. Every time you brush your teeth, the blood in your bathroom sink makes you cringe. If you floss a bit too aggressively, your gums become so tender and inflamed that they hurt. You may hate to admit it, but it's true: You have gingivitis, a chronic low-grade bacterial infection in your mouth. If you don't watch out, the next step will be full-blown periodontal disease, the number one cause of tooth loss in older individuals.

You can thank plaque for your problems. Gingivitis is caused by the buildup of a yellow or white gluey substance that forms naturally on your teeth and gums every 24 hours. Whether you eat or not, even while you are sleeping peacefully, this sticky bacterial film clings to the surfaces inside your mouth. It causes inflammation and decay if you don't remove it regularly. The bacterial buildup can stir up an acidic situation that will break down the enamel on your teeth and destroy gum tissue. Plaque can create pockets at your gumline where bacteria settle and infections grow. Eventually, gingivitis can lead to periodontitis, an irreversible stage of gum disease that can wreak havoc on your dental health. Periodontitis can destroy not only your teeth and gums but also the bony tissue in your mouth. Call your dentist. Get a checkup. Make sure to mention your concern about gingivitis. In the meantime, here are 12 steps to preserve your gums.

Brush often.

Your gums shouldn't bleed if you brush properly. Brushing correctly will help maintain the tone of your mouth tissue. It should be tight around each tooth. Inflammation doesn't come from overzealous brushing but from the bacterial infection. Gum tissue is a little like the tissue around your fingernails. There is an intermediate zone between the hard surface and the soft membrane. If this zone remains firm, making the seal tight, you are less likely to develop pockets of bacterial infection.

Time yourself in your current routine and you may be surprised at how quickly you race through it. Bring a clock or wristwatch to the bathroom so you can time yourself. Brush three times a day for three minutes each time. By all means, don't go to bed at night without brushing. A bedtime cleaning is most important because, if left alone over night, bacteria will find a warm, hospitable, airless environment in which to grow and multiply. Besides, better oral hygiene at bedtime is reflected in better breath in the morning.

Brush correctly.

Hold your toothbrush at a 45-degree angle against the teeth. Start at the gumline and use a gentle scrubbing action in a circular motion. Use short strokes and don't press too hard. Only the tips of the bristles actually clean the teeth, and a light pressure allows the bristles to move freely. Don't concentrate just on removing food particles. Too often the gums don't get enough attention. When you clean your top teeth, hold the brush so it points up toward your nose. When you clean your bottom teeth, point the brush down toward your chin. Don't tackle a big area in one stroke; cover one or two teeth at a time. And be kind to your mouth. You aren't scrubbing the bathroom floor. A gentle stroke is fine. Use the same motion on the inner surfaces of your teeth, both top and bottom. Maintain the 45-degree angle. Next, move back to the chewing surfaces of your molars. Hold the brush flat and move it back and forth. Now you are ready to clean the most overlooked terrain in everyone's mouth: the back side of your front teeth. Tilt the brush vertically and use up-and-down strokes. Use only the front tip of the brush. Clean the roof of your mouth and don't overlook rear teeth, which may need a slightly smaller brush for a thorough cleaning. What about a swipe at your tongue? The tongue is no stranger to plaque.

Floss.

Flossing is not just a way to remove pieces of meat or popcorn kernels. Dentists say flossing is absolutely the best way to clean plaque from between your teeth and under your gumline. Choose between waxed or unwaxed, flavored or unflavored. To floss correctly, start with up to two feet of floss. Use a clean section to clean each tooth; otherwise, you risk spreading bacteria from one spot to the next. And never save used floss for another day. Be sure to use a gentle sawing motion on every surface of every tooth, from beneath the gumline to the top of the tooth. Ask your dentist to demonstrate the best method for you.

Use a soft brush.

A soft nylon toothbrush with rounded ends and polished bristles is perfect for fighting plaque. If the bristles are too hard, they break down the enamel on your teeth and could form grooves on the surfaces. Replace your toothbrush every month and a half.

Buy an electric brush.

A recent study of elderly patients indicated that they often lacked the manual dexterity needed for thorough toothbrushing using regular brushes. Even if your finger strength and dexterity are fine, ask your dentist about the potential advantages of going electric.

Pick a good toothpaste.

Don't ignore what's printed on the side of the toothpaste box. Some ingredients are helpful at every stage of life. For instance, fluoride combines with minerals in your mouth to help keep your teeth strong as you grow older. And tartar (the calcified mineral deposits made of bacteria and plaque) can be held in check with the right toothpaste.

Water well.

After you brush and floss—not before—try an electric water-irrigation device to clean out debris from deep pockets and to massage your gums. If you don't want to invest in this type of appliance, rinsing your mouth vigorously with plain old water can help prevent bacterial buildup. Over-the-counter mouthwashes and rinses are not miracle cures for gingivitis. Good oral hygiene comes first.

Rinse with salty water.

Put half a teaspoon of salt in a full eight-ounce glass of warm water to make a saline solution. Take a sip and swish this mixture all around your teeth for 30 seconds. Salt water kills bacteria and soothes inflamed tissues.

Give up smoking.

A recent study of health problems caused by cigarette smoking revealed that, statistically, gum disease is right up there with cancer and heart disease. When dentists examined the gums of 59 nonsmokers and 75 smokers, more than twice as many smokers had significant gum disease compared to nonsmokers.

Adjust eating habits.

Limit sugary and sticky foods. Foods that stick to your teeth, like raisins and other dried fruits, are among the worst offenders. Crackers, cookies, and white bread are also poor choices because they all have a tendency to stick to the cracks and crevices of your teeth.

Chew sugarless gum.

Chewing gum stimulates the production of saliva, which cleanses your mouth and protects your teeth. Stick with sugar-free varieties, however.

Schedule regular dental checkups.

A professional dental hygienist should clean your teeth at least twice a year. And a dentist should examine your mouth for tooth decay and gingivitis at the same time.●

GOUT

10 WAYS TO TREAT GOUT

You've just learned that the pain in your foot—the foot you've been nursing for days—is not a broken toe, as you thought; it's gout. You're flabbergasted. You associated gout with elderly monarchs who ate and drank too much.

Surprise! Although age, weight, and alcohol consumption may lead to this condition, gout is actually a metabolic disorder. It results from a chemical imbalance in the body that causes recurrent bouts of acute arthritis. In the early stages gout usually involves a single joint, but in later stages it can lead to a chronic arthritis often associated with joint deformity. It appears more frequently in men after the age of 30 as a sudden inflammation of one joint, usually the big toe, although any joint may be involved. In women, attacks of gout usually don't begin until after menopause. The underlying chemical cause, high body levels of uric acid, is present throughout one's life. Thus, an attack may subside completely, only to occur again years later. Fortunately, once it has been diagnosed, gout can usually be treated successfully with proper medication.

Each day your body undergoes an amazing process of breaking down and removing old cells to make way for new ones. Your body changes the chemical content of these old cells so the kidneys can eliminate them. The natural chemical breakdown of purines, the building blocks of your cells' genetic information, results in the formation of uric acid, one of the body's waste products. When your body produces more uric acid than your kidneys can keep up with, the level of uric acid in your blood rises. And high levels of uric acid (a condition known as hyperuricemia) are often, but not always, associated with gout. You're also more prone to gout if your levels of uric acid rise—or fall—rapidly.

A gout attack is triggered when uric acid accumulates in or around the joints and forms tiny, needlelike crystals of sodium urate (a salt of uric acid). The accumulated uric acid irritates the nerve endings in the joint, resulting in the telltale signs of gout: The joint becomes painful, swollen, and inflamed, and the skin around the joint becomes tight and red.

Unfortunately, gout has a way of creeping up on you. The first episode, painful as it is, often subsides within a few days, even without treatment. You may think you've seen the last of gout, then weeks, months, even years later, the episodes return, often with a vengeance. Subsequent attacks tend to be more frequent, usually last longer (as long as several weeks) and are more painful. Progressively severe joint pain is accompanied by swelling and extreme tenderness, with redness of the skin and a moderate fever. The good news is that medication can usually relieve the symptoms immediately. But there is a negative side to the outlook for gout as well, because osteoarthritis often becomes a complicating factor.

When it comes to gout, a little prevention will truly yield generous dividends. Fortunately, there's a lot you can do to avoid flare-ups—and to nip them in the bud when they do occur.

Have your pain diagnosed correctly.

Simply knowing that gout is causing the pain is a good part of the battle. Once you know you have gout, you can take medications to reduce the pain, prevent recurrences, and keep your blood levels of uric acid at normal levels.

Take nonsteroidal anti-inflammatory drugs (NSAIDs).

NSAIDs are widely prescribed for gout these days. (Indomethacin is known to work especially well.) NSAIDs help to relieve attacks of gout by suppressing in-

---

WARNING!
• • •
Many physicians prescribe allopurinol as a treatment for gout for patients who show an increase of uric acid in their urine. And it is not unusual for these patients to continue taking the medication for years. Allopurinol does suppress the body's production of uric acid. However, something like 85 percent of those with elevated levels of uric acid in their urine will never have gout: They should not be taking this medication. If your physician is prescribing allopurinol to prevent gout attacks and you show no symptoms of the disease, it is probably a good idea to have a rheumatologist or other specialist diagnose your condition. Medication for gout tends to be overprescribed.

flammation and reducing pain, and most people can take them without side effects. A couple of things to keep in mind, however: Colchicine, which is not an NSAID, is known to be highly effective but produces such side effects as nausea and vomiting, while aspirin, which is an NSAID, is usually not recommended because it may increase the amount of uric acid in the blood.

Inquire about your hypertension medicine.

If you are on medication for hypertension, talk to your doctor about the effect it may be having on your gout. Most hypertension medicines are diuretics, which increase the flow of urine but can also raise blood levels of uric acid. It may be possible to reduce the dosage of your antihypertensive and bring about a lowering in the frequency and severity of gout attacks.

Eliminate alcohol.

Alcohol can slow the desirable excretion of uric acid. And an excessive amount of alcohol can promote acute gout attacks. Rather than take a chance on precipitating an attack, delete alcohol from your diet.

Lose weight slowly.

If you're overweight, one of the best things you can do for overall good health is to shed pounds. Do so slowly, though, because if you lose weight too rapidly you can develop ketosis, a condition that interferes with urate excretion and can trigger gout attacks.

Skip water pills.

Avoid nonprescription diuretics, commonly referred to as "water pills," for weight loss.

Avoid foods that are purine rich.

They include anchovies, asparagus, liver, mushrooms, sardines, and sweetbreads. Purines can trigger the production of uric acid and, therefore, gout attacks.

Rest after an attack.

To avoid a repeat performance, take it easy for a day or so after gout symptoms disappear.

Eliminate caffeine.

Most people can tolerate caffeine, at least in small amounts, but others can't tolerate any at all. Don't take a chance. Cut out all caffeinated beverages, including soft drinks and coffee.

Drink water.

Six to eight glasses a day is the recommended amount to keep your system cleansed of uric acid and other toxins.●

GRIEF

16 SUGGESTIONS FOR MANAGING THE PAIN

Few emotions are as devastating as the psychological and even physical suffering that accompanies the loss of a spouse, a child, or other loved one. For all the pain and suffering that accompanies grief, however, it is considered a healthy emotion because grief is a sign of healing. Having grieved, we can get on with life. But as normal and ultimately healthy as grief is, it is also difficult and painful work. With it comes very deep emotional pain that can last for months and sometimes years. Grieving also takes its toll physically, depressing our immune systems and leaving us vulnerable to a variety of ailments.

While there's no one, perfect way to cope with grief, here are some suggestions that may help you, your family, and friends to manage the pain a little more easily.

Maintain a balanced diet.

Preserving good health is important at all times; it is particularly important during the grieving process. One warning sign that you are not taking care of yourself is weight loss—if you drop ten or more pounds, see your doctor for advice.

Be careful about medication.

You may benefit from sleeping pills or tranquilizers on a temporary basis, but don't attempt to medicate yourself: Check with your physician first. It isn't realistic to believe you'll face up to your grief if you are continually sedated.

Be patient with yourself.

Grieving takes time, and you may not be very productive during the process. With its emotional toll, grieving often leaves you feeling preoccupied and uninterested in normal activities—but this should not make you feel guilty or less worthy. Just remember, there's no way to shorten the duration of your grief, but if you take care of yourself, you may be able to reduce its intensity.

Remember you're not alone.

Grief is an emotion that most of us experience at one time or another. Not that such an understanding lessens the pain associated with grief. After all, we all have our own unique emotional makeup, and every grief-evoking situation is unique—just as every death is unique, and our relationship to the deceased is special. Even so, it may help you to feel more hopeful about your future if you keep in mind that millions of people go through the pain of grieving, yet they recover over time.

Get enough rest.

Maintain normal sleeping patterns. Attempting to keep busy long into the night to keep your mind off your grief will just make you feel run down. When you become tired, give in to the urge to stop and get some rest. Rest will regenerate your mind and help you think clearly.

Exercise regularly.

You're going to need a healthy body to work through all the emotions that accompany grief and at the same time keep up a reasonable level of energy. Even if you've never been active before, this is an excellent time to take up an exercise regimen. And if you have been exercis-

ing regularly, try to continue doing so at a pace that's comfortable for you. Make arrangements to work out with a friend if you feel uncomfortable about exercising on your own. Be sure to consult with your doctor to establish a fitness program that is appropriate for your level of fitness.

Set up a nurturing social network.

This is the time you need the support of an understanding family and friends. Talk to others who have experienced a death and understand grief. Reaching out like this is something that women can often do more easily than men because women are more likely to be part of a nurturing social network that predated the grief-causing event. Studies show that as a result of this interaction women tend to recover from a time of grieving faster than men.

Manage your fatigue.

Not only is it normal to feel tired when grieving, but you may feel a great reluctance even to get out of bed in the morning. To sidestep this tendency—which is a way of avoiding reality and is counterproductive—assign yourself a task to accomplish every day.

Focus on concentrating.

You may find that you can't concentrate on anything for more than a few minutes at a time, and that even small tasks seem to require more time than ever before. In short, you're preoccupied with grief, and your preoccupation is simply a natural part of your attempt to deal with a loss. Just be patient, and make a little extra effort to concentrate fully.

Write it down.

Make notes about tasks that need to be accomplished. If you have difficulty sorting them out, ask a friend to help you decide which tasks have priority.

FIVE PHASES OF GRIEF

○ ○ ○

Psychologists believe that the grieving process—from the initial shock through the final acceptance—occurs in distinct phases, with one stage usually following another in a recognizable sequence, though the boundaries between the phases are sometimes blurred. It is important to recognize these stages and move through them toward healing.

Phase 1: Shock. Shock may last for a period of a few days to a month or two following a death. During this phase, your body functions to protect itself and give you time to adjust to the situation. You may even experience a sense of unreality and a feeling of numbness.

Phase 2: Disbelief. Although you know in your rational mind that your spouse or loved one has died, the second phase is characterized by an unwillingness to accept that fact. For months or even longer, you may think about the deceased all the time and feel a strong yearning to recover the lost person. You might feel angry at the loss and physically experience chronic fatigue and weakness. Keeping busy is one way to take your mind off the painful reality of your loss, but don't mistake your busy activity for recovery—you're not healed yet and are still experiencing considerable pain.

Phase 3: Relief. When a loved one dies after a long-term illness, in a sense you may have a feeling of relief. Although you may not have given up hope for a loved one's recovery, you may have started saying good-bye in your own small ways. In this phase you're beginning to accept the loss, but you're not quite ready to fully embrace the reality, and you may well continue to experience despair.

Phase 4: Guilt and Anger. It is normal to feel both guilt and anger when grieving. At first, you may wonder what you could have done to prevent the death, then you feel only anger when you try to come to terms with the loss. Remember, it's very hard for anyone to accept these emotions, so take your time and talk to others about what you may be feeling.

Phase 5: Resolution and Reorganization. Eventually, normal activities resume and you regain interest in the world around you. Occasional feelings of sadness, emptiness, and crying spells may occur, but they arise less frequently than before and with less intensity. This transition period can be an opportune time to let go of the past, embrace the present, and look forward to the future.

Cope with holidays.

Do what you need to do during holidays and significant anniversaries. Understand in advance that the time may be difficult and that you have to do whatever you can to get through the day. If you truly want to be alone, don't give in to the pressure of family and friends to join them—spend the day by yourself if that's what you really want. Cry if that helps. Part of learning how to live through grief is the realization that you won't forget your loved one. It also means you'll be able to handle being alone without feeling overwhelmed.

Pay attention to your emotions.

Grief revisits in waves. Often something that is said or something you see triggers the feeling of grief, and loneliness takes over. Try to be aware of what is taking place when that happens, and tell yourself that it's OK.

Help others to help you.

Realize that your friends may not know what to say to you. They care for you and want to help, yet they are uncomfortable with the situation. Let them know that you need to share your feelings with them. Tell them to:

- Call often.
- Make specific plans to do something or go somewhere together.
- Talk about their memories of your loved one.
- Not pity you.

- Express their caring even if it means crying together.
- Invite you to lunch or dinner.

Prepare for strong emotions.

Be prepared for the intense emotions that come with grief. You may feel exhausted all the time, and you may need to cry often. You'll also experience physical sensations that are probably just a sign of emotional duress. It's quite typical, for instance, to feel short of breath or experience a sensation of aching and tightness in the throat. Normal as these sensations are, see a doctor if they persist or worsen: They could be signs of a physical disorder, such as heart disease.

Write down your feelings in a journal.

You may feel angry at the person who died and blame him or her for leaving you alone to face such pain. Rather than channeling this anger inward, or turning to destructive behavior such as drinking or overeating, work your anger out. Give yourself permission to be upset and write down how you feel about the experience in a journal.

Get counseling.

Counseling may consist primarily of support from friends and family, from a member of the clergy, or from a health care professional. By talking to people about your feelings, you will find it easier to come to grips with your loss and adjust to the changes in your life.●

HEADACHES

---

12 WAYS TO TAME THE PAIN

If your head hurts, you have plenty of company. More than 70 percent of the population suffers from headaches—ranging from occasional and annoying episodes to chronic and severe ones. Doctors see as many as 50 million Americans each year complaining of headaches, and a billion dollars is spent annually for headache medication.

Most headaches are annoyances that go away by themselves. When they don't, a mild pain reliever is usually enough to handle the discomfort. Headaches can affect any part of the head as well as the neck, and they can be short-lived or last for days. Sometimes they are the first symptom that something is wrong with your health, and on occasion they can be disabling.

Science has learned much in the past decade about the causes and treatment of headaches. For instance, recent research demonstrates that high levels of stress don't necessarily accompany what are referred to as tension headaches. Indeed, headaches may not be caused by a tense, type A personality or by a particularly difficult day, as is commonly thought. For years, doctors suspected that people suffered from some type of character weakness that made them vulnerable to headaches. Currently it is believed that imbalances in the brain's chemical and nerve activity cause the pain, not stress and emotions, although the latter may serve as triggers.

Under normal circumstances, the sensation of pain begins when the endings of sensory nerves are damaged. Researchers focus on the trigeminal nerve system, an important track for pain transmission, as well as a neural chemical called serotonin as a set of possible triggers. The trigeminal nerve system ferries neural impulses that occur above the neck back into the brain. Serotonin is a neural chemical (neurotransmitter) that helps pain impulses move through that nerve system. Migraines may be caused by misguided nerve transmissions heading in the wrong direction along the trigeminal pathway, ending up inside the brain's defensive layer, or meninges, or even in the scalp. The affected blood vessels then swell and become irritated, causing the pain that we call headaches.

Researchers know that when migraines are present and blood vessels are distended, serotonin levels drop. Consequently the vast majority of migraine-relieving drugs attempt to increase serotonin levels in an effort to obstruct the pain impulse. There is also a theory that migraine and tension headaches may be variations of the same disorder, though tension headache is a milder version.

Although persistent headaches are a genuine medical problem, there are many ways to tame the pain.

Know when to see a doctor.

Make an appointment if your headaches are so severe you find yourself at maximum dosage of over-the-counter painkillers (acetaminophen, aspirin, ibuprofen, or naproxen) more than once every three days, or if the pain begins to strike more often or last longer than usual. Your doctor will want to rule out other possible medical conditions for which headache is a symptom.

Keep a headache calendar.

For a period of eight weeks or more, note the date of each headache and profile the kind of pain it brings: where it's located, how strong it is, how long it lasts, and any special characteristics. Pay particular attention to any headache triggers you can identify.

Exercise.

The cardiovascular benefits of regular aerobic exercise are well known. But there's an added benefit: Because it reduces tension, regular exercise may help prevent some types of headaches. Your headaches may also benefit from exercises that stretch the neck, shoulders, and back four or five times a week.

Take the cold-pack plunge.

Headache relief may be as simple as tucking an ice pack around your neck or ducking your head under a running stream of cold water. These tips are based on the theory that cold reduces circulation by restricting the size of capillaries (the smallest blood vessels) and thus reducing pressure on sensitive nerve endings in the head and neck.

Take a warm shower.

Some people prefer heat to cold as a headache treatment. Tension headaches may respond to a warm, wet cloth on the neck or a warm bath or shower.

TYPES OF HEADACHES

o o o

Experts do not agree on whether headaches represent many different disorders or one disorder that takes a variety of forms. Doctors continue to rank headaches by symptoms described by the International Headache Society in 1988.

Main types of headaches include:

- Tension headaches. Sometimes called muscle-contraction headaches, tension headaches constitute the most common form. The pain may be generalized or local, and it may appear on one or both sides of your face.

- Cluster headaches. More than one million Americans suffer from cluster headaches, especially men who drink and smoke heavily. Cluster headaches are usually located on one side of the head, usually in or around the eye. The pain can be excruciating—worse than a migraine. Duration runs from 15 minutes to three hours. They may occur one or more times daily in clusters, and the process can continue for weeks or months. Cluster headaches often strike at the same time each day and frequently begin during sleep.

- Migraine headaches. An aura is a visual indication, such as blurred vision or zigzag lights, that a migraine headache is on the way, though not everyone experiences an aura before a migraine strikes. Migraines cause throbbing or pulsating pain, and sometimes just pressure. They also cause sensitivity to light and sound and may be accompanied by nausea or vomiting. A migraine can be severe enough to force you to put your life on hold. Migraines usually affect one side of the head, in the area of the forehead or temples. The level of pain in a migraine headache ranges from moderate to severe. It can be incapacitating and might last for days.

Less-common types of headaches include:

- Postmenopausal migraines, as the name implies, begin to occur in some women with the decline of the hormone estrogen and are thus associated with menopause. The symptoms usually diminish as estrogen levels stabilize. Dietary measures and low-dose estrogen replacement therapy may help to control symptoms, but in some cases therapy with estrogen acts as a trigger, bringing on the headache.

- Post-traumatic headaches appear after a minor head injury that does not cause unconsciousness. They can persist for a year or more after the trauma.

- Ice pick headaches are experienced as sudden and severe stabs of pain, but their duration is short. They concentrate on a single point on the surface of the head.

Learn to relax.

Relaxation training and techniques to reduce tension may ease the suffering from headaches. Learn deep-breathing exercises to slow your breathing when you become rushed and stressed. Meditation, self-affirmation, and creative imagery are other ways to manage behavior and control headache triggers.

Get an eye exam.

An eye exam is in order when anyone over the age of 40 is bothered by headaches, since glaucoma (with its elevated pressure in the eyeball) could be the cause. If left untreated, glaucoma can lead to blindness, so check with an ophthalmologist.

Maintain a regular meal pattern.

Waiting too long between meals (more than five hours) often brings on headaches.

Read food labels.

You may get headaches as a reaction to ingredients in certain foods. Some of the most frequent headache triggers include caffeine; the sugar substitute aspartame; alcohol (particularly beer and red wine); chocolate; and certain food additives, such as monosodium glutamate (MSG) and sodium nitrite.

Get the right amount of sleep.

Sometimes either too much or not enough sleep can cause a headache. Most people should have between eight and eight and a half hours of sleep every night, but individual needs vary. Your headache calendar will help you determine how much is best for you. Contrary to popular belief, sleep requirements do not decline with age.

WARNING!
. . .
Take your headache seriously.

Headaches are often an important symptom of a larger problem, such as an infection or disease, including flu, Lyme disease, measles, meningitis, mumps, pneumonia, and tonsillitis, to name just a few. The mouth and eyes can also be sources of headaches as a result of a cracked tooth, jaw problems, or eyestrain. Some other conditions that include headache as a symptom are: aneurysm, brain tumor, glaucoma, head injury, and multiple sclerosis.

Know the side effects of your medications.

Some medicines can trigger a headache. Diuretics and the antihypertensive drugs hydralazine and reserpine are examples of such drugs. Some sinus and cold medications may also bring on a headache, particularly those that do not contain acetaminophen or aspirin.

Ladies, monitor hormone therapy.

As estrogen and progesterone decrease during menopause, about 50 percent of women begin to get serious headaches or migraines for the first time. Although a minority of women find that estrogen replacement therapy (ERT) helps to subdue headaches, for many others, ERT tends to intensify them.●

HEARING LOSS

8 HELPFUL HINTS

You're hearing differently. Sounds aren't quite as sharp or clear as they once were. This change has probably come about gradually. Perhaps you find yourself asking friends and relatives to repeat what they said more than once. You can't hear voices at a distance. You find telephone conversations easier than face-to-face communication, or vice-versa. Your own voice may sound unusually loud or strange even to you. People around you seem to be mumbling. You turn up the sound on the television, radio, or tape player. You feel shut out at a busy dinner table because the sound of your own chewing is louder than the voices around you. You hate to admit it, but you suspect that you have joined the ranks of millions of adults with hearing loss. (Researchers predict that more than 20 percent of all Americans will have hearing difficulties by the year 2000.) The first thing you must do is call an otolaryngologist—an ear, nose, and throat specialist—because you certainly shouldn't take hearing loss in stride or delay treatment out of embarrassment. Proper diagnosis is critical.

Basically, there are two types of hearing loss: conductive and sensorineural, or perceptive. If you have a conductive problem, a breakdown has occurred somewhere in your external canal, your middle ear, or your eardrum, the parts of the ear that send sound waves on to the inner ear so you can hear. Airborne waves of sound are not getting through. Noise is being shut off before it has a chance to reach the auditory nerves so it can be sent along to your brain for interpretation. A long list of disorders can bring about conductive failure, including chronic ear infections; ruptured eardrum; too much congestion, fluid, or pressure; or the abnormal growth of bone or tissue in the ear.

As an adult over age 50, you are more likely to be suffering some kind of sensorineural (perceptive) hearing disability, caused by aging nerves or damage to your inner ear. Have you noticed that the sounds of certain letters of the alphabet are more difficult to discern? In cases of sensorineural damage, consonants like *P, K, T,* and *D* don't come through loudly and clearly. Female voices, especially the higher pitched ones, are hard to hear, too. The words of others sometimes turn into mumbo-jumbo blends of nonsense. You can trace some of the blame for this kind of hearing loss to your age. Your hearing nerve is just not as efficient as it was when you were younger. You can also pin part of the blame for sensorineural damage on the after-effects of a lifetime spent listening to extra-loud noises. Then again, hearing difficulties can be caused by a blow to the ear, decreased circulation, high blood pressure, medications, the presence of a tumor, or a central nervous system disorder. If you have noticed problems with your hearing, read on for some helpful hints to deal with them.

Don't diagnose yourself.

See an otolaryngologist, who can test your hearing on a regular basis using sophisticated equipment. If you notice a change in hearing, ringing in your ears, or drainage from an ear, go right away. You can also call an otologist, an ear specialist. But don't delay taking action in the hope that your problem will miraculously correct itself: It won't. Your primary care physician can also help. Or you may be sent to an audiologist, a trained professional with a master's degree or Ph.D. Your loss will be measured in terms of decibels (the standard units of intensity of sound) and a course of treatment outlined. Surgery may be recommended for an implant or to correct bone growth in your ear. You may need a hearing aid, although hearing aids can't correct every kind of hearing loss. Some otolaryngologists and audiologists can fit you and sell the device. If you don't know where to find an expert, ask your doctor for a referral, call the nearest hospital, or check the yellow pages of your local telephone book under "Physicians—Otolaryngology."

Call 800-222-EARS.

Dial-A-Hearing Screening Test Hotline—800-222-EARS (800-222-3277)—is a toll-free telephone service approved by the Food and Drug Administration and sponsored by hospitals and hearing clinics throughout the United States. The operator can give you a local number to call for a quick hearing test conducted over the telephone—free of charge.

Anticipate slight hearing losses.

Some researchers suspect that the first symptoms of hearing loss will routinely show up in your 40s and 50s. A normal young person can hear the fullest range of sounds from the lowest notes of a pipe organ to the highest pitched sound of a shrill, screeching voice. By the time you reach your 60s, your range is not going to be as great even if you still consider your hearing to be good. Some doctors believe that this slight loss is due to less elasticity in all the parts of your ears and plain old wear and tear on your acoustic nerve.

Suspect earwax.

Not all cases of hearing impairment are traced to serious disabilities. In one study of people over age 62, a buildup of earwax had cut hearing acuity by 50 to 75 percent. While it's dangerous to poke or insert anything into your ear, you can gently rub around the external part with a wet washcloth. Some ear specialists recommend over-the-counter earwax removers such as Debrox, a dilute preparation of hydrogen peroxide. Or put a few drops of mineral or baby oil in your ears once or twice a month to keep the wax soft and pliable. In some cases, earwax is stubbornly difficult to remove: Don't hesitate to have your doctor handle it.

Keep the sound down.

Noise pollution can add to your hearing difficulties. Be aware of the level of sound around you, and avoid prolonged exposure to loud noises whenever possible. Normal conversation averages about 60 decibels, a vacuum cleaner generates 80 decibels, and a rock-band concert can expose your ears to 90 to 130 decibels. You put yourself in danger when you try to live with sounds above 85 decibels for any length of time, even in short spurts. Here's a good rule of thumb: If you have to shout over a sound to be heard, if your ears actually become painful, or if they seem to ring, then the noise level is too high for you. Turn down the volume if you can or move away. By the way, if you listen to music on headphones and have the volume set so loud that other people can hear it, then it's too loud. You are damaging your hearing even further.

Buy earplugs.

If you must remain in noisy circumstances, invest in some kind of sound-muffling devices to cover your ears. Some experts expect today's rock music fans to become tomorrow's victims of hearing impairment. Even if you don't find yourself in the midst of screaming music fans very often, other loud noises around you could be harmful. Did you know that the sound of an electric shaver has registered at 85 decibels? a jet plane at 140 decibels? Become more aware of these dangerous encounters of the noisy kind, and take precautions to cover your ears.

Check your medicines.

Before you go to the doctor for an examination, make a list of all your medications. Aspirin, diuretics, and some antibiotics can all have an effect on your ability to hear properly. But never discontinue any drug on your own. Tell your doctor if you have hearing difficulties and ask for an analysis of your medication.

Check out new technical aids.

Technology can come to your rescue in a variety of forms. Not only are today's hearing aids better than ever, but several other devices can take some of the sting out of hearing loss. Your telephone company probably offers a service commonly known as TDD, which stands for Tele-communications Devices for the Deaf. If you are hearing impaired and become a TDD user, your phone receiver will be adapted to fit into an acoustic coupler that has a typewriterlike device attached. You can then type messages to other TDD users and send them over the telephone lines. Telecaption decoders are devices that print subtitles on your television screen for programs advertised as "closed captioned." Light-signalling machines are also available for smoke detectors, door bells, telephones, and even alarm clocks.●

IF YOU NEED A HEARING AID

○ ○ ○

Not all types of hearing loss can be corrected by hearing aids, and you should never buy an aid without the advice of your doctor. First, get tested. Find out if your health insurance will cover the cost. Hearing aids can be purchased from a physician, an audiologist, or a hearing aid dealer certified by the National Hearing Aid Society. Some states license these dealers. In any case, the dealer should provide you with a written warranty. Repairs and adjustments ought to be made free of charge for up to 90 days after your purchase. In fact, if your aid needs repair and must be sent back to the manufacturer, responsible dealers will offer a loaner until your aid is returned. Ask about a trial period and other kinds of purchase-option plans. Some agreements charge a fee to let you try the device for a period of time, perhaps 30 days, to see if it improves your hearing. Here are some choices you may be offered:

- In-the-ear aids are small, light, and will fit into your ear canal. If your hearing loss is minimal, this may be your best option.

- Behind-the-ear models are a bit bigger but are able to correct a wider range of hearing loss difficulties, from mild to severe.

- Eyeglass hearing aids can be built into regular eyeglasses.

- On-the-body models come with large components for patients with severe hearing loss and are made of soft plastic that is form-fitted to your ear. You can carry the mechanism for this type of model in a pocket or attach it to your clothing.

HEARTBURN

15 WAYS TO TURN DOWN THE HEAT

There's nothing like a fiery bout of heartburn to remind us that our digestive tracts are a lot like a kitchen sink. Put too much—or the wrong things—down the drain and the plumbing backs up.

That's exactly what happens when you wake up in the middle of the night with a fire raging in your chest. Stomach acids—which outside the accommodating environment of the stomach are a lot more corrosive than you'd think—are backing up into your esophagus, creating a burning feeling between your stomach and neck so hot you can almost see your pajama top smoking.

Medically, this condition is called reflux, and it usually occurs after you've eaten too much of the wrong foods and eaten them too fast. You're more likely to experience heartburn as you get older, because with age the valve at the bottom of the esophagus becomes weaker and less able to prevent stomach acids from creeping north. While most people can expect to experience heartburn occasionally, there's a lot you can do to keep episodes to a minimum and to douse the flames when the fire flares.

Check your medicine chest.

Many medications, including some sedatives and antidepressants, can trigger heartburn. If you think your prescription drugs might be responsible for burning a hole in your chest, talk to your physician about alternatives.

Grab the antacids.

Maalox and other over-the-counter antacids really do work. They're especially helpful when taken before bedtime, when stomach acids are most likely to swim into your esophagus and do their dirty work. Take antacids exactly as directed on the package because an overdose can bring on diarrhea.

Be careful with aspirin.

Despite all their benefits, aspirin and ibuprofen can irritate the esophagus. Acetaminophen doesn't, so it's a wise choice if you're in pain and prone to heartburn.

Loosen your belt.

A tight belt—or girdle, pantyhose, or any other garment that pinches the waist—pushes your gut in. This you already know, but what you might not realize is that the pressure also forces stomach acids to drift upward into your esophagus.

Lose some weight.

A roll of fat around your middle has the same effect as a tight piece of clothing—it squeezes stomach acids upward. You'll feel a lot better in other ways, too, if you get rid of that spare tire.

Don't lie down.

Lying down and laying low for a while may seem like just the thing—perhaps the only thing—to do when heartburn strikes, but you'll only prolong the agony. When you sit upright or stand, you put the force of gravity on your side, making it harder for stomach acids to travel up your esophagus.

Change your bedtime or your mealtime.

If you eat late and retire early, something has to give. Lying flat on your back in bed with a full stomach is a surefire way to trigger heartburn. Wait a full two to three hours after eating before turning in. By the same token, flopping down on the sofa in front of the TV won't do: You have to sit upright. Better yet, step out for a little night air.

Slow down, you're eating too fast.

Gulping down a meal is like playing with matches. Your stomach can't easily accommodate the overload and starts secreting acids like mad; before you know it there's a fire in your chest.

Let your stomach be the judge.

While it's clear that some foods should be avoided by anyone who's prone to heartburn, other foods can set your chest aflame but may be mother's milk to someone else. This means that you may be able to eat spicy dishes or enjoy orange juice and other acidy drinks without a hint of heartburn. The trick is a little experimentation to separate the foods you can tolerate from those you can't.

Cut back on fat.

The stomach produces more acid to digest fatty foods, and the more acid you generate, the more likely you are to get heartburn.

Eat smaller portions.

The more food you send down to your stomach, the more acid it's going to produce. Try eating smaller portions at mealtime even if it means having an extra meal or two a day.

Watch what you drink.

Many drinks may trigger heartburn. The list includes: regular and decaf coffee, because the oils, not the caffeine, irritate the esophagus; alcohol, which churns up stomach acids and also relaxes the sphincter between the stomach and the esophagus, opening the floodgate to acids; and carbonated beverages, which can have the same effect on the sphincter as alcohol.

Drink plenty of water.

Pour some water down your throat, and you'll flush stomach acids out of the esophagus and back down where they belong. It's especially important to drink water with meals.

Get some exercise.

If you're more prone to heartburn when you're lying down, then the more you move around the less likely you are to

get it. Exercise helps a lot, and you don't need much to get heartburn-relieving benefits. Even mild exercise, such as a daily walk, may keep heartburn at bay.

Hold your head up high.

Unfortunately, stomach acids have a habit of creeping up on your esophagus when you're sleeping. The next thing you know, you'll be awakened by the sensation that something's burning a hole in your chest. One way to keep stomach acids in their place is to elevate the head of your bed. ●

WHEN IT'S MORE THAN HEARTBURN

○ ○ ○

It's easy to confuse the discomfort of heartburn with the symptoms of any number of serious medical disorders. While it's normal, for instance, to experience heartburn occasionally, persistent, recurrent heartburn can be a sign of severe esophageal inflammation or an ulcer. See a doctor without delay if what you think are heartburn pains are accompanied by any of the following:

- Crushing chest pain that may extend to the neck, shoulders, arms, jaw, or back, perhaps accompanied by shortness of breath—all of which are symptoms of a heart attack.

- Difficulty swallowing—can be a sign of severe scarring on the esophagus caused by repeated exposure to stomach acids; can also indicate the possibility of cancer of the esophagus.

- Vomiting—can be a symptom of ulcers or a bowel obstruction.

- Bloody stool—can be a sign of ulcers, inflammatory bowel disease, or cancer of the intestine.

HEART DISEASE

---

29 WAYS TO HELP YOU KEEP ON TICKING

Heart disease remains the number one cause of death in the United States, a dubious distinction that has continued throughout the twentieth century, with the exception of one year.

Heart disease comprises a number of disorders and diseases, but physicians and the public alike tend to associate the term most often with coronary heart disease (CHD). Coronary disease results from a buildup of fatty material in the arteries that channel blood to the heart (a process known as atherosclerosis).

CHD causes almost half a million deaths annually, many as a result of heart attacks. Roughly equal numbers of men and women account for CHD mortality. According to the American Heart Association, more than 11 million Americans have coronary disease.

That CHD remains a major health problem is both curious and disappointing. Medical research has clearly identified the factors that lead to coronary disease, and intensive public education and awareness campaigns have made the disease and its risk factors almost household names.

Some CHD risk factors can't be changed: genetics, male sex, and older age. But the impact of most major coronary risk factors can be modified or, like smoking, eliminated altogether. If you have the desire, the following tips can put you on the road to a lower risk for coronary disease.

Watch your blood pressure.

High blood pressure, or hypertension, is one of the most powerful risk factors for heart disease, heart attack, and stroke. The risk begins to rise any time blood pressure exceeds 140/90 millimeters of mercury (mm Hg). Studies have shown that even modest reductions in blood pressure can lessen the chances of developing heart disease or stroke. A variety of drugs can effectively control blood pressure, which also responds well to non-drug treatment, including weight loss, dietary changes, exercise, and smoking cessation. Many people can bring their blood pressure under control without the use of drugs. (See HIGH BLOOD PRESSURE.)

Don't smoke.

The prevalence of smoking in the U.S. has dropped from 50 percent of the population thirty years ago to 30 percent or less today. Even so, cigarette smoking continues to make a major contribution to disease risk. The contribution may be underappreciated for heart disease. If the entire population gave up smoking, between four and five years would be added to the average life span. On the other hand, if all cancer were eliminated, average life span would increase by two or three years. The difference results from the influence smoking has on heart disease. Within five years of quitting, an ex-smoker may have a 70 percent drop in the excess risk attributable to smoking.

Keep cholesterol in check.

Nationwide, the average cholesterol level among American adults is declining and now stands at about 200 milligrams per deciliter (mg/dL). However, an average reflects a balance between people with high and low levels. Many people still have cholesterol levels in the danger zone, above 240 mg/dL, and many others are in the borderline range of 200–239 mg/dL. In general, heart disease risk declines by two percentage points for each one-point decrease in a person's cholesterol level.

Don't go soft in the middle.

Excess weight is particularly harmful when it leads to fat accumulation in the abdomen (an apple shape), as opposed to the legs and hips (pear shape) or other sites in the body. Even people who are only modestly overweight may have a much higher risk for heart disease if they have a "spare tire." Exercise and weight control are especially important to combat the accumulation of abdominal fat.

EXERCISE: PLAN BEFORE YOU START

○ ○ ○

Of all the coronary risk factors, physical inactivity may be the most widespread. For a variety of reasons, many people have an aversion to physical activity. Common excuses include lack of time, the perceived need for special clothing or equipment, boredom, and discomfort.

In reality, most people who are unsuccessful at establishing a regular exercise program don't give enough thought to physical activity. They don't have a plan. Advance planning and thought can greatly increase the likelihood that you'll stick with a program once you start.

1. Consult your doctor. Everyone over the age of 40 should see their physician before starting an exercise program, even if they feel as if they're in great shape.

2. Read up on exercise. Fitness magazines and books offer a variety of tips for the beginning exerciser. Something may strike a responsive chord in you.

3. Be goal oriented. What do you hope to accomplish? Maybe you want to lose weight, have more energy, or enjoy retirement more. After starting to exercise, set other goals. For example, someone who jogs might eventually want to join in a 5K or 10K "fun run." Keeping an exercise log, a written record of steady progress, helps many people to achieve their goals.

4. Identify obstacles. If lack of time is a problem, look critically at your schedule to find the needed time (what is more important, another forgettable TV show or a brisk walk around the block?). If it's boredom, find an exercise partner, join a health club, or search more diligently for the right exercise.

5. Look for incentives. Riding a stationary bike might give you more time for reading. A regular walk or jog might give you more time to listen to music on a personal stereo, learn a foreign language, or listen to books on tape.

6. Know your likes and dislikes. Pick an activity you enjoy or think you might enjoy. Maybe you can learn to play tennis or relearn skating, even try those newfangled in-line skates. Don't sabotage your chances by building your plan around activities you're not likely to enjoy.

7. Be sensible. Start with a reasonable level of activity and build gradually.

Lose those extra pounds.

More and more authorities on coronary heart disease consider an excessive amount of weight to be the most dangerous of all the factors considered in evaluating the risk for disease. The numbers tell the story: Whereas today only a minority of adults smoke, the incidence of obesity has reached what many authorities consider an epidemic magnitude. Moreover, being overweight greatly increases the chances that a person will have other heart disease risk factors, namely, high blood pressure, high cholesterol, diabetes, and physical inactivity. You do not have to be clinically obese (defined as 20 percent above ideal body weight) to be at risk for heart disease; any excess weight adds to your personal risk.

Stay active.

Next to obesity, physical inactivity ranks as the risk factor that seems to be most out of control. Overwhelming evidence clearly shows that regular physical activity favorably affects weight, cholesterol level, blood pressure, and the risk of developing diabetes. Recent studies indicate that the regularity of physical activity, not the intensity of the workout, counts more in heart disease reduction. Most experts recommend a minimum of 30 minutes of activity at least three days a week.

Eat less fat.

Fat is the major culprit leading to higher cholesterol levels. Many foods that have no cholesterol in them may still have substantial amounts of fat. The American Heart Association recommends that everyone try to get fewer than 30 percent of their calories from dietary fat, and fewer than 10 percent from saturated fat (found in butter as well as meat and animal products).

Calories still count.

Watching fat intake is important, but everyone still needs to be aware of calories. Study the information on food labels about calories (and fat). No matter how little fat you eat, if your calorie intake exceeds your energy expenditure, you'll gain weight.

Go meatless for a day.

Meat, especially red meat, remains the major source of saturated fat in most diets. One way to cut back on meat is to have one or more meatless days each week. Many people are surprised to discover the variety of nutritious and filling meatless dishes that are available. Entire cookbooks now focus on meatless entrees.

Cut back on serving sizes.

Many nutrition authorities are fond of saying there are no bad foods. The statement reflects the widely held view that the amount of food a person eats, not the kind of food eaten, plays the key role in weight gain and its associated problems. To get a better handle on how much you eat, measure your servings for a week or two. A typical serving size is half a cup. For meat, a standard serving is three or four ounces.

Avoid quick fixes.

Extreme approaches that offer the promise of quick results have a high failure rate. Among the few who do succeed with them, the relapse rate is high. Some extreme approaches may even be harmful. Reducing coronary risk is a continual process, not a one-shot deal. Approaches that lead to gradual changes usually are easier to stick with and produce better results over the long term.

Consider aspirin.

Studies have shown that a baby aspirin a day or an adult aspirin every other day can significantly reduce the risk of heart attack. The benefits are clearest for men, but many coronary-disease experts recommend regular aspirin for all adults beginning at age 40. Be sure to check with your doctor before beginning aspirin therapy, however.

Eat more fruits and vegetables.

Nutrition surveys continue to show that many Americans do not eat enough fruits and vegetables. At a minimum, everyone should try to eat at least five servings daily. In general, fruits and vegetables are low in calories, rich in vitamins and minerals, and quite filling.

Drink lots of water.

At a minimum, everyone should try to drink eight glasses of water daily. In most instances, that minimum amount will just replace the water lost through perspiration and excretion. People who are very active or who live in warm climates may need even more. Water is filling, it promotes fat metabolism, and it should be an important part of any plan to control weight.

Go easy on the booze.

If you drink, keep alcohol intake to one or two drinks daily. People who exceed that limit have an increased risk of high blood pressure and heart disease, not to mention other risks of too much alcohol.

Keep diabetes in check.

Diabetes doubles a man's heart disease risk and increases a woman's risk by four to six times, essentially eliminating the advantage women enjoy before they reach menopause. About 95 percent of people with diabetes have what is known as type II, or adult-onset disease. Type II diabetes tends to be associated with a cluster of factors: older age, physical inactivity, and excess weight. Diabetes increases the risk of high blood pressure and high cholesterol; it is also an independent risk factor for heart disease (see DIABETES).

Hold the salt.

Excessive salt consumption may not cause high blood pressure, but salt (more specifically, sodium) contributes to the risk of high blood pressure and the ability to control it. Everyone should try to hold salt consumption to no more than one teaspoon a day. As an experiment in salt reduction, try omitting salt from recipes and then adding it when food is served.

Add antioxidants to your diet.

Population studies consistently show that people who eat more foods rich in antioxidants (beta carotene, vitamin C, vitamin A and its derivatives) have a lower prevalence of CHD. Fruits and vegetables are the major dietary sources of antioxidant vitamins.

Read labels.

The best way to become more familiar with hidden sources of fat and salt is to develop the habit of reading labels on food packages. Dedicated label readers learn to remember hidden sources of fat when they encounter the same foods out of their packages (in restaurants, for example).

Work on your muscles.

As people grow older, their metabolism slows and a change occurs in the ratio of lean mass (better known as muscle) to fat. In general, lean mass is lost and the proportion of fat increases. A modest strength-training program can help maintain that muscle. Benefits include lowering blood-lipid levels, improving control of blood sugar, and increasing aerobic endurance (making it easier to engage in aerobic exercise). Studies have shown that even very elderly people benefit from strength training. Increased muscle mass can lead to better mobility and reduce the risk of injuries from falls. Ask your physician for advice about how to start a muscle-strengthening program.

Take it easy.

Anger, impatience, hostility, and stress responses have an unclear association with heart disease. Studies have not proven beyond a doubt that emotions and mental stress increase the risk. However, many authorities believe that emotions and emotional responses may indirectly affect coronary risk by causing people to disregard other established risks, such as high blood pressure and cholesterol, excess weight, smoking, excess alcohol consumption, and physical inactivity.

Enjoy an occasional treat.

You don't have to feel like you're depriving yourself all the time. It's OK to indulge yourself occasionally. Skip your early-morning workout every once in awhile. Have eggs for breakfast sometimes or a juicy steak for dinner. The key is moderation. People become overweight or have high cholesterol or high blood pressure because they go overboard on a regular basis.

Take your medicine.

Drugs for high blood pressure, high cholesterol, or diabetes won't work if you don't take them. If you're having problems with cost or side effects, talk to your physician to resolve the problem—don't just stop taking the drug. You might be able to switch drugs or change to a different dose. Suddenly stopping some medications can be dangerous.

Keep track of drugs.

Give all your physicians a complete list of every medication you take (including nonprescription drugs). Interactions between two or more drugs can lessen their effectiveness or even bring about potentially dangerous interactions.

Women beware.

Heart disease kills almost equal numbers of men and women each year and causes far more deaths among females than breast cancer. Women should not be lulled into the false belief that they are immune to heart disease, although the

disease does tend to arise at a later age in women. Even so, women should start addressing coronary risks early so they won't have regrets later on in life.

Be reasonable.

Coronary risks don't go away overnight. But they can be diminished if you set realistic goals and build toward them gradually. If you need to address multiple coronary risk factors, set priorities and

WARNING!

· · ·

Is It a Heart Attack?

Would you know what to do if you had a heart attack? Quick thinking could save your life.

- Don't deny. The biggest delay in receiving treatment involves people who don't accept the symptoms and seek treatment.

- Call for help. Dial 911 for an emergency vehicle or call someone else who can take you to the hospital immediately.

- Don't drive yourself. A person in the throes of a heart attack is in no condition to drive. The risk of losing consciousness could endanger the victim and others.

- Sit down. Don't stand or move about.

- Take an aspirin. If you are having a heart attack, you'll get an aspirin as soon as you arrive at the hospital. Taking an aspirin yourself may be helpful if you're delayed.

- Try to stay calm. About 70 percent of heart attack victims survive the experience.

ESTROGEN THERAPY: A WOMAN'S DECISION

○ ○ ○

For years, medical experts and the general public alike operated under the assumption that heart disease was a disease of middle-aged men. Today we know that women are full participants in the problem of heart disease. The difference is that the disease tends to occur later in life for women, about ten years later than for men.

A number of studies have pointed to estrogen, the female sex hormone, as women's "heart guardian." The conclusion is based on the results of epidemiologic (population) studies showing two things: One, heart disease risk in women begins rising after menopause, when estrogen production ends. And two, women who take estrogen supplements after menopause have a lower heart disease risk than women who don't take supplements.

Given the weight of evidence, one could argue that all women should take estrogen after menopause. But the issue is not quite that simple. Recently, researchers have begun testing the assumption that estrogen replacement therapy (ERT) will reduce coronary risk in postmenopausal women.

Until the data are in from several large, ongoing clinical studies, the decision to take estrogen along with the hormone progesterone (a process referred to as hormone replacement therapy, or HRT) or to take estrogen alone (ERT) must be based on a woman's individual situation.

The evidence gathered to date shows that women who have a uterus should have HRT to reduce the risk of uterine cancer. Women who do not have an intact uterus may get estrogen alone.

A woman's individual risk for breast cancer must also figure into the decision-making process. Estrogen supplementation, either ERT or HRT, may entail a slight risk of breast cancer. But that risk may be increased if a woman has a family history of breast cancer or other factors that put her at a higher risk.

work on them accordingly. Don't overwhelm yourself by trying to do everything at once: Such an approach is doomed to failure.

There are no magic bullets.

Available medication should be viewed as nothing more than a supplement to lifestyle changes that are necessary if you're serious about reducing risk. For example, you have reason to be pleased if you've been able to lower your cholesterol level through medication, but that doesn't mean you are free to stop exercising or to abandon your low-fat diet.

It's never too late.

Even people who have severe heart disease can benefit from risk-reducing behavior. Studies have shown that heart attack survivors are much less likely to have subsequent attacks if they work at reducing risk factors.

Accept the responsibility.

No one forces you to adopt the lifestyle habits that can lead to coronary disease, nor should you expect anyone to lower the risk for you. Your doctor can provide advice and medication, but you have to take responsibility for making changes in your life.●

HEART PALPITATIONS

11 WAYS TO PUT YOUR MIND AND HEART AT EASE

Love isn't the only thing that can make your heart flutter. A wide range of factors other than Cupid's arrows affect your heartbeat and your awareness of that beat.

Normal heart function depends on the precise firing and co-ordination of electrical impulses within the heart. Misfires, interruptions, and other alterations in these electrical signals can affect both the speed and coordination of the heartbeat.

Emotions, activities, medications, circumstances, and a host of other factors can affect the heart's electrical signaling. Keep in mind, however, that skipping or racing occurs from time to time in perfectly healthy people. Potentially serious heartbeat disturbances, called cardiac arrhythmias, require prompt attention from and evaluation by a physician. Cardiac arrhythmias often are associated with coronary heart disease or some other form of heart disease. Ventricular arrhythmias, the most serious of these disturbances, often result in sudden death.

To be on the safe side, it's a good idea to notify your physician any time you notice a heartbeat irregularity, particularly if it occurs frequently. Benign, or harmless, palpitations usually can be diagnosed without an extensive workup.

To help keep your heart in good ticking order, and perhaps ease your mind about an occasional errant tock, take time to consider these 11 tips.

Don't assume the worst.

An occasional skip or flutter usually does not mean that serious heart trouble is on the horizon. Although concern is understandable, there is no reason to panic. Don't overreact. Changes in speed, force, or other aspects of heartbeat can and do occur in perfectly healthy people.

Don't play doctor.

Remaining calm about a minor disturbance of your heartbeat is not the same thing as ignoring it. Always let your doctor know. If the disturbance is an isolated event, you will probably be advised that it can be evaluated during your next regularly scheduled doctor's appointment. But if, on the other hand, the disturbance occurs more often, or if you are concerned for any reason, don't put off letting your doctor know the full story.

Be aware.

Does your heart race, pound, or skip a beat in certain situations? Do certain activities, people, or events seem to influence your heartbeat? Do specific foods, drinks, or drugs affect how your heart behaves? Try to develop a heightened sense of awareness when a heartbeat disturbance occurs. If a change in heartbeat is situational or otherwise tied to a specific factor, dealing with that factor may eliminate the problem. Knowing the context in which a heartbeat disturbance occurs can also help a physician to evaluate the nature and potential seriousness of the problem.

Don't panic.

Anxiety can speed up the heartbeat and make the heart seem to race and pound in an unnatural way. Panic attack, a severe form of anxiety, can produce additional symptoms—such as shortness of breath or chest pain—that can be mistaken for a heart attack. Don't be reluctant to discuss anxiety with your physician. In many cases, the condition responds well to therapy using medication or behavior-modification techniques.

How do you sleep?

Lying in bed on your left side can sometimes make you more aware of your heartbeat. You may hear the pounding in your ear, and you might even feel the force of each contraction. If these sensations bother you and interfere with sound sleep, try different sleeping positions to see if you feel more relaxed.

Say no to caffeine.

Too much regular coffee or other caffeine-containing beverages can give a person the jitters and cause the heart to race or skip a beat occasionally. The same reaction often follows consumption of other types of stimulants, which should be taken only in moderation.

Don't smoke.

In addition to constituting a significant risk for heart disease, cigarettes—more specifically, the nicotine they contain—act as a type of stimulant and thus should be avoided by anyone suffering heart palpitations. Of course, cigarettes should be avoided by everyone, not just those concerned about their heart. (See SMOKING AND TOBACCO USE.)

Drink in moderation.

Heavy alcohol consumption, especially binge drinking (when large quantities of alcohol are consumed over a short period of time, usually with the objective of reaching a drunken state), can disrupt the heart's normal electrical activity. If you drink, limit consumption to no more than one or two drinks daily.

Control your anger.

Like anxiety, anger and hostility can affect the speed and force with which the heart beats. Some evidence suggests that anger may have a "toxic" component that affects the risk of heart disease and heart attack, possibly through an interaction with conventional risk factors such as high blood pressure and high blood cholesterol levels.

What medications do you take?

Certain medications can affect heartbeat, especially antihistamines. Interactions between two or more drugs can also cause disturbances. Make sure your physician has a complete list of your medications, including nonprescription drugs.

Exercise regularly.

A heart that undergoes regular exercise is more likely to be a healthy heart. Exercise may also favorably affect other factors that can influence heartbeat, such as one's emotional state, one's eating and drinking habits, and one's incentives to quit smoking. Anyone over age 40 should remember to consult a physician before starting an exercise program.●

A "BEEPER" FOR THE HEART

○ ○ ○

People who experience heartbeat disturbances with some regularity may require analysis with a Holter monitor. That's a portable version of an electrocardiograph, which is an instrument used to record the electrical impulses generated in the heart and displayed on an electrocardiogram, or ECG. Typically, the Holter monitor records the heartbeat over a period of a day or two.

But what if you have only occasional racing or fluttering? Monitoring heart activity for a couple of days at a time might never detect that kind of irregularity. The elusive heartbeat disturbance may prove to be less elusive when a person carries a device known informally as a cardiobeeper. This instrument is designed for long-term use. Some models are about the size of a pager and can be carried easily in a pocket or purse. At the first sign of a heartbeat disturbance, the user can activate the cardiobeeper to record the episode. The data is then stored in the device for future evaluation by a physician.

Known in technical circles as transient symptomatic event recorders, cadiobeepers can help physicians distinguish between benign and potentially serious heartbeat disturbances. The devices also help identify changes that may be situational, such as those that occur during exercise or stressful situations.

HEAT EXHAUSTION

11 WAYS TO BEAT THE HEAT

You're halfway into your morning walk and already your legs feel like they weigh a ton. You're upset because you think you have the flu: Your head hurts, you seem a little woozy, and your skin is clammy even though it's sunny, hot, and humid. You may even feel confused and disoriented.

The flu? Think again. Summertime heat waves aren't just uncomfortable; they can be downright dangerous. What you may not realize is that the reactions you've noticed are some of the major symptoms of heat exhaustion (not to be confused with heatstroke, which is more serious, even life-threatening). Heat exhaustion doesn't happen immediately. At the onset of symptoms, stop to rest, and take in some fluids. Otherwise, you're likely to become severely dehydrated, and you may collapse.

The best way to avoid heat exhaustion is to limit hot-weather activity. If you're not in good physical condition and haven't been exercising regularly, you won't be capable of the same level of activity as you were 20 or even 10 years ago. Your ability to cope with heat has been reduced. Moreover, hot weather can spell trouble if you have chronic medical problems such as heart disease or diabetes. In addition, certain medications can reduce your ability to respond to heat. Diuretics, for example, promote the loss of fluid through urination, and without ample fluids it will be harder for you to cool your body by perspiring.

WARNING!

· · ·

When to seek medical help

The heat can lay you low, literally, and can pose a serious health risk. That's why it's so important to seek medical attention at the first sign of any of the following heat-related symptoms:

- Fever
- Nausea
- Fainting
- Extreme lethargy
- Confusion
- Muscle aches
- Convulsions

These symptoms are signs of heat exhaustion, heat syncope (fainting), and—in the worst case—heatstroke, a potentially fatal condition that requires prompt medical attention. In addition to the symptoms noted above, a victim of heatstroke is also likely to have a rushed, rapid pulse; a body temperature of 104 degrees Fahrenheit or higher; and flushed, hot skin.

On the other hand, if you are in good shape, exercise regularly, and don't have a serious chronic illness, your response to the heat at 50 could be as effective as it was when you were 30. Indeed, studies show that healthy people between 55 and 70 years of age who exercise regularly are just as capable of acclimating to exercise in the heat as younger people. To compensate for higher temperatures, being fit, avoiding overexertion, and drinking plenty of fluids (before, during, and after exercise) are the things to consider at any age.

Here are a number of other simple suggestions to take care of yourself during hot weather and to avoid heat exhaustion.

Take it easy in very hot weather.

It's best to lay low when temperatures get high. Take advantage of the cooler times in the early morning and evening to deal with the jobs and activities you just have to do outdoors.

Stay in the shade.

It's just a matter of common sense: Keep out of the heat of the sun. That might mean staying in the shade or, on extremely hot days, not venturing outdoors at all for any period of time. Move your regular walk from the neighborhood or local park to an air-conditioned shopping mall.

Get acclimated.

If you plan to be active and walk, bike, or play tennis in hot weather, shorten your sessions of activity until you get accustomed to the heat.

Turn on the air.

Air-conditioning, obviously, is the best way to keep the heat down. If you don't have air-conditioning, consider spending time, preferably the hottest part of the day, in a movie theater, restaurant, or other air-conditioned place. At home, the next best thing to AC is an electric fan. For quick relief, consider jumping into the shower or sponging yourself with cool water and then sitting down in front of a fan for a while.

Drink up.

When the temperature goes up, increase your intake of water, fruit juices, and vegetable juices. This is essential not only during periods of activity in the heat, but before and after as well. It's also important to drink plenty of liquids even if you're not exerting yourself. As a rule of thumb, once the temperature hits 90 degrees Fahrenheit or higher, you should increase your fluid intake to about a gallon a day (less if you remain in an air-conditioned environment). And remember, just because you're not thirsty does not mean you don't need to be drinking liquids—you can already be seriously dehydrated before you realize it.

Keep a sports drink on hand.

They replenish the electrolytes and carbohydrates you lose through sweating. As a result, they help fend off fatigue and make you less prone to heat exhaustion.

Avoid alcohol.

Tempting as a gin and tonic or a frozen daiquiri may seem in hot weather, try not to give in—alcohol is extremely dehydrating.

Be alert for other conditions.

Hypertension, coronary heart disease, diabetes, thyroid conditions, and kidney disorders are among the medical conditions that can make you more susceptible to the effects of the heat. Along with the medications you might take to treat them, these disorders can deplete fluid supplies or inhibit your sense of thirst. It's extremely important to speak with your physician about special measures you should take to cope with the heat if you have one or more of these conditions.

Skip salt tablets.

Don't take salt tablets unless instructed to do so by a physician. If you're on a salt-restricted diet, it's especially important to ask your physician about safe ways to replace salts lost through sweating.

Hit the showers.

Stepping under the shower or sitting in a tub of cool water will bring your body temperature down and make it a little easier to withstand the heat for a while after you get out.

Pay attention to your clothes.

Wear lightweight, light-colored, loose-fitting clothing. Cotton is ideal. Wear a hat on sunny days to keep your head cool.●

HEMORRHOIDS

---

17 WAYS TO BEAR THEM

Talk about a pain in the backside. Hemorrhoids are essentially varicose veins that form along the linings of the anal canal and lower rectum. Sometimes these bulging veins can protrude through the anus, or "prolapse," or they can pop up under the surface of the skin around the anal opening. Wherever hemorrhoids occur, they can burn, itch, bleed, and hurt like heck. They can make a bowel movement, which irritates them, an experience to be dreaded, and for most sufferers, they're just plain embarrassing, too.

Well, hemorrhoids should not be embarrassing. After all, they are among the most common of ailments, and most of us—as many as three-fourths of all Americans—develop hemorrhoids at some time. So, if you haven't experienced hemorrhoids yet, you still might. Indeed, we become more prone to hemorrhoids as we get older, because of ordinary wear and tear on the anal area over time and the general weakening of all body tissue that is part of the aging process. Besides, hemorrhoids are often triggered by the straining that accompanies constipation, a fairly common condition in the over-50 crowd.

The first sign of hemorrhoids is often a streak of bright red blood on the toilet paper, an alarming sight and possibly a symptom of more serious conditions, including colorectal cancer. Therefore, if you see blood and aren't 100 percent sure that hemorrhoids are the cause, see your doctor. But if hemorrhoids are flaring up, there's a lot you can do at home to get rid of them.

Don't strain yourself.

If you can read the newspaper during your stay in the bathroom, you're probably straining to have a bowel movement—and setting yourself up for hemorrhoids. One way to ensure that you are not straining is to breathe easily and evenly while moving your bowels. If you tend to huff and puff, you're straining and possibly injuring the veins in your rectum.

When nature calls, listen.

Whether you experience it once a day or twice a day or even more, the urge to eliminate is a perfectly natural sign that stool has entered your lower digestive tract and is ready to come out. The longer fecal matter remains inside the colon, the more likely it is to lose moisture and become hard, and the harder it will be to eliminate. So, when you gotta go, go...even if it's not always convenient.

Shift positions.

On a very personal note, sitting on a toilet seat may not be the best thing for your hemorrhoids because it can make elimination difficult. Squatting—the way our ancestors did and people in many parts of the world still do—to move your bowels can be a lot easier on the anal area than the customary seating position. Try a squat position in which you bring your knees as close to your chest as possible.

Watch what you eat.

If you have hemorrhoids, you'll feel the effects of certain foods as you eliminate them. Prime offenders are spicy foods, sugar-rich colas, and coffee—these can all irritate hemorrhoids on their way out of your body. Salty foods, like potato chips, are bad news for hemorrhoid sufferers, too, but for a different reason. Your circulatory system will retain excess salt, which can cause veins, including hemorrhoids, to bulge. And just as high-fiber foods are the easiest to eliminate, low-fiber foods (such as those high in sugars, fats, and proteins) are likely to produce hard stools that are difficult to eliminate.

Eat grain, don't strain.

Our digestive tracts do a great job of handling grains, oats, fruits, vegetables, and other fiber-rich foods. Fibery foods produce soft, bulky stools that are easy to eliminate and don't irritate the anal area on their way out. As a result, when you add these foods to your daily diet you'll

ADD FIBER TO YOUR DIET.

○ ○ ○

We hear a lot about the benefits of adding fiber to our diets—not only to prevent hemorrhoids but to stave off cancer and heart disease as well—but that can be easier said than done. The place to start is at the breakfast table, where a high-fiber cereal will provide part, but certainly not all, of your daily needs. It's also important to gradually include more fibery foods in the rest of your diet. Whole-wheat breads are good, easy-to-come-by sources, as is brown rice. You should also get sufficient supplies of fiber if you follow that basic health rule and eat five servings of fruits and vegetables a day. Fiber-rich vegetables include asparagus, broccoli, brussels sprouts, cabbage, carrots, green beans, and legumes such as chick peas and lentils. Apples, bananas, oranges, pears, prunes, raisins, and strawberries are high on the list of fruits that are rich in fiber.

strain less during a bowel movement. Fruits pack a double dose of relief—they supply fiber and contain their own supply of water to keep stools soft.

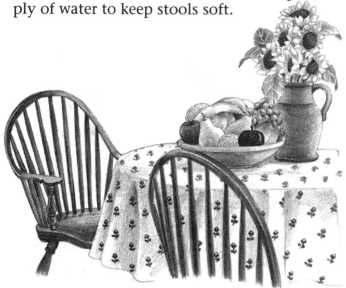

Watch your weight.

Yes, those extra pounds affect hemorrhoids, too—by putting extra weight on your anal area, causing veins to bulge.

Don't stand—or sit—too long.

Both positions are hard on hemorrhoids. When you sit for prolonged periods, blood moves sluggishly through your veins, causing them to bulge. And when you're on your feet for a spell, the pull of gravity causes blood to collect in the veins throughout your lower body, including those in the anal area. So, if you sit at a desk, use a computer, or watch TV for hours at a time, get up and move around every so often. And if you stand a lot, take a load off your feet—and other areas—from time to time.

Slurp it down.

Water, that is, and plenty of it. Six to eight glasses a day is the recommended dosage to keep your digestive juices flowing. Vegetable and fruit juices have the extra benefit of adding fiber and nutri-

ents to your diet. Water and juices alike will help your body absorb fiber and keep stools soft.

Keep moving.

Regular exercise keeps your digestive system in tip-top shape, helping food move through your bowels with regularity. As a result, you're less likely to become constipated and thus less likely to develop hemorrhoids. Avoid strenuous exercise that can irritate the anal area: A long ride on a bicycle is definitely not recommended. But walking and swimming are easy on the body and will keep your digestive tract moving.

Take a load off your duff.

Special doughnut-shaped pillows can be a hemorrhoid sufferer's delight. They allow you to sit while keeping your weight off sensitive areas.

Clean it up.

Not only is it important to keep the anal area clean—because fecal matter can irritate hemorrhoids—but the way you clean yourself makes a big difference, too. Dry toilet paper can scratch hemorrhoids, and the chemical additives in perfumed brands may sting. When feasible, it's best to stay with plain white, unscented paper and run it under warm water before use. Premoistened wipes and moistened facial tissues are other options, but some people find that these products irritate the already tender area.

Rinse off the soap.

While it's important to keep the area around hemorrhoids clean, too much soap and soap residue can irritate and cause itching. So rinse the anal area thoroughly. To be extra gentle, consider using a special perianal cleansing lotion, available over the counter.

Go soak.

A sitz bath spells relief for most hemorrhoid sufferers. Fill the tub with six inches of warm water, sit so your knees are raised, and just soak for a while. You can add half a cup of soothing Epsom salts if you want. But water alone will ease irritation and (in combination with your raised knees) increase blood flow to the anal area, which will take the painful bulge out of those swollen veins. And if it's not convenient to pop into a warm bath every time your hemorrhoids begin to irritate you, you'll get some relief by gently pressing a warm washcloth to the troubled area.

Be-witch them.

Witch hazel, that old medicine-chest staple, causes blood vessels to contract—that's why it stanches the flow of blood from a cut or scrape. A little dab on a clean cotton ball applied to an external hemorrhoid should do. This simple remedy can provide welcome, but temporary, relief from pain and keep hemorrhoids from bleeding for a while.

Beware of hemorrhoid preparations.

Most of the special hemorrhoid creams and lotions that fill drugstore shelves are not going to hurt you, and many will provide temporary relief from pain and itching. But they may not do everything they claim they will. None of them, for instance, will shrink hemorrhoids or make them disappear. And some can actually irritate hemorrhoids. Keep in mind that suppositories are likely to slip too far up the rectum to do your hemorrhoids any good. And a word of caution about cortisone creams: Though they are quite effective in reducing swelling, they may cause tissue to thin and pave the way for another bout of hemorrhoids down the road.

HOW CAN YOU TELL IF IT'S MORE THAN HEMORRHOIDS?

○ ○ ○

You can't tell easily, and that's a real health risk. The itching, pain, and bleeding you may write off as signs of hemorrhoids can also be symptoms of other, more serious conditions. These include parasites, perianal warts, intestinal polyps, and anal fissures. Rectal bleeding should always raise a red flag because it's one of the first symptoms of colorectal cancer.

So, if bleeding or any of the other symptoms of hemorrhoids persists for more than a few days, see your physician. And even if you suffer from hemorrhoids regularly, don't take it for granted that the telltale symptoms are just the sign of another flare-up. Get regular exams for colorectal cancer.

Go for a simple solution. Use petroleum jelly or zinc oxide paste. The moistening action of petroleum jelly inhibits bleeding and alleviates pain by preventing hemorrhoids from drying out.

Lay off the laxatives.

It's true that constipation is a major cause of hemorrhoids, but laxatives that act on the muscles of the rectum and colon are definitely not the solution. Such laxatives can seriously disrupt bowel function and irritate the anal area and hemorrhoids. What you want is a stool softener or a substance that bulks the stool.

Pop a pill.

Nonsteroidal anti-inflammatory drugs (NSAIDs) such as aspirin and ibuprofen (Advil, Motrin, and Nuprin are examples) should provide relief for the discomfort of hemorrhoids.●

HERNIA

8 TIPS TO MANAGE THE DISCOMFORT

You've noticed this dull ache and soreness around your groin for the past week. It's not bad, and it hasn't stopped you from doing anything. You're not really sure whether you should call your doctor, because the pain seems to go away when you lie down.

With symptoms like that, chances are good that you have a hernia, especially if you feel a slight bulge under the skin above and to either side of the pubic area—a definite signal to have your physician check this out.

Although hernias can be found almost anywhere in the body, most of us think of hernias as taking place in the groin or the inguinal (IN-gwen-al) area of the lower abdomen (the area where the abdomen and the inner thigh meet). That makes sense because as many as three fourths of all hernias are inguinal. Although anyone can get a hernia, including infants, hernias are most common in men over age 50.

In general, a hernia develops when an organ pushes through surrounding tissues and muscles that normally hold it in place. The only noticeable sign in an inguinal hernia is a bulge or swelling at the site. It usually appears gradually, enlarging slowly over several weeks. But sometimes a hernia can emerge suddenly. The bulge may feel slightly tender, and the pain is more noticeable when you stand, then eases up when you sit or lie down. You find yourself complaining that you feel a heavy or dragging sensation.

Hernias often occur later in life because the muscles and ligaments that support the abdominal wall weaken over time. They're more common in men than in women because the opening to the testicles makes that muscle area weak in males. In fact, there is a 50-50 chance that a man will have had a hernia by the time he reaches the age of 75. However, when women have a hernia it can be more dangerous. That's because the opening or tear is usually smaller in women, increasing the chance that the intestine that becomes trapped in the opening will become strangulated, or shut off from blood supply—a situation that requires medical attention without delay. Unless it's surgically repaired immediately, a strangulated hernia can cause intestinal blockage and a gangrenous bowel. In short, the condition can be fatal.

Given the risk of these potentially fatal consequences, surgery is usually recommended when an inguinal hernia is diagnosed. In fact, surgery—whether through traditional abdominal incision or using newer laparoscopic methods—is the only way to treat a hernia. In procedures performed under local anesthetic, usually on an outpatient basis, surgeons return the bulge of tissue back into place and often put plastic mesh over the tear in the abdominal wall to prevent recurrences.

Laparoscopic procedures, now widely used for many kinds of abdominal and orthopedic surgery, have many advantages over traditional surgery for the repair of hernias. In laparoscopic inguinal herniorrhaphy, a tiny camera is inserted through a small incision to provide a video image of the area. The surgeon then makes a few other small incisions to insert pencil-thin instruments to repair the hernia. Since incisions in the abdominal wall are kept to a minium, post-operative pain and recovery time are reduced significantly. It's not unusual for patients to be up and about within a few days, and full recovery often takes only a couple of weeks.

Since it's not known exactly what causes hernias, it's difficult to prevent them. Genetics sometimes plays a part, so if you have a family history of the problem you should be especially aware of the symptoms. Then again, it may arise simply as the result of some strain. Obesity, injury, repeated trauma, and lack of general physical fitness are additional possible causes. Still, there are many things you can do to reduce the risk of developing a hernia.

Keep the excess weight off.

It's just a matter of gravity: The more you weigh, the more strain you put on your organs and muscles, increasing your risk of developing a hernia. One of the best measures you can take to prevent a hernia is trying to maintain your ideal body weight (your physician should be able to tell you what you should weigh, based on your height, frame, and age). If you're overweight, try to develop a sensible diet and exercise regularly—you'll not only lower your risk of hernia, you'll help your heart, reduce your risk of diabetes, and improve your general health in many other ways, too.

Flatten your stomach.

Sit-ups, trunk-twisting stretches, and other exercises that build your abominal muscles not only help you get rid of a pot belly, but lessen your chances of developing a hernia by strengthening muscles throughout the abdominal region. Do your abdominal work carefully, though—it's important that you not overdo and put undue strain on your back.

Exercise carefully.

Remember, overdoing it can be danger-ous, because the extra strain you put on your muscles and organs can lead to a hernia. Overstretching or overzealous strength training can do more harm than good. If you're just beginning an exercise program, ask your local YMCA or gym about classes in abdominal strengthening, or ask your physician to recommend a physical-therapy program.

Lift gently.

To avoid the strain that can cause a her-nia, don't try to lift anything that's too heavy to manage comfortably. When you must lift something, lift with your arms and legs—being careful not to put too much strain on your back and ab-dominal muscles.

Eat a high-fiber diet.

If you strain to have a bowel movement, you're setting yourself up for a hernia. Chronic constipation often means you don't have enough fiber in your diet— add whole-grain cereals, raw vegetables, and other fiber-rich foods to your diet.

You'll feel better, avoid bowel problems, and help prevent hernias, too.

Don't fuss with a truss.

If your hernia is so painful that you feel you need one, what you probably need is surgery. In fact, a truss can be dangerous, because it impedes blood flow to the area of your hernia. Let your doctor decide if you need a truss.

Find out what's ailing you.

Varicose veins, phlebitis, a herniated disk, kidney stones, bladder infections, and other conditions can cause symp-toms similar to those of a hernia. So, if you're suffering from pain that suggests a hernia, get a complete workup to un-cover the real cause of the problem.

See a doctor if you think you have a hernia.

Common as hernias are, they can have dangerous consequences, such as stran-gulation of the intestine. At the first sign of symptoms, play it safe and see your physician.●

MYTH:
· · ·
I can't lift that— I'll get a hernia.

You can—and lifting can also worsen an existing hernia. But it's unlikely that you're going to get a hernia on the rare occasion you lift a heavy object. Only in cases where you continually put undue strain on the abdominal area are you likely to develop a hernia from lift-ing heavy objects. You should be more concerned about what the strain is doing to your back.

HIGH BLOOD CHOLESTEROL

22 APPROACHES TO CONTROLLING LIPIDS

Every year almost 500,000 Americans die from coronary heart disease—a number that represents about 25 percent of all deaths in the United States. And every year as many as 1.5 million people suffer the pain and fear from heart attacks, which constitute the leading cause of death for men and women alike.

The risks for coronary heart disease and heart attack have a clear association with levels of cholesterol in the blood. In general, as the cholesterol level rises, so does the risk. Keep in mind that cholesterol is just one of the risk factors for coronary disease and heart attack: High blood pressure, obesity, smoking, lack of exercise, diabetes, age, and genetic factors also come into play. And coronary risk factors often occur together, which greatly increases the overall risk.

A normal cholesterol level is less than 200 milligrams per deciliter (mg/dL). More than half of the adults in the United States aged 20 or older have cholesterol levels of 200 mg/dL or higher, according to the National Heart, Lung, and Blood Institute. And approximately 25 percent of adults have high cholesterol levels, defined as 240 mg/dL or higher.

Excess cholesterol in the blood tends to take up residence in the arteries, vessels that supply the body with oxygen-rich blood. Cholesterol accumulates in the walls of arteries to form a fatty substance called plaque. Significant buildup of plaque will obstruct blood flow through an artery. This can lead to stroke if arteries to the brain are affected, or to heart attack if coronary arteries are blocked. Coronary heart disease refers to a severe narrowing or obstruction of one or more of the arteries—the coronary arteries—that supply blood and oxygen to the heart. Most heart attacks occur when a blood clot plugs a plaque-clogged segment of a coronary artery.

Cholesterol is one of the factors you can control to reduce your risk of coronary heart disease and heart attack. The following tips show you how.

Turn over a new leaf.

Managing your cholesterol level requires a new mindset that emphasizes long-term lifestyle changes, not dietary fads that produce only short-term benefits, if any. Fad diets or extreme approaches to cholesterol management or weight loss fail to address the primary issue—the need to follow sensible lifestyle practices. And they may actually increase the risk for coronary disease and heart attack: People who repeatedly lose and gain weight (a phenomenon referred to as "yo-yo" dieting) may unintentionally cause their cholesterol levels to rise even higher, a so-called rebound effect.

Don't go it alone.

Encourage the whole family to make a commitment to risk-reducing lifestyle changes. Even family members at low risk today should be concerned about the years to come because the risk of coronary disease and heart attack increases as we age.

Safe may not be so safe.

Though high cholesterol is defined as more than 240 mg/dL, most heart attacks occur in people with cholesterol levels between 150 and 250 mg/dL. Only about 20 percent of heart attacks occur in people whose cholesterol levels exceed 240 mg/dL. The message: People with low or borderline cholesterol levels need to be concerned about how factors other than their total cholesterol level may influence coronary risk.

Don't shoot yourself in the foot.

Each year seems to usher in a new "magic bullet" to prevent coronary disease and heart attacks: rice bran, oat bran, fish oil, something else. The road to good health and lower cardiac risk

LIPIDS

∘ ∘ ∘

Most physicians look at more than total cholesterol when evaluating cholesterol as a risk for coronary disease. Several kinds of fatty substances—called lipids—may contribute to overall risk. As a result, physicians often evaluate a patient's "lipid profile," which may include several types of blood fats aside from total cholesterol.

LDL: Known as "bad" cholesterol, levels of low-density lipoprotein are closely associated with the risk of heart disease.

HDL: High-density lipoprotein is commonly called "good" cholesterol because increased levels have been associated with a lower risk of coronary disease.

Triglycerides: Triglyceride levels provide an indication of the total fat content of the blood.

CONSIDER THE NUMBERS

○ ○ ○

Sometimes a single number doesn't tell the whole story with respect to the link between cholesterol levels and coronary risk. A total cholesterol level of less than 200 mg/dL is associated with low risk for coronary disease, according to the American Heart Association and the National Institutes of Health. Cholesterol levels of 200 to 240 mg/dL represent borderline risk, while high risk refers to cholesterol levels that exceed 240 mg/dL.

Though not an absolute measure, total cholesterol does provide a starting point for defining risk. Across populations, every one percent increase in cholesterol level leads to a two to three percent increase in the rate of coronary disease. That means a cholesterol level of 220 mg/dL represents a 20 percent greater risk than a level of 200. At 250 mg/dL, the risk of disease is 50 percent higher.

Relationships among the different types of fat in the blood can also influence coronary risk, independent of total cholesterol level. For instance, a borderline cholesterol level combined with a low level of HDL can make for a high overall risk. Physicians are increasingly concerned about the ratio of LDL to HDL: The lower the ratio, the lower the risk for heart disease.

Ideally, a person's HDL level should exceed 50 mg/dL, while a desirable LDL level is less than 130. When the LDL level rises to 160 or more, the risk of coronary disease increases substantially. As with total cholesterol, these numbers should not be considered absolutes. For example, levels of triglycerides (another type of blood fat) can affect the risk associated with particular levels of HDL or LDL.

doesn't have any shortcuts. Focusing on fads detracts from the true task, which is to get at the root of the problem. In this case, that means the dietary and other lifestyle factors that influence cholesterol levels.

Focus on fat.

Many people erroneously think that high cholesterol levels result from eating cholesterol-laden foods. In reality, the major culprit is dietary fat, especially saturated fat (found in whole-fat dairy products and animal fats). Even products made from vegetable oil (which contains mostly polyunsaturated and monounsaturated fat) can contain hidden sources of fat. Hydrogenation, a process used to change a liquid oil into a solid (such as margarine or shortening), produces sub-

stances called *trans* fatty acids, which raise blood levels of cholesterol. The safest bet: Decrease total fat intake; when you do use fat, choose the ones that remain liquid at room temperature.

Study labels.

Labels make for interesting reading. But be wary of food package labels and advertising that tout a product as being low in cholesterol or cholesterol free. A close inspection of the label may reveal that the food contains a substantial amount of fat.

Know your meats.

Meat packages at the supermarket often contain U.S. Department of Agriculture labels that identify the meat as *prime, choice,* or *select.* While most people probably associate the terms with meat flavor and texture, the three meat grades also reflect fat content. *Prime* cuts contain the most fat (about 40 percent by weight). *Choice* meat cuts are 30 to 40 percent fat. *Select* cuts are about 20 percent fat. Even leaner cuts are available, with 10 percent fat or less. By using package labels to guide meat selections, you can reduce the fat content of each serving.

Add up the fat.

On average, Americans get about 35 to 40 percent of their daily calories from fat, which is up to one-third more than the American Heart Association (AHA) recommends. One way to become more familiar with your own fat consumption is to read food package labels, most of which list the grams of fat in the food, usually for one serving. The AHA diet defines fat consumption in terms of percentages of total calories. To convert fat grams into a percentage of calories, multiply your total daily calories by 30 percent (.30), then divide by 9 (the number of calories in a gram of fat). To calculate your daily allowance for grams of saturated fat, multiply your total calories by 10 percent (.10), then divide by 9.

The calculations show that someone on a 2,000-calorie diet should eat no more than 67 grams of total fat daily and no more than 22 grams of saturated fat. For 22 grams of saturated fat, you might be able to get more food than you think,

AMERICAN HEART ASSOCIATION DIET

○ ○ ○

The American Heart Association has developed some of the most widely recommended dietary guidelines for the prevention of heart attack, stroke, and other heart and blood-vessel diseases. The basic guidelines, called the Step I Diet, apply to healthy adults. If you already have evidence of heart disease or are at high risk, ask your physician for specific dietary recommendations.

1. Limit total fat intake to no more than 30 percent of calories consumed daily.

2. Limit saturated fat intake to no more than 10 percent of calories consumed each day.

3. Intake of polyunsaturated fat should account for no more than 10 percent of daily calories.

4. Limit cholesterol intake to no more than 300 milligrams (mg) daily.

5. Carbohydrates should account for at least 50 percent of total daily calories,

preferably more. Emphasize complex carbohydrates provided by fruits, vegetables, whole-grain products, and legumes (dried beans and peas).

6. The remaining calories (20 percent of daily calories or fewer) should come from protein sources.

7. Limit sodium intake to a maximum of 3,000 mg daily (a little more than a teaspoonful of salt).

8. People who drink alcohol should not consume more than two ounces daily. That translates into no more than two ounces of 100-proof whiskey, eight ounces of wine, or 24 ounces of beer.

9. Limit total calorie intake to the number needed to support your recommended body weight, as determined in the Metropolitan Tables of Height and Weight. Consult your physician for specific numbers.

10. Eat a variety of foods.

especially if you read labels and shop wisely. A tablespoon of butter in itself has about seven grams of saturated fat, but some margarines contain as little as a single gram per tablespoon.

Go for less.

How low can you go? Most experts believe we should try to get by with even fewer than the 30 percent limit for calories from fat in our diets. In particular, anyone who has additional risk factors for coronary disease should set lower targets for total and saturated fat.

Say yes to fruits, veggies, and grains.

Cholesterol occurs only in animal fat and whole-fat dairy products. The same products tend to have large concentrations of saturated fat. In contrast, plant foods are naturally cholesterol free and usually are low in fat. Moreover, vegetable fats tend to be of the polyunsaturated and monounsaturated varieties. Major exceptions are the so-called tropical oils—coconut, palm, and palm kernel oils—which contain large amounts of saturated fatty acids. Most fruits and vegetables are virtually devoid of fat. The same is true of grain products (cereals and breads) and legumes (dried beans and peas).

Fill up on "carbs."

People who consume lots of complex carbohydrates tend to have less room left over for fatty foods. Fill up on fruits, vegetables, pasta, whole grains, rice, and legumes.

Fire up the broiler.

How you cook meat has a definite impact on how much fat is left to eat. Frying—especially deep-fat frying—adds fat. Grilling, broiling, and braising remove fat during cooking. But avoid too much

grilling: It has been linked with an increased risk of cancer.

Skin those birds.

The skin of poultry is loaded with saturated fat. Remove it before cooking.

Shrink your meat portions.

For many people, the amount of food they eat is more of a problem than the kinds of food. That's especially true for meat. A "serving" of meat usually means only three to four ounces.

Say no to pastries.

Learn to distinguish between breads, which are usually low in fat, and pastries, which may appear breadlike but are often hidden sources of fat.

White is light, yolk is not.

Eggs are an excellent source of protein, but they're also high in fat and cholesterol. A typical egg yolk contains about 213 mg of cholesterol, more than two-thirds of an entire day's allowance in the

AHA diet. Fat makes up more than half the calories in a yolk. The AHA recommends a maximum of three whole eggs a week. Be sure to carefully check the labels on packaged foods, since yolks frequently show up as a hidden source of fat and cholesterol in prepared foods.

Go fishing for less fat.

As an alternative to red meat, fish offers lots of protein and a fraction of the fat. Don't squander the benefits of fish by frying it, however; grill, broil, or bake it.

Leave the organs behind.

Organ meats, such as liver, invariably are high in cholesterol and fat, more so than nonorgan meat from the same animal. Be extremely careful to limit your consumption of organ meats, and eliminate organ products altogether if possible.

Add fiber to your diet.

Fiber is the portion of plant foods (fruits, vegetables, and grains) that resists digestion. A number of studies have shown that increased consumption of soluble dietary fiber can help lower cholesterol. But most Americans consume only small amounts of fiber on a daily basis. One way to get more fiber is to eat more fruits, vegetables, and whole-grain products. Even then, however, fiber consumption may still fall short of what's been used in clinical studies. As a supplement to dietary sources of fiber, consider a daily dose of a bulking agent that contains the fiber-rich product, psyllium. (Metamucil is one of the best-known psyllium-containing products.) If you decide to increase your fiber intake, do so gradually to minimize concern about constipation, gas, and other digestion-related problems.

Take the nicotine cure.

Smoking is a major coronary risk factor, due in part to the fact that it lowers HDL-cholesterol, the "good" cholesterol.

Start exercising.

Regular aerobic exercise (the type that increases heart rate) has a number of beneficial effects on heart disease risk. Regular exercise boosts the level of HDL and promotes weight loss. These factors may in turn have favorable effects on cholesterol. Everyone should strive for at least 30 minutes of exercise, to be performed three times a week. The exercise doesn't have to come all at once or even take the form of classic exercise. For example, you can incorporate more exercise into your day by parking farther away than usual from your workplace and walking the extra distance. Or use the stairs in buildings rather than riding the elevator.

Start today.

Ideally, you should make the prevention of heart disease a lifetime objective. In reality, you can start anytime, and it's never too late. Even people who already have coronary disease or who have had a heart attack can benefit from lower cholesterol levels. People at especially high risk may need to aim for even lower cholesterol levels than those recommended for the general population, however.●

HIGH BLOOD PRESSURE

13 STEPS TO DEFLATE HIGH BLOOD PRESSURE

After an initial washing, that new cotton shirt or those jeans often don't fit as comfortably as the first time you wore them. With a bit of tugging, you can get the clothes on, but the fit is snug at best.

Similarly, the "fit" inside a blood vessel becomes more snug when a person has high blood pressure, or hypertension. Small blood vessels called arterioles constrict, or tighten, which increases pressure—and resistance to blood flow—throughout the circulatory system. As a result, the heart has to work harder to pump blood through the system.

As many as 50 million Americans have high blood pressure, according to the American Heart Association. The disease contributes directly to almost 36,000 deaths a year and plays an indirect role in thousands of other deaths. High blood pressure substantially increases the risk of heart disease (including heart failure), heart attack, stroke, and kidney failure. The chances of developing high blood pressure increase with age, as does the risk of complications associated with the disease.

Almost half the people who have high blood pressure don't even know it. In most instances, the disease causes no obvious symptoms, hence the nickname "silent killer."

The good news about high blood pressure is that the disease is very treatable. A variety of medications can effectively control blood pressure in many people. Even better, most risk factors for high blood pressure are controllable. Thus, in many instances, attention to

---

STROKE

○ ○ ○

Stroke risk increases with age, doubling with each decade after age 55, and high blood pressure is the single most important risk factor for stroke. Men have a 30 percent higher stroke risk than women, and African Americans have a 50 to 60 percent higher risk of stroke-related death and severe disability. Smoking is another major controllable risk for stroke, as is an increased level of red blood cells, which predispose a person to clot formation. Diabetes increases stroke risk, especially in women, even when blood glucose levels are well controlled. The presence of coronary disease also doubles a person's risk of stroke.

If you have any of the following warning signs of stroke, seek medical attention immediately.

- Sudden weakness or numbness on one side of the body, affecting the face, an arm, or a leg
- Sudden dimming or loss of vision, especially in one eye
- Difficulty talking or understanding speech or total loss of speaking ability
- Sudden, severe headaches that have no apparent cause
- Sudden, unexplained dizziness, unsteadiness, or episodes of falling, especially when accompanied by other stroke symptoms

(Source: *Heart and Stroke Facts* and *Heart and Stroke Facts: 1995 Statistical Supplement,* American Heart Association)

---

the risks can help a person manage blood pressure without the use of drugs. The following ideas will help to reduce some of the threats from high blood pressure.

Get with the program.

The large number of people who don't know they have high blood pressure suggests that failure to diagnose the condition is the biggest obstacle to effective treatment. However, many people refuse to believe they have hypertension, even when blood pressure measurements confirm the existence of the disease. To some extent, the denial is understandable. High blood pressure usually produces no symptoms until the disease has gone untreated for years and has begun to cause damage to the heart and other organ systems. An otherwise healthy person who feels fine may have a hard time accepting the fact that he or she has a potentially life-threatening disease. Effective treatment depends not only on early diagnosis but also on the transition from denial to belief. A true believer gets with the program: regular blood pressure checks, use of medication as prescribed, weight loss, exercise, and any other aspects of treatment that apply to a specific situation.

Pay now or pay later.

Buy a blood-pressure monitor to take measurements at home. Many physicians now recommend the devices, either to help confirm a diagnosis of hypertension or to keep closer track of a patient's blood pressure. At-home monitoring can warn you of a potentially serious increase in blood pressure or help you identify situations or times of the day when blood pressure may be higher or lower. By checking blood pressure at home, you can also reduce the number of visits to your physician's office and save money. The monitor itself costs about $20. Most home monitors are easy to use, but if measuring your own blood pressure makes you nervous, you can let your spouse or a friend or relative do the honors. If possible, take several measurements daily, at least initially, to see how your blood pressure fluctuates during the course of a day. Try to check your pressure at about the same time or times every day.

Take your medicine.

Even if you feel fine, the ravages of high blood pressure continue inside your body. If left untreated, hypertension can cause irreparable damage to blood vessels, the heart, and other organ systems. Antihypertensive drugs often bring blood pressure under control and reduce the risks—but only if you take them faithfully as prescribed. Stopping drug treatment carries the risk of a rebound effect: Blood pressure soars even higher than it was before treatment began. If a certain drug has caused bothersome side effects, don't give up on blood pressure medication altogether: You might be able to switch to an alternative that your system tolerates better.

Take a load off.

Excess weight increases blood pressure for everyone, including those with low and normal readings. Many overweight hypertensive people can substantially lower their blood pressure by losing weight. As a rule of thumb, blood pressure tends to drop two points for each pound of excess weight lost. In a severely hypertensive person, medication combined with weight loss may help bring blood pressure under better control. A person who has only mildly elevated blood pressure might be able to stay off medication altogether simply by losing weight. Mild hypertension, the most common form of high blood pressure,

increases stroke risk threefold. In many cases, the loss of only ten excess pounds can eliminate the added risk.

Exercise regularly.

Exercise affects blood pressure indirectly by promoting weight loss. But physical activity also has a direct effect that's independent of weight. At a minimum, a person should get 20 to 30 minutes of exercise at least three days a week. The U.S. Centers for Disease Control and Prevention and the American College of Sports Medicine recommend that all adults exercise moderately for 30 minutes on "most, preferably all, days of the week." Moderate-intensity exercises include brisk walking, swimming, cycling, calisthenics, and racket sports. Certain activities not normally viewed as exercise can also provide a moderate workout: lawn mowing, gardening, painting, and house-cleaning. The total amount of exercise, rather than the type, appears to be the key factor in staying physically fit.

Severely hypertensive people should postpone exercise until their blood pressure is better controlled. And anyone over age 40 should consult a physician before starting an exercise program.

Aerobic activities, which raise the heart rate, should be the focus of exercise. Anaerobic activities, such as lifting weights and doing push-ups, may be harmful to a person with high blood pressure and should not be performed without consulting a physician.

Say "when" after two.

Heavy alcohol consumption increases the risk of high blood pressure and can worsen existing hypertension. Limit yourself to no more than two drinks daily (including beer, wine, and cocktails) or less if that's what your physician recommends.

Go easy on the salt.

Americans eat too much salt—up to three teaspoonsful per day—and salt intake affects blood pressure in many people. From a nutritional standpoint, less than $\frac{1}{10}$ of a teaspoon of salt daily will meet the body's sodium needs. Besides, individual taste for salt is highly adaptable. Studies have shown that, over time, people who reduce the amount of salt in their diet find that less salt is needed to satisfy their taste for it. Everyone should try to limit salt intake to less than one teaspoonful daily (about 2,400 milligrams). If you have high blood pressure, talk to your physician about the need to aim for an even lower target for salt consumption.

Check the labels.

You control the amount of salt used in food you prepare at home. But what about the processed and prepared foods you buy in grocery stores? Many such foods contain gobs of salt. Even some nonfood items, such as antacids, may be loaded with salt. A word to the wise: Read package labels. Salt content typically is expressed in milligrams of sodium.

DEFINITIONS

○ ○ ○

For years, physicians used terms such as mild, moderate, and severe to describe high blood pressure. In 1993, new government guidelines for diagnosis and treatment of high blood pressure introduced the concept of stages to describe the severity of hypertension. As shown in the table below, the higher reading determines the category, so 160/92 would be stage 2, 180/120 would be stage 4.

Keep in mind that blood pressure consists of two components. Systolic pressure (the first number in a measurement) indicates the pressure inside blood vessels when the heart contracts. Diastolic pressure (the second number) is the pressure when the heart relaxes between beats. The numbers indicate how far a column of mercury (chemical symbol Hg) rises (in millimeters or mm) when exposed to the pressure. For example, a typical reading could be expressed as 140/85 mm Hg.

Category	Systolic	Diastolic
Normal	<130	<85
High normal	130–139	85–89
Hypertension		
Stage 1 (mild)	140–159	90–99
Stage 2 (moderate)	160–179	100–109
Stage 3 (severe)	180–209	110–119
Stage 4		
(very severe)	≥210	≥120

Kick the habit.

Cigarette smoking is arguably the single most harmful influence on blood pressure. Smoking increases the risk of heart disease, heart attack, and stroke, as well as the risk of lung cancer. Nicotine directly affects blood pressure and makes blood more prone to clotting. Clots plug arteries to the heart and brain, and they are the most common causes of heart attack and stroke. For a person who kicks the habit, the cardiovascular threats that are posed by smoking disappear fairly rapidly. Three years after quitting, an ex-smoker has almost the same risk of death from heart attack and stroke as a person who never smoked. If you are a smoker and you want to stop but are unable to, ask your physician for advice. Nicotine gum and patches are available by prescription to ease the stress of nicotine withdrawal. For information on smoking cessation programs in your area, contact your physician, hospital, or local affiliate of the American Heart Association, American Cancer Society, or American Lung Association. (See SMOKING AND TOBACCO USE.)

Peel a banana.

Increased potassium intake has proven useful in managing blood pressure. Bananas constitute one of the best known and most popular sources of dietary potassium. Other good sources of the nutrient include raisins and currants, milk, yogurt, and orange juice. People with normal blood pressure should try to include at least three servings of potassium-rich foods in their daily diets. Those with high blood pressure who are taking diuretics should try for twice that amount. Don't use potassium supplements without first consulting a physician, however, since the supplements can have potentially serious interactions with certain medications.

Drink milk.

At least some people enjoy a modest reduction in blood pressure from increased calcium intake. Milk and yogurt (regular, low-fat, or nonfat) rank at the top of dietary sources of calcium. Leafy green vegetables, especially spinach, also contain substantial amounts of calcium.

Check the fats in your diet.

Substituting polyunsaturated and monounsaturated fats for saturated varieties not only tends to reduce cholesterol levels, it can also help to lower blood pressure. Oils that are high in poly- or monounsaturated fat include canola, olive, and safflower. Some types of fish contain large amounts of omega-3 polyunsaturated fatty acids, which have also been linked with reduced incidence of heart disease in studies of Eskimos. Examples of fish that provide good sources of omega-3 fatty acids include albacore tuna, Atlantic salmon, and mackerel.

Take it easy.

The term *hypertension* refers only to blood pressure, not a person's emotional state. But it happens that many people with high blood pressure experience a great deal of stress. Chronic stress can jolt the body with large doses of adrenaline, which has the ability to constrict small blood vessels. Depending upon individual personality traits, a person with high blood pressure may benefit from training in stress reduction or relaxation techniques. Meditation, biofeedback, yoga, prayer, and other stress-reducing activities have been tried with some success in hypertensive patients.●

HIVES

7 SOOTHING STRATEGIES

Are you turning as red as the lobster you just ate? Does your skin feel the way your clawed friend probably did when it was plunked into that vat of boiling water? Well, that lobster is getting its revenge. You probably have hives, a common scourge that is triggered by certain foods (often shellfish), medicines, insects, you name it. In fact, depending on your immune system, an encounter with just about any type of flora, fauna, chemical, or even plain water or cold weather can trigger an outbreak of these itchy red welts on your skin.

When you encounter something to which you are allergic, skin cells release a substance called histamine. In turn, a buildup of histamine causes plasma to leak from blood vessels into the skin. The resulting welts can be as small as a penny or as big as a dinner plate. Although they usually disappear after a day, sometimes even within a few hours, new welts often continue to form for as long as a month to six weeks after the initial attack.

Hives, in case you haven't guessed, aren't much fun. But here are some things to do to avoid them and to make the ones you do get a little more bearable.

Don't scratch.

Scratching only increases the inflammation that accompanies hives and makes your problem worse.

Play it cool.

Blood vessels shrink in response to cooling, and as a result they release less hive-causing histamine. Apply a compress soaked in cool water or milk, an ice pack, or a bag of frozen peas to the area for about ten minutes, several times a day.

Soak your troubles away.

A soak in a tub of cool-to-tepid water can also help. Throw in some baking soda or oatmeal for extra relief.

Mellow out.

Stress can trigger an outbreak of hives, and stress—such as stewing about the itching—can make the hives you already have even worse. Therefore, when an outbreak occurs, don't let it get to you. Simply relax the best way you can.

Pop an antihistamine.

Over-the-counter oral remedies like Benadryl provide relief because they block the release of hive-triggering histamine.

Check your medicine chest.

If you take drugs regularly, you may be more prone to hives because this malady is often an allergic reaction to medications. Be especially wary of aspirin, because it is a common ingredient in so many over-the-counter medications. Read labels carefully.

Know the other triggers.

Some other common causes of hives are animal dander, certain foods (especially chocolate, nuts, shellfish, and tomatoes), exposure to extreme cold, insect bites, some plants, and household molds. A little knowledge may help you avoid a big nuisance.●

HOT FLASHES

8 TIPS TO COOL OFF

Y ou can feel one coming. Every woman is slightly different, of course. Your hot flashes can be extreme, slight, frequent, only at night, usually during the day, as short as three to five minutes, as long as an hour. They can be a drag on your life for years or gone almost as soon as your menstruation ends. Most women agree, however, that hot flashes don't feel anything like having a fever or being overheated after a fast game of tennis. While the rush of physical and emotional sensations involved is intense, there is nothing pleasant about this nearly universal sign of menopause.

Perhaps your first clue of an impending hot flash is a twinge of anxiety or a split second of dizziness, nausea, or tingling somewhere in your body. The heat definitely comes from within as your skin gets hot and your face and neck redden. If you are in your forties or fifties, if your periods have been arriving irregularly or not at all, then the signs are nothing extraordinary. During a hot flash you experience increased blood flow, a jumping pulse rate, a dramatic rise in skin temperature—up to eight degrees Fahrenheit—a corresponding flush of heat, then perspiration. All of which may be followed by the shivers as your body cools down. If it happens at night, experts call the experience night sweats. Real lethargy can make it difficult to get anything done. If you wake up at night drenched in sweat and in need of dry nightclothes, your lack of sleep can become serious. Headaches, itchy skin, a light-headed lack of equilibrium, sweating, grouchiness, and a red face can make you feel miserable.

Your body is adjusting to the drop in hormones women experience as they go through the menopausal years—from age 40 to 60. Women who have undergone surgery for removal of their ovaries can have intense hot flashes right away because of the sudden shift of hormones. When your system is short of estrogen, the brain's temperature-control center sends messages telling your body to move into cool-down mode, even when you aren't warm at all.

You have lots of tiny blood vessels beneath your skin. When blood vessels dilate, they relax, open up, and fill with blood. This makes your skin warmer, redder, and perhaps even swollen. In contrast, when blood vessels constrict, they narrow and empty. You get colder and paler. For complicated hormonal and biochemical reasons, this process is out of control during a hot flash. The messages being sent by your brain are in response to a hormonal switch and not in sync with the environment around you.

Here are 8 tips to help you cool off.

Ask about hormone therapy.

Most physicians agree that hormone replacement therapy is safe and effective for the majority of women, but not for all women. Many find relief from hot flashes when they take estrogen. Progesterone, the second major female hormone, is given with estrogen to decrease the incidence of endometrial cancer. Available in pills, patches, suppositories, and creams, these hormones can be prescribed to suit your symptoms and medical history. Such therapy isn't advised for every woman, however. If you've had endometrial cancer, breast cancer, stroke, any blood-clotting disorder, abnormal vaginal bleeding, or liver dysfunction, your doctor will advise you not to take hormones.

Track your flashes.

Keep a daily diary. Write down the circumstances surrounding your hot flashes. Knowing that you are in a pattern that repeats itself can help you prepare for the coming rounds.

Dress naturally in layers.

Wear cotton clothes because they let your skin breathe more easily than synthetics. Choose outfits so you can remove layers of clothing if you get hot.

Don't smoke.

Cigarette smoking constricts blood vessels and will intensify hot flashes.

Watch your diet.

Spicy, salty, and sugary foods can bring on hot flashes. Eating too much or drinking alcohol can have a similar effect.

Exercise.

Regular exercise will help your body more easily tolerate extremes of temperature. It also helps circulation and increases the level of estrogen in your blood.

Plan your cooldowns.

Put ice water next to your bed at night or on your desk when at work. Install a fan or an air conditioner and be ready to lower the air temperature.

Learn to relax.

Teach yourself some deep-breathing or meditative techniques to use the next time you have a hot flash. Consider signing up for a yoga course. While it may sound simplistic, relaxation techniques have proven to be clinically effective in shortening the duration of hot flashes and in minimizing the symptoms.

Here are a few helpful relaxation exercises taught by nurses to anxious patients. If you do them regularly before bedtime, you may be able to enjoy a good night's sleep—without interruption by night sweats.

Lie down in a comfortable spot and put one pillow under your head, another under your knees. Pick a quiet, peaceful place. In each of the exercises, you will contract and then relax the same muscle. Your objective is to relieve tension.

Head and Neck. Pull your chin down toward your chest as tightly as possible. Now, push your head back into the pillow. Turn your head from side to side slowly. Let your head rest in a comfortable position.

Shoulders. Shrug your shoulders and tighten the muscles. Hold for a few seconds, then let go.

Arms. Take one arm at a time. Bend your elbow and make a fist. Tighten the muscles. Then relax. Straighten your arm and spread out your fingers. Tighten the muscles, then let them go loose.

Legs. Take one leg at a time. Straighten and point your toe. Tighten. Then let go. Pull your toes back. Tighten and let go. ●

UNDERSTAND FLASHES

○ ○ ○

Most American women experience hot flashes during their menopausal years. However, there are a few reasons your symptoms could be worse than your neighbor's.

- *Are you thin?* The fatty layer just beneath the skin actually continues to produce estrogen after your ovaries have given up on their production of this hormone. The less fat you have, the less estrogen you'll have as you age and go through menopause. Thus, heavy women aren't always as troubled by hot flashes as other women because the drop in their estrogen just isn't as dramatic.

- *Do you sweat easily?* If generating perspiration has never been difficult for you, you may have an easier time dealing with temperature extremes. On the other hand, if you rarely perspire, managing hot flashes could be more challenging for your body.

HYPERVENTILATION

8 WAYS TO BREATHE EASIER

You feel like you're suffocating. Try as you might, you can't inhale enough air to relieve the discomfort. You're dizzy and everything appears blurry. Your heart is beating wildly, and your chest hurts. Is this the end? With symptoms similar to those of a heart attack, hyperventilation can unnerve the most stoic individual.

Despite your worst thoughts, you will recover. In fact, you'll probably be no worse for the wear: Hyperventilation ranks among the most benign of medical conditions.

Rarely a symptom of a serious medical problem (but see sidebar, "Risk Increases with Age"), hyperventilation most often arises from anxiety or fear. Distracted by the emotion of the moment, the victim typically fails to notice the increase in both the number and shallowness of breaths. Occasionally, hyperventilation results from an irregular breathing pattern.

The symptoms evolve from an imbalance of oxygen and carbon dioxide. Fear or anxiety can cause a person to exhale too much carbon dioxide. The body interprets the loss of carbon dioxide as a signal to prepare for action, commonly called a fight or flight response. Adrenaline is released in large quantities. Blood flow decreases to the brain, while the flow increases to muscles that would help a person confront or escape from a threat.

In some instances, hyperventilation may cause a person to lose consciousness. Before the situation progresses that far, give the following a try.

Know your sources of stress.

Make an inventory of the situations, events, people, and other factors that cause stress in your life. Write them down, study them, and decide which ones you can change or get rid of, then act accordingly.

Get organized.

Routines, schedules, and patterns bring organization to your life and help reduce stress. Try to establish realistic schedules for meals, sleep, chores, relaxation, and so on, then stick to your plan.

Distract yourself.

Force yourself to try to think about something other than the source of your stress.

Exercise.

Regular physical activity stimulates production of endorphins, the body's natural pain killers, or tranquilizers. Exercise also helps minimize the impact of stress. Less internalization of stress may lead to fewer episodes of hyperventilation.

Put it in a bag.

The most common remedy for hyperventilation is to breathe into a paper bag (not plastic). The bag captures the carbon dioxide you exhale, allowing you to breathe it back in. Eventually, blood levels of carbon dioxide should return to normal.

Understand the problem.

The knowledge that you're not dying, that you will recover, will help you through a scary bout of hyperventilation. If you have recurrent episodes, make sure your family understands your situation and is supportive.

Try therapy.

Ask your doctor for a referral to a qualified therapist, who will be able to guide you with relaxation techniques and perhaps utilize biofeedback (a system to monitor physical responses to stress).

Say no to stimulants.

Caffeine, nicotine, aspirin, diet pills, and decongestants are just a few of the items that can aggravate anxiety and possibly lead to bouts of hyperventilation. ●

RISK INCREASES WITH AGE

○ ○ ○

Though ordinarily not a symptom of a serious problem, shortness of breath should not be dismissed automatically as nothing more than a response to stress or anxiety. People of any age can experience anxiety or panic attacks, which can be difficult to distinguish from heart attacks. As you grow older, your suspicion of alternatives to hyperventilation should increase. Don't take chances. Let a physician make the diagnosis.

IMPOTENCE

24 WAYS TO COPE

Impotence: It's not a word any man likes to hear. Nor is it a condition that most men like to talk about or, even more so, be forced to cope with. Well, guys, now that the scary word's been uttered, you should face the fact that as you get older, chances are you will have to deal with impotence at least some of the time.

Impotence, the inability to achieve and maintain an erection, is not an inevitable part of aging, but the decreased muscle response and blood flow that come with wisdom and gray hairs do play a part. A lot of age-related ills, such as hypertension, hardening of the arteries, and diabetes, can also take a toll on a certain part of your anatomy, as can chronic pain, depression, and psychological factors like the fear of not being able to perform.

Perhaps the most important thing to know is that impotence doesn't have to bring down the curtain on your sexual performance. The more you know about impotence and the more you talk to your partner and physician about it, the better able you will be to do the right things. Here, as a starter, are some coping strategies to consider.

Keep up an active sex life.

Sexual closeness, whether it's intercourse or other physical expressions of affection, continues to be an integral part of a marriage or other intimate relationship at any age. Don't let impotence prevent you and your partner from partaking of one of life's greatest pleasures. In fact, research shows that remaining sexually active can keep penile tissue in shape, thus helping to prevent impotence.

Adjust to new situations.

The inability to maintain a rigid erection doesn't mean sex must grind to a halt. After all, there's more than one way to skin a cat. For instance, it may be necessary to manually insert the flaccid penis into the vagina or to achieve climax through touch. Sex may be more natural in the morning, because a man is more likely to have an erection after the beneficial effects of a night's sleep. Look at these adjustments not as compromises but as new wrinkles in your sex life.

Brush up on the facts of life.

You learned about the birds and the bees when you were a kid, and now it's time to learn some new facts. The more you know about how aging affects sexual response, the better prepared you'll be to enjoy sex on age-adjusted terms. Knowing in advance that it can take longer to get an erection or that there may be times when you may not be able to get one, for instance, can take the fright out of these situations as they arise.

Overcome performance anxiety.

Feeling anxious about an episode of impotence increases the likelihood that it will happen again. One of the best coping strategies is to simply avoid the situation for a while. If you're nervous about it, don't even try to have vaginal sex. Restrict your bedroom activity to enjoyable sessions of hugging and kissing until it seems comfortable to try again.

Remember, it takes two to tango.

It's difficult to talk about something that makes you feel as vulnerable as impotence does. But your partner has a stake

MEDICAL CAUSES OF IMPOTENCE

○ ○ ○

Some of the most common diseases that accompany aging can have a severe effect on a man's sexual function. These include hardening of the arteries (including the arteries in your penis), hypertension (which can also damage veins and arteries), diabetes (which can damage nerves and blood vessels necessary to achieve and maintain an erection), and Parkinson disease (which affects nerve function).

It's an unfortunate irony that many of the medicines used to treat erection-inhibiting physical conditions also interfere with a man's ability to get an erection. Many hypertension drugs, for instance, affect the nerve centers in the brain that also trigger the blood flow into the penis that's necessary to achieve and maintain an erection. The combination of physical factors and medications can put a big, double-edged crimp in your sex life—which is why it is so important to keep yourself informed about what's going on and to speak to your physician candidly about troubles you may be having with impotence. Alternative medications with fewer erection-inhibiting side effects are sometimes available, as are medical treatments that reverse or help mitigate physical factors that cause impotence.

in this, too, you know. Talk about the problem openly and work out possible solutions together. That feeling of cooperation may be all that's needed to overcome the problem.

Prepare for failure.

And let your partner in on your plans. If impotence is a recurring problem, don't climb into bed every night with high hopes. If you both recognize the fact that you might not be able to achieve an erection, you won't be setting yourselves up for disappointment and hurt feelings. Remember, the more comfortable you feel about the situation, the more likely you are to get an erection.

Relax.

When you're nervous—and that includes fretting about getting an erection—your body pumps out adrenaline, which floods many parts of your body. Unfortunately, your penis isn't one of them. In fact, adrenaline focuses so much energy elsewhere in your body that you may not be able to muster the responses necessary to have an erection. So mellow out. Enjoy your partner's company, let yourself go, ease into the mood, and try to keep your mind off that part of your anatomy.

Deal with depression head on.

Depression is one of the most common diseases of aging. Feelings of sadness and despair can put a damper on your sex life at any age, and as you get older you are likely to encounter personal losses that can lead to depression. Talking about these concerns openly and coping with depression, by seeing a therapist if necessary, can keep them from interfering with a pleasurable sex life. In fact, working through depression with a partner can enhance intimacy.

Don't go to bed angry.

It's hard to engage in happy sexual union if you're angry with your partner or hurt by something she's done. Making more of a regular effort at expressing these feelings as they arise can do a lot to prevent a frost from settling over the bedroom.

Don't let guilt get the best of you.

The failure to get an erection isn't something to feel guilty about, though men and women alike often feel guilty about an inability to perform sexually. Talking about erection problems with your partner openly and coming to grips with the fact that impotence is just a part of life can do a lot to help you overcome those harmful pangs of guilt.

Roll over and get a good night's sleep.

Fatigue is a major contributor to impotence. If you're just too tired to be interested in sex, don't even attempt it. Rest up and kindle amour for another time, when you feel up to it.

Get a little aerobic exercise.

No need to high-step to loud music in a fast-paced aerobics class. Taking a walk or engaging in any other kind of regular exercise that pushes up your heart rate will help keep the blood flowing briskly through your veins—in every part of your body.

Cool down from exercise before getting amorous.

Exercise can increase potency in the long run, but it is worthwhile to note that in the short term blood will be directed to the part of the body being exercised—not where you may want it to concentrate now.

MEDICAL REMEDIES FOR IMPOTENCE

○ ○ ○

The knowledge that there's a physiological cause to your impotence is hardly good news, but there's no reason for it to be devastating news. It is not a pronouncement that your sexual life is over—most forms of impotence can be remedied with devices and techniques that range from surgically implanted prostheses to other, less drastic, measures. New injection techniques, in which a man injects medication into his penis, can overcome many forms of arterial and nerve damage (you can uncross your legs now—it's not nearly as painful as it sounds). In fact, the Food and Drug Administration recently approved a new prescription medication for impotence called alprostadil (Caverject). New microsurgical techniques can help restore blood flow to the penis, and special vacuum devices can be used to draw blood into the penis temporarily. But if you choose to pursue that route, speak to your doctor about getting a medically approved instrument; don't look to advertisements in the back of a men's magazine. And just for the record, any type of homespun medical wizardry is to be avoided like the plague.

Don't cuddle after caffeine.

Coffee is a stimulant, to be sure, but the adrenaline it triggers can direct blood flow away from the penis to other parts of the body. A couple of cups in the morning is probably OK, but if you keep the pot percolating all day long you may not be in Casanova condition when you climb into bed. The same goes for swilling caffeinated soft drinks or cozying up over endless cups of caffeinated tea.

Eat a healthy diet.

You've been hearing this one for years, usually in connection with heart health. Well, high-fat, high-cholesterol foods can clog arteries anywhere in your body, not just the coronary arteries, and proper blood flow through penile arteries is what an erection is all about. It's never too late to change your ways. Eating wisely—getting no more than 30 percent of your daily calories from fat, keeping cholesterol intake to a maximum of 300 milligrams a day—may have a positive effect on your sex life.

Mix your martinis in moderation.

Booze might brazen your sexual bravado, but if you overdo it, you and your partner are in for a big disappointment. Alcohol is a nervous-system depressant, and the more you drink the more difficult it can be to get and maintain an erection.

Don't let your sex life go up in smoke.

Time was it seemed pretty sultry to look at your beloved through a haze of cigarette smoke. Now we know that smoking hardens heart arteries and obstructs blood flow, and, more to the point, it wreaks the same sort of havoc on the arteries in the penis.

Take your time.

As you get older, it takes a little longer to get an erection. Granted, this fact of life can be a little disturbing at first. But it is usually nothing to worry about, just a sign that it takes longer for blood to engorge the penis. In fact, this turn of events can add to the enjoyment of a sexual encounter. Make the most of the extra time to enhance the pleasure—kiss, hug, cuddle, engage in more foreplay.

Spice it up.

Variety is, after all, the spice of life. Trying new positions, making love at different times of the day, popping an adult video into the VCR, or checking into a hotel and ordering a bottle of champagne can recharge your batteries.

Don't strain to overcome pain.

You probably know how pain can take over mind and body and deaden any other sensation—and that includes the pleasurable feelings necessary for adequate sexual response. If you're hurting, leave the loving for another time.

Don't let arthritis put a dent in amour.

It might be full-scale arthritis or just general wear and tear, but painful joint inflammation is one of the most common curses of age. When it strikes, the last thing you want to do is rub your bones against someone else's. Find the right moments and the best situations when a flare-up isn't going to interfere with a pleasurable amorous encounter. Arthritis and other joint pain are likely to peak in the evening, after a day's exertion, so mornings might be a better time for lovemaking. Soaking in a bath might do a lot to lessen pain and get your mind on other things.

Improve your body image.

It's fine when the poets pipe of love being a soulful experience, but sex is also largely a physical activity. Accordingly, anything you do to make yourself feel good about your body can spruce up your sex life. Lose a few pounds, start an exercise regimen, take up yoga—as your body awareness increases, your sexual response might improve, too.

Beware of gimmicks.

Despite centuries of searching, humankind has yet to find a magic love potion. What we have come up with are a lot of gimmicks that don't work and can even be harmful. So give the Spanish fly and virility stimulants a pass. Plenty of safe, medically proven options are available. Talk to your physician and see the sidebar, "Medical Remedies for Impotence."

Talk about therapy.

If impotence is a big issue between you and your partner, it might be time to seek counseling. Your physician may be able to refer you to a qualified therapist, and large university hospitals often have sexuality clinics. Two shopping tips: Find a therapist who is experienced in dealing with impotence problems among couples your age, and make sure you are comfortable with your therapist—talking about impotence can be difficult.●

INCONTINENCE

16 WAYS TO END THE EMBARRASSMENT

This is an awkward subject for those who are affected. You understood that your body might change as you grew older, and you anticipated developments like graying hair, but you never figured on anything as embarrassing as urinary incontinence disrupting your life. (See sidebar, "When Your Bowels Bother You.") In fact, the very idea of wetting your pants in public—not to mention the reality—has become nightmarish. Do you dread simple physical acts—such as laughing too hard, sneezing, coughing, lifting, or jumping up too quickly from a chair—because urine is likely to leak out? Are you unnerved by the prospect of traveling in a car or train because you won't be close to a bathroom?

Don't worry. Loss of control over your bladder or, less frequently, your bowels, is not a curse you must endure silently. You don't have to closet yourself in a safe place so accidents won't ever happen. Actually, incontinence is not a disease in itself but rather a symptom. And incontinence is certainly not an inevitable part of aging.

Women are more likely to experience urine leakage than men for several reasons. The urethra, the tube leading away from the bladder, is much shorter in a woman than in a man. Childbearing can wreak havoc on pelvic muscles. You also may have lost critical muscle tissue if you recently experienced menopause. Experts say that this reduction in muscle mass is greatest in the first three years after your last period. In addition, the hormone, estrogen, helps the sphincter muscle (located at the base of the bladder) to do its job. Thus, when a woman's hormone levels drop, so does her ability to hold urine. Surgery, infections, medications, diabetes, problems with the uterus, and stress can also lead to incontinence.

Nor are men immune to this ailment. If you have prostate troubles or have undergone a prostatectomy (removal of the prostate), your bladder's efficiency can be impaired. For instance, an enlarged prostate gland can affect your physical ability to sense when you need to go to the bathroom.

Here are some ideas to help end the embarrassment.

Start a diary.

Not everyone suffers from the same type of incontinence, so discovering your particular problem is key. You may have stress incontinence. Do you wet yourself when you are exercising or sneezing or in response to some kind of physical movement? You could have urge incontinence. Are you struck with a sudden urge to urinate but can't always make it to the bathroom in time? Overflow incontinence means that your bladder is filled to the point of overflowing and thus is more likely to leak. Perhaps you are unable to sense the problem due to an enlarged prostate or other medical complication.

Keeping an accurate record for up to a week of occasions when you experience incontinence will help you learn to control it. Help for Incontinent People (HIP) is a nonprofit group that suggests making a written record each time you urinate—both on the toilet and accidentally—and noting the circumstances leading up to it. Include what you eat as well as what you drink. Keep track of activities you were engaged in, whether you experienced an urge to urinate, the amount of urine, and the amount of leakage, if any. Any other details that seem important should be jotted down, including medications.

Watch your fluids.

If you are drinking loads of water for another condition, you could be causing bouts of incontinence. Your diary will give you clues about dietary factors. However, don't give up water completely. Some people erroneously believe that if they don't drink anything at all, they won't have to urinate. Unfortunately, too little fluid can lead to dehydration, and dehydration can lead to constipation. When you get constipated, your urinary tract nerves can become inflamed: You might end up with the very incontinence you were trying to avoid. Therefore, think before you take a drink.

Sip throughout the day so your bladder never becomes overly full nor empty for very long. Slow up in the evening hours so your sleep isn't interrupted by rushed trips to the toilet. Aim for a fluid intake of six to eight cups a day.

Go often.

Your bladder will become irritated if you wait until the last minute to go. Be sure to get to a bathroom every two to three hours even if you don't have an overwhelming urge to void. Try anyway.

Go twice in a row.

Practice emptying your bladder. Women should practice standing up and then sitting down on the toilet once more to try again. Lean forward the second time to put pressure on the bladder while you squeeze to empty it completely.

Stay away from known irritants.

Some beverages are always going to be bad news because they are known to be diuretics. For instance, the caffeine in coffee could trigger your leakage. Experts believe that even decaffeinated coffee can cause problems. Grapefruit and tomato juices, tea, and carbonated sodas should be avoided, along with alcoholic drinks.

Drink these juices.

Cranberry, grape, cherry, apple, and orange juices will help quench your thirst and won't aggravate your condition. Orange juice, in particular, is metabolized by your body and turns into a more alkaline, less acidic, substance before it reaches the bladder. Hospital studies of cranberry juice have led experts to suspect that up to four eight-ounce glasses a day can actually help people suffering from urgent or too-frequent urination.

Don't smoke.

For one thing, the nicotine in cigarettes irritates the bladder. For another, the coughing spells that often accompany smoking mean trouble for those with incontinence.

Eat smart.

Your diary will offer the best information as to which foods irritate you the most. In addition, cut back on hot, spicy dishes and tomato-based entrées. Certain sugars can cause problems, too: Stay away from honey, corn syrup, and chocolate. Then watch for improvement.

Add fiber.

To help your digestive system and to take potential pressure off your urinary tract, make sure you get enough fiber in your diet each day. Check with your doctor first, of course, if you plan to adjust your eating habits in any drastic way. Here are foods that are high in fiber content: almonds, apricots, beans, blackberries, bran, brussels sprouts, coconut, corn, dates, and figs. Other possibilities include kiwi, lentils, parsley, peaches, pears, pineapple, pistachio nuts, popcorn, prunes, raspberries, strawberries, walnuts, and whole-grain products. You could end up feeling bloated and gassy if you jump into a high-fiber diet too quickly. Make the transition gradually.

Slim down.

If you are overweight, you put extra pressure on all your muscles, including the ones needed to urinate. Be sure to check with your doctor before dieting.

Be prepared.

If you know when, where, and why you experience incontinence, plan ahead. For instance, go to the bathroom immediately before you head for a walk in the park or to an exercise class. Shop for adult protection at the drug store in the form of panty liners, inserts, shields, or disposable pads.

Do Kegel exercises.

You can regain muscle power in your pelvic area by doing special exercises designed about 50 years ago by Arnold Kegel, M.D. If you are a woman, you can locate pelvic muscles by stopping the flow of urine midstream. Later, after you have finished urinating, tighten this ring of muscles and then relax. Don't tense up your buttocks or thighs. If you are a man, try imagining that you are holding back a bowel movement. You use the sphincter muscles circling the anus to do this. These are the same muscles that can help you to control incontinence. Practice tightening while counting slowly to four and then relaxing for a second count of four. Continue for about two minutes.

WHEN YOUR BOWELS BOTHER YOU

o o o

Not all kinds of incontinence are bladder-related. Occasionally, incontinence refers to loss of bowel control. Any disease that causes severe and regular diarrhea can bring on fecal incontinence, especially in elderly patients. Multiple sclerosis, spinal cord injuries, Alzheimer disease, diabetes, tears in the sphincter muscle, and surgical complications could all be factors, too. Your bowels could be irritated and inflamed because of blockage. When this happens, you are more likely to lose control and allow small pieces of feces to be released. Don't be embarrassed about speaking with your doctor. Therapy, diet adjustments, medication, enemas, and regular exercise can aid you.

Schedule three Kegel exercise sessions a day, repeating the contract-relax regimen 100 times.

Don't rush.

Racing to the bathroom in anxiety turns out to be a trigger for disaster. You put pressure on your bladder when you rush. Instead, when you experience the urge to go, relax, tighten your sphincter muscle, and use your pelvic muscles to hold your urine while you walk very slowly.

Put your "pelvics" to work.

As you tighten and build strength in your pelvic area with exercise, anticipate leakage by contracting those muscles whenever you need to sneeze, cough, jump, or perhaps even lift something.

Check into hormone therapy.

Estrogen can become a lifeline for women during the menopausal years. Bladder problems send many women over 50 to their gynecologist, so don't be shy about raising any questions you might have about hormone replacement therapy. Your urinary and genital tract membranes are thinning, and as they lose elasticity, this urgent need to urinate becomes quite common. Estrogen creams, suppositories, patches, or pills could ease your incontinence.

Call for help.

Dial 800-BLADDER and ask the experts at Help for Incontinent People (HIP) to send you the free package of pamphlets offering information about incontinence as well as services and products.●

INGROWN TOENAILS

9 WAYS TO NAIL THEM

So, what's the big deal? It's just an ingrown toenail, right? Well, if you're the one suffering from this common complaint, you know all too well that an ingrown toenail can be awfully uncomfortable. While not necessarily a serious problem under normal circumstances, for anyone with diabetes or other circulation problems, an ingrown toenail can lead to a major infection and some very serious problems indeed.

An ingrown toenail is simply an errant toenail that has decided to grow into the flesh surrounding the nail. With each millimeter of growth, the nail pushes deeper into the skin, causing pain that makes walking, wearing shoes, or just lounging around sheer agony. Fortunately, there's a lot you can do to prevent and treat ingrown toenails.

Go soak your feet.

If you are bothered by irritation from an ingrown toenail, consider a good soak. Fill a basin with enough warm water to immerse your feet. This practice should relieve your soreness and help to bring down any inflammation. Make this a routine by setting aside time for one ten-minute soak in the morning and a second in the evening. You can't overdo this treatment—it's fine to soak as often as you feel the need for some relief.

Get out the cotton pads.

After a good soak, insert a thin sliver of sterile cotton beneath the nail where it is burrowing into your skin. This way, you'll gently lift the nail and prevent it from becoming ingrown.

Let it breathe.

Fresh air, and plenty of it, is what your ingrown toenail needs to heal. And fresh air is one thing your nail won't get in the tight, damp environment inside socks and shoes. Instead, wear open-toed shoes or sandals whenever you can.

Get it straight.

Your first line of defense against ingrown toenails is cutting them properly. Jagged or rough nails are hot spots on your toes—these uneven edges can grow into the surrounding flesh. Begin a pedicure session by soaking your toes for five minutes or so in warm water. This will soften the nails, making them easier to cut and helping to prevent splitting. Then, using a sharp cutter, trim the nails straight across so there will be no curved ends to grow into the surrounding skin. Be especially careful not to leave any sharp edges that can pierce the skin as the nail begins to grow out.

File those ends.

After you've cut the nail straight across, take out a file or pumice stone and blunt both corners of the nail. This way, you'll eliminate the sharp surfaces in the corners that can cut into the surrounding flesh.

Protect your nails.

If you stub your toes or injure them in other ways, you may cause injuries that promote ingrown toenails. Be careful when walking barefoot, and always wear shoes with adequate toe protection when exercising, doing heavy work, or engaging in other activities, such as gardening, that put your toes at risk.

Choose your footwear carefully.

Your toenails demand one thing from a shoe—a roomy toe. If there's not enough room to move around down there, your toenail may decide to grow in the only direction it has to move, and that's into the surrounding flesh. Choose shoes, socks, and panty hose that don't pinch the toes. Women should be especially careful about high heels.

Spread on the ointments.

Products are available over the counter in drugstores that are specifically designed to relieve pain, and they do help to soften the skin around an ingrown nail and ease the discomfort. If the skin around an ingrown toenail is red, inflamed, and painful, however, it may be infected—which means it's time to see a doctor.

Beware of infection.

An infection can lead to very serious complications, including the loss of a toe. People with diabetes and those suffering from circulation problems are at special risk because the lack of circulation in an infected toe can lead to gangrene. What's more, if you suffer from poor circulation, you may not notice the pain associated with infection. That's why anyone who suffers from circulation problems should be particularly watchful and see a doctor at the first sign of an ingrown nail.●

INSOMNIA

21 WAYS TO MANAGE A GOOD NIGHT'S SLEEP

If you walk a hole in the carpet at night when you should be sleeping, or find yourself dozing during the day, you are probably among the almost 75 million Americans who live with disturbed sleep. And it's more than an inconvenience: As just one example of the consequences of not getting a good night's sleep, some 20 percent of drivers say they have nodded off at the wheel at one time or another. Sleep is a complex activity and researchers continue to learn more about the unique role certain stages of sleep play in maintaining health and functioning.

As you sleep, you actually pass through two major sleep phases: rapid-eye-movement (REM) sleep and non-REM, or quiet, sleep. You enter non-REM sleep as you begin to nod off, then progress through four stages. In the first stage of non-REM sleep, you begin to make the transition from being awake to drowsiness and light sleep. In stage two—actually, you spend about half the night in this stage—your heart rate begins to slow down and you don't breathe as rapidly. In stages three and four, brain waves slow down for deep sleep. Stage four is the deepest sleep, and although you slip into it for only brief, half-hour stretches throughout the night, stage four accounts for about one-fifth of total sleep time and provides the greatest rest. Not only does stage four sleep restore your energy and refresh you mentally, but this is believed to be the stage in which the immune system is activated to help the body ward off infection.

You enter REM sleep four or five times a night, but you only spend about one and one-half hours of your total sleeping time in this stage. An awful lot of activity occurs during REM sleep: Your heart beats away at the same levels it does when you're up and moving about, thoughts come and go, and your eyes move around as if your eyelids were wide open and your eyes were following a moving object. Dreaming occurs during REM sleep, restoring the mind and probably enhancing learning and memory.

As well-defined as the levels and stages are, we don't necessarily move through them in a logical progression. Instead, we alternate between REM and non-REM sleep, and sleep patterns vary widely from individual to individual. There are, however, some common patterns that seem to depend on age. In a young adult, most deep sleep occurs during the first half of the night, and periods of REM sleep get longer in the second half. By the time you reach middle age, you are likely to wake up more frequently during the night (often after only a few hours of sleep) and get less deep sleep and more light sleep. Women going through menopause awaken frequently due to hot flashes. After age 65, it takes longer to fall asleep, and it's more common to wake up frequently during the night. You don't actually lose sleep, though, and the notion that older people require less total sleep is a myth. Usually, you manage to catch up through napping and sleep the same total number of hours as someone younger.

Here are some suggestions that may help you manage a better night's sleep.

Cut back on caffeine.

Caffeine may make it tough for you to fall asleep, and once you do, your sleep may be shorter and lighter. For most people, avoiding caffeine for about six hours before bedtime is probably enough to nullify its effect on sleep.

Give up tobacco.

The nicotine in tobacco stimulates your central nervous system, making it harder to fall asleep. A smoker can also be awakened at night by withdrawal symptoms.

Drink alcohol in moderation.

Sure, a stiff drink will help you fall asleep. But chances are you'll find it difficult to stay asleep, and the sleep that you do get is likely to be lighter (alcohol suppresses REM sleep) and broken into shorter periods. Add in the fact that alcohol relaxes your nasal passages and throat, making it more likely that you're going to snore like a buzz saw. Maybe it's best to skip that nightcap.

Become active.

Use your muscles during the day and they'll relax more fully at night. That's why sedentary people are more likely to have insomnia than active people.

Exercise.

Work out more if you want to increase your amount of deep sleep. However, an evening workout can elevate your heart rate, increase your alertness levels, and in other ways keep you from falling asleep. Therefore, it's a good idea to not exercise during the five- to six-hour period before bedtime.

Get set for sleep.

Think about your bedroom: It should be soothing, quiet, not too bright, not too hot. It should be a place to sleep, to make love, to relax—and that's it. Get rid of the television set, the computer, even the telephone. For a better night's sleep, do everything you can to make your bedroom a retreat from the world.

MEDICAL PROBLEMS AND SLEEP

○ ○ ○

There are several medical conditions that may cause sleeping problems. And even though you are getting enough sleep, you may still feel very tired because of an illness. Some possible problems are listed below. Be sure to check with your physician if you believe you may be affected by any of them.

- Cardiovascular disease may cause extra body fluid to settle in your lungs, and as a result you may feel a shortness of breath when you lie down. Medication or supplementary oxygen can remedy the problem.

- Diabetes can disrupt sleep with night sweats and the need to urinate frequently. These problems are less likely to occur if you keep your blood-sugar levels in control.

- Heartburn, caused by stomach acid backing up into the esophagus, is provoked by heavy and fatty meals eaten too close to bedtime.

- Anxiety, depression, stress, and an intense state of worrying may easily exacerbate sleeping problems. If these problems bother you, see your physician before the situation gets out of control.

- Arthritis, with its accompanying musculoskeletal pain, can make it hard to find a comfortable position for sleeping. A sound night's sleep appears to be associated with less joint discomfort and more energy. Moreover, some medication, such as corticosteroids, may also contribute to insomnia. If you are sleeping poorly, tell your doctor. It may be necessary to adjust your arthritis medicines.

Slumber on schedule.

Maintain a regular sleeping schedule. Go to bed at the same time every night, and get up at the same time every morning, even on weekends and no matter how tired you feel after a sleepless night. By holding to a consistent schedule, eventually you'll be able to readjust to the 24-hour sleep-wake cycle.

Nibble.

Have a light snack if you're hungry before bed, but don't consume a heavy meal. Avoid the extremes: Don't go to bed hungry or too full.

Take a warm bath before hitting the hay.

And keep it a warm bath—not too hot, which can be invigorating, and not a shower, which may perk you right up.

Maintain the right weight.

Research shows that if you're overweight you are more likely to have breathing problems in the night, and that is almost guaranteed to keep you awake.

Go to bed when sleepy.

You're on the couch. You're feeling very sleepy. You know you should get up, brush your teeth, and go to bed. But it's so comfy stretched out on the couch watching TV. "I'll just doze off here," you say. Don't do it. When you feel sleepy, go to bed. If you find you can't sleep, get up, leave the bedroom, stay up until you're sleepy, then go back to bed.

Learn to relax.

It may be that your worst enemy is a busy and worried mind. Learn some basic relaxation techniques to help you unwind and make it easier to leave your worries behind you.

Check the light.

Light in the bedroom is a major problem for some people. If you're one of them, try installing heavier draperies, shutters, darker blinds, or some other window treatment that will do a better job of keeping out the light. A less expensive alternative is simply to don a pair of eye covers.

Squelch the noise.

Earplugs can effectively provide exactly the quiet environment you need to sleep. They can be uncomfortable, however, and you may have to try several different kinds until you find the ones that are right for you. As an alternative, some people prefer a "white noise" device that gives off a lulling sound to cover up disturbing noises.

Set the bed.

Find out what sort of pillow and mattress suit you best. If you prefer a hard mattress, chances are you're going to have trouble falling asleep on one that's soft and lumpy.

Be cool.

Good ventilation and comfortable temperatures are important for a good night's sleep. Also make sure that your night clothes are comfortable and not too confining.

MEDICATIONS AND SLEEP

ooo

It isn't unusual that drugs taken to deal with medical problems turn out to be more responsible for your sleepless nights than the problems themselves.

- Amphetamines, for instance, are powerful stimulants that may increase your wakefulness and hinder your ability to fall asleep.

- Medications to treat heart arrhythmias may also cause sleeping difficulties.

- Antidepressants such as fluoxetine (Prozac) and protriptyline (Vivactil) can disrupt sleep.

- If you take antihistamines for allergies or colds and feel drowsy during the day, ask your pharmacist or physician to recommend an alternative medication.

- Beta blockers for high blood pressure, angina, and irregular heartbeat (arrhythmia) can also promote insomnia.

- Corticosteroids such as prednisone, which is used to treat a variety of disorders, can cause jitters in the daytime and insomnia at night.

- Diuretics taken to rid the body of excess sodium and water can interrupt your sleep because you are likely to awaken during the night to urinate.

- Caffeine isn't limited to coffee, tea, and soft drinks. Many over-the-counter and prescription drugs contain caffeine. Study the labels.

Write it down.

Write down your major daily activities (meals, stressful events) in a journal. Then log the number of hours you sleep and how many times you get up during the night. See if any connection appears between those activities and your ability to sleep, and make changes accordingly.

Don't lose sleep to jet lag.

Drink lots of fluid on the plane, but leave out the caffeine and alcohol. If it's a brief trip, keep to your home schedule and make appointments for periods when you would be alert at home. If you're taking a longer trip, start adjusting your schedule to the new time a few days before you leave, and don't go to bed until bedtime in the new time zone.

Get counseling.

Insomnia that lasts more than seven days, accompanied by difficulty staying awake, can be a sign of a problem, not to mention a major inconvenience. See a physician to rule out any underlying medical conditions, and consider seeing a therapist if the problem persists.

Nix the pills.

Avoid the habitual use of sleep medications. Small amounts can help in a crisis, but you want to avoid relying on them for too long. If you do take sleeping pills, to minimize the risks and maximize the benefit, use them only for a relatively short period. Taken over the long term, sleeping pills may have serious side effects, including depression, disorientation, and confusion. Be mindful of problems brought on by combining sleep medications with other drugs you may be taking.

Understand the myths.

You won't be able to perform after a sleepless night. One night without sleep isn't going to have that much of an effect on your activities the following day unless it's driving a vehicle or operating machinery. In those cases you should exercise caution.

You need eight hours of sleep. Not so for everyone. You may need nine hours of sleep while your spouse can get along just fine with only six. Sleeping longer than the body requires increases the amount of time spent in very light sleep, and that may make you feel groggy when you wake up.●

WARNING!
・・・
Hold off on the Melatonin

Melatonin is a hormone, available in health food stores, that is supposed to promote sleep and limit jet lag. At night or in the dark your melatonin production rises, then lessens during the day. As you get older you seem to produce less of it, and jet travel appears to interfere with its production. Researchers are currently studying melatonin, and the consensus is that treatment should not be undertaken until more is known. Human hormones are powerful substances and often result in negative side effects during long-term use.

IRRITABLE BOWEL SYNDROME

14 WAYS TO CARE FOR IBS

Diarrhea, constipation, abdominal pain, indigestion, bloating, cramping, and embarrassing bouts of gas are symptoms you know well if you have irritable bowel syndrome (IBS). In fact, the term *irritable* is probably too tame to describe this ailment, which can easily make your life miserable. Sometimes known as spastic colon or spastic colitis, IBS is probably one of the most common reasons people throughout the United States go to their doctors. You are certainly not alone in your discomfort. Fortunately, IBS is an ailment that you can do something about on your own.

Your intestines and colon are overreacting to a variety of factors. Everything from the food you eat to the stress of your working life could be causing bouts of IBS. Normally, the food you eat is pushed along through your intestines by waves of regular muscle contractions. If you have IBS, those muscular waves aren't coordinated or regular at all. Going to the bathroom to empty your bowels becomes nightmarish because there is no predicting when your urge to go will occur. Symptoms vary from case to case. More women than men have IBS, but if you've never had twinges of this disorder before in your early adult life, you probably won't get it now that you are past 50. For those who have it, try these methods to trick your bowels into behaving better.

Watch what you eat.

Buy a little spiral-bound notepad and start keeping a record of what you eat. Not everyone with IBS is adversely affected by the same foods, so your doctor can't prescribe a diet that will help without your input. Take a look at the types of foods that seem to aggravate digestive and intestinal tracts in the following remedy. Then start eliminating the potential culprits one by one. This will help you narrow down the ranks of likely offenders.

Check your reaction.

Not all people who suffer from irritable bowel syndrome react to the same diet in the same manner, though some foods seem to bother a great many people. Look out for:

- Dairy products: A physician can test you to see if you are intolerant of lactose, the sugar contained in milk products.

- Spicy foods: You could be sensitive to peppers and other hot stuff.

- Wheat products: Start reading labels. Wheat can turn up in odd places; this could be the culprit you need to avoid.

- Citrus fruits: Oranges and tangerines set off symptoms in some people.

- Sugar: You may be reacting to fructose, a kind of sugar included in many foods, not just fruits.

- Chocolate: Chocolate is high in sugar, fat, and caffeine.

- Gas formers: broccoli, brussels sprouts, cabbage, cauliflower, chives, dried beans, garlic, melons, onions, radishes, and rutabaga are among the gas formers. Also avoid barbecued meats, chili, hot dogs, lasagna, luncheon meats, ravioli, sauerkraut, sausages, and spaghetti with meat sauce. These

are more of the many foods that can cause gas, according to experts. (Tip: Soak beans before you cook them and change the water used for soaking several times. You will eliminate the starch that your body finds difficult to digest. Then, cook them slowly.)

Get serious about stress.

In some cases, emotional stress is directly linked to acute bouts of IBS. Think back to the last time your bowels acted up. Did you experience something stressful beforehand? If so, take steps to learn how to handle your life's ups and downs with ease. Sign up for a yoga course at your local YMCA or community center. Buy a book on relaxation techniques. Use visual imagery by recalling the most pleasant experiences of your life: a day at the beach, a visit with family or grandchildren, a sunny day in your garden. The next time something sends you into a panic, take a deep breath, close your eyes, and relax. Just two minutes of deep, slow breathing can interrupt your stress response. Put on soft music. Turn off the radio or news broadcast if you know the talk will only upset you. Keep a book of poetry or jokes at your desk to make you smile or laugh when the going gets tough.

Exercise moderately every day.

Your digestive system will work much more effectively if you move your muscles. Not only will the muscles in your intestinal walls have a better chance of getting in sync, but exercise has been known to release endorphins, hormones that are known to control pain. Don't go crazy, however. Long-distance runners who push themselves beyond reasonable limits have been reported to suffer from IBS. But when women between ages 56 and 87 were put on a regular walk-jog routine that also included light stretching and calisthenics, muscular signs of nervous tension diminished in just six weeks. That same kind of nervous tension could be making your bowels act up.

Add fiber.

Increasing fiber intake is one of the more effective ways to combat IBS symptoms. Fruits, vegetables, oat bran, and cooked beans and peas are essential to better bowel function. Be careful about adding too much bran too fast, however. Give your body time to adjust to any change in diet, especially bran foods, which can end up giving you more gas than you may already have.

Go for pectin.

Cooked grains like rice and barley contain pectin, which may be able to absorb the bad bacteria and help the good kind grow in your system. Sip some of the water used to cook the rice or barley as well. Bananas are also good sources of pectin, as are carrots. One old-fashioned remedy for diarrhea calls for eating mashed, cooked carrots. If you don't want to go to all that trouble, buy strained carrots in the baby-food section of your grocery store.

Eat yogurt.

Natural, unsweetened yogurt that contains "active cultures" can help restore the bacterial balance in your digestive and intestinal tract. Even people with lactose intolerance can handle such yogurt. For more information about lactose intolerance, check with your doctor (also see LACTOSE INTOLERANCE).

Drink.

All adults should try to consume at least eight 8-ounce glasses of cool water every day for general health and to help keep their bowels hydrated.

Don't drink.

Beer, red wine, and too much alcohol can cause diarrhea.

Cut caffeine.

Coffee, tea, and sodas with caffeine will stimulate your gastrointestinal system.

Eat slowly.

Racing through a meal will put your entire digestive system under stress. Slow up, eat smaller meals, and chew thoroughly. Dine, don't gobble.

Give up smoking.

Cigarettes definitely affect your digestive system. You don't need them.

Give up gum.

Sorbitol, one of the main ingredients in artificially sweetened chewing gum and some candies, can cause diarrhea.

Try peppermint.

Fresh peppermint leaves as well as peppermint oil or extract used to make a tea

drink could help control diarrhea, intestinal cramping, and indigestion. If your IBS acts up when you travel, remember to pack peppermint tea bags or carry a little vial of peppermint oil. First check with your doctor or pharmacist to make sure that this herbal remedy doesn't interfere with any of your current medications.●

ITCHING

11 STEPS TO SOOTHE ITCHY SKIN

Got an itch? Just thinking about this annoying sensation is enough to set off a bout of itchiness. Lay the blame on the thousands of nerve endings that lie beneath the surface of your skin all over your body. It doesn't take much to get them feeling fidgety. Itching, especially as you get a little older and your skin produces fewer soothing oils, is often the result of dry skin or dermatitis and eczema. Itching also frequently results from an allergic reaction to the flora and fauna that share our space—to an insect bite, for instance, or to a brush with poison oak or poison ivy.

Well, take heart. Whatever is causing your itch, relief is usually close at hand.

Try a cool compress.

It doesn't really matter whether it's an insect bite or extremely dry skin or something else causing an itch—applying a compress soaked in cool water can take the heat out of irritated nerve endings. Using a cool compress will also help to reduce any swelling.

Go for the bigger chill.

An ice pack is another tool to have at hand when itching gets the best of you. Simply put a few ice cubes in a towel and hold it over the area for a few minutes. A bag of frozen peas that is loosened so it becomes pliable can also be placed over the site of the itching. This alternative is handy and works well for cooling.

Calm with calamine.

It comes in the form of ointments, lotions, and powders, and the zinc oxide and ferrous oxide it contains cool irritated skin and relieve itching. Calamine soothes the itchiness that accompanies dermatitis and eczema, insect bites, poison ivy, sunburn, and other itch-provoking conditions.

Baste with baking soda.

It can soothe the irritation when the venom of an insect or the chemicals of poison ivy and poison oak get under your skin. Mix baking soda with a little water and apply it to the affected area.

Get creamed.

Ointments and creams containing cortisone (available in lower strengths over the counter at drugstores) help relieve the itching associated with allergic reactions—from insect bites or run-ins with poison ivy, for instance. Don't overuse these creams, though, because repeated use can thin the skin.

Wear no wool.

It doesn't really matter what's actually causing your itch. It just happens that wool, more than any other fabric, is going to feel scratchy.

Don't sweat.

Perspiration can irritate an already inflamed patch of itchy skin. You won't be able to staunch the flow of sweat entirely when the weather is warm, but having an itch is good reason to lay off strenuous activity for a spell.

Play some mind games.

Once nerve endings decide to go into itch mode, it's hard to wrap your mind around anything else. So do your best to take your mind off it—throw yourself into your work or a hobby or try some other diverting activity.

Go ahead and scratch, but be gentle.

If the preceding steps don't help, it's OK to scratch lightly. If you scratch too hard, you might irritate and even break the skin; that would leave it open to bacterial infection.

Take an oral antihistamine.

This group of drugs helps counteract itching caused by allergic reactions. Antihistamines block the release of histamine, a chemical released in reaction to an encounter with a foreign substance, and prevent it from affecting nerve fibers and triggering an itch. They can help to relieve the itchiness associated with irritants such as hay fever, insect bites, and reactions to poison ivy.

Check your medications.

If you have an itch and just don't know what's causing it, check with your doctor. Also consider your medications. If you've just started a new prescription, your itchiness could be a reaction to it. Better yet, make an inventory of all your medications, including what you've acquired by prescription as well as over the counter. Keep it up to date, and have your physician or pharmacist check it periodically.●

KIDNEY STONES

8 WAYS TO STOP THEM

The pain is legendary. No one ever plagued by kidney stones could ever forget it. Not only can your lower abdomen be in agony, but sharp, unrelenting pain in your back and also at your side near your waistline can be so excruciating that you are literally doubled over. Kidney stone symptoms can leave you gasping for breath and praying for relief.

Why you? Experts don't really know precisely why. What they do know is that kidney stones are tiny, hard deposits of salt and minerals that form in the kidney ducts and end up in the tube leading from the ducts to the bladder. Your doctor will do an analysis to figure out what your stone is composed of. A genetic predisposition may be a factor, so if someone else in your family has kidney stones, you have a higher chance of developing them than the average individual. More men than women get stones, and first-time victims are usually between 30 and 40 years old. Unfortunately, once you've experienced an attack of kidney stones, it's more likely to occur a second time. After a first stone appears, you have a 10 percent chance of getting one again within a year and an 80 percent chance of ending up with a new stone within 15 years. If you have reached the age of 50 without a case of this kidney ailment, you may be home free. Prescription medication can help prevent them from forming, but it still pays to practice a little preventive medicine. Here are a few ideas that could help keep stones away.

Drink lots of water.

Water will dilute your urine and can help interrupt the formation of crystals that turn into stones. Aim for two or even three quarts of liquids a day. If you can't stomach that much plain water, turn to juices and sodas. But don't drink a lot of milk: You are trying to cut down on your calcium intake.

Measure your flow.

If you find it difficult to remember exactly how much fluid you drink each day, try testing your urine flow. In fact, output of urine is always a better gauge of fluid in your system than input. Keep an empty plastic container with marked measurements in the bathroom you use most frequently. Experts insist that you should be reaching at least two quarts a day in order to keep stones away. Sometimes sweating can steal fluids from your system. That's why you may need to increase your fluid intake in hot weather or after periods of heavy exercise. Once you become accustomed to what your body

needs in order to produce at least two quarts, you can set aside your bathroom measuring routine.

Stay away from milk products.

A doctor should do a chemical analysis of any stone your body has formed in order to determine exactly how to treat you. However, calcium is often a major factor in stone formation. You may hear the terms *calcium oxalate* or *calcium phosphate* mentioned in your case. If either of these diagnoses turns up, avoid excess calcium. Restrict milk products such as butter, cheese, cream, ice cream, and milk. Speak with your doctor about any long-term dietary restrictions you impose on yourself. The failure to take in enough calcium over a period of time could force your body into an unhealthy chemical state.

Check the medicine cabinet.

If you've been taking antacids to treat stomach upsets or heartburn, you may be upping your calcium intake without even realizing it. Some common antacids are high in calcium, so check the ingredients listed on the container. If you find that your antacid is an offender, stop taking that particular brand and look for one that is not calcium-based.

Watch your protein.

Studies have shown that people with kidney stones tend to eat too much animal protein. Experts are still debating the exact nature of the relationship between diet and the body's tendency to form stones, but cutting down on meats, poultry dishes, and even fish could help. Don't cut out protein completely, however: Too little animal protein could be more harmful than too much.

Be picky when you pick fruits and vegetables.

Not all fruits and vegetables are created equal if you've suffered with a stone. Stick with dark-green, yellow, and orange vegetables like broccoli, carrots, pumpkins, and sweet potatoes, which are high in vitamin A. Cranberries, including cranberry juice, are reputed to prevent problems in the urinary tract. The medical jury is still out on the exact nature of the cranberry-juice connection, but this fruit can certainly help the acidic balance in your body and it won't hurt you. If your urine is highly acidic, it's supposed to be less hospitable to bacteria.

Steer clear of what are considered to be oxalate-rich foods, especially during an acute stone episode. Oxalates include celery, citrus fruits, grapes, green peppers, parsley, rhubarb, and spinach. Be cautious about drinking cola and tea, and cross chocolate off your snack list, too.

Use salt in moderation.

There is a direct connection between excessive salt intake and calcium-based kidney stones. Be moderate. Too much salt will make your tissues retain water, but too little will dehydrate you. That can upset your fluid balance and increase the likelihood of stone formation. Limit yourself to 2 grams a day (for comparison, a teaspoon contains between 2 and 2.5 grams). But beware: The salt in your shaker isn't the only way you are satisfying those tastebuds. Here are just a few foods to avoid: luncheon meats like bologna, ham, salami, and sausage; olives; pickles; relishes; and snack foods such as chips, pretzels, salted popcorn, nuts, and crackers. Cheeses can also be high in sodium content. Read labels on prepackaged foods because salt doesn't always appear as plain old salt. Did you know that any of the following could add to your sodium intake: monosodium glutamate (MSG), brine, sodium propionate, sodium citrate, sodium nitrate, sodium sulfite, sodium hydroxide, sodium alginate, disodium phosphate, sodium saccharin, and sodium caseinate? Opt for lemon juice or vinegar, flavored peppers, lite salt, herbs, or spices to satisfy your appetite.

Exercise.

Regular physical activity speeds up your metabolism and helps to keep calcium and other minerals on the move through your system. Check with your doctor first, and if it's OK, start walking, biking, swimming, or cycling. If you are a couch potato, your kidneys are more likely to collect stones.●

STUDY YOUR ABCs

○ ○ ○

Vitamins A and B, especially B$_6$, will help inhibit stone formation. Magnesium is also important, and you can find extra magnesium in whole-grain breads, cereals, and nuts. You definitely need a multivitamin because, if following doctor's orders, you are drinking so much liquid that you run the risk of washing nutrients right out of your body. Meanwhile, according to some theories, vitamin C may not be a wonder drug as far as your condition is concerned. In your body, vitamin C has the potential to change to an oxalate. So stick to the RDA of 60 milligrams. Reports indicate that vitamin D is another vitamin that can lead to trouble: Never get more than the recommended daily amount of 400 international units.

KNEE PAIN

18 STRATEGIES FOR HANDLING SORE KNEES

Crawling around on the floor to play with the baby grandson has been tougher lately. Your knees seem a bit stiff, and they hurt when you get up off the floor. Well, sorry to say it, but you may be experiencing one of the normal effects of aging. With normal wear and tear, as well as the onset of chronic ailments such as osteoarthritis, by the time you reach 50 it is not unusual to experience knee pain. You may have a genetic predisposition to knee problems, be plagued by an injury you incurred playing sports in school, or be paying the piper for lack of activity, which can cause the muscles that help support the knee to become weaker. Maybe you've always been bowlegged or knock-kneed, and over the years these conditions have put excess strain on your knees. Whatever the cause, those old reliable knees of yours can swell, become stiff, and in other ways be a source of pain.

Some knee problems may be related to the basic structure of the knee itself. Think of it as an elaborate hinge with many parts. The major components include the menisci, two disklike pieces of cartilage. Menisci are located just above the tibia, the larger bone that extends beneath the knee to the foot, and below the femur, the thighbone that extends above the knee to the hip. The job of the cartilage is to prevent the tibia and femur from rubbing against one another. Then there's the kneecap (patella), or front of the knee, which is a little like a piece of protective equipment that safeguards the knee joint from injury.

Ligaments are the bundles of fiber that help hold the different parts of the knee in place. They connect the knee to the femur above the knee and to the tibia and the smaller fibula below the knee. Tendons are fibrous bands that attach different groups of muscles in the legs to the kneecap and cross the knee to attach leg muscles to the femur and tibia. They also hold the kneecap in position.

Given this elaborate array of cartilage, ligaments, tendons, and bones, it is not surprising to realize that a lot can go wrong in and around the knee. Add to the complexity of these many parts the fact that you are continually putting just about all of your body weight on your knees. They also act as shock absorbers, taking the brunt of all your leg movements. Walking, climbing, jumping, kicking, stepping, you name it, you are continually putting wear and tear on what amounts to a relatively small part of your body, and one that relies on vulnerable soft tissue like cartilage, ligaments, and tendons for much of the support it provides. Little wonder, then, that sore knees are so common.

Here are some useful ideas to help protect your knees from strain and to keep them in good shape.

Stretch your leg muscles.

A habit of mild stretching will help you retain the flexibility in your knee joint. Remember, tendons and ligaments connect the knee with the three major muscle groups in the legs—quadriceps (the muscles in the thighs), hamstrings (the muscles in the back of your thighs), and calf muscles. The trick, then, is to keep muscles throughout your legs flexible so they don't tighten across your knee and cause pain. Simple stretches like standing on the tips of your toes (to stretch the calf muscles and hamstrings) and lifting your foot and pulling it back to-

ward your buttocks (for your quadriceps) can do a lot to keep these muscles from becoming tight and causing knee pain (see "Exercises").

Warm up prior to exercise.

A preexercise warm-up of five to ten minutes gets the blood flowing to your muscles, so they remain more flexible. A little gentle exercise will also prime the knee for action. And *gentle* is the key word for warming up: Save the strenuous workout for the regular exercise period that follows. It's best during your warm-up time to use the same muscle groups you'll be using in the exercise period that will follow.

Increase your workout levels in stages.

If you suddenly decide to work out harder and longer than you normally do, your knees may pay the price. Your knee joint, tendons, and muscles may just not be able to adapt to the added exertion so quickly. Instead, add a few extra minutes to your run or other exercise regimen each time out and see how your knees respond. If you experience pain, pull back. If you think it's safe to do so, continue adding time and increasing intensity as you see fit, making sure all along that your knees are holding up.

Beef up those quadriceps.

The muscles on the front of the thigh have a lot to do with how well your knee functions. They lend a lot of support to the knee and also affect its general mechanics, determining, for instance, how flexibly the knee cap moves. In other words, the better shape your quadriceps are in, the better shape your knee will be in. Bicycling, walking up hills, and climbing stairs are all good ways to strengthen the quadriceps, as are specific weight training exercises that concentrate on these muscles (ask a trainer or physical therapist about weight machines and free-weight exercises that can help strengthen your quadriceps).

Give your leg muscles a cooldown.

Stretch your muscles after exercise, too. This way, they are less likely to become stiff later and tighten around the knees.

Check your feet.

If you have foot problems, you may have knee problems, too. That's because a chronic condition like flat feet is going to put added stress on the knee joint.

Arch supports and orthotic devices will not only help your feet; they may prevent you from developing problems with your knees as well.

Invest in good exercise shoes.

Ill-fitting, worn out exercise shoes can put a lot of extra wear and tear on your knees. If you're going to exercise, invest in the proper footwear.

Shun high heels.

The footwear you wear day to day also has a lot to do with how well your knees function. Topping the list of stressors are high heels, which pitch your feet and legs in an unnatural way, putting a lot of extra stress on your knees. Low heels are much more sensible and better for all-around foot and knee health.

Lose some weight.

Your knees bear most of the brunt of your weight. So, it only follows that the heavier you are, the more stress you put on your knees.

Adjust your bicycle seat and gearing.

Too high or too low, an improperly adjusted bicycle seat is going to put a lot of unnecessary stress on your knees. Ideally, your knee should be only slightly bent when your foot reaches the bottom of the range of motion of the pedal. If the seat is too high, your leg won't bend enough; if it's too low, it'll bend too much. In either case, you'll be putting excess stress on your knees.

After you've settled on the correct seat height, be mindful of the correct gear when riding your multispeed bicycle. Though it may be fun to zip along with higher gears engaged, note that the higher gears tend to increase the pressure on your knees. For the sake of your knees, stick with more revolutions and lower gears when out on your bike.

Take pain medication with care.

Yes, ibuprofen, aspirin, other nonsteroidal anti-inflammatory drugs (NSAIDs), and even corticosteroid injections can go a long way toward lessening painful inflammation in the knee joints. But remember, any drug taken over long periods of time can have unwanted side effects. Besides, if you are in chronic pain, surgery, special exercises, or other treatments may be in order. See a physician if knee pain persists.

Don't jog on pavement.

Running on a hard surface is a little like pounding on your knees continually with a hammer. It's much better to run on dirt or grass, which absorb the shock and put less strain on your knees.

Get back on your feet after surgery.

Lying around with your knee out of action is one of the worst things you can do following surgery. Instead, pursue an exercise plan you work out with your physician, and get your knee back into action—gradually. This way, you'll prevent muscles, tendons, and ligaments from tightening.

Don a knee brace for security.

If you've injured a knee, a neoprene sleeve that slips over the knee or a hinged brace that wraps around the knee to minimize side-to-side movement can provide a lot of security. These braces aren't foolproof and they're not necessarily going to prevent further injury. Aside from wearing thick knee pads, for instance, there's not much you can do to minimize the effects of a slip on the ice.

But braces do provide some major benefits. They minimize movement in the knee, giving ligaments and tendons a chance to heal, for instance, and they can make your knee feel better simply because of the warmth and compression they provide.

Do some water exercises.

Working out in water after an injury or surgery is a great way to get your knee back in action. Water workouts benefit the knees in two ways: The gentle resistance of water boosts the effectiveness of exercise, and the buoyancy protects the knee from excess stress.

Alternate muscle groups.

When you use the same muscle groups day in and day out, you're just looking for knee trouble. All that wear and tear on the surrounding muscles is bound to result in strain and pain in the knees. It's best to alternate exercise routines so you avoid using the same muscle groups more than every other day. One good way to ensure this is to bike, jog, or do some other form of aerobic exercise one day and strength training the next. Or mix up your biking routine with swimming. The point is, just don't overdo.

PRICE your knee when recovering from an injury.

Protect. Immobilize your knee to prevent further injury. Try walking with a cane to reduce weight.

Rest. A light pain in the knee tells you to slow down. A severe pain says stop. If it's not serious, the pain will go away. If it doesn't go away, check with your doctor.

Ice. Cool the knee by wrapping some ice in a cloth and rubbing it on the area in a circular motion for about 15 minutes.

Numbness will set in and the swelling should go down.

Compress. Wrap an elastic bandage tightly around the knee and keep it in place for about half an hour to reduce swelling. Alternate compression with the application of ice.

Elevate. Raise the leg above the level of your heart to minimize swelling. Gravity is what's working in this situation.

If pain persists, gets worse, or prevents you from carrying out your normal activities, check with your doctor. Sometimes pain in the knee points to trouble elsewhere in your body, such as arthritis in your hip or a pinched nerve.

Exercises

To shape up your knees so they are strong, flexible, and in balance, try the following exercises on a regular basis:

- Wall sit. To strengthen the quadriceps and gluteal muscles, lean with your back against a wall, and lower yourself into a squatting position in which your upper legs are positioned at a 45-degree angle to the wall. Tighten your buttocks and hold the position for one minute.

- Knee extension. For overall strength in the knee joint, attach light weights to your ankles (no more than a few pounds). While seated in a chair, slowly straighten one leg so you can extend the knee without locking it, and hold the position for five sec-

onds. Lower slowly and repeat ten times, then switch legs.

- Leg raise. To stretch and strengthen your hamstrings, lie on your back, straighten your left leg, and rest it on the floor. Bend your right knee so your right foot is flat on the floor. Now bend your left leg and bring your left knee toward your chest. Then straighten your left knee so your left leg is pointing directly upward. Lower your leg to the floor, repeat the exercise six to ten times, and switch legs.

- Quad stretch. To strengthen and stretch the quadriceps muscles, begin by holding on to the back of a chair or other sturdy surface for support. When you feel you can do so without losing your balance, curl one leg back and grasp the ankle. Then, pull your ankle forward until your foot touches your buttock. Hold the position for 30 seconds and then curl the other leg back.●

WARNING!

• • •

Recovering from a knee injury? Don't think about resuming your exercise regimen until you have the all clear from your physician. And never exercise if you are experiencing knee pain.

LACTOSE INTOLERANCE

10 WAYS TO LIVE WITH IT

Milk—it's wholesome, it's good for you, and it tastes good. But if you're like a lot of folks, milk and other dairy products can seem like poison. They can make you feel bloated and full of gas, give you diarrhea, and jolt your stomach into turning somersaults.

If you just can't stomach the stuff, chances are you're one of the 50 million Americans with lactose intolerance. That means your body does not produce enough of the enzyme, lactase, which is necessary to break down the sugar, lactose, that's present in milk, most cheeses, and other milk products. As a result, lactose is not absorbed into your bloodstream but goes right to your gut, where it causes its discomfort-producing mischief.

"But I drank milk by the gallon when I was a kid," you may well say. That's because most people don't begin to suffer the effects of lactose intolerance until they hit their 20s. And while people of Jewish, Asian, African, and Hispanic descent are most prone to the condition, just about all of us find it harder to digest milk as we get older.

So, lactose intolerance may well be the cause of the discomfort you feel after eating a slice of cheesy pizza or a bowl of ice cream. But don't despair. Even if you are lactose intolerant, there are ways you can still enjoy milky indulgences—and get the health benefits of dairy products, too—without paying the piper.

Stick to small amounts.

Don't give up on milk altogether just because you get a tummy ache after eating your way through a pound of creamy cheese and washing it down with a gallon of milk. Chances are, you may be able to handle some lactose, just not a big dose of it at one time. Try drinking your daily glass of milk in three installments, part with each meal. Or, if you can't resist a piece of pizza, simply remove some of the cheese. The thing to remember is that your body produces just so much lactase, and you are going to be able to handle only a corresponding amount of lactose.

Find your lactose-tolerance level.

If you suspect that you have a tough time digesting dairy products, find out just how much you might be able to tolerate. First get all the lactose out of your system by staying away from dairy products altogether for two weeks. Then reintro-

MAKE SURE IT'S REALLY LACTOSE INTOLERANCE

o o o

The intestinal upsets triggered by lactose intolerance can also be a sign of a lot of other maladies. Irritable bowel syndrome is chief among them (see IRRITABLE BOWEL SYNDROME). The bloating, changes in bowel habits, and other symptoms of lactose intolerance are associated with a long list of problems ranging from stress to an allergic reaction to many different kinds of foods. So, don't be too quick to write off your intestinal malaise as lactose intolerance. If you cut back on dairy foods and find that your symptoms disappear, great. But if they persist, see your doctor.

duce them into your diet, but proceed slowly. When you can enjoy milk and dairy products without suffering any ill effects, you'll know you've found your level of tolerance.

Add a dab of lactase.

So what if your body is stingy in providing lactase? Not to worry—you can add your own. There are a number of different lactase products on the market, available at most drugstores. You can, for instance, sprinkle lactase enzyme powder into your milk or add a few drops of the liquid form; it will predigest the lactose for you. You can also chew a lactase tablet just after you eat a dairy product. And if these measures seem like too much trouble, look for lactose-free milk—it costs a bit more, but the manufacturer has already done the work of taking the lactose out for you.

Switch to buttermilk.

Sounds crazy, but buttermilk has less lactose than whole or two-percent milk, and less fat and cholesterol, too.

Fall in love with an aged cheese.

Swiss, aged cheddar, Parmesan, and other hard, aged cheeses contain only tiny amounts of lactose—most of it is lost during the long aging process. Chances are you'll be able to tolerate these cheeses better than others.

Add yogurt to your diet.

There are some very good reasons to stock up on yogurt (look for "live and active culture" on the label). For one thing, yogurt is an excellent source of the calcium you'll need to replace if you're not eating other dairy products. Second, you'll probably be able to tolerate yogurt because it contains a lot less lactose than milk does. Plus, the bacteria in yogurt

HOW NOT TO SHIRK ON CALCIUM

o o o

Yes, you'll be doing your tummy a favor if you lay off dairy products, but don't let your bones suffer from a lack of calcium. In fact, if you're reducing your dairy intake, it's essential that you make sure you get plenty of calcium from other sources. This is especially important for women, who run the risk of osteoporosis. Fortunately, a lot of foods other than milk and cheese are calcium rich. High on the list are broccoli, most greens (excluding spinach), whole grains, nuts, lentils and other legumes, and some fish, including sardines, anchovies, and salmon.

If you're cutting back on dairy products, you should also speak to your physician about calcium supplements.

produce lactase that naturally helps you digest the lactose it does contain. However, you may not find it as easy to digest frozen yogurt because, before it's frozen, it's often repasturized—a process that kills the lactase-producing bacteria.

Eat a meal with your glass of milk.

You may find it easier to digest milk and dairy products if you eat them in combination with other foods. That's because the more food you put in your stomach, the slower it empties, giving your digestive system more time to absorb the lactose you take in.

Read the labels on medications.

A lot of medications, both prescription and over the counter, contain lactose as a filler. If you take one or several medications every day, you may be getting enough lactose from them to cause intolerance symptoms. Be advised that manufacturers are not required to list lactose as an ingredient, however. If you think your medication may be the hidden source of your lactose problems, ask your pharmacist or contact the manufacturer directly (many have consumer hot lines).

Read the labels on processed foods, as well.

It's not just milk and other dairy products that you should watch out for. Cake mixes, frozen breakfast foods, TV dinners, canned soups, and many other prepared foods contain lactose, too. Read labels carefully, and if you find that to be a bore, here's a better idea—switch to fresh foods. You'll know for sure what you're eating, and they're better for you.

Check out menus.

Wonder why your stomach was in an uproar and you tossed and turned all night after that big dinner in the fancy restaurant? Well, that delicious repast you ordered may have been loaded with milk or cream—you know, the fettucine alfredo, clam chowder, Dover sole in cream sauce. If you're lactose intolerant, do yourself a favor and ask your waiter if any dish you're not sure about is made with dairy products.●

LARYNGITIS

12 WAYS TO REGAIN YOUR VOICE

When you open your mouth to speak, nothing but a raspy, croaky, whispery sound emerges. You certainly don't recognize your own voice, if you can hear it at all. If you spent last night screaming for your team to win, then you may have isolated the reason. Laryngitis is an inflammation of the larynx, or voice box. Besides all the stressful ways the voice can be stretched to its breaking point, laryngitis can also be caused by an upper respiratory infection such as a cold. Smoking and heartburn can bring on laryngitis as well. Symptoms to watch for include: pain, a scratchy feeling, a dry tightness in your throat, a cough, or a persistent urge to clear your throat.

You can credit your larynx for the sound of your voice. Located at the base of your throat, this boxlike contraption has openings at its top and bottom. It's about two inches long in women and a bit longer in men. Made of fibrous muscle, the box houses strips of tough, membrane-covered muscles called vocal cords. Like the strings of a guitar, these cords create sounds by vibrating back and forth when air passes through the box. The sound varies in pitch depending upon how tightly or loosely the cords are stretched. To hit a high note, the muscles need to be pulled very tightly. For a low sound, the cords are slack.

Irritated, inflamed, and swollen vocal cords can't vibrate properly. To regain your voice, try these tips.

Keep silent.

Rest your voice for several days. If you have to speak, use a soft, modulated voice, but don't whisper. Whispering can actually strain your voice. If you have a presentation, or some other situation that calls for your complete verbal participation, cancel or reschedule. A simple case of acute laryngitis is not serious, but if you push yourself, you might damage your vocal cords in more complicated ways. Take the situation seriously.

Check your medicines.

Drugs can dry out the membranes in your throat. Are you taking antihistamines or medication for high blood pressure or for your thyroid? Diuretics, which are often prescribed by doctors for hypertension, can dry the membranes and cause laryngitis. Tell your doctor about losing your voice, and ask him or her to take a long look at possible side effects for every drug you may be taking, both prescribed and over the counter.

Take water breaks.

Fluids will soothe a dry throat and keep the tissues hydrated. Can you manage eight to ten glasses a day? At least aim for that amount. Juices are fine. Alcohol is a no-no, so abstain until you can speak again. Wine, beer, and hard liquors dehydrate the body and irritate the tissues of the throat. Ice could aggravate your problem, so don't suck on chips or cubes. But warm drinks are wonderful for a cold.

Try steaming yourself.

During the winter, when laryngitis is more prevalent, indoor heating systems can take moisture out of the air you breathe. Put some back in by using a humidifier or portable steamer. Make sure you keep the machine clean by using

fresh water, however. You don't want bacteria or mold to find a happy home in your humidifier. Stand in a hot shower for a while, or make a steam tent for yourself: Put a towel over your head and lean over a pot of hot water. Breathe deeply. Be careful not to burn yourself.

Schedule tea times.

Stay away from caffeine, however. Make decaffeinated tea with lemon. Did you know that lemon in any form stimulates the flow of saliva?

Use pursed-lip breathing.

Keep your mouth closed and slowly breathe in through your nose. The air will be warmed, filtered, and humidified right there in your nose before it heads toward your hurting larynx. If you lean slightly forward, you will be able to take in even more oxygen. Now, exhale through your mouth with your lips pursed. To picture pursed lips, think of kissing or whistling. Blow the air out in a steady stream through the center of your lips. Don't open too widely and don't try to push the air out. Just relax. Exhale easily. Try to time the duration of exhaling so it lasts twice as long as the time of inhaling.

Get away from smoke.

If you are a smoker, stop right away. If you live or work with smokers, ask them not to light up when you are near. Any kind of smoke, even the passive kind, will irritate your larynx.

HELLO, DOCTOR?

○ ○ ○

Acute laryngitis is not usually something for adults to fear. In children, it can signal croup (a serious medical situation), but if you are over 50, you generally don't have to worry. There are certain times, however, when you might need to alert your doctor. A bacterial infection should be treated with an antibiotic. Polyps, or nodules, on your vocal cords could make them vibrate slowly, changing the sound of your speaking voice. Cancer of the larynx has also been known to appear initially as laryngitis. Contact a physician:

- If the loss of voice lasts more than seven to fourteen days.
- If pain won't go away.
- If you have an upper respiratory infection and you are also running a fever.
- If you can't breathe deeply.
- If you are coughing up blood.
- If you are a smoker and you've noticed a major change in the pitch of your voice.

Don't clean.

Dust can irritate your larynx; if the air is dry, you compound the problem. Set aside your cleaning chores until you can speak clearly again. If you work in a dusty environment, stay home sick. You are. You have laryngitis.

Stop clearing your throat.

Constantly trying to clear away mucus won't help or hurry your recovery. Try to resist that urge and give your larynx a chance to rest.

Gargle with salt water.

Add half a teaspoon of salt to a cup of warm water, then gargle. Don't make it too salty, which might be irritating to your throat.

Learn how to protect your voice.

Clergymen, politicians, and anyone who must speak regularly in public can get chronic laryngitis from overuse. If you make a living using your voice and you seem to be losing it more than you'd like, find a voice trainer. You may be stressing your vocal cords in ways that can be easily corrected.

Don't go flying.

The dry air inside an airplane can be hard on your voice. If you must travel by air, chew gum or use throat lozenges. Stay with honey or fruit-flavored varieties, however, since mentholated varieties aren't as good at keeping your membranes moist. Suck on hard candies to keep the saliva moving.●

LOSS OF SEXUAL DESIRE

14 IDEAS TO HELP KEEP THE FLAME BURNING

You don't have to outgrow sexual desire. As you get older you may become a little less interested in sex and lose some of your former ability to express yourself sexually, but you are just as capable of giving and receiving sexual satisfaction as you were when you were younger. Contrary to myth and common misconception, sexual desire doesn't evaporate as you get older.

As in other stages of adult development, sexuality has a continuity across one's life span that reaches far into old age. The fact is, sexual decline as you get older is often less a function of biological changes and more a reflection of poor health, social prohibitions, and, often, the lack of a partner.

It's important to remember that for men and women alike the sexual drive reaches far beyond the need to reproduce. The way you look and behave continues to reflect your sexuality at any age. Likewise, sexual desire is an interest in sexual activity; it isn't the same as actually having or participating in sexual activities. Nor is the lack of desire the same as impotence or the inability to obtain an erection, although these are affected by lack of desire.

If your partner exhibits more sexual desire than you do, it doesn't necessarily mean you have a problem with your level. It simply means that a difference exists, and the two of you have to talk about it and attempt to come to a mutually satisfactory understanding.

The loss of sexual desire—marked by a level of interest in sex that is inadequate for engaging in sexual activities—can be caused by physical factors, nonphysical factors, or a combination of the two. Physical causes for a decreased sex drive in both women and men include: hormone imbalances, undiagnosed physical conditions, kidney and liver disease, medications, alcohol, depression, stress, and fatigue. Nonphysical factors include absence of a suitable partner, lack of information, want of privacy, and a conflict of values.

Chronic illness is more likely to produce difficulties with sexual desire and arousal than with orgasm. General symptoms of chronic illness such as fatigue, stress, and pain may diminish a person's energy in general and capability for sexual expression in particular. Changes in physical appearance such as those caused by arthritis, weight loss, or surgery may reduce self-esteem and alter your body image, indirectly influencing your sexual desire. And a chronic or continued lack of sexual drive may have an impact on your relationship. It should also be remembered that changes in sexual desire are simply a part of aging. Such changes needn't put an end to your sexual life. For even if your interest in having intercourse may have declined, it doesn't mean you've lost interest in other kinds of physical and emotional intimacy.

Here are a number of ideas you and your partner can use to help keep the flame burning.

Communicate with your partner.

Don't expect your partner to read your mind. Establish an atmosphere in which both of you feel secure enough to speak freely and won't have to hold back your true feelings. If you want your partner to take a different approach or a more active role, then say so.

Have a physical checkup.

Get a complete medical examination if you feel you are losing your sexual desire and can't figure out why. Eliminate the possibility that an illness or some other condition may be the underlying cause of your problem.

Continue to court one another.

The dating game never goes out of style. Enjoy a special dinner together, see a romantic movie, bring home flowers, and hold hands. Be mindful of the little things that show you care deeply.

Don't be afraid to say no.

In the past, many women felt pressure to engage in sex whenever their husbands wanted it. And men may be burdened by an imagined macho role that requires them to perform whether or not they really want to. The time is past for both partners to be reluctant to admit their true feelings. Perhaps the formation of a mutual pact would make it easier for each partner to respect the right of the other to behave more honestly.

Make time for sex.

If you're still working or taking care of your elderly parents or your young grandchildren, you are probably not burdened with an excessive amount of free time on your hands. But sexual intimacy should be given a high priority. If necessary, set some special time aside for just the two of you.

Guard against routine.

Avoid allowing relations to become too predictable. Don't get together only at the same time on the same night week after repetitive week. Change the time and place. Take full advantage of opportunities for romance when on vacation.

Understand how your body changes with age.

Knowing the effects of aging on your body is key to accepting the fact that sex may be different later in life than it was in your youth. Lifestyle changes, stress, and medications can also affect how people function sexually.

Consider HRT.

Women should consider hormone replacement therapy (HRT) after menopause. As a woman ages, the production of hormones declines, just as it does in men, but the effects are different. The hot flashes, night sweats, mood swings, sleeplessness, heart palpitations, headaches, urinary incontinence, and vaginal dryness that may occur after menopause also play havoc with sexual desire.

HRT restores the hormones that decline during the aging process, thus diminishing some of the unwelcome aspects of menopause. Quality of life and the interest in and enjoyment of sexual intercourse can improve markedly for women on estrogen replacement. In fact, some women report that sex is more enjoyable after menopause because pregnancy is no longer a concern.

Although levels of testosterone, the male hormone, do decline with age, most men retain levels adequate to maintain an interest in sex. But if you are concerned, check with your doctor about your testosterone level.

Use it or lose it.

It's well established that an active sex life can help postmenopausal women maintain vaginal lubrication and retain the elasticity of vaginal tissues. Likewise, it's also believed—though it's not known exactly why—that prolonged abstinence from sex is one of the underlying causes of impotence.

Respect one another.

Remember that the foundation of good sex is respect and trust. That means treating each other as equals and knowing that your partner considers your best interests.

Be realistic.

Don't expect sex to be great all the time. After all, you don't expect anything else in life to be perfect; your sexual relations are no exception.

Maintain a healthy outlook.

Depression often produces a loss of appetite—whether for food or sex. As you grow older, given the losses you are likely to experience, it is difficult to avoid some encounter with a depressed state of mind. Choose to deal with these losses rather than to succumb. Think of them as challenges. Overcoming depression goes a long way toward restoring interest in sex. If necessary, seek professional counseling for guidance through a depressed state.

SEX AND ILLNESS

○ ○ ○

An illness or physical disability can have far-reaching effects on many aspects of your life—on your self image, for instance, as well as on your physical response to sex and on your interest in sex altogether. However, you needn't let an illness or disability affect your sexuality or throw your sex life out of balance. Here are some things to keep in mind:

- A loss of sexual desire or impotence can be a side effect of many commonly prescribed drugs. Medications can reduce desire, impair the ability to achieve or maintain an erection, and inhibit vaginal lubrication. The list of such drugs includes beta blockers and other medications used to control high blood pressure, antihistamines, drugs used to treat depression, and drugs that block secretion of stomach acid. Your doctor or pharmacist should be able to tell you what the effects of drugs or other treatments might be. They can also explain what you might be able to do to overcome or minimize undesirable side effects and what alternative medications you might be able to take.

- Speak frankly about your reservations. For example, you're in pain and won't enjoy sex, let your partner know. There's no reason for you to suffer through what should be a pleasant experience, and a frank discussion of the basis for your lack of enthusiasm will help your partner overcome any feeling of rejection.

- Check with your doctor first, but you can anticipate getting full approval for the resumption of sexual activity within a month or so after experiencing a heart attack or bypass surgery.

Exercise.

Work out regularly, both aerobically and with weights. Chances are you will have a healthier self-image along with a healthier body when you exercise, both of which can enhance sexual interest.

Get a good night's sleep.

Changes in sleep patterns as you get older can be disconcerting. You may find yourself sleeping fewer continuous hours at night but taking short naps during the day. Sleeping excessively and feeling fatigued despite a good night's sleep are often symptoms of depression and can detract from a vigorous sex life.

Keep up your appearance.

Good hygiene and attentive grooming add to your sex appeal. Vanity does not disappear with advancing age.

Do some research.

Plenty of books are available from bookstores and public libraries on sexual self-expression. Look over some of the options, choose one or two that appeal to both partners, and study them together. A number of videos are also available.

Get creative.

As your research will show, a multitude of ways exist to express sexual interest and affection, and many of them are not limited to sexual intercourse.

Limit alcohol.

Chronic alcohol and drug abuse can lead to psychological and neurological problems that are related to impotence and a lack of sexual desire.●

Low Energy

18 Ways to Beat the Low-Energy Blues

You feel run down, worn out, and after lunchtime you are tired, drained, and simply exhausted. Work, play, and the activities you used to enjoy have lost their appeal as you find yourself dragging during the afternoon. You keep worrying: "Am I sick? What's wrong with me?" Frustrated, you let your doctor know that you always seem to feel tired these days.

You're not alone. Fatigue is one of the most common reasons why patients over 50 go to see their doctors; it's right up there with the sniffles, headaches, fever, and muscle pain. There is nothing wrong with being tired once in a while, of course, especially when you know you're not getting enough sleep. But persistent tiredness that no amount of sleep can address could lead to depressive moods and a sense of helplessness.

You may be tired because you work too much or too little. You may be depressed and not even realize it. Fatigue can easily be caused by chronic anxiety, for example. An undiagnosed chronic illness such as diabetes, an underactive thyroid, anemia, or an infection can be causing the problem. So you're examined and the doctor concludes that there aren't any physical causes for your lack of energy.

It may be that you just have too much going on in your life. Excessive demands on your energy can produce a kind of "brownout" by overwhelming you, physically and psychologically. You can suspect a low energy level if you experience fatigue, especially in the morning; lethargy; and a significant decline in both physical and mental activity. Psychologically, you will find it hard to concentrate and to remain motivated.

The truth is, if you're like most people, your fatigue probably results from less-than-healthy habits rather than actual illness. You can change this behavior, especially when you understand that getting older does not necessarily equate with being tired. With a less physically demanding lifestyle you don't need as many calories as when you were more active, but you still need certain vital nutrients.

Moreover, you still need your sleep. As tempting as it is to squeeze in an extra hour of work or reading at the end of the day, that regular hour adds up to a significant amount of sleep deprivation over time.

Weakness and the feeling of exhaustion, whatever the cause, can be demoralizing. Thus it's important to manage the specific underlying conditions, whether emotional or physical. The recommendations that follow get you started in the right direction.

Visit your doctor.

Find out if your loss of energy is the result of disease or just caused by your current behavior. It's common to be listless and lack focus for a day or two occasionally. And it's normal to be tired after an illness or a significant change in your life, such as starting a new job. But when you have no logical explanation for several weeks of fatigue, that's when a more careful look at your health picture is in order.

Set aside more time for sleep.

Keeping late hours at the office and having an active social life can wreak havoc with your sleep time, so something in your schedule may have to give. You can prepare yourself for a busy week by allowing more sleep time on weekends. You may think you will be refreshed on six hours of sleep or less, but most people need between eight and eight and a half hours of sleep every night.

Exercise in moderation.

Physical activity provides an outlet for the relief of tension and mental fatigue and is important for weight control. Just don't overdo it. If you feel tired for several hours after working out, you're pushing too hard. However, just 30 minutes of aerobic activity three times a week will increase your energy level by increasing the flow of oxygenated blood to your tissues.

Manage your stress.

Ease up on your workload. Your heart responds to stressful situations by pumping harder, and your nervous system becomes hyperresponsive under constant stress. This energy overload leads to exhaustion if you keep it up. Take time out to read a book or go for a quiet walk.

Maintain a network of family and friends.

Perhaps your low energy is related to unresolved personal problems. Discuss such problems and fears with people close to you to place them in a better perspective. Sometimes just talking problems out and using friends as a sounding board eases your mind.

Don't skimp on food.

Food is fuel. You may be so busy that you skip breakfast or lunch and then feel drowsy in the morning and sluggish in the afternoon. A healthy breakfast sets the stage for an energetic morning. And a sensible lunch will make you more productive during the day.

Eat a smaller dinner.

If you overeat at dinnertime, it may make falling asleep a lot harder. To get a better night's sleep, skimp on dinner and eat more during the day.

Eat the right foods.

Keep up your intake of vitamins, especially those found in most vegetables and grains. Eat foods that are naturally rich in potassium (bananas and potatoes) and brimming with magnesium (leafy green vegetables). These nutrients are instrumental in extracting the maximum energy from food.

Stay away from alcohol.

There are many reasons to be careful about your alcohol intake. Experts generally agree it's okay to drink in moderation, but too much alcohol actually inhibits restful sleep. If you have a low energy level to begin with, be extra cautious about any alcoholic beverage.

Plan a diet high in fiber.

Consuming foods rich in fiber enhances your general health by helping to lower cholesterol levels, protect your heart, and reduce the risk of cancer. The strongest evidence of a major reduction in risk comes from studies of diets that are rich in high-fiber foods. Such foods should supply 20 to 35 grams of fiber each day. You can get these recommended amounts by eating five servings of fruits or vegetables along with six servings of whole grains or beans on a daily basis.

Control your caffeine intake.

If you use caffeine to keep you going during the day, make sure you're taking it at the right level and at the right time, when it doesn't make you nervous and jumpy and doesn't prevent you from going to sleep at night. A single cup of coffee will circulate in your body for three hours. If you can't quit regular coffee, reduce the amount of caffeine by mixing decaffeinated blends with regular ground coffee. Drink decaffeinated colas.

Reduce excessive noise.

Even if you aren't actually awakened by noises coming from the street or inside your own home, they can limit the restfulness of your sleeping hours. Try to drown them out with a steady, humming noise, such as from an air conditioner or fan, which will be more soothing than the disruptive sounds.

Get involved.

Make a commitment to become actively involved in volunteer work at a local hospital, help at a charity that is meaningful to you, or get a job. A sense of purpose may heighten your sense of self esteem and actually make you feel up to doing more.

Find an afternoon pick-me-up.

Avoid refined foods and sugars. The sugar will pick you up for the first hour, but then it's all downhill. Try an apple or other fresh fruit as your snack instead.

Learn how to relax.

People exhausted by stress may choose inappropriate ways to relax, such as by binging on sweets, smoking, or drinking alcohol. Learn deep relaxation techniques such as yoga instead, and find an activity or hobby at which you can become engaged and truly relaxed.

Lose weight.

Carrying more pounds than your body is able to handle will make you tired faster. Moreover, you're probably more sedentary than you should be. Become active, engage in a physical fitness program, and figure out how much exercise you need to use up more of the calories you're taking in.

Balance your vitamin intake.

Fatigue may be caused by too many or too few vitamins. Keep in mind, however, that you can't make up for poor eating with an army of vitamin supplements. If you enjoy a well-balanced diet, most experts agree, you don't need any supplements. If you are concerned that you aren't getting enough vitamins, a multivitamin with minerals is a good choice.

Manage your time.

Time management can help busy people weed out the clutter in their lives to make more time available for pleasure, leisure, and rest. Disorganized and bored people can use time management to schedule interesting activities and become more productive. A daily time log will help you understand how your time is used and whether or not it is being spent efficiently.●

CHRONIC FATIGUE SYNDROME (CFS)

○ ○ ○

CFS is characterized by an extreme weakness and debilitating fatigue that sometimes lasts for months or even years. People grow so weak that normal activities become impossible.

No reliable diagnostic test exists for CFS, so a diagnosis is usually made by ruling out other possible illnesses. The Centers for Disease Control and Prevention established a set of criteria for CFS that includes a chronic or recurring fatigue that doesn't go away even with proper rest and is severe enough to keep a person from doing half of his or her usual activities. In addition, a patient must experience most of the following minor symptoms that persist or recur over six months: mild fever, sore throat, painful lymph nodes, generalized muscle weakness, muscle discomfort, prolonged fatigue, pain in joints without swelling, disturbances in sleep patterns, and depression.

The fatigue that is associated with CFS is unlike normal fatigue in intensity and duration. The patient is so tired that he or she is often confined to bed. The illness affects more than physical health; it depletes emotional and spiritual resources as well. Rest and patience seem to be the best antidotes.

LOW VISION

11 SECRETS FOR BETTER SIGHT

Most people would probably agree that sight is the most important of the five senses. In fact, the area of your brain that deals with vision is larger than the parts involving taste, smell, touch, or hearing. Your ability to see with clarity affects almost everything you do. Can you imagine not reading the newspaper or magazines, not watching television, not driving a car, not preparing dinner, not being able to "read" the love in the faces of your family and friends? Without sight, even the simplest acts can become troublesome.

You may be worried. From the time you hit age 40 your vision has been changing. That's because the lenses in your eyes have been slowly losing elasticity, which makes it more difficult to focus quickly. The front page of the paper is blurry and letters dance a bit—unless you hold it at arm's length. Perhaps you need reading glasses or bifocals; maybe you use a magnifying lens for small type. Experts say these changes in the lenses of your eyes (a condition called presbyopia) may be one of the few universal signs of normal aging. While you may not be happy about any vision impairment, correctable or not, you can at least be comforted by the fact that you are not very different from any other human being who has celebrated a fiftieth birthday.

Other sight changes can be more serious. Diabetes, arteriosclerosis, malignancies, and other factors must be taken very seriously if you expect to keep good vision. The four eye diseases most commonly associated with aging are: cataracts, macular degeneration (a blurring of central vision, though peripheral vision remains clear), diabetic retinopathy (deterioration of the retina due to problems in its blood vessels), and glaucoma. Rest assured that many medical problems, injuries, and abnormalities involving your sight can be prevented, stopped, or sometimes reversed. For example, modern medicine has made marvelous strides in the treatment of cataracts, a clouding of the lens. Is your vision watery or blurry? Do you find yourself needing stronger and stronger prescriptions for your eyeglasses? Are you experiencing difficulty seeing in bright light or driving at night? Has the color of your pupil changed? Answering yes to any of these questions might indicate that you are developing cataracts.

Meanwhile, some people just don't see well in special circumstances. If your eyes are slow to adjust to the dark—in a darkened movie theater, for example, or while driving at night on a moonless, unlit highway—then you may have night blindness. Anyone over 40 should schedule regular eye examinations at least every two years with an ophthalmologist, even if they believe their sight to be normal. Preventive eye care can help to preserve your sight. Here are 11 secrets for better vision.

Get tested.

While it's easy to postpone doctor's appointments and pick up cheap reading glasses in your local drugstore or supermarket, you need an examination by an ophthalmologist to rule out serious eye diseases. Low vision may be on your list

EYEDROP ANXIETY

○ ○ ○

If you need to use medicated eyedrops for glaucoma or another eye condition, you may be experiencing problems getting the drops into your eyes correctly. If so, you aren't alone. A study of older users of eyedrops turned up the fact that the majority had trouble unscrewing the cap on the bottle, tilting their heads back far enough, lifting their shoulders as they positioned their bodies for the drop technique, pulling the eyelid back far enough, and aiming the dropper itself. Ask your doctor to take you through each of these steps in the office.

of complaints, but the doctor will be interested in diseases that have no symptoms. Glaucoma, for instance, sometimes has no symptoms, usually appears after age 60, and can cause blindness if left untreated.

Pay attention to vitamins and nutrients.

Many nutrients play a role in your eyesight. What you eat and drink can affect how well you see. Your eyes are nourished by your blood supply, and even fluctuations in blood-sugar levels will result in fuzzy or double vision. People deficient in vitamin A and suffering from night blindness have responded well to large doses of this supplement.

The best approach is to concentrate on a healthy diet, and, with your doctor's OK, back that up with a regular multivitamin and mineral supplement.

Quit smoking.

Cigarette smoking contributes to poor health in general and can lead to problems with circulation and high blood pressure, both of which can be hazardous to your sight. Smoking has also been implicated in macular degeneration, which leads to blurring of central vision.

Rest your eyes.

Take rest breaks throughout the day if you are working at a computer, reading, watching television, or doing any kind of hand work that requires intense focusing and concentration. Don't continue such activity for more than two or three hours at a time without a break. Simply close your eyes for five or ten minutes to relax the muscles. Put the palms of your hands over your eyes. Blinking also refreshes your eyes; it is a way to "massage" tired eyes.

Check your lighting.

Soft lights provide more contrast for tasks that require visual concentration. Light that reflects off the ceiling is preferred so the glare isn't shooting straight into your eyes. Good lighting is essential throughout your home, especially if you have low vision. Think of your well-being first; don't think about turning lights off to save money on electric bills. You don't want to fall because you were unable to see a step. Put night-lights in hallways and bathrooms. In the bedroom, install two-way switches so you can turn lights on at your bedside or at the doorway.

Be prepared.

If your night vision isn't what it used to be, think ahead to prepare yourself for situations that might pose an unwelcome challenge. Avoid driving at dusk. When rainy or foggy weather is a factor, use public transportation, catch a ride with someone else, or try to postpone the trip altogether. Slow down when driving at night, and think about your route before you leave so you know it perfectly.

Perhaps a passenger can assist in navigating. Special glasses are available that are designed to help with night vision: Ask your eye doctor about them.

Beware of dusk.

The time of day when the sun goes down may present challenges to clear vision. All landscapes look grayish and dim. You can see best in dim light by not looking directly at objects, but to one side. As you get older, your eyes require more light to see, and you could develop vision difficulties if you always wear tinted or dark glasses. Your eye is designed to appreciate light, especially when the outside temperature is neither too hot nor too cold. If you are on the beach on a bright sunny day, in the mountains at a high altitude, on the water, or driving a car in bright sunlight, dark sunglasses are fine. Otherwise, take them off.

Get a good night's sleep.

Your eyes, along with the rest of your body, need eight to eight and a half hours of sleep each night. Not only will your eyeballs be rehydrated while they are closed beneath the lids, but the six eye muscles deserve a break each day as well. Did you know that this team of muscles—some connected to the top, bottom, and sides of the eyeball—are unique? Human beings are among the few creatures on earth who can turn their eyes to see something without even turning their head. Look up, down, or sideways. When you take care of them, your eyes work together perfectly—in tandem like binoculars.

Check your medicine cabinet.

Are you taking medication for depression? Some tranquilizers can cause blurred vision. Older people are more likely to be vulnerable to such drug side

CALL THE EYE DOCTOR

○ ○ ○

Your eyesight is much too valuable to take for granted. A wait-and-see attitude about any eye problem may be quite dangerous. You should schedule regular eye exams at least once every two years after age 40 with an ophthalmologist. Here is a list of signs that should send you straight to the phone to arrange for an immediate checkup:

- Are you suddenly or painfully sensitive to light?

- Do you have severe eye pain?

- Have you lost part or all of your vision?

- Do you have double vision?

- Are you seeing flashes of light?

- Are there halos around objects or lights in your vision?

- Are your eyes bulging or protruding from the sockets?

- Is there a foreign body embedded in your eye?

effects, especially as the medication builds up in their bodies. Ask your doctor if any of your regular prescriptions could be contributing to your low vision.

Check your glasses.

Wearing eyeglasses with the wrong prescription can hinder your vision. Glasses are designed to focus rays of light onto your retina. The image on the retina is sent to the brain, which interprets what you see. The wrong prescription can't cause eye disability, but it could make you uncomfortable, blur your vision, and irritate your eyes. You can end up with headaches and even nausea. If you are experiencing difficulties with your vision, your physician may have sugges-

tions regarding alternatives, such as visual aids, contact lenses, laser surgery, or other special treatments.

Look for low-vision aids.

Inquire at your local drugstore or ask your eye doctor about special devices that can enhance your low vision. A variety of magnifying lenses are available, from common hand-held magnifying glasses to lenses that can be positioned on the chest to help with hobbies such as knitting and needlepoint. Other lenses fit over regular eyeglasses. Check at lighting stores for lamps with built-in magnifying lenses, lamps using halogen bulbs for intense clean light, and light fixtures for

use on tables and the floor that have flexible necks to position the light exactly where you want it to be. There is even a gadget that fits over the numbers on a standard telephone that has larger buttons and numbers that are easier to read.

Computer users can usually increase the size of the characters displayed on the screen and show them in boldface while at work, then reduce them to a smaller size when the time comes to print the results.●

LUPUS

---

13 IMPORTANT INSIGHTS

Your symptoms are confusing. Perhaps your joints ache. An overwhelming fatigue is making life miserable. Sometimes you think you have arthritis. The chest pain you feel whenever you try to breathe deeply is a real worry. Muscle aches, dry eyes, and a dry mouth may also be on your list of complaints when you speak with your doctor. Fever and swollen lymph glands are common complaints. Even seizures are possible, though uncommon. Are you feeling a little off; unable to think straight? Do your fingers and toes turn blue or white when it's cold? You're hypersensitive to strong sunlight, and a bright red rash that spreads across the bridge of your nose and cheeks is embarrassing. This last symptom is the most characteristic of what you may have: lupus erythematosus, often simply called lupus. Your facial rash, caused by sensitivity to sunlight, is the hallmark of lupus and is alleged to resemble the markings or bite of a wolf. Sometimes the rash takes on the shape of a butterfly.

Lupus is a chronic, immune-system disorder that causes inflammation in various parts of the body. Experts call it an autoimmune disease because the body is automatically making war upon itself. Your immune system ordinarily protects you from foreign influences such as viruses and bacteria. When you have lupus, it is ironic that the immune system, which is designed to help you, actually attacks you.

There are three types of lupus. The first is discoid lupus erythematosus (DLE), which involves the skin only and can leave you with crusty red lesions on the bridge of your nose and cheeks. Scarring and pigment changes also appear on other parts of your body exposed to the sun. The second type is systemic lupus erythematosus (SLE), a variation of the disease that includes some of the symptoms described above and involves many other parts of the body. Finally, there is drug-induced lupus, which affects older people most often and is caused by complications from medication.

Lupus was once believed to be a rare disorder, but recent studies show that it may be even more prevalent than muscular dystrophy, multiple sclerosis, cerebral palsy, cystic fibrosis, or leukemia. More than half a million Americans have lupus; 90 percent of them are women in their child-bearing years. Lupus can occur at any age, however, and affects men and women of all races. Fully 15 percent of cases occur after age 55, and at this age, too, more women than men are victims. The prognosis for lupus patients is better than ever, and there are a number of steps you can take to help bring the disease under control.

Call 800-558-0121.

This information hotline is available 24 hours a day, seven days a week, and is operated by the Lupus Foundation of America, Inc. (LFA), a nonprofit agency. LFA will send you an Inquirer's Packet describing lupus in easy-to-understand language. The warm voice on the end of this line can direct you to experts and local support groups and can even prepare you for a visit with your doctor. Since there are 90 local chapters of LFA in the United States and 73 in countries around the world, you may be able to locate help right in your own neighborhood. After all, the more you know about your symptoms, the more helpful your physician can be in bringing your problem under control.

See a doctor.

Living well with lupus is going to require teamwork. You need a medical professional who understands you, your medical history, and exactly how you react to various triggers—those factors that affect your lupus. A family doctor may be fine, but if you feel the need for a specialist, don't hesitate to ask for a referral. Many lupus patients use rheumatologists or clinical immunologists who specialize in lupus. Your local hospital or medical society—as well as the Lupus Foundation—can help you find the right person. Not only should the personal physician you locate be able to keep track of the physical outcomes of your disorder, but he or she ought to be familiar with your usual mood and personality. Depression can become a problem for patients with lupus, and having someone you trust who can recognize your normal ups and downs can be critical to your quality of life. You certainly don't want someone who dismisses any of your complaints or suspects that you are neurotic.

Keep a disease diary.

What triggers lupus in another patient may not be a factor in your case. Experts refer to lupus attacks as flares or flare-ups. If you can keep an accurate physical, emotional, and biological record of what happened before, during, and after a flare, as well as information as to when your symptoms began, how long they lasted, and how you coped, you'll have valuable pieces of your health puzzle. Don't trust these facts to memory, however. Write everything down whenever possible. (See sidebar, "Signs That Signal a Flare-up.")

Check your medicine cabinet.

Drug-induced lupus occurs more often in older people who may have preexisting medical conditions. Do you have high blood pressure? Heart disease? These problems sometimes require medications such as hydralazine, procainamide, and isoniazid, all of which have been implicated in lupus flare-ups. Tell your doctor of your concerns immediately. Lupus symptoms should fade gradually once your medication is changed or discontinued. Don't stop taking any medicine without first checking with your doctor, however.

Stay out of the sun.

In susceptible people, lupus may be triggered by three different factors: drugs, infections, or exposure to sunlight. In fact, sunlight exposure is the most common reason for flare-ups in a large percentage of cases. Even if you don't have a rash or lesions to worry about and your

disease is confined to an internal complication, sunlight is often a key factor. Use sunscreen both summer and winter, and pick one with the most protection possible against ultraviolet (UV) light: Choose a sunscreen with a sun protection factor (SPF) of at least 15. Be certain that your choice has been tested, and labeled accordingly, and don't buy sunscreens through the mail.

Apply sunscreen in the morning. If you wear makeup, let the sunscreen dry thoroughly for at least 20 minutes before applying anything over it. If you are headed for a pool or the beach, or if you are involved in physical activity that will cause you to perspire, reapply every two hours. Use clothing for more protection. Wear a hat and long sleeves and look for other ways to block the harsh sunlight. Wear sunglasses. If possible, stay inside between 10 A.M. and 2 P.M.

Beware of *all* ultraviolet light.

Ultraviolet rays are invisible light rays responsible for tanning, sunburn, and, regrettably, many cases of skin cancer. If you have lupus, UV rays can be particularly dangerous. Too much exposure—even if you are wearing protective gear or sitting behind a pane of glass—can increase skin rashes, fatigue, weakness, joint pain, nausea, and vomiting. Moreover, a bright, sunny day is not the only source of UV light. Unshielded fluorescent lights in offices and buildings also give off UV rays. Beauty shops often offer unshielded ultraviolet lamps for facials. Sunlamps emit even more ultraviolet rays than sunlight, and three to five minutes of exposure to a sunlamp can equal 15 minutes outside. Ultraviolet radiation increases at higher altitudes, and the rays can be reflected off snow, water, sand, glass, and cement, compounding the danger. Even an overcast sky offers little relief. Medications like sulfa, phenothiazines, chlorothiazides, griseofulvin, or tetracycline, can further increase photosensitivity to UV rays. Stepping straight out of a hot shower or sauna and into the sunlight can also increase the danger.

Join a support group.

Meeting and interacting with other people who have lupus can help you and your family manage the disease. Support groups not only share the newest information about treatments, but members improve coping skills and bolster each other's self-esteem and morale.

Learn more about helpful drugs.

There are several categories of drugs that could become extremely important. You need to know as much as you can about each category, not only to help get well but also to help your doctor keep lupus under control. No matter what type of drug your doctor recommends, ask why the drug was chosen for your case and make notes of any side effect mentioned or experienced. Early intervention and drug therapy can decrease your risk of organ damage and sometimes shorten flare-ups.

Nonsteroidal anti-inflammatory drugs (NSAIDs) are prescribed for numerous diseases. NSAIDs include aspirin, ibuprofen (Motrin), naproxen (Naprosyn), indomethacin (Indocin), sulindac (Clinoril), and tolmetin (Tolectin). When your muscles or joints ache, NSAIDs could be just what are needed. Incidentally, if aspirin irritates your stomach, taking it with meals, milk, or antacids will minimize the problem.

Acetaminophen (Tylenol) is a mild analgesic that can take pain away. It won't help much with inflammation, however.

Corticosteroids, or steroids, are actually hormones that can reduce inflammation and work on the immune system. A common prescription form is prednisone. Steroids have side effects that can worry you, especially if your doctor keeps you on a steroid regimen for long periods of time at high doses. Weight gain, a round face, acne, easy bruising, brittle bones, high blood pressure, cataracts, onset of diabetes, increased risk of infection, and stomach ulcers have been associated with steroids.

Antimalarial medications such as chloroquine or hydroxychloroquine are often used to treat lupus, especially for joint or skin symptoms. Antimalarials can't eliminate signs of lupus immediately; sometimes it takes months to show beneficial effects. And side effects can be worrisome. If your doctor has prescribed an antimalarial, watch for diarrhea, rashes, and eye problems. Your doctor may advise you to see an eye specialist regularly if you are on antimalarial medication.

Be prepared.

Always take your medicine with you when away from home. Let "be prepared" become your daily motto. Getting ready for a doctor's appointment, for example, should include the preparation of a list of current problems as well as an updating of your diary. If medications are causing side effects, be specific.

Eat right.

If you are nutritionally deficient, your immune system will not be able to fight off infections, and viral invasions are just one of the triggers for lupus flare-ups. Don't follow fad diets proclaiming to be cure-alls for lupus. Fish oil has been touted as a wonder treatment for lupus sufferers, but scant scientific evidence exists to support those claims. Hy-

SIGNS THAT SIGNAL A FLARE-UP

○ ○ ○

Learn how to recognize early symptoms of lupus activity. Your physician may order tests to determine precisely what, if anything, these signs represent. Perhaps only a change in drug therapy may be called for. In the meantime, be alert for the following symptoms. Any could be a warning of an impending flare-up, according to the Lupus Foundation of America, Inc.

- Persistent fatigue, out of proportion with what you would expect based on your usual activity level
- Persistent weakness
- Aching all over
- Fever, which may be slight to high
- Persistent loss of appetite
- Involuntary weight loss
- Increasing hair loss
- Recurring nosebleeds
- A sore on the roof of the mouth, which burns with spicy foods
- Any unexplained skin rash
- Sores on the skin
- Painful or swollen joint(s)
- Stiffness of the joints when waking up in the morning
- Chest pain that increases with breathing
- Shortness of breath
- Coughing up blood
- Persistent unusual headache
- Recurring or persistent abdominal pain
- Persistent, increasing swelling of the feet and legs
- Puffy eyelids
- Blood in the urine

drazines, the chemicals believed to be responsible for drug-induced cases of lupus, are found in mushrooms, tobacco, and tobacco smoke. Some food dyes, such as tartrazine, have been linked to lupus flares. Reduction in fatty foods, caloric intake, and saturated fats may help decrease the severity of flares.

Don't smoke.

Not only is cigarette smoking hazardous to your health in general, but hydrazines are in tobacco smoke. Stay away from secondhand smoke, too.

Exercise.

Stay reasonably active. Though rest may be what your doctor ordered, especially during periods of extreme fatigue, with the doctor's approval there is no need to cut out all activity. A program of regular walking, swimming, or bicycling can tone your muscles and increase your overall feeling of well-being. If you are out of shape, you also add to the risk of joint pain, muscle weakness, and fatigue. Aim for a balance between activity and rest periods. Don't push yourself beyond your natural limits, but do get up off the couch.

De-stress your life.

Doctors who treat lupus agree that emotional stress can add to the risk of flare-ups. Your immune system certainly reacts in times of emotional or physical stress overloads. If you have lupus, the effects can become complicated. Learn how to let go of anxiety through deep-breathing techniques, by pacing yourself, or by meditating. By taking time to care for your mental health, you will increase your stamina, vitality, and confidence. You will feel less like a helpless victim if you can put the areas of stress in your life in perspective and take one problem at a time.●

MEMORY PROBLEMS

26 WAYS TO BE UNFORGETTABLE

Yﾞou run into a former coworker at a wedding and you can't re-call her name. You remember she has three children and her hus-band is an engineer, but you still can't think of her name, though it's on the tip of your tongue. You feel frustrated, attributing your lapse of memory to the fact that you're getting older.

But anyone—of any age—can draw a blank. Younger people may see their memory lapses as amusing or at worst annoying. You, on the other hand, may react with embarrassment and con-cern, responding to the false stereotype that old age causes loss of memory, and memory loss means the onset of senility.

You need to understand that everyone has trouble remember-ing some things: where they parked their car, whether or not they paid the water bill. This is called benign forgetfulness, often caused by stress, depression, or the simple failure to pay attention. Indeed, it's very likely that you think your memory is a lot worse than it actually is.

It is true that just as muscle tone is lost as you get older, many of your brain neurons (the circuits that control memory) have been dying. Between the ages of 40 and 50, you may have noticed that it takes a little longer to learn something new, and your abil-ity to memorize information seems to have lessened a bit. Your brain has so many cells, however, that even if you lose thousands of them per day over a 70-year span, the total loss would amount to only a small percentage of your total supply.

With America's growing population of healthy seniors, it is increasingly apparent that while some people suffer substantial memory losses, many do not. Recent studies show that as you get older you can still learn and use your memory in disciplined ways. When learning something new seems important, older people catch on very quickly. In fact, lack of motivation is probably a bigger factor than memory problems in learning difficulties among older students.

Other studies indicate that there is a difference between the abilities needed for long-term memory versus short-term memory. Basically, only recall skills are required to extract data from long-term memory, since it was placed in memory some time ago. But successful short-term memory requires skills in both storage, or acquisition of data, and recall. Though some older people experience difficulty with short-term memory skills, it is small or nonexistent for those who are mentally and physically active. If you don't remember recent events, it's more than likely because you weren't paying attention at the time or it just wasn't important to you.

At any age, absentmindedness can result from automatic or routine behavior and from not paying attention. You might notice that memory lapses seem to occur more frequently as you get older, and that it becomes a little harder to pay attention to more than one thing at a time. It's not so much your memory that's declining as it is your ability to process incoming information quickly. In addition, as you grow older you may not have the energy it takes to remember things (remembering actually takes quite a bit of physical energy). As a result, it might take a little longer to learn something new and longer, too, to recall something.

Part of the problem is that while your memory bank grows each year, your ability to access memory might diminish a bit. Slower recall, therefore, seems to be a normal phenomenon of aging. On the other hand, many experts believe this doesn't have to happen.

The suggestions that follow will help you to keep your memory in shape and provide ways to remember better.

Get a complete physical.

See your doctor to rule out any physical cause for losing your memory.

Check out your vision and hearing.

Sometimes you may fail to get the message, not because of a problem with memory, but because you weren't able to take in the information to begin with. Have your sight and hearing tested, and take the necessary steps to have any problems corrected.

Eat a well-balanced diet.

Good nutrition contributes to overall health, including a properly functioning memory.

Avoid alcohol.

Alcohol is a depressant and will slow you down generally. You may find that you have less tolerance for alcohol as you get older, so its effects occur after a single glass of wine instead of the two you used to drink.

Pay attention.

Devoting adequate attention to what you want to remember will eliminate some instances of forgetting.

Block out distractions.

When you go into a room to do something, don't think about anything else until you've completed the task you set out to do. Don't allow yourself to become distracted until you have finished the job you intended. It's especially important to give your undivided attention to situations that could be dangerous, such as driving and cooking.

Believe that you can.

Don't say, "I can't remember anything anymore." When you expect to fail at something, you usually do.

Remember to take prescribed medication.

Keep your medication near something you use routinely, like your alarm clock or toothbrush. Set medications out each night so they will be ready to take the following day.

Emphasize actions.

Pay more attention to things you want to remember. For example, if you often wonder whether you locked your door, focus on the action. Say to yourself, "I'm locking the door now." To help you remember that you're doing it today, not thinking about what you did yesterday, note the weather or what you're wearing at the time you act.

Set aside essentials.

For example, keep keys and glasses in a specific location whenever they are not being used. Don't deviate. And designate a fixed place for anything you'll want to take with you when you go out (such as mail to be posted).

Reserve slots.

Decide where things belong so when they're not there, you'll notice it. For example, keep your briefcase on the front seat of your car whenever you go out. If you're used to seeing it there, you'll instinctively check the front seat whenever you get in the car.

Set habits.

Get in the habit of doing things at the same time each day. And get help from reminders, such as feeding the dog when the evening news comes on.

Take notes.

Keep records of what you've done. These will be helpful at your work or at home. If you're not sure whether or not you called the plumber, just refer to your notes. Be sure to put notes (sticky notes work well) where you can see them.

- Keep a small notebook or tape recorder with you—even by your bed at night—to make notes about things to do.
- Keep a list of health questions you want to ask your doctor.
- Keep a list of books you want to read and movies or videos you want to see.

Keep records.

Record appointments in a portable date book, which is also handy for phone numbers, addresses, and notes to yourself. Also keep a calendar or special notebook just for birthdays and anniversaries. Make a list by month and place it where it can be seen, like on the refrigerator door.

Be patient.

Especially with yourself. It may take a little longer to learn new information, but once you know it, you will have learned it as well as someone younger.

Don't pressure yourself.

Becoming agitated about your inability to remember something doesn't help matters. Relax and ease your mind. If you feel you're forgetting too much, give yourself time. If the name of your friend doesn't come to the surface, don't make a fuss over it. Just admit you've forgotten. You can't remember every little thing.

Do one thing at a time.

Stay focused. Doing several things at the same time makes it easy to forget something important.

Watch out for prescription drugs.

You may be taking a combination of medicines to deal with your health situation. The more medicines you take, the greater the chance for side effects, such as increased or decreased appetite, drowsiness, and nausea. Some may cause a slowdown in your recall. Tell your doctor about all the medications you take to control this potentially disruptive factor.

Exercise your memory.

Practice. Keeping your body in shape means working out on a regular basis. Keeping your memory in shape also requires daily activity. Keep intellectually involved through reading books, magazines, and newspapers; following news stories that interest you; doing crossword puzzles; or perhaps playing cards.

Position objects as memory aids.

Change something in your surroundings to jog your memory. Put the clothes to take to the cleaners in front of the door and stick a note on your steering wheel so you'll stop at the bank.

Associate.

Connect new information to something you already know. Link someone you meet with a place; associate a special date with an event. Repeat the association several times either in your head or out loud. This technique can be used to remember a name, street, title of a movie, and even directions to your destination.

Visualize.

Create a mental picture of what you want to remember. Generate an image in your mind of a task, a number, a name, a word, or an abstract thought. Hold the picture for a few seconds to lock it in.

Use reminding devices.

Dial your own phone number and use your answering machine to leave a reminder for yourself. In addition, carry a little notepad or a small tape recorder to record messages.

Focus and rehearse to remember names.

- Before you go to a party, think about who might be there and practice linking their names and faces.

- Ask people you've just met to repeat their names, then repeat the names to yourself several times.

- If you can, say the person's name out loud several times in the course of conversation.

- Make it a point to introduce the person by name to other people.

WHAT IS MEMORY?

○ ○ ○

Neuroscientists who study learning and memory divide memory into three categories to explain how your brain selects and stores information:

- The mind discards much of what you see and hear. Only a small part is recorded in what is known as sensory memory. When you pay attention to a particular sensory impression, you then enter the second stage, called short-term memory.

- The conscious thoughts you are carrying around with you right now are stored in what is known as short-term memory. Some items you will remember years from now, others may vanish within minutes.

- Items from short-term memory are stored in your long-term memory. Items in your long-term memory bank span the years of your life. Some are from childhood, others are from hours, even minutes ago. These items are not in your conscious thoughts but can be recalled.

When you learn and store information so you can recollect it at a later time, you are undergoing the process of remembering. Successful remembering means getting information into long-term memory and retrieving that information when it's needed.

Researchers use the term *encoding* to describe the process of getting the information into long-term memory. Encoding consists of many mental tasks including: paying attention to information, reasoning through it, associating it with something you already know, analyzing it, and elaborating on details.

You move items from your long-term memory into your short-term memory (your conscious thought) through a process known as retrieval. There are many ways to retrieve memory: A sight or other sensation may simply make you recall something; you may consciously scroll through your long-term memory for a piece of information ("Where was I the day Kennedy was shot?"); or you may come across information that you realize you already know, a process that is known as recognition (for instance, someone may happen to mention a place that you once visited).

- At a social gathering, concentrate on learning a few names rather than trying to remember everyone.

Group first letters.

Quick—How do you remember the names of the Great Lakes? Combine the first letters of each and you have the word HOMES (Huron, Ontario, Michigan, Erie, Superior). Using the first letters in a list of words to form another word or sentence is a great memory tool.

Observe actively.

Then think about what you want to remember. Consciously pay attention to the details of what you see, hear, or read. Think about the meaning of the subject, how you feel about it, how it affects you, and whether you want to remember it. Ask yourself questions that will reinforce its meaning.●

MOBILITY PROBLEMS

---

16 WAYS TO MANAGE

The experts are still trying to figure out theories for successful aging. What they have arrived at so far is that if you continue your interests, activities, and attitudes through middle age and beyond, you have a better chance of staying active and managing the changes that take place in your life. In other words, an active lifestyle may be more important than your date of birth.

To stay active means being able to move around independently. Let's face it. If you want to stay in charge of your life, you have to keep moving. Mobility means getting to the grocery store and cooking your own meals as well as keeping your driver's license. It means staying flexible enough to accomplish your daily chores plus having enough energy left over for leisure activities.

The problem is that getting older brings with it an increased probability for illness that may leave you with some physical limitations that can lessen your mobility. As you move on in years, for instance, your body starts showing signs of wear and tear and you lose some bone and muscle mass. You experience some vision and hearing loss. Your nutritional needs change, too, as your body becomes less efficient at absorbing vitamins and minerals from food.

While you can't prevent these normal signs of aging altogether, you can slow down the process. You can also avoid behavior that would tend to speed up the process. What's more, there's plenty you can do to keep problems relating to aging from affecting your mobility.

Keep in mind that dealing with mobility problems presents different problems for different people: What your friends do may or may not work for you. Tell your doctor about any unexplained dizzy spells or faintness, your eating habits, whether your eyes are irritated by the glare from lights. If you find that it's harder to use reverse gear when driving because you can't turn your head very well, tell your doctor. Let the doctor guide you in setting up a wellness program that will help keep you mobile and in greater control.

Following are a number of ideas that may make it a little easier for you to get around more easily and safely.

Have your vision and hearing tested.

Do this on a regular basis. Wear a hearing aid and glasses if necessary to correct any problems. Have cataracts removed if that's what you need to see what you're doing.

Learn about side effects.

Are you tired because you're ill, or is one of your medications causing you to feel sleepy? Understand the side effects of all your medications—how they might affect your energy levels, coordination and balance, vision, and other functions. Alternatives are often available that have fewer side effects.

Use pain relievers properly.

Aches and pains that can slow you down are common with age. Fortunately, any number of over-the-counter pain relievers can make it a lot easier to live with such problems. For example, nonsteroidal anti-inflammatory drugs (NSAIDs) include aspirin, ibuprofen (Advil, Nuprin), and naproxen sodium (Aleve), which can help relieve pain and bring down inflammation. Acetaminophen products, including Tylenol and Panadol, reduce pain but do not affect inflammation. Be sure to use these products wisely: Read labels and instructions carefully, and do not take more than one type of pain reliever at a time. Remember, too, that time-released versions provide more relief over time and are especially effective for muscle soreness.

Limit alcohol.

It's not that you shouldn't drink at all—just keep consumption to moderate levels and remember that even a small amount of alcohol can upset your balance and slow your reflexes. Also note the warnings about alcohol consumption that are noted on the labels for all medications you take.

Don't smoke.

In addition to the many other well-known reasons not to smoke, you should also know that smoking can accelerate disk degeneration associated with back problems and loss of mobility.

Don't be too cool.

You'll feel more comfortable and active, especially as you get older, if you keep your house at 65 degrees Fahrenheit or warmer. When you're in an environment cooler than that for long periods, you may experience a drop in body temperature that could result in dizziness and, possibly, a fall.

Wear supportive low-heeled shoes.

The right shoes can make it easier to get around and help prevent falls, especially on stairs, slippery floors, and uneven ground. Be especially wary of wearing socks or slippers with slick soles around the house, where you can easily take a spill on waxed floors.

Use a cane or walker.

Don't shy away from using one if it helps keep you mobile and independent. A cane is especially useful when walking outdoors on uneven ground.

Get your weight down and keep it there.

The more you weigh, the more strain you put on your heart, muscles, and joints. You are also more prone to debilitating illnesses such as diabetes and hypertension.

Maintain good posture.

Spine straight, shoulders back—that's the proper posture to help maintain good balance and prevent the falls that can cause fractures. With age, you may have to make a conscious effort to maintain good posture, because changes in your musculoskeletal structure may take a toll, causing your spine to weaken and your shoulders to round a bit. One way to achieve a better posture is to clasp your hands behind your back for about five minutes as you walk. This simple exercise helps to straighten your spine and to keep your shoulders level rather than rounded.

Keep up good eating habits.

Good nutrition is important at any age, especially as you get older and your body becomes less efficient in absorbing nutrients from food. If you're not eating properly, you may feel run down and become more prone to illnesses.

- Eat lower-calorie meals and snacks. As you grow older, you need fewer calories, but your need for good nutrition doesn't decline. That means concentrating more diligently on choosing meals and snacks that are low in calories to get the most from your food.

- Eat a high-fiber diet. This will help your digestive tract keep things moving along. It's also a good idea to reduce the amount of fat in your diet, especially saturated fat, along with cholesterol.

- Read medication labels carefully and ask your doctor and pharmacist how they might interact with your diet. Drugs can affect nutrition in two ways: Some drugs can decrease the nutrients you are able to absorb from food, and some can lose their effectiveness when eaten with certain foods.

Check blood pressure and cholesterol regularly.

High blood pressure and other coronary ailments are major causes of mobility problems. To maintain a healthy heart, check your blood pressure regularly; you can buy a sphygmomanometer (blood-pressure testing device) at most drugstores. Many community organizations offer regular blood pressure and cholesterol screening.

BECOME PHYSICALLY FIT

○ ○ ○

If you don't keep physically active, muscles, tendons, and ligaments tend to weaken. The result is stiffness, a lack of flexibility and coordination, and a limited range of motion. The ideas below should help to achieve fitness.

- Begin an exercise regimen. Your goals should be to improve endurance, build strength, and enhance flexibility. Medical problems needn't stand in the way of exercise, for you can still find a level of activity that provides benefits.

- Keep your sense of balance. By strengthening muscles and tendons, whether through aerobic activities like walking or using weights and machines, you can sharpen your sense of balance and overall agility and at the same time increase bone density.

- Get aerobically fit. Even walking, for at least 20 minutes at a time and repeated several times a week, can help improve cardiovascular fitness. When you feel up to it, you can gently progress to more strenuous activities like biking or jogging.

- Work out in water. The advantage is that you get a great cardiovascular workout, and the buoyancy of water makes exercise easier on the joints.

- Stretch. Yoga and stretching exercises can do a lot to relieve stiffness and make you more flexible. Try doing simple stretching exercises at home several times a week. Your goal is to feel the stretch mildly—but not so it hurts—and to hold the stretch for several seconds.

- Warm up before you exercise, cool down afterward. By doing so, you'll get the most out of exercise and prevent soreness later. Warming up and stretching the muscles before exercise gently raises the heart rate and brings nourishing blood supplies to the muscles you'll be working out. A cooldown period (light exercise that helps your heart rate return to normal range) followed by stretching gives muscles and tendons a chance to return to their normal state, so you won't feel post-exercise stiffness.

- Do abdominal exercises. This is important, because your abdominal muscles help support your spine. Lie so your lower back is flat on the floor, bend your knees, place your feet flat on the floor, and clasp your hands gently behind your head. Exhaling, bring your shoulders several inches off the floor and raise your chest toward the ceiling. Don't pull on your head or neck, and keep your lower back pressed to the floor. Inhaling, return to the starting position. Repeat 10 to 15 times.

Use adaptive devices.

For people who have limited flexibility in their hands, there are a number of household devices especially designed so they are easier to hold and use. Some options include vegetable peelers and knives with thick rubber handles that are easier to grasp and manipulate, a jar opener that reduces the effort needed to twist, and an electric can opener.

MAKE YOUR HOME SAFER

○ ○ ○

Here are a few simple steps that will make your home more user friendly.

- **Light it up.** To prevent falls and other mishaps, outfit lamps and fixtures with brighter bulbs.

- **Keep a light burning.** Night lights in hallways can make a nocturnal trip to the bathroom a lot safer. Kitchens, bathrooms, and stairways are other prime places for night lights, and it's a good idea to have light switches at both the bottom and the top of the stairs. Illuminated switches make it easier to find a light in the dark (you can achieve the same effect by putting fluorescent tape around your electrical switches).

- **Beware of cords.** Keep electrical cords and telephone cords tucked away so no one can trip over them. You may want to have them affixed to baseboards.

- **Select functional furniture.** Some things to keep in mind: Make sure chair arms are long enough to pro- vide leverage so you can push yourself from a sitting to a standing position; make sure cushions are firm enough to prevent you from sinking into them so far you can't get up easily; and make sure chairs and couches provide solid back support.

- **Install handrails on stairways.** Put them on both sides of the stairs to ensure the greatest safety.

- **Tack down carpeting.** Anywhere in the house, especially on stairs, loose carpeting can be a hazard. If you have area rugs or runners, use rubber matting or apply carpet tape. Be careful of throw rugs, which can be hazardous because they tend to slide.

- **Install nonskid strips and grab bars in and around the bathtub.**

- **Maintain outdoor steps and walkways** so surfaces are level, smooth, and in good repair.

- **Don't take chances when reaching to high places.** Keep a sturdy stepladder with handrails in the house.

Wear adaptive clothing.

Buttons, zippers, and snaps can be difficult to manage if it is painful to use your hands and fingers. Instead, have easy-to-use hook-and-eye fasteners put into your clothing. And look for clothing that fastens in the front, not in the back.

Change your driving habits.

If neck and vision problems make it difficult to see properly when driving, train yourself to use your rear- and side-view mirrors to monitor traffic. You may have to limit your driving—staying off expressways during rush hours or giving up night driving—but by making a few adjustments you may be able to continue behind the wheel and maintain your independence.

Keep moving.

In other words, use it or lose it. By keeping active, you will help maintain muscle tone and flexibility. It's just a question of finding the activities that you feel comfortable doing, whether it's gardening, swimming, or a daily walk.●

MOTION SICKNESS

---

13 WAYS TO SQUELCH THE QUEASINESS

It's a queasy sensation you know too well. Your stomach starts flipping, then churning and turning. You break out in a sweat, become lightheaded, and feel a desperate need for fresh air, even if you are already outside. Whether on a boat or a train, in a car or a plane, those signs make you want to cringe because you fear what's coming. Oh no, you may lament, not again. The nausea and all the other accompanying symptoms of motion sickness are hard to ignore. Once these stages are set in motion, however, there's usually no stopping the sequence until you get sick to your stomach. Doctors believe there may be a genetic tendency to suffer from motion sickness, but simply knowing it runs in your family doesn't make traveling any easier.

Some student pilots have to drop out of flight school because of motion sickness. During training, astronauts are put into a cargo plane actually called the "Vomit Comet" to prepare them for the worst, which almost always happens—everyone throws up! Remember those splashdowns when Mercury, Gemini, and Apollo astronauts landed in the ocean? Well, reports indicate that these pilots gave up the contents of their stomachs in service to their country. Astronauts in space are constantly fighting this dangerous side effect, which can be brought on by weightlessness. Inside the confines of a space suit, nausea from motion sickness could be truly lethal.

Doctors suspect that motion sickness is brought on by mixed messages being sent to your balancing system. To maintain your body's equilibrium, your senses constantly monitor information about your environment. It is filtered through your inner ear, then whisked to your brain. When you experience motion sickness, your eyes are telling you one thing and your inner ear is insisting on another. The brain responds to these confused messages by creating its own chain of reactions, and you end up feeling like you have to throw up. To stop this chain of events before it starts, try these suggestions:

Focus on the horizon.

Some researchers believe that motion sickness is as much a visual problem as it is an inner-ear condition. Face forward if you are moving forward, and look into the distance to steady your sight. This will help to counter the conflicting reports your brain is receiving from the bobbing, listing, rising, or falling of your surroundings.

Remain topside.

If you feel a hint of *mal de mer* on a collision course with your next cruise to the South Seas, leave your stateroom and all lower deck areas behind and head for the upper decks. For one thing, staying below decks is likely to intensify feelings of seasickness. Moreover, going topside allows you to concentrate on the horizon and to feel the refreshing breezes of the ocean.

Drive.

Research has shown that you are less likely to become carsick if you do the driving. If that's not possible, at least get settled in the front seat where you can anticipate the turns, hills, and bumps in the road.

Sit near the wing.

In an airplane, the wing is the most stable spot. Choose a seat in the midsection of the cabin and, if possible, make it next to a window so you can look out.

Don't look back.

Concentrate on the road, sea, or sky ahead when you travel. Especially while at sea, looking forward will take your eyes away from any busy up and down movement going on to your right or left.

Sit down.

Simply standing upright in a moving vehicle can bring on motion sickness. Subway riders know how you can be jostled around when trying to stand on a train that is swinging through curves, accelerating, and then stopping at stations along the way. You are more stable when seated and less likely to feel upset.

Fast.

Don't fill your stomach just before traveling. If you need food for energy, stick with plain crackers or a piece of toast. An empty stomach isn't as apt to become upset. Above all, stay away from fatty, spicy foods, because the very smell can make you sick.

Avoid others who are sick.

If you're feeling a little queasy yourself, the last thing you need is exposure to the sight, sound, and odor of someone else throwing up. For your stomach's sake, try to avoid contact with sick strangers, friends, or even relatives.

Don't drink.

Alcoholic beverages go straight into your bloodstream and will affect your inner ear. If you are prone to motion sickness, you are asking for the worst by drinking when you travel.

Wear a band.

Elastic wrist bands (sold in pairs by drugstores for around $10) are supposed to suppress the feelings of nausea from motion sickness. Each band contains a small plastic button that presses against a specific spot on the wrist. When positioned on the wrist as described in the instructions, these bands have proven successful for many sea and air travelers. In addition, by using a device of this sort rather than medication, the bloated feeling that sometimes accompanies over-the-counter motion-sickness remedies can be avoided.●

Stay still.

At the earliest sign of queasiness, keep very quiet and calm. You may be able to ride out the sensation without getting sick. Think happy thoughts. Some research indicates that motion sickness is in part psychological.

Don't read.

Reading in a moving vehicle forces your eyes to move back and forth while your body senses that it's moving straight ahead. For some people, this kind of sensation can overwhelm their equilibrium.

Stop smoking.

Smokers may be anxious to light up in a desperate effort to fend off feelings of nausea. This is a big mistake because cigarette fumes are likely to just add to their sick sensations.

STOMACH SETTLERS

○ ○ ○

1. Cola: Cola syrup is prescribed as a panacea for nausea. Drink a cola after it has gone flat.

2. Ginger: Powdered gingerroot capsules sold in natural food stores have proven effective for many people in curing motion sickness.

3. Soda crackers: The bicarbonate of soda and cream of tartar in these basic crackers help settle your digestive system and absorb any excess fluid sloshing around in your poor stomach. Many an old sailor has calmed a queasy stomach with a handful of crackers.

4. Cinnamon in tea: Rumor has it that in ancient times King Solomon recommended ground cinnamon in tea for nausea.

5. Mint: Chew a bit of fresh mint.

6. Water: Sip water.

MULTIPLE SCLEROSIS

7 WAYS TO COPE—PLUS NEW REASONS FOR HOPE

To understand what multiple sclerosis (MS) is and how it should be treated, it helps to think like an electrician for a minute. That's because MS affects the central nervous system (comprised of the brain and spinal cord), which resembles a complex bundle of electrical wiring. Both depend upon the smooth, uninterrupted transmission of electrical impulses to operate properly. And, just as electrical wires are shielded with rubber insulation to keep them from short-circuiting, the nerves are sheathed with a layer of insulating material, a fatty substance known as myelin. MS is a progressive, often debilitating, disorder that occurs when the protective myelin is destroyed at various sites throughout the central nervous system and replaced by hardened patches of useless scarlike tissue. This process is referred to by physicians as sclerosis.

Just like wires that have been stripped of their insulation, nerve fibers that have lost patches of healthy myelin are prone to "shorting out" at the sites where sclerosis has occurred, so that messages traveling to and from the brain or spinal cord might not reach their destination. Since the nervous system branches out to essentially every part of the body, MS can cause quite a wide range of symptoms, depending on which specific nerves are affected.

Initial attacks, which usually strike between the ages of 20 and 50, may produce slurred speech; pain and impaired vision or blindness (usually temporary) in one eye due to inflammation of the optic nerve (optic neuritis); muscle weakness in one or more of the extremities; tingling, numbness, or a "pins and needles" sensation; spasticity and loss of coordination; unsteady gait; and extreme fatigue. Problems with bladder control and constipation are also common. Sometimes, in more serious cases, one side of the face or body becomes partially or totally paralyzed. Over time, if certain nerve areas in the brain are affected, emotional depression, mental confusion, mood swings, or memory loss may result.

Symptoms—which vary widely from one patient to the next—typically flare up and then fade away in seemingly random, unpredictable cycles. Indeed, approximately 70 to 75 percent of patients have a form of the disease known as relapsing-remitting MS, characterized by sudden attacks of symptoms that intensify for several days, stabilize, and then gradually ease over a period of four to eight weeks. Such attacks are interspersed with remissions—periods of partial or complete recovery that can last for months, years, or indefinitely. Relapses tend to be more frequent during the first three to four years after the initial attack, although in some cases a second attack may not strike for 10 to 20 years. Even though symptoms may virtually disappear during a remission—particularly after early attacks—recovery tends to be less and less complete with successive bouts, and cumulative damage eventually leads to permanent disabilities. Another form of the disease, chronic-progressive MS, is characterized by gradual but continuous deterioration, without remissions. This form is most common among those whose first symptoms appear after age 45.

Except in very rare cases when the disease progresses rapidly, MS is not likely to affect life expectancy to any great extent. The majority of patients survive at least 35 years after their initial diagnosis, although quality of life is often compromised to some degree.

The precise cause of MS remains unclear, but it is now known that the body's own immune system is implicated. It seems that certain cells in the bloodstream that normally attack and vanquish hostile foreign invaders (such as viruses and bacteria) mistakenly begin to destroy myelin, too. While there is no known cure for MS, there are a number of ways to interfere with this overzealous immune response, reduce the severity of attacks, and relieve the problems associated with progressive neurological damage. People diagnosed with MS can aid the course of their own therapy by following these tips.

Stay cool.

MS patients are notoriously sensitive to heat. They commonly report that symptoms worsen or recur when they become too warm, and they may experience heat-induced exhaustion or temporary loss of muscle control when they exercise too vigorously. It seems that increased body temperature only further interferes with the chemical transmission of electrical impulses along affected nerve fibers. Visual problems, numbness, and pronounced loss of muscle control may result. Therefore—especially in hot summer weather—avoid sunbathing, heavy exertion, and hot baths. Try to stay in air-conditioned environments whenever possible. Frequent cool baths or showers are also helpful. These precautions can ease or prevent symptoms; indeed, the purchase of air-conditioning systems for the home or car may be considered a justifiable medical expense for heat-sensitive patients. Check with your tax advisor.

Fight a fever.

Since increased body temperature can have such adverse consequences, fever is a particular cause for concern. For example, urinary tract infections are unusually common among those with MS, and such infections often produce a fever. Those who are particularly sensitive to heat can quickly become debilitated or even fall into a coma when body temperature rises too high. Thus, during a flare-up of symptoms, check your body temperature regularly. If a fever is present, fight it aggressively. Both aspirin and acetaminophen (the so-called antipyretic, or fever-reducing, drugs) are effective in bringing body temperature back down to normal; cool, damp compresses can speed the process. If a urinary tract infection or other bacterial infection is the cause of the fever, your doctor can prescribe antibiotics to cure it promptly.

Stay active.

A program of regular, moderate exercise can help to preserve muscle strength and flexibility. (However, heavy exercise is discouraged, for the reasons cited above.) If even light exercise seems too strenuous, listen to your body—don't push yourself too hard. Simply taking a leisurely walk or spending some time gardening can be beneficial. Your doctor may refer you to a physical or occupational therapist who can devise an individualized program of special exercises that will help you build up alternative muscles to compensate for lost strength in others and to prevent stiffening and atrophy (wasting away) of muscles. Doing exercises in a cool bath or swim-

ming pool can enhance their therapeutic effect. Occupational therapy—designed to help you adapt to the everyday demands of the home and workplace—is often the key to maintaining a relatively normal quality of life.

"Bee" wary of unproven or fad remedies.

People suffering from a chronic illness for which there is no cure are often willing to try anything that promises even a glimmer of hope for improvement. Unfortunately, hucksters and even well-meaning lay practitioners may be steering people with MS the wrong way by hawking remedies that, at best, have not been proven effective, and, at worst, may actually do harm. Case in point: Bee venom therapy is a highly touted folk remedy that typically requires the recipient to endure a series of multiple bee stings. The problem is that no bona fide scientific studies have ever confirmed the usefulness of bee venom, and the successful results can be attributed to a number of possible explanations. For one, MS—by its very nature—is known to flare up unexpectedly and then, just as unexpectedly, to subside. So the remission of symptoms may simply occur anyway, regardless of whether or not a remedy is used. Another explanation is the well-established placebo effect, in which patients genuinely begin to feel better, even though the apparent treatment turns out to be an inert substance (such as a sugar pill). The harm in trying even a questionable therapy like bee venom (not to mention countless others) is that by spending time, money, and energy on an unproven method, patients may miss out on other, more established, and ultimately more effective treatments. And, the financial and emotional costs of investing in a so-called remedy that fails to yield any positive results can be demoralizing. Someday, reliable scientific studies may prove that bee venom or other folk remedies are useful after all. But until then, it's best to rely on established treatments.

Work with your doctor.

As important as your own efforts are in the success of your treatment, multiple sclerosis is a serious medical condition that requires careful monitoring and the expertise of a well-trained, experienced doctor. Your primary care physician is likely to refer you to a neurologist (nerve specialist) for a complete evaluation. And in the event of an acute flare-up, a neurologist is generally best equipped to know how to manage the symptoms. In such instances, treatment may involve the administration of corticosteroids (powerful hormones normally manufactured in the cortex of the adrenal glands, located above either kidney), or ACTH (adrenocorticotropic hormone), which

GREATER HOPE THROUGH RESEARCH

○ ○ ○

Scientists are tirelessly searching for new and better ways to treat multiple sclerosis, and every now and then their efforts pay off. Recently, the U.S. Food and Drug Administration approved the first new drug in 25 years scientifically proven to ease the course of MS. The drug, interferon beta-1b (distributed under the brand name Betaseron), was shown in clinical trials to reduce the frequency and severity of attacks specifically in patients with the relapsing-remitting form of MS who could still walk under their own power. (The drug is not approved for use in bedridden patients or those with the chronic-progressive form of MS.) Interferons are proteins genetically engineered to be identical to proteins produced by the body's immune system. The exact mechanism of Betaseron's action is not fully understood, but it appears that the synthetic protein suppresses the immune response that makes MS worse. Although Betaseron did not eliminate flare-ups altogether, patients taking it had less frequent attacks, milder symptoms during attacks, and fewer hospitalizations.

Brain scans also revealed a significant reduction in the progression of the disease in those receiving high doses.

Unfortunately, since the time of the drug's approval, Betaseron has not quite turned out to be the wonder drug initially anticipated. It seems a number of patients using it stopped taking it, primarily due to side effects, which can include skin reactions at the injection site, stiff joints, incontinence, and flulike symptoms.

Nonetheless, there are continued reasons for hope. For one, many patients taking Betaseron are getting good results. Furthermore, early test results with a new drug called copolymer 1 showed it to be nearly as effective as Betaseron, but with far fewer side effects. Copolymer 1 and Betaseron fight the disease in two entirely different ways, and scientists believe that combining the two drugs could produce results even greater than what could be achieved by either drug alone. Such ongoing research might offer new hope to MS patients in the near future; FDA approval for copolymer 1 could come within a year or two.

stimulates the body's own production of natural corticosteroids. These hormones reduce the inflammation associated with MS flare-ups and thus can shorten the duration and reduce the severity of attacks. Since treatment with corticosteroids (such as prednisone) can be taken in pill form, it is generally simpler than ACTH treatment, which is given by injection and typically requires hospitalization. However, many physicians feel that ACTH may be more reliable. In either case, therapy lasts from two to four weeks. Despite the often dramatic effectiveness of ACTH and corticosteroids, their long-term use is not advised due to the risk of potentially serious side effects.

Talk to your doctor about other medications.

Many different classes of drugs are prescribed to help ease the symptoms of MS. Immunosuppressives (such as azathioprine and cyclophosphamide) may be used to dampen the immune system's attack on healthy tissue—including myelin—although results with these drugs have been mixed. Antispasmodics or tranquilizers (such as baclofen or diazepam) are used to alleviate muscle spasticity. The chronic fatigue that commonly accompanies MS can be treated successfully with the drug amantadine, while symptoms of depression and other changes in brain function may respond well to antidepressants. The bottom line: Only your doctor can determine which medications are appropriate for you—and only your doctor can write the necessary prescriptions.

Get support.

The emotional and psychological aspects of MS are as significant and as potentially debilitating as the physiological problems. In fact, up to 54 percent of MS patients battle with an episode of major depression at some point. And it's no wonder why: Threats of disability, loss of work, increased dependence on others, sexual dysfunction, or prohibitive financial burdens loom over the majority of MS patients at one time or another. Consequently, ongoing psychiatric support can be of utmost importance to patients and their family members. The National Multiple Sclerosis Society is an excellent source of information on all aspects of the disease and can provide referrals to qualified professionals—such as social workers, local community agency workers, psychologists, and other specialists—who are specifically trained to help MS patients cope with these crucial issues. The national society's headquarters is located at 733 Third Avenue, New York, NY 10017-3288, and representatives can be reached by telephone at 800-344-4867.●

MUSCLE PAIN

11 WAYS TO MEND IT

Your leg cramped so badly you had to stop playing catch with your granddaughter. This, after working out yesterday with an extra ten pounds added to the leg press. You didn't think you were overdoing it, but, come to think of it, you didn't spend much time stretching after your last workout, and you felt a little stiff this morning.

Consider yourself fortunate. Your muscle cramp sounds simple enough, but some can be complex and dangerous. It all depends on the cause.

Yours, like most common cramps, was brought on by minor physical exertion and overuse. Less common is muscle pain that results from nutritional deficiencies of potassium, salt, or magnesium. No matter what the cause, here are some ways to deal with muscle pain.

Warm up.

It's the golden rule of exercise. Before any kind of prolonged exercise—be it jogging, strength training, or even a stretching routine—warm up for a few minutes first. This might mean walking at a slow pace, riding a stationary bike at low speed, or doing any other mild exercise that gets blood flowing to your muscles, making them more pliable and less prone to strain.

Stretch.

Once you've warmed up, stretch before you play or work out. For safe stretches, hold a mild-to-moderate stretch for 15 to 30 seconds, long enough for the muscles to receive the signal to lengthen.

Go easy.

Don't overdo it, especially if you're just getting into an exercise routine. Your muscles are unaccustomed to the wear and tear of even moderate exercise, and you may experience pain and cramping as a result. Also take it slow when jogging or doing other aerobic exercise if you have new shoes. If you don't give yourself time to adjust to the shoes, you may strain muscles in your legs.

Cross-train.

Mix up your exercise routine to avoid putting strain on one group of muscles. If you jog, try swimming or bicycling on alternate days. The point is to avoid using the same muscles in the same way all the time.

Dress warmly.

Be mindful of the weather if exercising outdoors in the cold weather. Your muscles are much more likely to cramp in the cold, so it's important to dress appropriately.

Massage with ice.

Ice helps reduce the swelling and inflammation associated with muscle strain, but apply it carefully. Applied directly to the skin, an ice treatment can be painful. Instead, use an insulated ice pack, or wrap some ice cubes or even a bag of frozen vegetables in a towel. Then, for the best results, try rubbing the area lightly with ice. About 20 minutes of this easy treatment should bring relief.

Put on the pressure.

If you're having a muscle cramp, try this quick, easy remedy. Locate the area that's cramping and, using your thumbs, apply gentle but steady pressure to the tender spot for about ten seconds, then release. Repeat again after a few minutes, and continue in this way until the cramping stops.

Have a banana.

Cramping is more likely to occur if you're not getting enough potassium, especially if it's hot and you're losing a lot of fluid through sweating. Diuretic medications, such as those you might take for hypertension and other conditions, can also rob you of potassium and cause cramping. To avoid cramps related to potassium deficiency, make sure your diet includes bananas, oranges, potatoes, and other potassium-rich foods.

Get your calcium.

Leafy green vegetables, dairy products, including yogurt, and other calcium-rich foods are not only good for your bones, but they help prevent muscle cramps.

Drink lots of fluids.

Drink water, and plenty of it, before, during, and after exercise. This way you'll avoid the dehydration that can contribute to cramps.

Get a good physical checkup.

If the aching muscles persist, see your doctor. Make sure your condition is not a symptom of arthritis or another disease that can cause joint and muscle pain.●

NAUSEA AND VOMITING

---

8 WAYS TO QUELL THE QUEASINESS

Your stomach is jumping up and down even though you're not. You feel clammy from your forehead to your toes, and you think you're going to throw up. Well, go ahead and do it—as they say, we've all been there, and you're going to feel a heck of a lot better afterward.

Nausea and vomiting are simply the stomach's way of saying no to one of any number of offenders—it might be a 24-hour bug, a case of food poisoning, or the price you pay for eating or drinking too much. The sensation is just awful, but whether you're feeling a little queasy or are nauseated beyond the point of no return, there's plenty you can do to get yourself in the pink again.

Get a handle on the problem.

Sometimes you know all too well why your stomach is turning somersaults: It's the extra-large pepperoni-and-pineapple pizza you just wolfed down. You may also conclude that your nausea was caused by one of the many other well-known stomach upsetters: food poisoning, a hangover, the side effects of a headache, motion sickness, or an ulcer.

Get out the crackers.

Provided your stomach is not too far gone, having something bland to soothe it may help quell your queasiness and keep you from vomiting. If you think you're going to vomit, though, refrain from eating anything—not that you'll particularly want to. After vomiting, give your stomach a break by limiting your menu to gelatin desserts, crackers, or other plain foods for a few hours.

Sip on a liquid.

Ginger ale or other sodas can be just the thing for a queasy stomach. They'll be easier to keep down if you let them defizz first and leave out the ice: Warm drinks are easier to digest. Liquids are especially important after a bout of vomiting because they help prevent dehydration. First wait an hour or so to give your stomach a chance to calm down, then try slowly sipping a drink. Your system will be better able to absorb sugary drinks, such as diluted fruit juices, weak tea with a little sugar or honey, or sports drinks, which also help replace sodium, potassium, calcium, and other electrolytes.

Stay still.

If you're nauseated, your churning stomach doesn't need any extra commotion. Lie flat, raise your knees to relax your stomach muscles, and try not to think of creamed crab and hot tamales. Engaging in a conversation, listening to music, or watching television may get your mind off your stomach until the nausea passes.

Don't fight it.

Vomiting is your stomach's way of emphatically saying good-bye to unwanted visitors. Trying to hold back is likely to only prolong your nausea.

Don't induce vomiting.

"Okay," you might reason, "if I'm going to vomit, let's get it over with," then stick your finger down your throat. Stop. Don't do it. You might put an end to your misery, but inducing vomiting can be unnecessarily painful, irritate your stomach, and cause damage to your esophagus. Besides, it's going to be over pretty soon anyway.

Avoid the offenders.

Nausea and vomiting are signs that your stomach isn't up to snuff, so treat it kindly. Avoid smoking; drinking alcohol or coffee; and eating rich, fatty, or spicy foods; all of which can irritate your stomach further.

Consider the pink stuff.

Pepto-Bismol, Maalox, and other over-the-counter stomach settlers coat the stomach and may bring some relief from nausea, but usually only if it's caused by excess acidity. Alka-Seltzer, on the other hand, may irritate the stomach with its aspirin and bubbles. None of these medications will prevent you from vomiting if the urge is fully upon you.●

WHEN VOMITING IS MORE THAN UNPLEASANT

○ ○ ○

Yes, we all have to vomit sometimes—it's only normal. But it's not normal to vomit regularly or for a prolonged period of time, nor is it normal to frequently feel nauseated. If nausea and vomiting persist for more than a day, if you're vomiting violently, or if you're vomiting blood, don't take any chances—call your doctor.

NOSEBLEEDS

7 TIPS TO NIP THE FLOW

Your nose is lined with veins and capillaries lying just beneath the thin membrane in your nostrils. Tiny arteries and veins in the center of your nose are extremely fragile, ready to break and bleed at even the slightest show of force. A punch in the nose; blowing boisterously when you have a cold; sneezing too hard; being exposed to dry air, dust, or dirt; or even picking your nose can bring on a bloody reaction.

When you were a kid, a bloody nose may have been the result of an encounter with schoolyard enemies. As an adult, frequent nosebleeds indicate more than a people problem. You might have a vitamin deficiency, for instance. If you are undergoing cortisone therapy, taking antibiotics, or using aspirin regularly, your blood may not be clotting on cue. Whenever blood vessels are torn or break open, cells in your blood called platelets should get right on the task of stopping the flow. Clots begin as patches of fibrin that plug up the holes in a damaged blood vessel. But if you are low in vitamin K, then your blood is slow at clotting. Nosebleeds can also be a sign of high blood pressure or heart problems. If your nose begins to bleed after an injury; if the flow hasn't stopped within ten minutes after it began; or if you are also sleepy, vomiting, or have a headache—seek medical attention. In the meantime, try these techniques to nip the flow.

Pinch your nose.

While sitting up with your head tilted slightly forward, pinch the soft section just below the bridge of your nose with your thumb and forefinger. Breathe through your mouth. Maintain this pressure for up to 20 minutes. The forward position of your head will keep blood from going down your throat. Sitting up will decrease the blood flow to your head and nose. Don't lie down. Release the pressure and check to see if the bleeding has stopped.

Ice it.

Put a cold compress on the bridge of your nose, your forehead, the back of your neck, or under your lower jaw. If you don't have one of those handy over-the-counter medicinal ice packs, try wrapping ice cubes or a bag of frozen vegetables (peas are good) in a towel.

Blow . . . then don't blow.

If the nosebleed has just begun, try one decent blow before you put on the pressure. This one-shot step could dislodge a clot that is keeping a blood vessel open. Once the bleeding has subsided, how-ever, leave your nose alone even if it feels stuffed by clots. It can take days for the delicate skin to heal completely, and you don't want to do anything that might disrupt the healing process.

Stay away from aspirin.

Because it is an anticoagulant, aspirin thins your blood. If your nose is extrasensitive, regular doses of aspirin could be aggravating the lining of your nose. If you are taking any prescription anticoagulants, they do the same thing. Nonsteroidal anti-inflammatory drugs (NSAIDs) and ibuprofen may also cause problems. Talk with your doctor if you are experiencing frequent nosebleeds, and review all your current medications.

Take your vitamins and minerals.

Vitamin C and zinc are essential to your body. If you aren't getting enough of them, nosebleeds could be a warning sign. Eat a balanced diet and consider a daily multivitamin supplement to boost your immune system.

Humidify your home.

Dry air, especially during winter months, can dry out your nostrils. Conversely, breathing damp air will moisten them and may make you less prone to nosebleeds. Use a vaporizer or a cool- or warm-mist humidifier, or simply boil a pot of water to create steam. Also try some moisturizer just inside each nostril.

Plug it.

Wet a bit of plain, sterile gauze and put it in the bleeding nostril. When the bleeding has stopped, the gauze is likely to have dried out. To avoid renewed bleeding, wet the gauze before taking it out by tilting your head back and using a nosedropper, or hold a wet washcloth to your nose.●

OSTEOPOROSIS

16 WAYS TO DEAL WITH POROUS BONES

Getting older does not have to mean developing a round-shouldered appearance, losing five inches in height, or acquiring a dowager's hump. These conditions result from osteoporosis, one of the most severe and crippling disorders that affect older women and men. Nearly one in four white postmenopausal women over 50 suffers from some degree of osteoporosis. About ten percent of them will live in pain and become immobile.

The human body changes as it ages, and the skeleton is no exception. As a child grows, the changes are very visible. As adults grow older, the changes still occur, but they're less obvious.

Both men and women lose bone as they age; women just do it at a much faster rate, particularly during the first five to six years following menopause. Between the ages of 50 and 80, women lose about 30 percent of their skeletal mass because of the decline in estrogen—a hormone that maintains bone density in women. Those affected by osteoporosis lose bone mass faster than their bodies can manufacture it. The bones become increasingly porous and fragile. They also become more susceptible to fractures, most often in the hips, forearms, and the spine.

Don't think you have nothing to worry about if you happen to be male. Men account for some 25 percent of broken hips and about one-seventh of vertebral fractures. Although men start out with more bone than women, this gradual age-related loss of skeletal mass can be enough to seriously weaken bones in men.

Sex hormones are important in maintaining bone strength in both sexes. In most cases the decrease in bone strength takes longer in men because testosterone usually doesn't begin to decline significantly until after age 65. Even then, the reduction is slow.

Risk of osteoporosis varies with age, sex, racial group, body build, and family history. Petite, fair-skinned women whose mothers had osteoporosis are likely candidates.

Osteoporosis is a silent disease that often remains undiscovered until a fracture occurs. The first symptom is usually lower back pain, because the vertebrae are usually the first to show signs of the disease. As they become more porous and weak, the vertebrae go through various stages of structural deformity and actually collapse. Vertebral fractures can occur spontaneously—without any particular trauma but simply from the weight of the body.

The following suggestions may help to manage osteoporosis.

Exercise regularly.

It's a lifetime commitment. If you've been diagnosed as having osteoporosis, find professional rehabilitative therapy. Exercise slows bone loss and helps build new bone. A recent study indicated that women over 65 who walked regularly for exercise were less likely to fracture a hip than their counterparts who did not exercise.

Include weight-bearing exercise.

Weight-bearing exercise such as walking, jogging, weight-training, and aerobic exercise help build and preserve bone mass. Recent research has shown that women who engage in strength training show an increase in bone density in the hips and spine.

Work with a pro.

Contact your physician for a referral to a qualified physical therapist. The routine developed for you should encompass not just aerobic exercise but stretching and strengthening workouts as well.

Stretch for flexibility.

Doing your stretching exercises for only five minutes a day, three times a week, will limber you up. But spending more time on them will produce even more benefits, particularly if you do them right after aerobic activity.

Balance your diet.

A healthy lifestyle requires a balanced diet. The development and maintenance of sound bone structure require a variety of nutrients, including calcium, vitamin D, and fluoride.

Increase calcium intake.

The recommended daily allowance for adult women who are not pregnant is 800 milligrams (mg) per day. Because

ALTERNATIVE TREATMENT

○ ○ ○

Once you lose bone mass it can never be fully replaced. Estrogen, the only medication used to prevent the condition, can be effective at reducing the rate at which bones weaken. For women who don't take estrogen, two other options are available.

- Biophosphonates are the drugs most frequently selected after estrogen. The only approved biophosphonate, etidronate, comes in tablet form and is taken for 15 weeks at a time. Studies show some slow-down in the loss of bone mass. Luckily, there aren't many side effects, but etidronate does seem to become less effective over time.

- Calcitonin is a thyroid hormone currently available only by injection. It's used to help people whose bones build up and break down at an exceptionally rapid pace. The down side is that it's very costly and can cause nausea. It, too, tends to lose effectiveness after long-term use.

Etidronate and calcitonin work for men, as well as women. A small number of men can also benefit from supplements of testosterone, the male hormone.

there is some indication that calcium requirements increase with age, the recommended daily dosage for postmenopausal women is 1,500 mg. It is desirable to use food to get as much of your calcium requirement as possible, because food (as opposed to supplements) provides additional vitamins, minerals, and trace elements. The body also absorbs calcium more reliably from food than from supplements. Dairy products are the best dietary source.

Take a calcium supplement.

If you don't eat or drink dairy products, you'll probably need supplements or fortified foods to get an adequate supply of calcium. Studies show that for those who don't get enough calcium in their regular diet, supplements can decrease the loss of bone in arms and hands by up to half. They also have a beneficial effect on the spine. Since most people don't get enough calcium in their diets, consider taking a supplement of 1,500 mg daily, but discuss it with your doctor first.

To maximize absorption, take your supplement with meals or at bedtime, but don't take it at the same time as you take iron-containing supplements, since calcium makes it harder for the body to absorb iron.

Drink plenty of water.

You should drink at least eight 8-ounce glasses of water per day, since about half of bone tissue consists of water (with about 20 percent made up of calcium).

Spend time outside.

Sunlight helps the body produce vitamin D, which your body needs to process calcium. If you're reasonably active, you probably get enough vitamin D from sunlight along with the small amounts contained in fortified milk and cereals. But you should spend about 20 minutes outside every day. If you don't, talk to your doctor about a supplement.

Start ERT early.

Estrogen keeps bones strong by decreasing the rate at which calcium is lost. Early estrogen replacement therapy (ERT) can reduce fracture risk for women (ERT is not available for men). If you have osteoporosis, taking estrogen, whether by itself or in combination with the hormone progesterone, can help minimize bone loss. There are certain risks involved with this type of therapy, however. Be sure to discuss the matter carefully with your doctor.

Combine exercise and estrogen.

Women who exercise and also take estrogen show an increase in bone density.

Increase magnesium in your diet.

Your diet should feature at least 400 to 600 mg of magnesium (about half as much as your calcium intake). Among the prime sources for this nutrient are bananas, cashew nuts, dry beans and peas, oats, and okra.

Limit or avoid negative behavior.

Quit smoking, limit caffeine or eliminate it from your diet, and restrict your consumption of alcohol, which decreases the amount of calcium that is absorbed through the intestines.

Bend properly.

When you bend to lift something, place your feet shoulder-width apart and bend your knees. Keep the natural curve in the lower part of your back, while maintaining a straight spine.

Avoid accidents and falls.

For a person with brittle bones, a fall can cause a fracture that might lead to lifelong disability and pain. Take these precautions:

- Exercise to strengthen muscles and to improve coordination and balance.
- Go for regular eye checkups. If you need glasses, wear them.
- Use handrails to get into and out of bathtubs and when using stairs.
- Install nonslip surfaces in tubs and on steps.
- Talk to your doctor about alternatives to drugs that may cause dizziness.
- Avoid slippery surfaces, including icy sidewalks, whenever possible. If you can't avoid them, be very careful.

Work on good posture.

In a physically fit person, the upper back is flat, not curved forward. Shoulders are pinched back slightly and the lower back is not arched excessively. With good posture there is less stress on the spine, you breathe deeper, and even digest your food better.

To maintain good posture, bolster your lower back when sitting by placing a rolled-up towel or pillow behind it. Use neck rests in the car, and don't lean over to read or do work—keep your spine as straight as possible. Don't sit for long periods without a break; periodically get up and move; and exercises.

Your standing and walking posture should involve holding your head high, keeping your chin in, and maintaining your natural lower-back arch. If you find yourself standing in one place for more than a few minutes (as when ironing), elevate one foot by placing it on a stool. If you're standing at the kitchen sink, you can open a lower cupboard door and place one foot on the cupboard shelf.●

POOR APPETITE

23 WAYS TO ENJOY FOOD AGAIN

It's one of the ironic twists of life: You might have spent much of your youth trying to resist temptation, fighting hard not to eat too much, and now that you've passed 50 and have a better sense of what good food really is, you just don't seem to have as much interest in eating as you once did.

A decrease in appetite can be a normal part of getting older, due to any number of social and physical factors. You might, for instance, be suffering from empty-nest syndrome and find it less enjoyable to cook for one or two than it was to put food on the table for the whole family. Physical factors, such as a gradual decrease of the sense of smell that is a natural part of aging, might make food seem less enticing. The medications you take may also decrease your appetite, and clacking dentures may make the prospect of eating less inviting.

If you've lost your appetite, it's important to know why. While an occasional—and temporary—lack of interest in cooking or sitting down to a meal is completely normal, a prolonged loss of appetite could be the sign of a serious condition. In addition, going without food can have serious implications if you have diabetes or take medications that cannot be metabolized properly on an empty stomach. If your interest in food doesn't return within a few days, talk to your physician about possible causes.

It's important to remember, though, that sound nutrition is essential to good health at any age. Food is one of the great pleasures of life: A good meal is something to be enjoyed, even if you are eating alone. Here are some tips that will help you eat healthfully and maintain a good appetite. *Bon appétit.*

Enjoy your meals.

If it's pleasant to be sitting at the table, you're likely to want to linger and nosh. Make breakfast a time to read the newspaper or work on a crossword puzzle. At dinnertime, light some candles, put on some soft music, and pour a glass of wine. Make it an occasion—even if you're dining solo.

Try to eat with others.

Good company makes a meal more enjoyable. If you live alone, arrange to eat with friends or family members whenever possible. Preparing meals for others can add to your enjoyment of and renew your interest in food.

Cook with someone else.

It can be fun, and there's another advantage, too: When you do all the cooking yourself, by the time you sit down to eat you may have already been "filled up" just by the sight and smell of the food you've been preparing. If someone else has done at least part of the cooking, you'll probably come to the table with a different perspective along with a bigger appetite.

Eat more frequently.

Add snacks to your everyday eating routine—a piece of fruit midmorning, a muffin and tea in the afternoon, some yogurt after dinner. You may find these small treats more appetizing than a big meal, and they can provide some good nutrition.

Set established mealtimes.

By making mealtimes a regular part of your schedule, you'll be more likely to sit down and eat even if you are not hungry.

Mix up the menu.

If you eat the same thing day in and day out, you're going to become bored with food and either skip meals or fill up on unhealthy snacks. Eat something different every day.

Crack open some exotic cookbooks.

Or join a cooking class. Even if your sense of taste has diminished a bit, you'll stimulate your taste buds with new foods, and by experimenting with new dishes you'll make eating exciting again. Try a new dish or two a week, or branch out into a cuisine, such as Indian or Chinese, that you've never prepared before.

Buy some freezer bags.

Cook double portions so you can keep home-cooked food on hand and reheat it for an easy meal on another day.

Put some color on your plate.

The more interesting food looks, the more likely you are to want to eat it. Add some red peppers to a green salad, serve fish on a bed of lettuce, and dress up the plate in other ways so your meal looks more appealing.

Add some flavor.

Since your senses of smell and taste tend to diminish with age, compensate by adding more flavor to food. Dress a salad with flavorful herbs or add some bacon bits. Pour some good maple syrup over your oatmeal. Ketchup and mustard are readily available low-fat flavor enhancers, and you can make many tasty dressings from low-fat yogurt. By adding spices to your cooking, you can sharpen flavor and make food smell enticing while it is cooking.

Sauce your foods.

A good sauce can not only make almost any dish seem more appealing, it can also contribute some extra nutrients. Search through your cookbooks to find sauces that are healthy and easy to prepare. A parsley sauce, for instance, is a nice accompaniment to many fish and chicken dishes. Avoid sauces that are heavy in artery-clogging cream and butter and that may be hard to digest as well. Look for those made with fat-free yogurt or small amounts of oil.

Sprinkle, don't pour, the salt.

If the goal is to make meals more flavorful, you might be thinking, why not just add more salt? Because when you eat too much sodium, you can elevate your blood pressure and increase your risk of stroke and other cardiovascular diseases. The recommended daily intake is no more than 2,400 milligrams of sodium,

just a little more than a teaspoon. Try using herbs instead, or some pepper—but remember, pepper can be a gastrointestinal irritant, so sprinkle it on sparingly.

Go ahead, have a drink.

Many studies suggest that moderate intakes of alcohol are not harmful to your health and may even provide health benefits. The key word is *moderation*, which means no more than two beers, two glasses of wine, or two ounces of hard liquor. But there are many variables, including the interaction between alcohol and any medication you may be taking. Get advice from your doctor as to your own limits.

Plan menus in advance.

This is a good way to make eating a priority, and it can put the fun back into cooking and eating. Set aside one day a week to plan meals for the week, then do the shopping. This way, the food will be in the house, and if you know in advance what you'll be preparing, you'll be less likely to shrug off a meal.

Make a list before you shop.

Include protein (fish, poultry, and lean meat), nonfat dairy products, breads and cereals, and fruits and vegetables. This way, you'll be less tempted to fill the cart with fast foods and salty canned goods, and you'll come home with the makings for healthy, well-rounded meals.

Make an event of shopping.

If you enjoy buying food, you will probably enjoy preparing it and eating it more. Try to make your shopping rounds more interesting: Shop with a friend, try a new supermarket now and then, and make several different stops to make the

WHAT CONSTITUTES A HEALTHY DIET

○ ○ ○

If you're not eating as much as you once did, it's especially important that what you do eat constitutes a healthy, well-rounded diet—one that provides protein, carbohydrates, fiber, vitamins, and minerals. It's also important to limit your intake of fat, sugar, cholesterol, and sodium. According to the dietary guidelines established by the U.S. Department of Agriculture and the U.S. Department of Health and Human Services, a good daily diet should include the following: two to three servings a day of dairy products (milk, yogurt, and cheese); two to three servings a day of protein (meat, poultry, fish, eggs, dried beans, and nuts); three to five servings a day of vegetables; two to four servings a day of fruit; and six to eleven servings a day of fiber (bread, cereal, pasta, and rice).

outing a little more colorful—at a fruit and vegetable market, a meat market, a bakery.

Ask for smaller portions.

You may find it hard to shop for one or two people, but don't let that stop you from buying foods you're used to—for example, ask the butcher to cut a roast into small portions that you can freeze individually.

Stock up on easy-to-prepare foods.

If you have food on hand that can be prepared easily, you'll be less likely to skip meals on those occasions when you don't feel like cooking. Stock up on healthful canned and frozen foods.

Sample the salad bar.

Many supermarkets and delis now have them, and they're great places to stock up on a variety of healthy vegetables. You'll probably find it much more economical to create a salad this way than to buy large quantities of produce that may go to waste in the refrigerator.

Make sure your dentures fit well.

It's hard to enjoy a meal if your dentures are clacking away, and you're likely to end up with a bout of indigestion (which only decreases your appetite) if you can't chew your food properly.

Don't compensate with unhealthy foods.

It's easy to do: You're not really hungry, so you grab a bag of potato chips or a handful of cookies. Not only will you be eating empty calories—that is, adding calories but doing nothing to supply your nutritional needs—but fatty foods also raise cholesterol levels, increasing the risk of heart disease.

Take supplements, but don't rely on them.

Taking vitamin and mineral supplements should never replace a healthy diet. If you realize that you are not eating a well-rounded mix of the foods you need, however, a supplement may help supply essential nutrients. The best supplement is one that supplies 100 percent of recommended daily allowances—and no more than that.

Add a little activity to your schedule.

There's nothing like a little exercise to work up an appetite. Even an easy walk or gentle swim can get you in the mood to eat.●

POOR CIRCULATION

16 TIPS TO ENHANCE YOUR COMFORT

Poor circulation encompasses a spectrum of symptoms and conditions that result from a reduction in the flow of blood. The term applies specifically to blood circulation to the extremities—the arms, legs, hands, feet, fingers, and toes.

Symptoms of poor circulation include numbness, stinging, pain, and increased sensitivity to cold. Loss of all feeling may occur. Depending upon the cause of the problem, the skin in affected areas may discolor, turning blue or white or red.

Two major causes of poor circulation are peripheral vascular disease (PVD) and diabetes. PVD evolves from the same processes that cause coronary disease, except that in PVD the result is obstruction in blood vessels of the leg rather than arteries in the heart. The most common symptom is pain that occurs with standing or walking and is relieved by sitting or lying down (a condition known as intermittent claudication). Poorly controlled diabetes can lead to nerve and blood-vessel problems that pose special risks for the lower legs and feet. Less commonly, poor circulation may result from Raynaud disease, which affects the hands and fingers and involves extreme sensitivity to cold.

Poor circulation may also arise from age-related changes in the body. As people grow older, the heart's ability to pump blood may decline. Perhaps more importantly, the body's metabolic rate decreases, resulting in a slowdown in the release of energy and heat. This slowdown can increase sensitivity to cold.

VEINS CAN BE AFFECTED, TOO

○ ○ ○

The human circulatory system consists of two basic types of blood vessels: arteries and veins. Arteries carry oxygen- and nutrient-rich blood away from the heart to the rest of the body, while veins return oxygen-depleted blood to the heart and lungs.

The term *poor circulation* tends to be associated with blood flow through arteries, but circulatory disorders may also affect the veins. Two common problems of venous circulation are phlebitis and varicose veins.

Phlebitis refers to the development of a clot within a vein. The condition usually causes pain, inflammation, and swelling in the area of the obstruction, typically the lower leg. A physician can often make the diagnosis by probing the affected area and locating the clot by touch.

Phlebitis tends to be associated with an extended period of inactivity or bed rest, as might occur after an injury or surgery. In people who have a history of phlebitis, clots may even arise during long trips on airplanes or trains. In most cases, treatment for phlebitis consists of leg elevation, warm compresses, and anti-inflammatory drugs.

Varicose veins occur when valves in the veins malfunction. Blood pools in the veins, causing them to enlarge and become twisted. Sometimes they become dark blue in appearance. Pregnancy, obesity, and phlebitis may also play a role in some cases.

Supportive stockings or elastic bandages are a mainstay of treatment for varicose veins. Physical activity—such as walking, swimming, or biking—can help reduce pressure inside the veins. Leg elevation also helps reduce discomfort.

To guard against swelling and discomfort, avoid sitting or standing for long periods of time. Flex the feet and ankles periodically, and try to get up and move about from time to time whenever you spend a considerable amount of time sitting.

Here are 16 suggestions to help reduce the chances that poor circulation will knock you out of circulation.

Control your cholesterol.

A high cholesterol level is well known as a risk factor for coronary heart disease; it is also an important risk factor for PVD. Most people can reduce their risk and maintain a safe cholesterol level by following the daily dietary recommendations of the American Heart Association: no more than 30 percent of total calories as fat, no more than 10 percent of calories as saturated fat (found mainly in meat and animal products), and no more than 300 milligrams of cholesterol.

Stop smoking.

The link between cigarette smoking and PVD is at least as strong as between smoking and heart disease. Smoking cessation is important for relieving symptoms and limiting progress of PVD.

Watch your weight.

Excess weight increases the risk of high cholesterol and has a strong association with type 2 (adult-onset) diabetes. Extra weight also puts more strain on the cardiovascular system and can worsen the lower-leg pain associated with PVD.

Get enough exercise.

Regular exercise promotes weight loss and plays a role in controlling cholesterol, blood pressure, and diabetes. In people who already have PVD, exercise may help improve circulation by promoting the development of new blood vessels in the legs (a process called collateral circulation). In most instances, a daily brisk walk of 30 to 60 minutes' duration can greatly reduce the risk of PVD and provide relief of symptoms in people who already have poor blood circulation in the legs.

Don't ignore your muscles.

Modest weight training can help people maintain a better balance between muscle and body fat. As people age, their percentage of fat tends to increase, while muscle mass decreases. Muscle has a higher metabolic rate, which means it uses more energy (calories) and generates more heat. Increased muscle mass can therefore help to better regulate the body's internal thermostat and make people less sensitive to temperature, especially cold. Modest weight training does not mean heavy-duty weight lifting. Ask a physician, physical therapist, or fitness consultant for advice about how to incorporate weight training into your regular activity schedule.

Pay attention to nutrition.

As people grow older and their metabolic rate decreases, they often find themselves weighing more even though they're eating less. Thus, older people need to make a special effort to restrict their intake of high-fat foods but at the same time continue to eat adequate amounts of fruits, vegetables, and grain products.

Watch out for diabetes.

Diabetes greatly increases the risk of poor circulation, especially to the lower legs and feet. The risk of developing PVD for people with diabetes is two to three times greater than for those who do not have diabetes. And diabetes is the leading cause of lower-extremity amputation in the United States. In fact, the risk of amputation is 17 to 20 times higher compared to people who do not have the disease.

Take care of your nails.

Ingrown toenails, in particular, can pose a serious problem for people with diabetes and other problems that affect circulation to the lower legs and feet. Keep your nails clean and properly trimmed at all times. If arthritis or any other condition interferes with nail care, schedule pedicures on a regular basis.

Check your feet.

Poor circulation to the feet and toes can lead to complete loss of feeling, especially in people with diabetes. In some instances, a blister or some other sore may not be noticed until it has caused considerable damage to the skin and underlying tissue. If you have a history of poor circulation, inspect your feet regularly for sores, cuts, or breaks in the skin, all of which can lead to more serious problems if not treated.

Be alert for "bald toes."

Some medical experts believe that loss of hair from the feet or toes may indicate poor circulation. If you notice such hair loss, ask your physician about the need for an exam to check the circulation in your lower legs and feet.

Don't ignore symptoms.

Ignoring pain or loss of feeling is a risky business. If you have unexplained pain, numbness, or other potential symptoms of poor circulation at any time, notify your physician and let him or her decide on a proper course of action. Ignoring warning signs when they first appear can lead to serious problems down the road.

Keep warm clothes handy.

If you're chronically cool when others are comfortable, make sure that you keep various items of temperature-regulating clothes available for use—gloves or mittens, jackets, sweaters, shawls, and so on. When leaving the house, be sure to take them with you.

Check your house.

A drafty house or balky furnace can result in cooler indoor temperatures and add to the discomfort brought on by poor circulation. Have your house looked over to reveal drafts and other sources of uncomfortably cool air.

Don't compromise comfort.

When sitting around the house, if people around you are burning up with the heat while you feel just right, try using an afghan or a lap blanket to warm your personal space. This will allow your family to be comfortable and make you warmer. In addition, in the long run, adding a layer will be cheaper than turning up the heat.

Do you need aspirin?

If you have PVD, a blood clot can shut off blood flow through the affected blood vessel. Regular use of aspirin (usually one baby aspirin a day) can lower the risk of clot formation. If you're not already taking aspirin regularly, ask your physician about the wisdom of starting.

Take your medication.

A drug won't help you if you don't take it. If your physician has prescribed medication related to poor circulation, take it and take it on time—including aspirin. And don't stop taking it without first discussing the matter with your physician. If the drug is too expensive or causes side effects, suitable alternatives may be available.●

THE HIGH PRICE OF DIABETES

o o o

Poor circulation can lead to especially dire consequences in people who have diabetes. If left unchecked, tissue damage related to diabetes can predispose a person to severe infection, gangrene, and even amputation of a foot or lower leg. Every year diabetes accounts for more than 55,000 amputations, half of all amputations performed annually in the United States. Any person who has had one diabetes-associated amputation remains at high risk for tissue damage that will result in a second amputation.

POSTNASAL DRIP

7 STEPS TO THIN IT OUT

Gobs of sticky, gluey mucus stick to the back of your throat, and occasionally you are able to force them up, out, or down toward your stomach—by coughing or a gulping sort of hard swallow. You don't have a cold, your sinuses aren't hurting, your nose isn't even running, and you already had the flu. Why, you wonder, are you plagued by a constant drip of phlegm down the back of your throat? Sometimes you even feel a bit nauseated.

Postnasal drip is a purely modern expression, probably coined by someone in pharmaceutical advertising trying to sell decongestants. What it means is that your body simply isn't taking care of secretions in your nose and throat without a lot of hacking, sticky hassle.

The nasal membranes are lined with tiny, hairlike threads called cilia. The cilia wave back and forth as they trap particles and keep the passageways clear. Inside your nose, air is moistened and warmed up as it moves on to your lungs. Glands, located in your nasal passages as well as in the sinuses of your face, produce a thin and usually clear mucus that lubricates the membranes of your nose, mouth, and throat. If this mucus dries out or becomes irritated, it thickens, turns gluey, and gets stuck in your cilia. When this happens, you end up with an abnormal, bothersome drip instead of natural, harmless drainage—postnasal drip. The following steps will help to thin it out.

Drink fluids.

Water, tea, fruit and vegetable juices, and lemonade, can all help keep your membranes moist so cilia will be better able to perform their "housekeeping" job, sweeping passages clean. Drinking also helps soothe your throat if it's sore from coughing or clearing. And fluids will flush your digestive system.

Keep your nose clean.

Blow your nose often to clear out dried mucus. For a really thorough rinsing, try using a saline solution to get rid of phlegm. Nurses at LUNG LINE, a hot line operated by the National Jewish Center for Immunology and Respiratory Medicine in Denver, Colorado (800-222-LUNG), offer this recipe: Mix half a teaspoon of uniodized salt in an eight-ounce glass of warm water, and add a pinch of baking soda. Make a fresh solution daily, and store it in a clean glass or plastic bottle. Don't use salt substitutes, they warn, which will cause irritation. Pour some solution into the palm of your hand and "snuff" it up one nostril at a time, then spit it out through your mouth and blow your nose lightly afterward. It works best when your head is down and you are bending over a sink. You can also use a rubber syringe from the pharmacy. With your doctor's approval, do this once a day or as otherwise directed. Gargling with this solution can also help. Ask your doctor to provide other recommendations as well.

Turn down the heat.

Postnasal drip is often worse in winter months, and overheating your home doesn't help matters. Too much heat dries your membranes. As a result, secretions get thick and can't easily slide away. They start to stick, and you end up with the nasty drip.

Moisturize the air.

Look for a cool- or warm-mist humidifier or vaporizer, which can add important moisture to the air you breathe.

Beware of over-the-counter cures.

Nose drops, decongestants, antihistamines, and any other medicines supposed to stop postnasal drip shouldn't be used for more than a few days. If your doctor has diagnosed a sinus condition, decongestants can help thin mucus. But if you don't have a professional opinion about your postnasal drip, be careful.

Consider hormones.

Reports indicate that estrogen has an effect on mucus linings throughout your body. If you are a woman going through menopause, the normal drop in this hormone could be affecting your nasal passages. Raise this possibility with your doctor.

Exercise.

Your muscular, respiratory, and circulatory systems desperately need regular, vigorous use. Check with your doctor before starting an exercise program, however.●

PSORIASIS

---

22 WAYS TO TREAT IT

For millions of Americans, the heartbreak of psoriasis is an all-too-real fact of life. This chronic, incurable skin condition is seldom life-threatening and only rarely causes severe disabilities. But the unsightly outbreaks it produces on the skin can be painful, inconvenient, and emotionally devastating.

Men and women are prone to psoriasis in equal numbers and at any age, although outbreaks are more common in people in their 20s and in their 50s. Heredity is thought to play some role in the tendency to develop psoriasis, though some sufferers have no family history of the condition.

The first signs of psoriasis are tiny red dots on the skin. Over a few days these enlarge and become covered with silvery scales. Outbreaks can occur on almost any part of the body, but commonly they show up on the knees, elbows, scalp, hands, and feet, and sometimes on the arms, legs, and genitals. For most people, psoriasis outbreaks are limited to only a few patches of skin. But for others, the patches can cover large parts of the body.

What causes psoriasis is not thoroughly understood, but it is known that something about the body's biochemistry triggers abnormal skin-cell growth. It takes about 30 days for a normal skin cell to develop. In psoriasis, the cells mature in just three days, causing them to pile up on top of the skin to form the scaly plaques.

Sometimes an outbreak will subside on its own, not to reappear for many years. In other cases, the condition lingers on and on. Whenever the condition strikes, there is plenty you can do to treat psoriasis and keep it from getting the best of you.

Become a sun worshiper.

We hear a lot of sound advice about the dangers of taking in too much sun, but if you have psoriasis, moderate sunlight can be your best friend. Ultraviolet light from the sun appears to slow skin-cell growth and can have a wonderful effect in clearing up psoriasis outbreaks. However, be careful. Approach your sun therapy sessions as if you were trying to tan very gradually, taking in the sun a little at a time. Be aware that as helpful as the sun is for your psoriasis, it remains public enemy number one for your skin generally. Cover exposed skin that is not affected by psoriasis with sunscreen, and take the usual precautions when spending time in the sun.

Step into the tanning parlor.

Light treatments with artificial light can also be effective in fighting psoriasis. However, since exposure to ultraviolet light sources can damage skin, consult your physician before beginning such a regimen. Often a physician will suggest that you combine light treatments with medication. The oral medication psoralen, for instance, taken a short time before treatment, has been shown to enhance the effectiveness of light therapy.

Moisten up.

Lubricating your skin regularly will reduce inflammation and scaling, and it may prevent a psoriasis outbreak from progressing. Dry and cracking skin also leaves you vulnerable to secondary infec-

tions, which can be especially troublesome during a psoriasis outbreak. Any moisturizer should do, but try this rule of thumb: the heavier and greasier it is, the better. Heavy hand creams and plain old petroleum jelly work very well.

Slather on medicated creams.

Creams and shampoos containing salicylic acid can be very effective in clearing up psoriasis outbreaks, as can topical cortisone creams. Lower-strength preparations are available over the counter, and you may want to ask your physician about a prescription for higher-strength concentrations. Some potent, high-strength steroid creams, available only by prescription, may be particularly effective in treating psoriasis. Another often-prescribed medication is anthralin, a strong topical ointment that is highly effective but must be used judiciously because it can stain the skin.

Try tar.

Coal tar is an age-old remedy for psoriasis, and it seems to go a long way toward reducing itching and scaling. Creams, shampoos, and bath oils containing coal tar in limited amounts are available over the counter, and more concentrated preparations are available by prescription. Psoriasis sufferers often apply a coal-tar cream directly to the affected area or soak in a bath to which a coal-tar solution has been added.

Wrap it up.

To optimize the effects of topical treatments and moisturizers, try wrapping the affected area in plastic wrap or in a skin patch (sold over the counter) after you apply the cream or lotion. The wrap will seal in moisture and help the medication penetrate deeper into the psoriasis lesions. Don't overdo it, though—when the skin becomes too soggy, it is prone to secondary infections.

Check the other medications you take.

Certain medications can aggravate psoriasis. The risk list includes certain blood pressure and heart medicines, including some beta-blockers; lithium; and anti-malarial medications. Give your dermatologist a rundown of the medications you take: If a conflict arises, a substitution can often be made with a drug that doesn't aggravate psoriasis.

Don't hide out.

If you're like many people with psoriasis, you may be tempted to wear concealing clothing that will cover up the outbreak or to hole up indoors, out of public view. Try to overcome your self-consciousness, because exposing the affected area to sunlight is one of the best things you can do to speed recovery. Getting out and going about your normal business will also help you cope better psychologically with psoriasis.

Relax.

There's evidence that psoriasis outbreaks are stress related, so avoiding stress and learning how to cope with it may be other ways to prevent outbreaks. Unfor-

tunately, the appearance of psoriasis is not the sort of thing that's likely to reduce your stress level. And the more concerned you are about the unsightly sores, the more likely you are to notice the discomfort they can cause. Try to take it easy and be kind to yourself. Listen to your favorite music, read an engrossing novel, spend some time pursuing your favorite activities, take a walk—do whatever it takes to calm yourself down and make it easier to weather the storm of a psoriasis outbreak.

TRY SOME OLD-FASHIONED REMEDIES

o o o

You may need to look no further than your kitchen cabinets to find some tried and true remedies for psoriasis. Remember, a good part of the battle is keeping the affected area lubricated to prevent itching. So bring out the artillery of anti-itch treatments your grandmother may have used.

- Before you settle into the tub for a soothing soak, try adding any of these to the bath water: a cup of white vinegar, some Epsom salts, a handful of oatmeal, or a couple of teaspoons of olive oil mixed with a glass of milk.

- Dissolve three tablespoons of boric acid in 16 ounces of water or 1½ cups of baking soda in 3 gallons of water, soak a sterile cloth (like a gauze bandage you buy at the drugstore) in the mixture, and apply it to the affected area as a compress.

- If you have a psoriasis outbreak on your scalp, try this gentle shampoo treatment: Heat a little olive oil until it is warm but not hot, gently massage it into the affected area, then rinse. The olive oil may help loosen the pesky scales.

Take a trip.

If you're suffering from a psoriasis outbreak, there may never be a better time to head for sunny climes, especially during the winter months.

Beware of achy joints.

About ten percent of psoriasis sufferers develop psoriatic arthritis, which may damage joints, especially those in the hands and feet. If you feel any joint stiffness or notice that your joints seem to be inflamed, see your physician immediately.

Nip infections in the bud.

An infected tooth, a chronic sinus infection, a systemic infection like strep throat, or any other infection can trigger a psoriasis outbreak. If you're prone to psoriasis and develop an infection, see your doctor without delay.

Protect your skin against injury.

A scratch, cut, or even the irritation from tight clothing—and that includes tight-fitting shoes—can bring on a psoriasis outbreak. Take special care to avoid activities that might put undo pressure on your skin.

Stock up on gentle soaps.

Harsh soaps can irritate psoriasis. Use a mild moisturizing soap, such as a soap formulated for dry skin, or a soap-free cleanser. And however mild the soap product you use, be sure to rinse well: Soapy residue may cause itching.

Stop that itch.

Tempted as you'll be to scratch that patch of psoriasis, understand that scratching will only make it worse. When the itching gets the best of you, try taking an over-the-counter antihistamine. Cap-

saicin creams, derived from hot peppers, have been found to be especially effective in stifling the psoriasis itch.

Soak your troubles away.

A warm, soothing bath can be just the thing when psoriasis flares up. A shower, swim, or session in a Jacuzzi or whirlpool can do the trick, too. These hydrotherapy sessions will bring relief in several ways. A good soak rehydrates the skin, soothes irritation, helps reduce itching, and takes some of the redness out. The water will also gently dislodge the plaques that build up on a psoriasis outbreak, so you'll get more benefit from the healing effects of the sun. Your skin will also appreciate the moisturizers and topical medications you apply after soaking. Since a soak is likely to draw oils from your skin, it's very important to apply moisturizing creams as soon as you step out of the water—within three minutes or so. Otherwise, your skin may dry out. That's when you should apply medicated ointments, too, before scaly plaque (which acts as a barrier to medication) has a chance to build up again.

Kick the smoking habit.

Some research shows that smoking may increase the risk of developing psoriasis. In addition to all the other health benefits that come with quitting, then, you might also reduce your chances of having to cope with this painful condition.

Slim down.

There appears to be some link between carrying excess weight and the frequency and severity of psoriasis outbreaks. A low-fat diet and regular exercise may lessen the effects of psoriasis and do your heart a lot of good, too. Other benefits of a weight-loss regimen will help you cope better with psoriasis, as well: The exercise will help you relax (and stress is a factor in psoriasis), and the weight loss will do wonders for your self image.

Cut back on alcohol.

Alcohol is thought to be another factor that might contribute to psoriasis. And drinking may act as a double whammy for the psoriasis prone: Since alcohol is a depressant, it may contribute to the feelings of depression that can accompany a psoriasis outbreak.

Put fish on the menu.

Some research suggests that the omega-3 oils in salmon and other cold-water fish may be beneficial in keeping psoriasis at bay. But caution is the buzzword here. It appears that a lot of fish oil is needed to provide the antipsoriasis benefits, so you should talk to your physician before going on this "fishy" regimen. Besides, you don't want to risk overdosing on vitamins A and D.

Crank up the humidifier.

Dry air will aggravate your psoriasis. This is of special concern in the winter, when the heat is on and the air in your home and office is likely to be unusually dry. Use room humidifiers and try putting pans of water on radiators or near heating ducts to add that extra bit of moisture to the air.

Think positively.

It's hard enough to live with any chronic condition, not to mention one like psoriasis, which can not only be painful but also unsightly. And it's liable to make you feel like a bit of an oddball. Psoriasis can have a negative effect on your mood, get in the way of your social life, and even affect your job performance. The trick is not to let psoriasis get you down. This is easier said than done, of course, but when an outbreak flares up, try to think positively and keep the following thoughts in mind:

- You're not alone. It's estimated that nearly five million Americans suffer from periodic bouts of psoriasis. (See sidebar, "Help Is Only a Phone Call Away.")

- It's not contagious. Psoriasis can't be passed on, so don't let an outbreak keep you from spending time with understanding family members and friends.

- Psoriasis is not self-inflicted. Your outbreak has nothing to do with your sanitary habits or failure to maintain proper levels of cleanliness. So don't hang your head in shame.

- No matter how bad the outbreak, the situation is not hopeless. There's a lot you can do to treat the problem. Any of the ideas mentioned here, or a combination of them, may work for you. And researchers continue working to find new treatments and potential cures.●

HELP IS ONLY A PHONE CALL AWAY

○ ○ ○

The National Psoriasis Foundation in Portland, Oregon, is ready and willing to help you with loads of informative brochures, physician recommendations, and referrals to local support groups. You can reach the not-for-profit organization at: 6600 Southwest 92nd Avenue, Suite 300, Portland, Oregon 97223, or by telephone at 800-248-0886 or 503-297-1546.

RESTLESS LEGS

12 WAYS TO GET RELIEF

It seems to happen when you least expect it. Last night this strange twitching and jerking feeling, this restless sensation—as if someone had placed jumping beans in your lower legs—started when you were at the movies and became worse despite your attempts to concentrate fully on the screen. You may be one of the approximately 15 percent of the people (mostly women) in their 50s and beyond who experience restless leg syndrome (RLS), and you've learned that the only way you're going to get relief is by moving around.

The episodes can take place just when you're trying to fall asleep or in the middle of the night, or both, and sometimes during the day, though daytime symptoms don't seem as bad as the ones that wake you at night. There is no warning, and you never know how long they will last—a few minutes or a few hours. But it is known that RLS runs in families and tends to get worse as you get older.

The major problem for most of those who have RLS at night is that the episodes occur frequently, taking away any chance you might have of a good night's sleep. This leads to all sorts of undesirable consequences, including depression, the possibility of insomnia, and an increased risk of accidents because you're frequently tired.

Here are some ways to seek relief from this troublesome malady.

Get fit.

Aerobic exercise will help your circulation and add to your overall well-being. Walk, jog, bike, or swim. But not within two hours of bedtime.

Strengthen and stretch.

Do some of your walking with weights on your ankles. Use the fitness machines at your local community center or work out with elastic bands. Do stretching exercises for your calf muscles when you get up in the morning and before bed.

Seek support.

Support hose help improve circulation in your calves. They are available at medical supply stores.

Start walking.

When symptoms begin, get up and walk; it may relieve tingling.

Choose a good spot.

In a theater, plane, or bus, choose a seat on the aisle. That will allow you to stretch and move your legs easily—or even get up and walk around.

Massage your legs.

Poor circulation may be a factor that brings on symptoms. Massage warms leg muscles and increases circulation.

Check your diet.

Make sure you're getting enough vitamins and minerals. RLS has been associated with diets lacking in some of these vital nutrients, particularly vitamins B and E, iron, and magnesium.

Avoid caffeine.

Skip coffee or soda in the evening. And cut down on caffeine intake during the day, including chocolate. Check your medications for caffeine content; ask for a caffeine-free substitute.

Consider aspirin.

Many people counter RLS with two aspirin before bed; others say aspirin has no effect. It's worth a try, but check with your doctor first.

Wrap 'em up.

You'll get some relief from symptoms by covering your lower legs with warm damp towels for five to ten minutes. Try this a couple of times a day.

Soak in a warm tub.

It may provide some relief before bed, particularly if you have circulation problems.

Seek help from a pro.

Many people have found relief with medical treatment, so call your family physician and explain the symptoms. If your doctor is not familiar with the condition, contact a sleep disorders specialist.●

RINGING IN THE EARS

7 STEPS TO STOP IT

Absolute inner quiet is something you crave desperately because of the nearly constant ringing, roaring, buzzing, clicking, or hissing inside your head. Tinnitus, the technical name for ringing in the ears, is a real torment for millions. In some cases, the sounds are so constant and so overpowering that leading a normal life becomes impossible.

The outside of your ear is shaped like a funnel. It gathers sound waves and directs them down a tube to your eardrum. Tiny hairs line this canal as well as the fluid-filled chamber behind the eardrum. Vibrations and electrical impulses are picked up by these delicate sensors so messages can be passed along via the auditory nerve to your brain. Your brain interprets the sounds and tells you what you hear. Occasionally, hair cells are damaged and don't know when to stop sending signals. A little muscle called the tensor tympani inside your ear acts like a shock absorber. If you rock your eardrum with extremely loud sounds, sometimes this little muscle keeps moving and flexing even after the sound has stopped. Continuous electrical pulses and vibrations keep your auditory nerve standing on end, even when noise ceases. Overexposure to loud noise, an abundance of earwax, ear infections, a perforated eardrum, fluid in the ear, or problems with the middle ear bones are among the possible causes. See an ear, nose, and throat specialist to rule out serious medical problems. In the meantime, the following tips may help.

Quiet down.

Is the sound on your television turned up as loud as it can go? Do you listen to audio equipment at the highest volume? If so, turn down the sound. Continued exposure to loud noise damages the tiny hair cells in your ears. Give your body a chance to heal those hair cells.

A decibel is the smallest measure of sound that can be heard by the average human ear. In normal conversation, voices register 60 decibels, while a tractor trailer might hit 100, and live rock music registers at between 120 and 140 decibels. Wear earplugs to protect yourself from sounds higher than 90 decibels.

Check your medicine cabinet.

Be particularly mindful of your aspirin intake, for example. High, regular doses of aspirin for arthritis, chronic pain, or a heart condition can cause tinnitus. That little muscle in your ear, the tensor tympani, also reacts to very high doses of aspirin. Call your doctor and, if possible,

lower your intake to see if the ringing stops. Many over-the-counter medicines for pain contain aspirin as an ingredient, so be sure to read labels before you look for alternatives. Ringing in the ears can be a side effect of other drugs, such as barbiturates, quinine, and systemic aminoglycosides (streptomycin and oral neomycin, for example).

Take your blood pressure.

Ask a physician to measure your blood pressure. Ringing in the ears is one possible symptom of high blood pressure, or hypertension, which is a serious medical condition that affects millions of people but often has no symptoms.

Rest.

A rundown body is more likely to fall victim to colds, infections, and influenza, which can aggravate tinnitus. Ringing in the ears has been related to exposure to stress as well.

Cut the caffeine habit.

Caffeine has been identified as a tinnitus culprit. Eliminate all caffeine for a few days to see if your condition clears up.

Exercise.

Start a regular regimen of walking, jogging, or some similar exercise. In addition to its many other benefits, exercise can help with the problem of poor circulation that could cause tinnitus.

Compete with the buzz.

Ask your doctor about electronic devices that look like hearing aids but generate pleasant, competing sounds capable of masking the troublesome buzzing or ringing in your ears. Or simply cover up your tinnitus with soft background music.●

SEASONAL AFFECTIVE DISORDER (SAD)

12 APPROACHES TO MANAGING SAD

You are really feeling down. Nothing seems to make you smile, and it's taking all the strength you can muster just to get ready to see your grandchildren. You just don't feel like going outside. It's been cold and wet and gloomy for the past 6 weeks and there's still another 12 weeks before spring arrives.

Believe it or not, there's a name for what you're feeling: seasonal affective disorder, or SAD. At one time reports of cyclical mood patterns were brushed aside as baseless or inconsequential. But not any more. SAD is now recognized as a depressive syndrome that ranges in severity from mild to incapacitating. Its symptoms embrace all the characteristics of full-blown clinical depression, including sleep disorders, changes in eating habits, loss of energy, loss of interest in sex—even suicidal thoughts.

SAD follows a seasonal pattern, with symptoms of depression in autumn and winter, a return to equilibrium in the spring, and quite often the joy of "up" moods during the summer months. If you have it, you probably start feeling sad during wet or overcast periods in early September. Laziness or apathy is often the first clue. If you're usually very active, you may find yourself starting to put off some tasks because you lack sufficient energy and can't concentrate. Or you may feel irritable and more easily angered. It's not uncommon to feel depressed, tearful, angry, hostile, and just overwhelmed in general. Many people with SAD say they tend to feel unhappy and withdraw from family and friends.

Interestingly, four times as many women as men are affected, although the reasons for this are not understood. For the majority of SAD sufferers, symptoms are at their worst at the very beginning of the new year, in January and February.

An accurate diagnosis is the first step toward treating SAD. Typically a positive diagnosis requires evidence of major depression at least once in your life, an autumnal/winter depression for two consecutive years, and the absence of other factors (such as psychiatric problems) that could explain your mood swings. If you have to deal with SAD in yourself or others, keep in mind that the problem is very treatable.

Here are a few approaches to managing your SADness.

Light up your life.

Use phototherapy treatment. Many people get relief by soaking up light from special fluorescent bulbs that shine 5 to 20 times more brilliantly than the usual household bulb. Studies show that for approximately three-quarters of SAD sufferers, basking in such light for a mere half-hour to several hours each morning can relieve symptoms in only a few days. (In some cases, additional late-afternoon

---

WARNING!
. . .
There are side effects to phototherapy

It is possible to use this treatment to excess. Begin to suspect overuse if you develop headaches, eyestrain, or mild nausea or if you become easily aggravated and distressed. The solution is to simply cut down on exposure time.

---

or early-evening sessions may be necessary.) It is believed that as the winter progresses and the days shorten, it may be necessary to increase the time of exposure to phototherapy to keep pace with the reduced amount of sunlight.

Relax.

Stress is the major cause of fatigue and anxiety, and one way to cope with it is to practice stress-reducing techniques. Try a class in relaxation; borrow a book or a tape from the library on how to relax using yoga, meditation, or perhaps the Chinese martial art of T'ai Chi Chu'an; take a long weekend just for yourself; or go to a spa. Such techniques are useful at any time for stress reduction, but they can be especially valuable during those depressing gray winter days.

Exercise.

Exercise relaxes muscles, reduces fatigue, and promotes sound sleep. People who exercise regularly report feeling more self-confident and more productive in their work—all of which may help fight the winter blahs. And if you can exercise in a natural setting outdoors, so much the better. You may benefit every bit as much from walking in fresh air and sunlight as from light therapy.

Get counseling.

Many health care professionals are well informed about SAD and experienced in treating its symptoms.

Take vacations in sunny, warm climates.

Aside from the break provided by the change in climate, the travel and the departure from your usual routine may have rejuventating effects that last long after the photos pasted in an album. Be sure to wear a sunblock to protect your skin from too much sun, however.

Modify your home.

Maximize window exposure and increase the quality and intensity of interior lighting. Use an array of plants as reminders that spring will arrive before long. Paint the interior of your house in light colors to maximize light reflection indoors.

Get outside as much as you can.

Make a point of using your lunch hour to expose yourself to some strong noontime daylight. Bundle up if necessary, and get walking shoes if you need them, but get out for a brisk walk before or after lunch.

Maintain a good social network.

Some of the best buffers against depressive moods are convivial friends, warm family bonds, and a host of social engagements that keep you active. Get involved in activities at your church, temple, or mosque. Join a social club. Invite family and friends over for dinner.

Dodge certain foods.

Learn which foods can affect your moods, then avoid them. Among the most common offenders are alcohol, chocolate, and sugar.

Keep in shape.

Fight bad moods with sensible eating. Carbohydrates, when eaten in reasonable amounts, may lift your spirits, but be moderate in how much you eat. You don't want to lift your depression from SAD only to create new problems by becoming overweight.

Be an informed consumer.

Mood disorders can be complex illnesses with multiple causes and complicating factors. Since doctors and other health-care providers differ markedly in their responses to SAD, you need to inform yourself about the syndrome and act as coordinator of your own care. Ask your doctor for guidance. And understand that more than one factor could be involved. For example, you may be bothered by SAD, but you might also be experiencing a problem that actually results from a thyroid disorder.

Take prescription antidepressant medication.

Under the careful guidance of your physician, a regimen of medication specifically designed for the control of depression may be recommended. If so, be sure to take it exactly as directed and be alert for side effects. Consult with your doctor about potential interactions with other medications.●

SENSITIVE TEETH

6 TIPS TO MAKE YOU SMILE

Seemingly simple acts can send you through the roof: drinking an icy cold soda, sipping a hot cup of tea, or crunching down on a bite of granola in your cereal bowl this morning. If you have sensitive teeth, ordinary eating and drinking can drive you crazy, sending shivers of real pain up your spine. Even exposure to cold air can make the act of opening your mouth something you would rather avoid.

According to dental experts, there are no easy answers to explain this phenomenon. As we age, our teeth are beset with various problems that can nudge them up the sensitivity scale. The root of the problem can be anything from a single damaged tooth to erosion of tooth enamel, especially at the point where the gums may be receding. Dentin, the material underneath the tooth enamel, has microscopic nerve endings that will make you cringe when they are exposed. You aren't alone, because age is often a factor in tooth sensitivity. And don't be shy about bringing up this question at your next regular checkup. Sensitive teeth could signal a serious problem requiring root-canal surgery. The promising news is that, in many cases, the older you get, the less sensitive your teeth become. Meanwhile, if your pain is severe and lasts longer than an hour, consider it a dental emergency.

Teeth can become sensitized because of pressure somewhere inside your jaw. You may have chewed on something too hard recently, jamming a tooth out of its place. Or perhaps you are in the habit of unconsciously grinding your teeth. People who tend to clamp their jaws together can end up with extrasensitive teeth, too. If your pain shows up only occasionally—when you eat or drink something hot, cold, or sweet, for example—then you probably don't need to worry. If you feel persistent pressure, however, you may have cracked or broken a tooth. In addition to making a dental appointment, you can try these tips.

Use special toothpaste.

Several brands of toothpaste contain an ingredient that actually fills up the worn-down spots on your enamel as you brush. Buy one and use it for at least two weeks. Besides putting it on your toothbrush for your regular cleaning, squeeze a little of this paste on your finger and run it over your teeth before you go to bed. Spit out any excess, but don't rinse your mouth.

Clean your teeth often.

Plaque, the yellow, gummy buildup on your unbrushed teeth, not only causes cavities, it can make sensitive areas even more agonizing when they are stimulated. If plaque is given free rein and destroys enamel in your mouth, it also creates an acid that can irritate teeth. Fight back by brushing and flossing daily.

Use a soft toothbrush.

A hard-bristled brush being used the wrong way and too abrasively on older teeth can actually break down enamel and expose the softer dentin underneath. If you are an overzealous scrubber, you may do more harm than good.

Rinse.

Use a fluoride rinse at least once a day, especially if your teeth are decayed.

Watch what you eat and drink.

Stay away from extreme temperatures as well as extra sweet or sour foods and drinks. Don't suck on hard candy, for instance, because it could be causing abrasion of the enamel.

Relax.

An unhealthy dose of stress can actually affect your dental health. Saliva will become more acidic when you are stressed to your outer limits. When you grind your teeth or clamp them closed, the pressure can cause the teeth to ache. Check with your dentist about what may be unconscious habits wreaking havoc in your mouth. In the meantime, learn how to relax. When you feel your body tense, your teeth clench, or your neck and shoulder muscles tighten, try to let the anxiety go. Relax.●

SHINGLES

12 WAYS TO COPE

You wake up one morning feeling a little achy and not quite yourself. You might notice a slight tinge on one side of your torso or face or on one of your legs. Within a few days, purplish itchy blisters erupt in the same area and you begin to experience pain—not just any pain, but perhaps some of the most excruciating pain you've ever had to endure. There's a good chance, especially if you're over 50, that you have shingles.

Shingles blisters often begin to subside after a week or so and are not too likely to make a repeat appearance. But the bad news is that some shingles sufferers, especially those older than age 60, develop a painful nerve condition called postherpetic neuralgia that can persist for years.

The spots and itching of shingles may well remind you of your childhood bout with chicken pox, and there's a good reason for that. Your case of shingles is a reactivation of the same virus, herpes zoster, that triggered your case of chicken pox and has remained with you through the years, lodged in nerve cells. Although you can develop shingles at any age, you are more prone to an outbreak as you grow older and your immune system begins to weaken. Likewise, diseases that impair your immune function, such as some forms of cancer, may also leave you prone to shingles.

Unpleasant as a case of shingles can be, there is medical help for the disease, as well as many measures you can take at home to help the blisters subside and to make the pain more bearable.

Get your doctor on the phone.

If you suspect you have shingles, the first order of business is to see your physician without delay. The sooner you get treatment, the better the chances are that you can avoid the long-term pain that can accompany a shingles outbreak. Some studies show that the antiviral drug acyclovir, taken early in the course of shingles, may help reduce persistent shingles pain by preventing the spread and limiting the severity of the disease. Other antiviral drugs may help, too.

Watch your eyes.

If shingles flares up on your face, forehead, or anywhere near your eyes, there is a risk of impaired vision due to damage to the cornea. See your physician without delay.

Wrap up your blisters.

For relief from itching, burning shingles blisters, try dipping a clean towel or cloth in ice water or cold milk and wrapping it around the affected area. A bag of frozen peas, wrapped in a towel, will also do the trick. Whatever method you select, leave the compress on for 20 minutes, take it off for 20 minutes, and repeat the sequence for as long as the treatment spells relief.

Take it easy.

One way to restore a flagging immune system—and shingles acts up when your immune defenses are down—is to get plenty of rest. A little R&R should also make it easier to cope with the pain.

Take a couple of aspirin.

Or take ibuprofen, acetaminophen, or any other over-the-counter pain killer that usually works well for you. Ibuprofen, provided you're not allergic to it, may

be especially beneficial—it has the added advantage of reducing the inflammation that can accompany shingles blistering.

Slather on relief.

Treatment with any number of topical ointments may calm your blistered skin. Local anesthetic creams may work, but beware of Benadryl or ointments ending in "-caine," which may trigger an allergic reaction, the last thing you want to deal with when you're battling shingles. Calamine lotion may help dry up oozing blisters and ease the pain a bit. Domeboro, an astringent available at drugstores and applied on a compress (follow the instructions on the package), also helps dry out blisters.

Keep your hands off 'em.

Strong as the temptation is to pick, scratch, or pop your blisters, don't do it. You will only irritate them and put yourself through more agony. Besides, the blisters will go away sooner if you leave them intact and let them heal.

Keep your blisters out in the open.

Tempted as you may be to cover up those ugly blisters, don't hide them under bandages or restrictive clothing. The fresh air will help them heal faster. Of course, shingles may occur on certain parts of the body that out of modesty you'll want to keep covered in public. Just remember that tight-fitting clothing can irritate shingles blisters; opt for loose-fitting cotton apparel.

Beware of secondary infections.

Any sores on your skin can become infected, and that goes for shingles blisters, too. Try to keep the affected area clean, but use mild, nonabrasive soap so you don't irritate the blisters. If you think the sores might be infected (if they become enlarged or begin to ooze pus, for example) speak to your physician, who may suggest that you use an antibacterial ointment or may prescribe an antibiotic.

Thanks for not sharing.

While shingles is not contagious, the herpes zoster virus that causes shingles and chicken pox, its partner in crime, is highly contagious. So keep your distance from children who haven't been exposed to the virus as well as from anyone whose immune system is severely compromised—someone with AIDS, for instance, or someone who has recently received a transplanted organ.

Pepper the pain.

Capsaicin cream, derived from the same plant family that produces red peppers, has been shown in several clinical studies to provide relief to people suffering from postherpetic neuralgia, the painful condition that can linger on long after shingles blisters go away. Capsaicin,

A RAY OF HOPE?

○ ○ ○

The recent development of a chicken-pox vaccine may be good news on the shingles front. Since shingles is linked to the same virus, there is some evidence that what works for chicken pox may work for shingles, too. Accordingly, clinical trials involving thousands of older people are now underway to determine what, if any, protection the new vaccine may provide against shingles. Stay tuned.

which is sold over the counter for muscle aches and pains, can burn like the dickens when first applied. But if you can tolerate the initial discomfort, capsaicin may well bring long-term relief. Talk to your physician before beginning a capsaicin regimen, and don't use it until all the blisters have healed.

Ask your doctor about antidepressants.

Even if you're not depressed, these medications may help you deal with the emotional strain of ongoing pain. And some antidepressants may actually lessen pain by increasing brain levels of a chemical agent (a neurotransmitter, to be precise) called serotonin, which is believed to weaken pain signals reaching the brain.●

SINUSITIS

8 WAYS TO FACE IT

Your nose feels stuffed up, though you don't really have a cold anymore. A pain comes and goes across your cheekbones and up around your eyes and forehead. When you lean forward, it hurts. Your headache is worse in the morning. Your face is painful, perhaps a bit swollen or sensitive when touched. Postnasal drip is driving you crazy as gobs of mucus slip down the back of your throat, upsetting your stomach and making you cough. To compound the problem, friends have been complaining about your bad breath. What's the cause? Sinus problems...and you are certainly not alone. In both its acute and chronic forms, sinusitis (the formal name for an infection of one or more of the sinuses) may be more common than arthritis.

Your sinuses may be out of sight, but when you are hit with an infection in these hollow facial cavities, they are certainly not out of mind. Here's the layout—you have four pairs of sinuses: 1) frontal sinuses above your eyebrows, 2) maxillary sinuses underneath your eyes inside your cheekbones, 3) ethmoidal sinuses between your eyes and nose, and 4) a pair of sphenoidal sinuses back behind the ethmoids. The sinuses act as a resonating chamber for your voice. They also lighten the skull because they contain air. They even play a role in warming and humidifying the air you take in through your nose, but it is minor.

All sinus infections begin as infections in the nose. Bacteria; viruses; and particles of dust, pollen, or other allergens get trapped in the mucus of your irritated nasal passages or in any one of those sinus cavities, allowing nasty infections to brew.

Call your doctor if the pain lasts for more than three days, if you are running a fever, and if the mucus is thick and yellow, brown, or green. Healthy mucus is clear to white and watery. If you have asthma, don't wait for three days, phone immediately because sinusitis can trigger asthma episodes. In the meantime, don't take this kind of pain passively. Here are eight ways to "face" the situation.

Unstuff your sinuses.

Moisture and plenty of humidity can keep mucus moving. Take a long, steamy shower or a hot bath, and blow your nose while the bathroom is foggy.

Drink water.

At least eight tall glasses of water a day will hydrate your system, thinning the phlegm. Keep a tall bottle of cool water nearby at all times. Try sipping mugs of warm fluids like hot tea or soup. Cradle your cup and sniff up the steam.

Beware of over-the-counter medications.

Decongestants (sometimes referred to as sinus pills) can relieve sinus pressure and break up congestion by opening those clogged cavities and easing your pain. Antihistamines, however, may dry your nose and actually thicken nasal secretions, worsening the problem. So choose your over-the-counter relief carefully, and be sure to follow the directions for use. Keep in mind that nose drops and nasal sprays that contain decongestants can hurt more than they help if used for an extended period. When the drops wear off, you may experience a rebound effect—more swelling, more congestion, and the same old symptoms. So never use over-the-counter nasal sprays for more than three days. If your condition hasn't cleared by then, see your doctor.

Don't combine.

Combining any over-the-counter medication with other regular prescriptions can be dangerous. For instance, if you are being treated for glaucoma, medicines commonly taken for hay fever or sinusitis can raise the pressure in your eye. If you have emphysema or chronic bronchitis, taking something for a case of sinusitis without telling your doctor could cause other problems. Sinus medicines might dry the mucus in your chest and bring on breathing difficulties; they should not be taken if you are using an antihypertensive medication. And don't take decongestants or antihistamines if you are using antidepressants, tranquilizers, or sleeping pills, or if you have prostate problems. Some sinus medications have been known to raise blood pressure in otherwise healthy adults.

If you want to try an over-the-counter sinus medication and you have a medical condition or are taking prescription medications, consult your doctor or pharmacist first. And be sure to read the labels carefully and follow directions. Some contain aspirin or another pain reliever, so you'll want to be sure you don't take any additional pain medicine at the same time.

Take preventive steps.

Enhance your body's ability to fight off infectious invaders by eating a balanced diet, exercising, getting enough sleep, and taking your health seriously. Stay in good shape and you'll also lessen the severity of any infection that blows in your direction.

A Salty Solution

○ ○ ○

Cleaning out your clogged up nose could be key to ending your sinusitis. Here are two doctor-recommended ways to irrigate nasal passages, keep sinus swelling down, and wash out mucus or bacteria. Mix a teaspoon of salt in 16 ounces of warm water. Add a pinch of baking soda. Make a fresh solution daily, and store it in a clean glass or plastic bottle. Don't use a salt substitute, which will irritate your nose.

1. Pour some of this mixture into the palm of your hand, lean over the sink, and "snuff" it up one nostril at a time. Blow your nose gently, then spit.

2. Buy a large rubber syringe, fill it with the salty solution and lean over a sink. Pinch your nose a bit and insert the tip just inside one nostril while you gently squeeze the bulb several times. Your aim here is to make the solution go up your nose and over the roof of your mouth. Now do the other side.

Recognize early signs of infection.

Treat cold and flu symptoms without delay, following your doctor's orders.

Avoid allergens.

If possible, stay away from triggers that make you feel terrible. Avoid cigarette smoke, and don't go outdoors when air quality is poor.

Ozone, which is the major component of smog, is the byproduct of the sun's action on automobile exhaust. If you live in a sunny area with lots of car traffic, then you may be inviting trouble with your sinuses as well as other, more serious, breathing difficulties. For example, sinusitis is considered a trigger for asthma. Other air pollutants that can cause problems are sulfur dioxide, a gas produced in heavy industry, and nitrogen dioxide, a product of gas stoves and a possible cause of indoor air pollution.

Whenever you hear the words "air pollution alert" on your radio or television, the American Academy of Allergy and Immunology suggests these precautions: Avoid unnecessary physical activity. Stay inside and put on an air conditioner if you have one. Avoid smoking and smoke-filled rooms. Keep medication handy for any breathing problem. Avoid dust and other irritants.

Stay away from sick people.

A surgical mask offers the most protection from another person's bug. In lieu of such total coverage, avoid standing near people who are sneezing or coughing. When friends or family members have a cold or the flu, don't drink from the same glass or share silverware. Avoid close contact. Ask others to dispose of used tissues properly and to cover their sneezes and coughs. And most of all, wash your hands frequently.●

SMOKING AND TOBACCO USE

11 WAYS TO BREAK AN OLD HABIT

You've smoked for more years than you care to remember. You can't imagine going through a day without a cigarette, and you have all the traits of an inveterate smoker—the extra wrinkles, the stained teeth and fingers, the ever-present hacking cough. So you figure what's the point in quitting now? Isn't the damage already done? Well, think again. Not long ago, a report from the Surgeon General of the United States systematically reviewed all the reasons why kicking the tobacco habit offers major and immediate health benefits to people over 50—even if they already suffer from smoking-related diseases.

For example, on the very day you quit, your circulation will begin to improve. Your lungs will immediately start to repair themselves, even after years of abuse. Your senses of taste and smell will be revitalized. You'll soon cough less, have more energy, and feel like you have greater control over your life. Then, within a year, your risk of heart disease will be reduced by half. Within ten years of quitting, you will have dramatically cut your risk of debilitating chronic health problems, including lung cancer, stroke, and emphysema. Finally, for those who smoked no more than a pack a day, within 15 years of quitting the risk of heart disease will be nearly the same as that of someone who never smoked.

No matter how much improvement you can expect in your quality of life—and life expectancy—by kicking the habit, how do you go about it after so many years of lighting up? Granted, it's not easy. Statistics show that even though 1.3 million of the 46 million Americans who smoke are able to quit every year, that's still less than 10 percent of the 18 million who try to quit (the remainder of whom return to being regular smokers). And of the 13 million smokers over the age of 50, 65 percent say they'd like to quit, but most don't follow through. Nonetheless, you can join the ranks of successful quitters if you are serious. Experts agree that permanently breaking the habit requires four distinct stages: having the sincere desire to quit, properly preparing to quit, going through with it, and then sticking with your commitment forever. The following tips will guide you through these stages.

Get motivated.

Giving up a drug as powerfully addictive as nicotine after many years of use takes a lot of resolve. You have to have a strong desire. Your state of health may be your primary motivation (see sidebar, "Medical Reasons to Quit"). But if that's not enough, there are plenty of other compelling reasons. Consider the money that's going up in smoke. A pack-a-day habit costs more than $800 per year. Consider your family. You want to be healthy and with them for a long time—especially if you have grandchildren. And if you smoke around your grandchildren, you're subjecting them to dangerous second-hand smoke. Children who regularly spend time with smokers have up to twice the incidence of colds, flu, ear infections, allergies, and lung diseases. Quit for the children's sake if not your own.

Set a target date.

For many smokers, it's not realistic to say you'll just stop smoking tomorrow. You should give yourself ample time to prepare for the big change you're about to make in your life. Give yourself a few weeks or months, or choose a day of special significance, like your birthday or your grandchild's birthday. Once you set the date, however, vow that you'll honor it and let nothing stop you. In the meantime, you can physically and mentally condition yourself to quit.

Get others involved.

Tell your family members, close friends, and the people you work with about your plan, including your target date. The people who care about your welfare can help you live up to your commitment and be a reassuring source of support during times when you might be tempted to light up.

Taper off with intelligence.

Find a brand of cigarettes you don't enjoy as much as your usual brand. Choose low-tar and reduced-nicotine varieties, but don't inhale them more deeply than your usual cigarettes. Challenge yourself to wait longer and longer each day before having your first cigarette. Smoke only when you feel you absolutely must; stop when you catch yourself lighting up out of habit or reflex. Gradually, your dependence on nicotine will wane. When you cut back to seven or fewer cigarettes a day, you're ready to quit completely.

Quit for a day.

A few days before you finally quit, resolve to go an entire day—or as much of the day as you can—without smoking a single cigarette.

Live up to your promise.

On the date you've set to quit, follow through! Get rid of all of your cigarettes, matches, lighters, and ashtrays. This will be a tough day, so make it a special one. Buy yourself something nice or find some other way to reward yourself. Above all, stay very busy—anything to minimize the opportunities to light up—and spend plenty of time with people who can offer support.

Be prepared for the worst.

Yes, if you've smoked for a long time, you can expect withdrawal symptoms—physical responses to the absence of nicotine in your system. But be assured that these will be strongest during the first week or two after you quit, then rapidly subside. Symptoms commonly include restlessness; disturbed sleep; hunger; dry mouth; sore throat, gums, or tongue; headaches; fatigue; constipation; irritability; and coughing. Exercise, warm baths, relaxation exercises, and plenty of sleep can ease headaches, mood changes, and fatigue. Sucking on cough drops or hard candy can help with mouth and throat irritation. Drink lots of water, and eat fresh fruits, vegetables, and whole-grain cereals to prevent constipation.

Don't let fear of weight gain stop you.

Not every ex-smoker gains weight—and for those who do, the average amount is a modest five pounds. Sometimes the oral gratification is all you need. (To satisfy this craving, try noncaloric substitutes or hold a toothpick between your teeth.)

Lead yourself not into temptation.

Try to change or avoid the circumstances that typically trigger your desire to smoke. For example, if you're used to lighting up after a meal, get up from the table immediately after eating, brush your teeth, then do something that will distract you from thinking about smoking. Be on your guard when drinking coffee or alcohol—beverages that many associate with smoking and that increase the desire to light up. For the first three weeks or so after you quit, avoid places and situations where you will be among smokers. Instead, spend time where smoking is not permitted: museums, libraries, and so forth.

Remember, a slip is not a fall.

Most ex-smokers attempt to quit several times before they are rewarded with permanent success. In fact, the average ex-smoker needs three or four attempts before quitting permanently. So don't give up hope if you have a momentary lapse. The important thing is to identify what triggered your setback and then get back on track before you become dependent on nicotine again. Don't become obsessed about never smoking again. Take it one day at a time.

MEDICAL REASONS TO QUIT

○ ○ ○

Smokers who quit after the age of 50 are unlike their younger counterparts in several ways. One major difference is the reason most older smokers give for kicking the habit: their health. Indeed, risks for the following major health problems can be substantially reduced by giving up tobacco for good:

- *Emphysema and Chronic Bronchitis.* The mortality rate from these progressive, incurable, and debilitating lung diseases is up to 25 times higher in smokers as compared with those who don't smoke.

- *Other Respiratory Ailments.* Smokers have double the usual rate of infections of the upper respiratory system and other breathing problems.

- *Lung Cancer.* The risk of lung cancer is seven times greater than normal for those who smoke less than half a pack per day, 12 times greater for those who smoke a pack or two packs per day, and 24 times greater for those who smoke more than two packs.

- *Other Cancers.* Some 30 percent of all cancer deaths (85,000 per year) are tobacco-related. Tobacco products promote cancers of the bladder, pancreas, mouth, and throat.

- *Heart Attacks and Strokes.* These are among the most serious consequences of smoking. Cigarettes are a major factor in the progression of atherosclerosis (hardening of the arteries) and other chronic circulatory problems. Consequently, smokers suffer 70 percent more heart attacks than nonsmokers, and 30 percent of all deaths from heart disease (that's about 170,000 deaths per year) are attributable to smoking. Women who smoke are particularly at risk, with triple the rate of strokes and up to ten times the rate of heart attacks compared to women who don't smoke. For all smokers, a pack-a-day habit carries three times the normal risk of a heart attack, while 25 or more cigarettes per day boosts the rate to ten times. For those who have already had one heart attack, continuing to smoke raises the risk of having a second attack dramatically.

- *Immune System Damage.* The chemicals in cigarettes can have a negative impact on how well your immune system protects you against infections—whether minor ones like colds or potentially life-threatening ones like pneumonia.

Pat yourself on the back.

Experts agree that indulging in plenty of self-praise for your accomplishment ensures greater success. You might start by calculating all the money you're saving—not just on tobacco and related paraphernalia, but on the costs of extra health care and damage to clothing and furniture. Then use the money for a gift to a charity, a family member, or yourself. Even more importantly, you should be proud to know that no other thing you can do for your health—not even exercising or dieting—can so quickly and profoundly improve the length and quality of your life as giving up smoking. Mark your progress periodically—and celebrate your success.●

SNORING

11 WAYS TO STOP THE NIGHTTIME RACKET

You might sleep like a baby every night, but just ask your bed-mate: There may be times when you sound like a baby, too—a baby rhino, that is, snorting and rumbling the night away.

Just about everyone snores sometimes, and about 50 percent of people snore regularly. Snoring is caused by air working its way past the tongue and tissue in the throat and upper airways. You're more likely to snore as you get older, because with age this tissue, like all body tissue, begins to lose its elasticity and become more lax. As you breathe in and out in your sleep, this tissue flaps in the breeze, so to speak, creating the various noises we call snoring.

Severe, continual snoring can be a sign of serious medical conditions. Foremost among them is sleep apnea, a disruption of breathing patterns that can be a sign of cardiovascular problems and have other life-threatening consequences as well. Often, though, the only consequence of snoring is annoying your bed-mate.

If you snore, take heart. There's a lot you can do about it. The following noise-abating techniques may go a long way toward en-suring nighttime peace and quiet in your home.

Keep off your back.

When you lie on your back, your tongue is likely to fall back into your throat and create a nearly perfect woodwind instrument as escaping air rushes over it. Your airways will remain clearer and you'll keep the volume down if you sleep on your side or stomach.

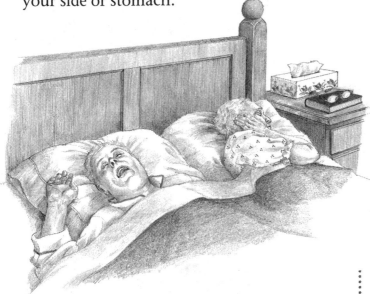

Take some tennis balls to bed.

It's one thing to settle into a good night's sleep curled up kittenlike on your side, but you may well roll over onto your back as soon as you begin sawing logs. Here's one sure way to keep off your back: Sew a long, tight pocket onto the back of a T-shirt or some pajama tops and put two or three tennis balls into it. Rest assured, every time you flop onto your back you'll be so uncomfortable you'll roll right over again.

Say no to a nightcap.

In fact, it's best to lay off booze for three to four hours before you go to bed. Alcohol is a major contributor to snoring because it relaxes the muscles of your throat and jaw, creating a virtual wind tunnel for each escaping breath. Sleeping pills can have the same effect.

Quit smoking.

Kick this habit, too, because smoking irritates the airways and makes nighttime breathing more difficult and noisier.

Don't fall into bed exhausted.

The more tired you are, the more likely you are to breathe deeply in your sleep and, as a result, to snore. Try to get eight to eight and a half hours of sleep a night.

Shed those extra pounds.

Your snoring problem may be yet another warning sign that it's time to lose weight. Fat around your neck puts pressure on your airways, constricting airflow. As a result, each intake and outflow of breath can sound like you're sucking and blowing through a wet straw.

Keep your head up.

If your head is elevated, you're more inclined to keep your neck straight and your jaws closed—the perfect no-snoring position—because the tissue in your airways is not as likely to vibrate. If you have an adjustable bed, you can raise your entire torso, which is the best way to keep your airways open. Some snorers get the same effect by putting a few bricks under the legs at the head of the bed. A still easier course of action is simply to use an extra pillow or two. For the best results, move your head up as high as you can on the pillows, so your torso, and not just your head, is elevated.

Take care of allergies.

When your nose is stuffed up, you are more inclined to breathe through your mouth and more likely to snore. Medications might help you cope with your allergy symptoms and your snoring, but be careful about the ones you use. Antihistamines, for instance, can have the same sedating effect as alcohol and exacerbate

SOME ANTISNORING EXERCISES

○ ○ ○

The following exercises, developed by Dr. Rosalind Cartwright, director of the Sleep Disorder Service and Research Center at Rush-Presbyterian-St. Luke's Medical Center in Chicago, may muffle your snoring considerably. Do them twice a day, once in the morning and again at night just before turning in. According to Dr. Cartwright, you and your bedmate should begin to notice positive developments in about four weeks.

Exercise One: To tighten jaw muscles. Hold a pencil, tongue depressor, or a flat-handled wooden spoon between your teeth. Bite down firmly but not too vigorously. Reduce pressure if you feel any pain in the teeth themselves. Keep bearing down for about five minutes, even though the muscles around the hinges of your jaws may begin to feel fatigued.

Exercise Two: To firm the muscles that keep your lower jaw from slacking backward when you relax. Place several fingers from each hand against your chin and press backward while holding your jaw firmly forward. You'll probably feel your jaw involuntarily sliding backward. Using your jaw muscles, try to resist the pressure and keep your jaw steadily in place for two or three minutes.

Exercise Three: To strengthen the muscles at the back of your tongue. (The stronger these muscles are, the less likely your tongue will be to fall back toward your throat when you sleep.) Firmly press your tongue against your lower teeth. You might begin to feel an ache at the back of the tongue, but keep up the pressure for three to four minutes.

snoring by relaxing the muscles in your jaws and throat. Ask your doctor about allergy medications that don't have sedating effects. You may also want to unclog your nose before bedtime with a nasal spray.

Buy a firm mattress.

The firmer the mattress, the greater the chance that your neck will be straight and your airways unobstructed. You'll be doing your spine a favor, too.

Check out antisnoring products.

Your physician or dentist may be able to prescribe a mouth guard to hold the upper and lower teeth together. It prevents the lower jaw from sagging and causing airways to flap. Gadgets referred to as "breathe-rights," which are popular with professional athletes, fit across the bridge of the nose and hold the nasal passages open. They're inexpensive and sold over the counter. Special antisnoring pillows, often sold in drugstores, hold the head rigid so your jaws remain closed and your neck stays straight.

Beware of sleep apnea.

It's easy to laugh your snoring away as a comical and harmless habit, but keep in mind that your nighttime breathing problems may be a sign of a serious medical problem. Sleep apnea, for example, is especially common among overweight, middle-aged men. People with sleep apnea literally stop breathing for short periods as they sleep—sometimes with serious consequences. See your doctor if you suspect the presence of this disease.●

SORE THROAT

8 SOOTHING STEPS

That scratchy, raw pain in your throat could be the first sign of a cold brought on by any one of more than 200 viruses ... but not necessarily. Throats also get irritated, inflamed, and swollen with the flu, laryngitis, or even a strep infection brought on by the dreaded *streptococcus* bacteria. Did you scream too loudly at a football game or strain your vocal cords singing along with your favorite oldies? Spending too much time in a climate with low humidity can also dry out those membranes. Allergies can irritate your throat, as can tobacco smoke or foods with sharp edges. A piece of chicken bone or even a rough potato chip can actually tear the throat's delicate lining. In the meantime, when you're suffering from a sore throat, talking and swallowing become less unconscious reflexes and more hurtful chores.

A sore throat doesn't stand alone. In fact, it's usually a symptom of something else happening. If your throat has bothered you for more than two or three days, if you are running a fever, and if you feel achy all over, call the doctor. While he or she won't be able to prescribe an antibiotic for a viral infection, a professional may culture the infection to rule out strep, which should be treated to avoid more serious problems. If your pain is mild, however, you might want to try fighting it from home using these 8 soothing steps.

Slow up.

By resting and deliberately taking it easy, both physically and mentally, you'll give your body's own immune system a chance to come to your defense.

Sip hot stuff.

Warm tea, chicken soup, hot lemonade, or a mug of almost any hot fluid will soothe your sore throat as you swallow. Mix hot tea together with lemon and honey. This wash of moist heat on your inflamed tissues works its healing magic rather mysteriously, but it does work.

Gargle.

Put a teaspoon of salt into a full eight-ounce glass of warm water, and slosh it around your mouth and throat several times a day. Don't waste money on medicated mouthwashes.

Take a painkiller.

Aspirin, acetaminophen, or ibuprofen can make your throat feel better fast. No matter which pain reliever, or analgesic, you choose, make sure it won't interfere

with any other condition you may have or with any other medication you may be taking.

Pop a cough drop.

Some work as mild anesthetics, numbing the soreness so your throat doesn't feel so irritated. But be careful—cough drops can trigger allergic reactions.

Drink lots of liquids.

Fluids help your membranes remain hydrated, washing bacteria and excess mucus out of your system. Aim for eight to ten glasses a day...or as much as you can handle without floating away.

Spritz the soreness.

Over-the-counter analgesic sprays are available that will relieve the hurt. Unfortunately, the effect doesn't last very long.

Turn up the humidity.

Breathing moist air will speed your recovery along, whether generated by a home humidifier or by a home-made steam tent. Make one by putting a bath towel over your head and sitting with your face above a pot of steaming hot water. You can also soak in a hot tub or stand in a hot shower.●

STOMACH UPSET

12 WAYS TO QUIT YOUR BELLYACHING

Quit your bellyaching? Oh, if only you could. Nothing throws you off keel like an upset stomach. Unfortunately, an occasional stomachache is just part of life. It might be the feast you just ate, or that little tiff you had with your spouse. It could have been caused by a bout with a 24-hour bug or a normal but annoying buildup of digestive acids. It could even be the side effect from some of the medications you take. A lot of different factors can have an upsetting effect on the stomach. And whatever causes your tummy to feel rummy, you just want it to feel better—soon.

Well, in most cases, the pain, cramps, and discomfort of an upset stomach will soon pass. If they don't, see a doctor. For temporary discomfort down there, these tips may help.

Identify the offenders.

Feel queasy every time you eat cream sauce? Bloated and squeamish after munching on broccoli and beans? Try to identify the foods that are likely to send your stomach into fits and cut back on them. A hint: You'll probably notice that fatty and refined foods in general are difficult to digest. This is also true of dairy products for many people.

Go easy on the aspirin.

One a day probably won't bother you—and it can be great for cardiovascular health—but too much aspirin may irritate your stomach. If you can't handle aspirin but need a pain reliever, try acetaminophen, which is easier on the gastrointestinal tract, or ask your physician to recommend an enteric-coated aspirin, which is easier on the stomach.

Eat slowly and chew your food.

When you take time to chew each bite thoroughly, your stomach won't have to contend with large chunks of food that are harder to digest.

Avoid the known culprits.

When your stomach's acting up, lay off coffee, alcohol, cigarettes, and acidic beverages like orange juice: They're all known gastrointestinal irritants.

Pop open a soda pop.

A glass of ginger ale or cola will help settle the stomach. Don't plunk in a couple of ice cubes, though, because cold drinks jolt the stomach. And let a carbonated soda defizz for a few minutes so the bubbles don't add to the commotion in your tummy.

Sip some soothing tea.

It can help. Make sure it's peppermint or another caffeine-free herbal brew, and drink it lukewarm rather than hot, because hot beverages can trigger stomach spasms.

Have a light snack.

Provided, of course, you're not so nauseated from overeating that you just can't imagine putting anything else in your stomach. Otherwise, a bland repast of toast, crackers, or gelatin dessert may be just the thing to settle you down.

Try an antacid.

If your stomach hurts even though you haven't eaten, excess acid could be the reason for your troubles. An antacid will probably soothe your stomach by neutralizing out-of-control acids.

Take a deep breath.

Inhale slowly and deeply, then exhale slowly. This simple exercise will relax muscles in your abdomen, easing the tightness in your stomach. It will also help relieve tension, which is often a cause of stomach upset.

Take a walk.

The age-old remedy of walking off a heavy meal really works. A little exercise keeps things moving in your digestive tract, so your stomach will process food faster, smoother, and without pain.

Check your medications.

If you feel queasy after taking prescription drugs, your stomach may be telling you that it's not able to handle them. Ask your physician for an alternative that may be less irritating.

Know when to call the doctor.

Intense stomach pain may be a sign of appendicitis or even a heart attack. If pain persists—and especially if it gets worse—call your doctor immediately. Do not apply cold to the area if you are having abdominal pain; it can mask the symptoms of appendicitis.●

STRESS

29 APPROACHES TO CONTROLLING STRESS

It's ten minutes after two in the afternoon, and no one has delivered the new washing machine that was promised by noon. You rearranged your entire week to create the time to stay home for this delivery, and now you're upset. You feel it's almost impossible to rearrange your life again. You are stressed, and you don't feel in control.

You realize that to be alive in these busy times means you're going to experience anxiety and stress from time to time. What you may not know, however, is that the way you cope with stress may well determine if you're going to lead the kind of life you want to live.

For our purposes, stress refers to your body's response to a physical or emotional threat, whether it is real or perceived. The body shifts into high gear when faced with stress. This process goes back to prehistoric days when, simply to survive, cave men and women had to respond quickly to the threats presented by wild beasts and other dangers. They developed a fight-or-flight response that is still with us. It demands more energy, a greater supply of blood, and more oxygen because physiological changes take place as the muscles tense for action. This reaction may have helped our ancestors escape from saber-toothed tigers, but it doesn't do much for us today when there's a mix-up on an appliance delivery.

Stress is your body's response to such circumstances. Problems develop when the stress in your life is prolonged and intense. When that happens, evidence points to stress as a common underlying factor in many health problems. Prolonged stress has been shown to weaken body defenses, for example. If you're under constant stress, expect to have more colds and other chronic illnesses. Indeed, it appears that stress makes you more vulnerable to physical and emotional problems, particularly when stress becomes chronic and your body feels as if it's constantly responding to emergencies. Moreover, under stress your immune system becomes less effective, weakening the antibodies that fight bacteria and viruses.

You may find that some stress marks the beginning of a new challenge, especially when the experience taxes but doesn't exceed your adaptive resources to respond. Some amount of stress is right—it excites your senses, enables you to work and play hard, and helps you adapt to your environment. But too much stress, whether externally created or self-imposed, can cause permanent physical and mental damage. Here are some ideas on how to control it.

Learn how your body reacts to stress.

You may react differently than your spouse or friends because of your individual situation and coping skills. The following symptoms may indicate that you are experiencing acute stress:

- Poor concentration, difficulty remembering, anxiousness, avoidance of responsibility
- Low energy, lack of normal motivation, feeling tired most of the time, and rarely feeling properly rested, even after a full night's sleep

- Feelings of tension, worry, restlessness, and depression; never feeling relaxed
- Difficulty sleeping, strained face, grinding teeth, clenched fists
- Changes in eating and drinking habits, nausea, vomiting

Develop a stress strategy.

Plan an overall strategy for managing stress by reviewing your options when you start feeling swamped.

Identify sources of stress.

Keep a journal of the events that take place in your life and note your feelings and reactions to them. Note your response patterns to discover what sets you off. Then try to change those patterns.

Find a hobby.

Hobbies provide time to lose yourself and offer an opportunity for relaxation.

Take time for yourself.

Designate a time for yourself each day. If you're very busy, schedule time for yourself just as you would set aside time for a business appointment.

Assume responsibility for your actions.

When you catch yourself blaming someone or something else for your choices, reflect on what you can do to change the outcome of your behavior.

Use the relaxation response.

Everyone has a protective mechanism that allows them to turn off the fight-or-flight response. This counteraction lowers your pulse rate, slows your breathing, and brings your body into better balance. (See sidebar, "A Relaxation Technique—Progressive Relaxation.")

Learn breathing methods.

When you're in the middle of a stressful situation, inhale for a count of three, then exhale for a count of two. This will help at least temporarily.

Practice yoga.

Concentrate on relaxing and stretching your muscles. This will get you focused on something other than your problems.

Visualize.

Use your imagination to relax. Picture yourself at the beach with ocean waves lapping the sand, enjoying freedom from pressure. Gradually shift your focus to the situation that's causing stress, and try to visualize the outcome you desire.

A RELAXATION TECHNIQUE—PROGRESSIVE RELAXATION

○ ○ ○

In addition to relieving stress, relaxation positions and relaxation breathing can give you a boost when you feel tired.

Lie comfortably on your back in a quiet place. Take a few deep breaths and relax into a natural breathing rhythm. Tense and release groups of muscles—one at a time. Beginning with your feet, tense the muscles, hold for a count of five, then release. Move up to your lower legs. Tense, hold, and release. Continue to move up your body—upper legs, buttocks, abdomen, arms, chest, shoulders, hands, and face.

Notice what the tension feels like as you contract each muscle group. Focus on letting go of this tension as you relax parts of your body. Practice this relaxation technique once or twice a day for five to ten minutes.

Learn to meditate.

Find a quiet place and make yourself comfortable. Concentrate on a phrase or word and repeat it in time with your breathing. Maintain a passive attitude. Empty your mind of all thought. Meditating once or twice a day for 10 to 20 minutes brings relief from chronic stress and will increase your stress tolerance.

Change the stress factors you can.

For example, if you find commuting stressful and have control over your schedule, adjust your driving time to avoid traffic congestion. Break down big jobs into more manageable portions and delegate responsibility. Think of other ways to make adjustments to reduce stress.

Recognize stress you can't change.

It is a special kind of maturity that enables some people to distinguish stressors they can change from those they can't. Give careful thought to sources of stress in your life, try to separate the ones you can't avoid, then learn to try to accept them as best you can.

Exercise.

Exercise has a positive effect on mood and mental well-being. In addition to distracting you from your troubles, it has a relaxing effect and can reduce anxiety, depression, and tension. Research shows that aerobic exercise has a quieting effect that helps people handle stress calmly for hours afterward. A growing body of evidence suggests that regular exercises can help people stay healthy under stressful conditions.

Get enough sleep.

Sleep is often an early casualty of stress. Sleep deprivation, in turn, magnifies the problem.

Set priorities.

It is imperative to learn the difference between high and low priorities in your life to avoid being torn in several directions at once. Failing to do this not only makes it harder to complete the most important tasks, but the frustration itself adds to your stress level. Make a list of your priorities, post it, and keep it up to date. And learn to completely eliminate tasks that are of very low priority.

Create a "worry time."

If you're the worrying kind, set aside a certain amount of time each day just for worrying. Write down and contemplate two or three concerns for the day. Then put them behind you and devote the rest of the day to more positive thoughts.

Be aware of good nutrition.

Good nutrition is vital to optimum health for everyone, whatever our level of stress. But when someone is under unusual stress, it is especially important to manage factors that can be controlled. Nutrition is one of these. Eat properly and your body will be better able to support you in times of stress. Similarly, there are some foods to avoid: Loading up on sugar or alcohol during stressful periods may create false energy and only complicate the stressful situation.

Take one step at a time.

Several problems that come along all at once can overwhelm even the most perfectly adjusted individual. Focus on the project you're working on now, decide on the first step, then proceed.

Speak up.

In some cases, avoiding conflict may actually add to your stress. That's the time to be more assertive. Training in assertiveness is available to learn specific skills for managing difficult interactions with other people. Exercise your personal right to state your opinion or feelings while respecting the rights of others to do the same.

Anticipate stress.

If you think ahead about possible stressful events and plan ways to handle them, you will often find the actual situation is not as stressful as anticipated.

Don't strive for absolute control.

You just waste time and effort. Sometimes the only possible way to cope is to withdraw from the situation.

Set a buffer.

List all the tasks that you hope to have completed within a given time frame. Estimate the time needed to complete each one, then increase that time by a good 10 to 15 percent to allow for unexpected problems. This extra time provides a buffer that will help eliminate a tremendous amount of stress.

Talk it out.

Talking out problems helps relieve stress and can put problems in their proper perspective. Your ability to handle problems usually expands when you can talk about them.

Maintain a sense of humor.

Research shows that a sense of humor can be the best medicine. Learn to laugh at the small stuff. Then tell yourself that it's all small stuff.

Take short breaks.

Even a short break, particularly if well timed, can take your mind far away from the problem at hand and help create a fresh perspective.

Think positively.

Your ability to do this fosters constructive thoughts and feelings and is known to decrease stress.

Use biofeedback techniques.

Biofeedback is a technique to monitor physical responses to stress and to feed the information back to the subject. As you try to relax, an immediate response is available to indicate how effective your relaxation efforts are. With the appropriate equipment and practice, you can learn to exert a degree of control over your heart rate, breathing, and blood pressure through biofeedback. Ask your doctor to refer you to a professional who is trained and qualified in the techniques of biofeedback.

Find help.

Take stress seriously. It's not all in your head, and not dealing with it can cause some real damage. When stress threatens to overwhelm you, get professional help.

Consult with a counselor, a member of the clergy, a mental-health professional, or a doctor.●

WARNING!
...
Stress, hypertension, and other medical problems

Your body handles the perceived "emergency" of stress with massive secretions of stress hormones called cortisol and adrenaline. This causes levels of blood sugar and blood pressure to rise, and it increases heart rate and muscle tension. These challenges to the system may endure for hours, long after the original stress-causing event has ended. Even sporadic episodes of stress can result in long-term high blood pressure by creating permanent changes in your arteries; stress over a long period of time—whether in your personal or professional life—can be even more destructive. Thus, there's evidence of a strong link between long-term stress and chronic hypertension.

Other conditions have been linked to stress; two of the most far-reaching are heart disease and colon cancer. Because the immune system is weakened by stress, it can also make you more vulnerable to infections; stress can also boost your cholesterol readings. Finally, stress often plays a role in backaches, persistent fatigue, gastrointestinal problems, headaches, sleep difficulties, and even asthma attacks.

STROKE

---

13 STRATEGIES TO FEND OFF A BRAIN ATTACK

Mention a heart attack and virtually everyone knows what you're talking about. Mention a brain attack, and you're likely to draw blank stares. Yet a growing number of medical experts are using *brain attack* as a means of describing a stroke. The term is appropriate: A heart attack is an interruption in blood flow to or through the heart; a stroke results from a disruption in blood flow to the brain.

Every year, according to the American Heart Association, half a million Americans have a stroke. More than 143,000 people a year die from stroke, which ranks third behind heart attack and cancer among leading causes of death in the United States.

Death from stroke has decreased 70 percent since 1950. The number of strokes (incidence) has not changed, however, and stroke remains the leading cause of serious disability in this country.

Still, public awareness of stroke has lagged considerably compared to awareness of heart attack. A public-opinion survey co-sponsored by the National Stroke Association revealed that only three percent of adults could identify even one stroke symptom; only one percent identified stroke as a leading cause of death.

Some risk factors for stroke can't be changed: If you are black or elderly or male or if you have diabetes, then you have a higher risk. But other major risk factors can be controlled, greatly reducing the chances of stroke, even in people who have risks that can't be modified. Here's a blueprint to help fend off a brain attack.

Keep your blood pressure in check.

High blood pressure, or hypertension, has emerged as the single most important factor in stroke risk. The generally accepted definition of hypertension is blood pressure that is 140 over 90 (140/90) or higher (that is, a systolic pressure equal to or greater than 140 or a diastolic pressure equal to or greater than 90) for long periods of time. Keeping blood pressure below 140/90 can lower the risk of stroke by 75 to 85 percent. Better control of blood pressure is generally credited for the dramatic decrease in stroke-related mortality over the past four decades. Between one-third and one-fourth of all adults in the United States have high blood pressure, even though the condition responds well to a variety of drug and nondrug therapies. (See HIGH BLOOD PRESSURE.)

Stop smoking.

In comparison to nonsmokers, cigarette smokers have about a 60 percent higher risk of stroke. Smoking increases the risk of high blood pressure and the tendency

TIA: A WARNING AND AN EMERGENCY

∘ ∘ ∘ .

About ten percent of stroke victims have a warning attack that precedes the actual stroke, according to the National Stroke Association. More than a third of the time, the warning, called a transient ischemic attack (TIA), will be followed by a stroke within a month. The occurrence of a TIA increases stroke risk by ten times. Yet, for a variety of poorly understood reasons, many people fail to report the TIA to their doctor.

The most common warning signs of a TIA are:

- Numbness, weakness, or paralysis, especially on one side of the body and affecting the face, arm, or leg

- Sudden blurring or loss of vision, especially when only one eye is affected

- Difficulty in speaking or in understanding speech

- Dizziness or loss of balance or coordination, especially when accompanied by any of the other symptoms.

TIAs result from a temporary blockage of blood flow to the brain (usually caused by a particle of cholesterol-containing ma-terial). A TIA may last anywhere from only a couple of seconds up to 24 hours. In some instances, a person may temporarily lose consciousness.

If you experience TIA symptoms, report them immediately to a physician. A failure to report the warning signs can prove fatal.

to form blood clots, two factors closely associated with stroke. Virtually all of the excess risk associated with smoking can be eliminated within two or three years after quitting. (See SMOKING AND TOBACCO USE.)

Stay active.

Recent evidence indicates that regular physical activity can reduce stroke risk, perhaps to the same extent as quitting smoking. Some of the evidence also suggests that heavy workouts aren't necessary to get risk-reducing benefits for stroke. Walking, riding a bike, and working in the yard are just a few examples of activities that can produce an adequate workout. Increasingly, studies indicate that the regularity of moderate physical activity, rather than the intensity, seems to be the key.

Keep diabetes in check.

Diabetes increases the risk of stroke by 300 percent. People with high blood-sugar levels often have strokes that are more severe and more debilitating. On the other hand, better control of diabetes can help reduce stroke risk. Keep in mind that the vast majority of people with diabetes have what is known as type II or adult-onset disease. Type II diabetes is closely associated with risk factors that can be controlled: obesity, physical inactivity, high cholesterol, and high blood pressure. (See DIABETES.)

Be kind to your heart.

Heart disease substantially increases the risk of stroke. By attending to the risk factors for heart disease, you get the added benefit of a lower stroke risk. Potentially overlapping, controllable risk factors include high blood pressure, smoking, high cholesterol, physical inactivity, high blood sugar, and excess weight.

Go easy on the alcohol.

Heavy alcohol use (defined as more than two beers, two glasses of wine, or two ounces of hard liquor per day) increases the risk of high blood pressure, which in turn increases the risk of stroke.

Eat more fruits and vegetables.

Some recent studies have shown a lower stroke risk in people who have a higher intake of fruits and vegetables, although the formal connection between stroke risk and eating habits remains to be fully developed. It is possible that increased fruit and vegetable consumption may simply reflect a lifestyle that is healthier overall.

Don't ignore your cholesterol level.

Cholesterol's relationship to stroke is not as clear as its link to heart disease. However, some stroke experts believe that a high cholesterol level plays a role in the development of carotid atherosclerosis, a build-up of fatty material in the carotid arteries, the blood vessels that supply the brain. The narrowing of these arteries brings about a significant increase in stroke risk.

Don't ignore flutters.

A fluttering heart, palpitations, or other suspicious sensations in the heart may mean trouble. Atrial fibrillation, a type of rapid, irregular heartbeat, poses a special risk for stroke. During an episode of irregular heartbeat, a blood clot can be ejected from the heart and shut off blood flow in an artery leading to the brain. And that can result in a stroke. The condition is more common in older people. Inform your doctor as soon as possible if you experience any unusual heart sensations.

ALL STROKES ARE NOT ALIKE

○ ○ ○

Strokes occur in two basic ways:

1. A blood clot plugs an artery leading to the brain or in the brain itself and shuts off the flow of blood. Clot-related brain attacks are responsible for more than 80 percent of all strokes, according to the National Stroke Association.

2. A blood vessel in the brain leaks or bursts.

Clot-related strokes frequently are called ischemic strokes, derived from the word *ischemia*, which means deficient blood flow. Ischemic strokes can be either embolic or thrombotic. An embolic stroke occurs when a clot travels through the bloodstream from another part of the body to the brain. Many of these clots originate in the heart, especially in people who have a history of heart attack. A thrombotic stroke results from a clot that forms on fatty deposits that can clog one or more of the arteries that carry blood to the brain.

Two types of hemorrhagic, or bleeding, strokes also can occur. If a blood vessel on the surface of the brain bursts or leaks, a subarachnoid hemorrhage is the result. Bleeding from a vessel within the brain is called an intracerebral hemorrhage and is extremely serious.

In general, the risk factors are similar for the different types of stroke. However, high blood pressure has an especially strong association with intracerebral hemorrhage.

Take your medication.

For reasons that aren't clear, many people stop taking medication for high blood pressure, high cholesterol, and other conditions. In fact, some people never even fill their first prescription. Failure to take medication as prescribed may result in a worsening of the condition being treated, further increasing the risk of stroke. If side effects, cost, or other factors interfere with your drug therapy, it is very likely that your doctor can prescribe a different drug or find other ways to cope with the problem. If you're on medication, take your drugs as directed, and don't stop unless you first consult with your physician.

Younger women beware.

Stroke is more common than heart attack in women younger than age 45. The risk is exceptionally high among women older than age 30 who smoke and use oral contraceptives. If you have symptoms that may represent a stroke, don't take any chances just because you're not the "right" age. Seek medical care immediately. Overall, women account for 43 percent of the strokes that occur each year, but 60 percent of stroke-related deaths involve women.

Talk "aspirin" with your doctor.

Regular aspirin (even a baby aspirin) reduces the risk of heart attack, especially in men. The evidence is less clear for stroke. Aspirin does seem to protect against recurrent strokes in people who have already had one stroke, but studies have yet to prove that aspirin reduces the chance of a first stroke. Ask your doctor about using aspirin to head off a stroke.

Think "emergency."

A stroke or a TIA is a bona fide medical emergency. Treat either event with the same degree of seriousness you would devote to a heart attack. Specifically, get to an emergency room as soon as possible. Don't be embarrassed if the symptoms you experience turn out not to be stroke-related. It's better to be safe.●

TENDINITIS

---

15 WAYS TO CARE FOR IT

I t doesn't seem fair. Two years ago you made up your mind to get off the sofa. You've been working out regularly—jogging, stretching, playing golf and racquetball. Today you're sidelined. That pain in your right shoulder was diagnosed as rotator-cuff tendinitis and the soreness in your left leg as Achilles tendinitis.

Tendinitis occurs when tendons (fibrous bands that attach muscles to bones) are strained, stretched, or injured from too much pressure. As a result, they become inflamed and painful. Any kind of activity that involves repetitive motion can injure tendons anywhere in the body, though tendons in the ankles, knees, and elbows are especially vulnerable. That's because they are attached to the muscles that come into play during most sports. Tennis, swimming, and golf are common culprits because they involve so many repetitive movements.

At one time the treatment for tendinitis meant complete immobilization. Today, it's considered wise to get back into the swing of things as quickly—and carefully—as possible, because being idle is only going to make it harder to regain strength and mobility in the affected area.

The good news is that you can recover from tendinitis with proper treatment, and you can prevent many tendon injuries, too. Here are some ways to help.

Find out what's causing the pain.

Let a professional tell you if your golf swing or tennis backhand is mechanically wrong and causing the injury. Or it might be that you've increased your jogging routine from three times a week to six, and your ankles aren't adapting well to the added pounding. Or perhaps those extra 15 pounds you've added to your shoulder press have caused some trauma. Whatever you think it might be, change the activity or stop it altogether.

Know when to stop.

It only makes sense. If you feel pain, stop the activity that's causing it. Unfortunately, that's sometimes easier said than done. But listen up: It's not likely that you'll be able to "run through" the pain you feel in your knees when jogging or simply wish away the pain that sears your elbow every time you swing a tennis racket. Stop at the first sensation of pain, keeping in mind that the injury will heal quickly if you treat it early.

Elevate.

Raise the area that's sore. This is another way to keep the swelling down, especially in the legs.

Apply a compress.

To keep the swelling down, wrap the affected area with a cloth bandage and secure it with tape. The extra warmth should also help keep the affected muscle from stiffening. Be careful not to wrap so tightly that you restrict circulation—especially if you have any problems with poor circulation.

Ice it.

Regular ice massages can do a lot to reduce pain and swelling. Here's a good way to administer ice treatments. Fill several paper cups with water and let them freeze. Tear away paper from the cup as needed to expose the ice, and massage the area for about 20 minutes, keeping the ice moving. Do this several times a day.

Wear protective gear.

Knees and elbows are especially vulnerable to spills, knocks, and impacts from playing basketball and racquetball. For protection from these mishaps, check

---

WARNING!
. . .

Be careful with ice. Don't allow ice to remain in direct contact with the skin for more than ten minutes without moving it. One approach is to wrap some ice cubes or a bag of frozen vegetables in a towel and gently the rub the affected area. Or freeze some water in a paper cup and apply it as needed. Remember, gel packs that can be refrozen are often colder than regular ice and, when applied directly to skin, can cause pain and injury.

out knee and elbow pads, like the ones that in-line skaters wear, and put them on any time you engage in an activity that's likely to put your knees and elbows in harm's way.

Do flexibility exercises.

Muscle strengthening is just part of the battle. While jogging strengthens your leg muscles, it also causes them to become shorter and tighter—and this tightness can lead to a tendon injury. With proper stretching (before and after working out) and range-of-motion exercises, you can maintain flexibility in muscles and tendons, no matter how strenuously you exercise, and protect yourself from injury.

Mix up the exercise menu.

To avoid the repetitive motion that can lead to tendinitis, mix up your exercise regimen. If you're a jogger, consider swimming or bicycling on alternate days. This way, you'll be using different muscle groups, avoiding the risk of overusing one set of muscles.

Reduce the inflammation.

Anti-inflammatory drugs such as aspirin and ibuprofen can reduce swelling and attendant pain considerably. Take them only after exercise, though, never before: Since they can mask pain, you could injure a tendon during exercise without realizing it.

Do some strength training.

Strengthen affected muscles around the joint and tendon. Use free weights and weight-resistance machines to gradually strengthen both the upper and lower body. Don't forget about your aerobic workouts, though: They're great for car-

diovascular conditioning and for muscle endurance.

Make sure the shoe fits.

The right shoes can do a lot to prevent injuries by absorbing the shock of exercise, which can lead to injury. Know what kind of shoe you need for protection. You may, for instance, need extra arch support. As a rule of thumb, soles should not be too stiff to prevent you from flexing your foot easily, and the toe box should be loose enough to give your toes room to move.

Do a warm-up.

The higher your body temperature, the warmer your muscles will be—and warmer muscles, infused with blood, are less prone to injury. Even before you start stretching, ride a stationary bike or use a treadmill for several minutes so your muscles are warmed up and can be stretched without injury.

See a physician.

If your acute pain doesn't respond to rest, see a specialist such as a doctor that handles sports-related problems.

Think about orthotics.

Podiatrist-prescribed orthotics (devices that are custom made to ensure foot comfort and are worn inside your shoes) may help chronic tendinitis. Orthotics may correct a tendency to lean inward (pronation) or to favor the outside of your feet (supination), which can place additional stress on your tendons.

Don't rush into a new sport.

Make the transition to a new exercise regimen gradually. That way you'll give your muscles and tendons a chance to develop the flexibility and strength necessary for the activity.●

TOOTHACHE

6 ANSWERS TO THE ACHE

A throbbing toothache shuts off your ability to concentrate on anything else. It really hurts, and you simply can't ignore the pain. Could it be a cavity? Of course. Even adults over 50 can develop cavities that act up. Perhaps bacteria has invaded a tooth, causing an infection or an abscess. If you have an abscessed tooth, pus is filling the gum tissue at the root, making it inflamed and tender. Look inside your mouth. Can you pinpoint the problem or see any redness? A loose filling, a cracked tooth, damaged pulp inside a tooth, a sinus infection, or something as simple as sensitive teeth could also be making your mouth hurt.

Think back to what preceded your toothache. Did you eat something too cold, too hot, or too sweet and then feel a stabbing twinge? It's probably sensitive teeth. Is the pain mainly confined to your top teeth? Sinuses are likely sources of that kind of discomfort. Did you jam anything into your gums or mouth recently? If so, an injury could be making your teeth ache. Does it hurt only when you bite down? A cracked tooth might be the answer. Did you try to eat something hard, sticky, or rough-edged and sense that you loosened a filling? You might have lost that filling, exposed the nerve, and increased the tooth's sensitivity.

No matter what's at the root of your dental dilemma, make an appointment with your dentist right away for professional attention. But if it's 4 A.M., here are some steps you can follow immediately to ease the ache.

Take a painkiller.

Aspirin, acetaminophen, ibuprofen, or any other nonprescription drug you use to relieve headaches can help. Make sure your choice doesn't interfere with other medications you might be taking. Ibuprofen may be the most effective medication when it comes to curbing the inflammation that accompanies a toothache.

Rinse your mouth.

If the ache is caused by a small piece of trapped food, a thorough rinsing with warm water might dislodge the debris. Put a teaspoon of salt in the water while you're at it to soothe any inflammation.

Floss.

If a tiny chunk of food is stuck between your teeth, use floss to remove it. But go easy. The gums surrounding your sore tooth may be irritated. Try a toothpick or the rubber tip on the end of your tooth-

---

TOOTHACHE DO'S & DON'TS

○ ○ ○

DO: Get an exam even if the tooth stops hurting. Pain anywhere in your head or neck should never be ignored because it could be a sign of something more serious. Even heart problems can cause pain in the lower jaw. See your dentist to identify or rule out problems with your teeth. Then check with a doctor for other possibilities if the pain persists.

DON'T: Place an aspirin directly on the aching tooth. This commonly accepted practice is a myth: It will not ease the pain and could end up giving the surrounding gum tissue a nasty burn. Aspirin works best for toothache when swallowed. It is not designed for topical pain relief.

---

brush. Flossing is critically important in controlling plaque, which should be removed from your mouth at least once every 24 hours.

Dab with oil of cloves.

If you can get to a drugstore, buy a little bottle of this old remedy. Dab your affected tooth with a bit of cotton dipped in the oil to numb the tooth. Don't put it directly on the gum, however, because it can irritate the tissue.

Don't eat on that side.

If you have a damaged or cracked tooth, using it to chew may make it worse. Stick to your safe side until you can get to the dentist.

Try special toothpaste.

If your pain isn't severe but comes and goes depending upon exposure to air or contact with heat or cold, then you may be one of the millions of people with hypersensitive teeth. Buy a paste designed for sensitive teeth and use a soft toothbrush. If the pain continues, see your dentist.●

TRAVELER'S DIARRHEA

8 Ways to Prevent and Treat It

Was it the enchiladas in chocolate sauce or the raw scallops? Frankly, when you're coping with a bout of turista, as traveler's diarrhea is universally known, you probably don't care what caused it—you just know that you're finding it impossible to be away from the toilet for any length of time.

What you're dealing with is foreign bacteria that have thrown your intestines for a loop. If it's any consolation, many, many travelers experience the runny stools, cramps, and other symptoms of turista. Chances are, your bout of turista probably will subside in a few days. In the meantime, there's a lot you can do to prevent it from getting to you, to slow it down if it does, and to cope with any serious side effects that may arise.

Don't drink the water.

This age-old traveler's adage is based on the fact that most travelers pick up their bugs when quenching their thirst. Although you can purify water by boiling it for five minutes or using purification liquids or tablets (available in sporting goods stores), use your common sense and avoid drinking the local water—in any form. The best advice about tap water is to use it for washing and flushing only—don't drink it. Instead, make sure your drinking water has been com-mercially bottled or canned and purified, and clean the lip of the container you drink from. Make sure you are the one to open the cap on a bottle of water to be sure that it wasn't opened and refilled before it was served to you.

Be on guard for water, water, anywhere.

The list of water-related *don'ts* is lengthy. Don't use ice cubes made with tap water. Don't drink lemonade and other drinks made with water or add a splash of water to an alcoholic drink (despite what you may have heard, alcohol does not kill bacteria). Don't brush your teeth with tap water or even open your mouth when you're in the shower. And don't drink from streams and other natural sources, no matter how clean they look.

Pass on the salad.

Or anything else that hasn't been cooked or boiled (both processes kill bacteria). Fruits are okay, but stick to oranges, bananas, grapefruit, and others that you peel yourself.

Stock up on yogurt.

For an extra dose of prevention, you can add yogurt or acidophilus milk (fermented milk, available in health food stores) to your daily diet a few days before you leave on a trip and keep it up until you return. The bacteria in these products will act as bodyguards and help fend off foreign bacteria.

Drink safe water.

If you're victimized by traveler's diarrhea, drink safe water and plenty of it—about a glass an hour. Forget all the jokes you've heard about Montezuma's revenge. The dehydration diarrhea causes can be very serious, especially for anyone with circulatory problems—the loss of fluids can lower blood pressure dangerously and raise the risk of stroke, heart attack, and kidney failure.

Start ORT.

That's oral-rehydration therapy. It replaces the electrolytes and minerals you lose with diarrhea and helps you absorb water better. ORT solutions are widely available over the counter in the United States and abroad. You can also get some of the same benefits by drinking fruit juices (but not prune, apple, or berry

juices, which are likely to have a laxative effect), weak tea with sugar or honey, water with a tablespoon or two each of salt and sugar, sports drinks that contain electrolytes, and broth.

Go for the bland to fight diarrhea.

Your mom probably called them "foods that bind"—toast, gelatin dessert, soda crackers, bananas, rice, and other bland alternatives. You'll be better able to digest foods like these, and they won't irritate your poor intestines. Acidophilus milk and yogurt are especially good additions to an antidiarrheal diet because they contain natural bacteria that will help squash those foreign bugs.

Arrest your diarrhea with antibiotics.

A dose of antibiotics can be just the thing to kill off the bacteria that's wreaking havoc with your system. But take antibiotics with care: They can interfere with your other medications and have side effects of their own, including diarrhea. Before you leave home, ask your doctor to prescribe an antibiotic that will be safe for you if turista strikes.●

ULCERS

8 WAYS TO MANAGE THEM

Food, of course, is one of life's greatest pleasures. But if you have an ulcer, anything you send down to your stomach might start a volcanolike reaction that can ruin the pleasure of a fine meal. In fact, even when you haven't eaten anything your stomach juices often keep churning away. Gnawing away is more like it, because an ulcer is the result of overactive juices that consume the digestive tract itself. They literally chew a hole in your innards.

No miracle cure is available for ulcers, nor is it even known what causes them. It's suspected that ulcers may be brought on by an overproduction of certain stomach acids or by bacterial infections.

If you suspect you have an ulcer, the first thing to do is see a doctor. Then, simply learn the best ways to live with it. And take heart—with a little care, ulcers are manageable.

Spread out your meals.

Ulcer sufferers have this in common— their digestive juices are busy all the time, even when they don't have a supply of food to break down. So keep your juices well supplied with something to munch on. Break meals into smaller installments, and eat frequently.

Check out your drugs.

Many drugs, including aspirin and anti-inflammatory arthritis medications, irritate the stomach. If you take medications regularly and have an ulcer, talk to your doctor about your ability to handle them. There may be alternative drugs that are easier on the stomach.

Leave the milk in the fridge.

It wasn't so long ago that ulcer sufferers were told to drink milk and plenty of it. It was thought that milk was a soothing agent because it coats the stomach. Which it does—for a little while, at least. But before you know it, the calcium in milk begins to stimulate stomach acid, which has an effect on your ulcer that's not soothing at all.

Follow your gut.

Gone, too, are the days when doctors put all ulcer sufferers on a diet that was bland, bland, bland. The rule these days is simply to find the foods that you enjoy and can eat without irritating your ulcer, while avoiding foods that cause your ulcer to act up.

Relax.

Does stress cause ulcers? The jury is still out, but it's widely thought that you're more likely to produce extra stomach acids when you're under stress. While you're not going to be able to avoid stress in your life, you can learn how to handle it better. Try some moderate exercise, yoga, or any other relaxing activity.

Put out the puffs for good.

There's a clear link between cigarettes and ulcers. If you smoke, you're more likely to get ulcers, and they take longer to heal.

Reach for an antacid.

Over-the-counter antacids can be a godsend when an ulcer acts up. Not only do these products relieve discomfort, but there's some evidence that by neutralizing stomach acid they can speed ulcer healing. Great news, but take antacids with care: Check with your doctor to see if they might interfere with other medications you take.

Be on the lookout for signs of trouble.

If your ulcer perforates and starts to bleed, you can lose so much blood that you run the risk of going into cardiac arrest. Your risk of blood loss increases if you take blood thinning agents such as aspirin and warfarin (Coumadin). If you experience intense nausea, pass blood in your stool, or vomit blood, you need to see a doctor at once.●

URINARY TRACT INFECTIONS

17 SOOTHING STEPS

You feel like you have to go to the bathroom all the time. When you get there, not only is it hard to go, but the little bit of urine that does come burns like crazy. These are just two of the symptoms of a urinary tract infection (UTI). In the mildest stage of this infection, called urethritis, the problem is confined to your urethra, the small tube leading away from your bladder. If the infection has traveled farther, the infection can affect the bladder itself, a condition known as cystitis. In even more serious situations, the kidneys can be involved. Much more frequent in women than in men, urinary tract infections can be accompanied by fever and chills. Your urine might be strong-smelling or even a bit bloody. You are uncomfortable, especially in your abdomen, which is painful and heavy. You may be experiencing back pain.

Women are more prone to bladder infections because the urethra, through which your urine flows on its way from the bladder to the toilet basin, is much shorter in women than in men. This proximity to the outside world leaves your urinary tract more vulnerable. Bacteria, normally present in your rectum and anal area, can easily travel and find a hospitable setting in your urinary tract to grow and multiply. Infection can then spread upward and inflame the lining of the urethra on its way to the bladder itself.

In men with prostate gland problems or urinary tract abnormalities, bladder infections can pop up. But they are uncommon. For a woman, loss of estrogen makes your situation more difficult as you move through the pre- and post-menopausal years. Estrogen, one of the primary female hormones, helps keep the organs and lining of your urinary tract firm and functioning normally. When hormone levels drop, membranes can thin, making you more susceptible to infections. Allergies, sloppy toilet habits, an underlying structural problem in your urinary or genital tract, a sexually transmitted disease, or a reaction to a birth control device can also be behind your UTI. In many cases, a UTI comes from the bacteria on your own body. Though it may not be any consolation to you, most women experience at least one infection during their lifetime, and many are plagued with recurring UTIs. However, you should never hesitate to call the doctor immediately. You may need antibiotics to clear up the problem. You may also want to discuss the various options for hormone replacement now available to women over 50. In the meantime, here are some soothing suggestions.

Drink lots of water.

The first time you get a twinge of a symptom, start guzzling water—lots of it. An eight-ounce glass every hour will dilute your urine and wash out bacteria. Experts say that women who suffer repeat infections don't drink nearly enough liquids. Even when you aren't experiencing any UTI symptoms, if you've had one of these infections in the past, make it a habit to drink eight tall glasses of water each day. Diluted urine offers bacteria a less-than-perfect growing situation.

Don't hold it in.

Go to the bathroom often, even if it hurts. Pain can occur just as you begin to pass urine and the bladder muscle contracts, touching the inflamed lining. Or the pain may be worse when you are nearly finished and the muscle is trying to squeeze the final drops out of your bladder. In either case, this memory of pain could make you want to put off using the toilet. Try not to let it stop you, however. When your urine collects and stays in your bladder for long periods of time, it becomes more concentrated, and concentrated urine is a good place for bacterial growth. By keeping your urine diluted with lots of liquids and moving it out of your body regularly, you help shut down the bacteria's ability to multiply.

Consider your hygiene.

Take a long hard look at personal habits that could be hurting you. For instance, have you been wiping yourself after a bowel movement with a back-to-front swipe of toilet paper? This apparently harmless habit could be costing you a lot of aggravation because you inadvertently move tiny particles from your rectum in the back to your vagina up-front. Change your toilet-paper technique to a front-to-back motion. Meanwhile, if you use pads during your period and have recurring infections, you might want to consider tampons. Conversely, if you are a tampon user, switch to pads to see if there is a difference. Experts just aren't certain why some women seem to end up with UTIs, so it's up to you to exam-

WHEN MEN GET UTIs

○ ○ ○

Men are much less likely to get urinary tract infections than women because in men the urethra, or tube leading from the bladder, averages about eight inches in length. Bacteria don't find it easy to make their way up this distance to the bladder. However, if you have a prostate infection, a bladder infection can follow. The prostate gland sits at the bottom of the bladder, on top of the urethra. Occasionally, if the prostate infection is aggravated, bacteria enter the bladder. If you are a man with a bladder infection, think back: Did you go bike riding or experience some kind of trauma that might have caused trouble?

Your symptoms are similar to female UTIs. You have the urge to urinate frequently with that same burning sensation. A prostate infection can make you feel like you are sitting on a brick and are in pain in your lower groin area. Don't let symptoms persist for more than a day. Call your doctor if you don't feel better within 24 hours.

ine your behavior to uncover sources of possible infection.

Each time you use the toilet, wash your hands with warm soapy water afterward. Before you make love, make sure both you and your partner have been extra careful about cleaning up your "private parts."

Take a painkiller.

Aspirin, acetaminophen, ibuprofen, or any painkiller that does not interfere with other medications you may be taking on a regular basis can help relieve bladder pain. Check with your doctor if you aren't certain about which painkiller to trust.

Wear cotton underpants.

Synthetic fabrics don't allow air to reach your genital area. You can stay drier with cotton panties than you can with silk or synthetic ones. Men troubled by bladder or prostate difficulties should opt for cotton boxers for the same reason.

Drink cranberry juice.

The connection between cranberry juice and urinary tract infections is still being debated. Nevertheless, several studies suggest that a minimum of two glasses a day could help acidify your urine and flush your system of bacteria.

Use the toilet after intercourse.

After you make love, head straight to the bathroom and urinate, especially if you suffer from stubborn UTIs. The flow of urine could help flush out troublesome bacteria.

Don't make love.

If you have an acute case of cystitis, lovemaking could be terribly irritating. Hold off until you feel better. If your infection turns out to be sexually transmitted, be sure to tell your partner. Antibiotics may be necessary for both of you.

Take a shower.

In addition to its usual refreshing effect, a warm shower will help to ease the itching of a UTI, at least for a while.

Rest.

If you have a slight fever, are feeling fatigued because of the infection, and simply need to stay close to your bathroom, don't feel guilty about taking the day off. Pick up a good book, rent a video, or just spend the day lounging in bed, being good to yourself. You will speed up the healing process.

Give up alcohol.

Beer, wine, and hard liquor are urinary tract irritants in both men and women.

Watch your caffeine.

Though you should increase your fluid intake, don't fill up on caffeinated drinks like coffee, tea, or cola. Caffeine stimulates your kidneys and makes them fill up your bladder, which could make your symptoms worse.

Wear loose clothing.

Extra-tight clothing, panty hose, underwear, or slacks can irritate your urethra. Opt for a loose look and feeling to help ward off attacks of UTI.

Debate your birth control.

If you rely on the diaphragm for birth control, speak with your gynecologist about another method. Because of the way the diaphragm is inserted and where it sits in your vagina, it could be a major factor in UTIs.

Eat yogurt.

If you are taking antibiotics for your infection, all the bacteria in your urinary tract are being destroyed. This sounds like a great idea, but in reality it's not. You need healthy bacteria to maintain the right balance and keep your system running smoothly. Look for cartons of unsweetened natural yogurt with *Lactobacillus acidophilus* and eat one a day.

Don't forget your vitamins.

First, check with your doctor to make sure that any antibiotics prescribed for your infection won't be hampered in their work. Extra vitamin C—up to 1,000 milligrams a day—can help acidify your urine to keep bacteria from growing. If

HELLO, DOCTOR?

○ ○ ○

Here are serious symptoms that can accompany a urinary tract infection and call for immediate medical attention. If not treated, infections of the bladder have been known to involve the kidneys. Call the doctor right away if you have or suspect you have a UTI and:

- You have any kind of kidney disease.
- You have diabetes.
- You have high blood pressure.
- You are terribly shaky and nauseated. (You could be coming down with a kidney infection or with septicemia, a potentially dangerous bacterial infection in your bloodstream that responds well to treatment.)
- You suspect that you have a sexually transmitted disease.
- Your symptoms have gotten worse during the few hours that elapsed since you tried to treat it at home.
- You are male and over 50.
- You have blood in your urine.

your body is fighting off an infection, a regular multivitamin mineral supplement could also help you stay strong while your system is healing. Ask your physician about vitamin E, which seems to help women with dropping estrogen levels.

Look in your medicine cabinet.

Some medications prescribed for depression can cause urinary difficulties. When you call the doctor to describe your urinary problem, bring up the possibility of a drug interaction.●

VAGINAL DRYNESS

---

13 WAYS TO FEEL BETTER

Vaginal dryness is not a topic many women discuss openly with each other or even with their physicians. Rest assured, however, that this unspoken topic is a common problem during menopausal years—anytime between the ages of 40 and 60. And there are definite steps that can be taken to alleviate this annoying problem. The thinning and drying of your vagina are directly related to the decline in female hormone levels in your body. Estrogen is especially important. When estrogen drops, all the reproductive organs are affected. Your cervix, ovaries, and uterus diminish in size. Your breasts can change and become less firm. The vagina—an expandable, resilient, muscular passage that is several inches long and lined with moist, sensitive tissue—actually becomes slightly smaller in both width and length. The outer lips of your vagina may thin and shrink. The clear or whitish acidic discharge produced by the vagina to help protect you from infections begins to diminish. This tendency toward drying also affects the way your body produces moisture during sexual arousal to prepare you for intercourse. Keep in mind that while these changes may be frustrating, they are all normal, and you have plenty of company. Don't be shy about speaking with your gynecologist. Here are some suggestions to make you feel better.

Use a gel, cream, or moisturizer.

There are several over-the-counter products that can bring back much-needed moisture, including K-Y nonpetroleum jelly, Replens, or Astroglide. Look for a water-based product because water will plump up your skin's tissues. Don't buy oil-based products or resort to baby oils: This type of coating on your vaginal walls is not recommended. Not only will a smearing of such oil promote infection, it can also inhibit your vagina's own lubricating response even further. Petroleum products can also destroy the latex in a condom. Ask your physician for a recommendation. Some vaginal moisturizing gels are designed to be applied externally and internally. Positive effects can last several days. Others come in tamponlike packages which, for full benefit, are inserted two or three times a week.

Investigate hormone replacement therapy.

Many women have discovered that replacing the hormones that are lost during menopause can eliminate bothersome symptoms like vaginal dryness. Speak with your physician and find out what might be right for you. The medication is available in the form of pills, patches, creams, suppositories, implants, or tablets. Giving women regular doses of estrogen in combination with progesterone has revolutionized the way menopause is approached. But not all women or their physicians are convinced of the need for hormone replacement therapy, and it is certainly not the right medical route for every woman. If you have a history of endometrial cancer, breast cancer, stroke, a blood-clotting disorder, abnormal vaginal bleeding, or liver dysfunction, your doctor will probably say no to hormone replacement therapy. Other factors to consider in your medical history that might warn you away are: diabetes, sickle-cell anemia, high blood pressure, migraines, uterine fibroids, fibrocystic disorders of the breast, endometriosis, gallbladder problems, family history of breast cancer, or habitual cigarette smoking.

In the meantime, the dose of estrogen in hormone replacement therapy is so low it is safe for most women, especially if they are monitored closely by their doctors. Many women rave about the return to normalcy they experience once they begin hormone therapy. Talk to your physician.

Stay away from perfumed products.

Toilet paper, bath soaps, oils, and talcum powders that are scented can dry and irritate your sensitive genital skin. Stop using them.

Don't douche.

Advertisements for personal hygiene products can be misleading. Routine douching with harsh, scented products can change the normal pH level of your vagina, which should remain at around 4.5. If you are experiencing vaginal dryness, don't turn to a douche for freshness; such products are more likely to have a drying effect.

Wash with water.

The vagina actually cleans itself. Organisms live in the vagina and keep it slightly acidic to prevent the growth of microbes. If you get carried away with your cleansing routines, you could destroy the natural balance and upset the mucous membranes that line the vagina. You should keep clean, of course, but harsh soaps are not necessary. Always use a gentle soap and don't scrub vigorously. If you are in the habit of cleansing your-

THE EXERCISE CONNECTION

○ ○ ○

In recent years, studies have shown that regular, vigorous exercise can have a multitude of positive effects on menopause. Not only can exercise help lift any tendency toward depression, but getting out to walk briskly, play tennis, swim, cycle, or take an aerobic dance class can help conquer fatigue and increase your body's ability to produce estrogen.

Exercise could be one of your best weapons for fighting aggravating symptoms of menopause like vaginal dryness. When you exert yourself physically, your adrenal glands are stimulated to convert a male hormone in your body called androstenedione into estrogen. Exercising four times a week for at least 30 minutes each time can pump up the estrogen quotient in your body.

Exercise can also be invaluable for your cardiorespiratory health. The benefits to your heart as well as your lungs have been documented in study after study. The older you get, the greater the loss of overall strength and flexibility you are likely to encounter. Exercise can keep you limber and strong and stop the loss of bone, a normal side effect of aging.

Osteoporosis is a real concern for inactive women over 50. If you've been active during your 20s and 30s with walking, running, and training with weights, then you've managed to increase your bone density. Even if you haven't exercised as much as you could have in the past, by starting a regular exercise program later in life you can still restore small amounts of bone tissue.

self thoroughly every time you go to the toilet, stick with water alone for that kind of cleanup. Remember to wipe from front to back so bacteria are less likely to travel from the anus to the genital area.

Stay sexually active.

Research indicates that women who continue to have sexual intercourse or to masturbate several times each month experience less drying and shrinking in the vagina. Sexual activity may actually be

the impetus for production of more estrogen. The muscle contractions and increased blood flow that come with an orgasm help keep vaginal tissues in shape.

Accentuate foreplay.

Past age 50, women take longer to lubricate when sexually aroused. (Men take longer to achieve an erection, too.) Your own body may have a better chance to release natural vaginal lubricants if you slow up and spend more time in foreplay before trying to have intercourse. Experts insist, however, that your mental health is also a critical factor in your ability to lubricate. If you are feeling angry, inadequate, or plain old bored, then no amount of foreplay will be enough. The problem of a dry vagina is certainly not all in your head, but psychology does play a role.

Avoid caffeine.

Coffee, tea, and sodas that contain caffeine take even more moisture from your drying membranes. You may think you are adding useful fluids when you consume these beverages, but caffeinated drinks don't add to your level of hydration at all. So skip that extra cup of coffee or switch to decaffeinated alternatives. Make it your business to start reading food labels for caffeine content.

Check your medication.

Antihistamines and diuretics can rob your body of water. Check with your physician before adjusting any medication you take on a regular basis, but inform the doctor of your concern.

Drink lots of water.

Keep your whole body hydrated by sipping water. Drink at least eight 8-ounce glasses of water each day.

Cut out alcohol.

Drinking alcoholic beverages can dehydrate you.

Consider extra E.

Some experts suspect that vitamin E may have chemical properties similar to estrogen. Though this hypothesis has not been medically proven, vitamin E has helped many women with hot flashes and has relieved vaginal dryness. Ask your doctor about adding E to your regular regimen of vitamin and mineral sup-

plementation. And eat more green leafy vegetables, cereals, dried beans, whole grains, and bread—natural sources of vitamin E. Women taking certain medications for high blood pressure, diabetes, or some heart conditions have to be careful about vitamin E because it could interact with those medications. They should check with their doctors about what would be the appropriate amount of E for them, if any.

Don't cut too much fat.

Yes, it is true that eating too many fatty foods is not good for your overall health. If you cut out all essential fatty acids from your diet, however, you will see detrimental changes in your skin, hair, and especially in your genital tissues. Add nuts and seeds to your salads. Sesame, pumpkin, and sunflower seeds are all good sources. Eating fish is a great way to get more essential oil into your diet. Try salmon, trout, tuna, mackerel, and sardines.●

FEED YOUR BODY RIGHT

○ ○ ○

As you age, your digestive tract becomes less efficient. It takes longer to digest meals, and your body doesn't even need as much food. You may be cutting back on calories and harming yourself nutritionally if you aren't careful. You still require the doctor's recommended allowance of vitamins and minerals, even more so now that you are experiencing frustrating menopausal symptoms.

VARICOSE VEINS

11 WAYS TO LIVE WITH THEM

Whether it's sagging skin or a drooping bottom, you've probably noticed how gravity begins to take its toll on your body as you get older. Well, if you have varicose veins, and about 25 percent of women and 15 percent of men do, think of them as the victims of gravity, too. Over time, valves in the veins in your legs begin to wear out from all the exertion it takes to combat the forces of gravity and pump blood all the way back up to the heart. As a result, blood pools in the veins and out pop those bluish, bulging, knotty outcroppings on your legs. They may be accompanied by thin, weblike spider veins that can also show up on the legs, as well as on the neck and face.

While spider veins are painless and relatively unnoticeable, the same can't be said of varicose veins. They can make you feel uncomfortable about your appearance, they can throb and just plain ache, and they can make your legs feel like listless, lifeless stumps.

There's not a whole lot you can do to avoid varicose veins. If there's a strong history of varicose veins in your family, you may well develop them, too. Short of surgery, there's a lot you can do to manage your varicose veins, from keeping the swelling down to lessening the pain they can cause.

Wear sensible shoes.

OK, they may not be the most fashionable-looking footwear in town, but you'll be doing your legs a big favor if you opt for flats, sneakers, sandals, or other comfortable walking shoes. That way, you'll be putting less pressure on your legs and varicose veins.

Get off your duff; get off your feet.

Sounds like a contradiction, but the rule here is to find the right balance. When you stand for long periods, blood has a harder time making the return trip back to your heart, so it pools in your legs, putting a lot of strain on your veins. The same thing happens when you sit for long stretches, too, because your bent knees and waist form a dam against normal blood flow. So if you have to stand a lot, sit down and put your feet up occasionally or alternate your weight from one leg to the other. And when you're sitting for a spell, take a stretching break every so often.

Sport support hose.

These stockings exert continual pressure on your legs, giving blood a gentle push back toward the heart. They also shore up bulging veins, easing the throbbing and pain. Any support hose will help, but you'll pack a bigger punch with special compression hose available by prescription from surgical supply houses.

Lift your feet for a spell.

Throw yourself back in that reclining chair, lie on the couch with your feet propped up on pillows, stretch your legs out on a footstool—find any comfortable position in which your legs are elevated above your hips. You may even want to lie on the floor with your legs raised and propped against a wall. The idea here is

to move the blood that pools in the veins of your legs and get it flowing back to the heart.

Get some exercise.

Exercise is the best way to get your blood flowing and to keep it on the move. It primes the pump, so to speak, and helps the heart to do a better job of keeping the blood circulating through your veins. In fact, the heart-pumping effects of aerobic exercise last for hours after you stop. Find an exercise you enjoy and find comfortable. Riding a bike and using a stair machine work for many people. Swimming and water aerobics are ideal because they work your legs but may put less strain on your veins. Plain old walking is also excellent and doesn't put undo strain on your body.

Beware of long journeys.

Sitting for hours in a car or on a plane can be torture if you have varicose veins because blood pools in your lower legs. Take a few countermeasures that will cause the muscles in your legs to contract, squeezing the blood out of your

WHEN VARICOSE VEINS BECOME DANGEROUS

○ ○ ○

You'll probably be able to find ways to live comfortably with your varicose veins, year in and year out. But if clots form or if a varicose vein ruptures, seek medical help immediately.

You might be able to see a clot. It will form a red lump that doesn't go away, will be tender and sore to the touch, and will cause a painful, throbbing sensation in the area. Clots can also form out of sight on veins deep in the leg, causing pain and swelling. If you suspect you have a clot, see a doctor immediately. If left untreated, a clot can travel to the lungs and cause a pulmonary embolism (a clot that blocks an artery in the lungs) or travel to the heart and bring on a heart attack (by blocking a coronary artery).

A varicose vein, especially one located around the ankles, may also rupture. If it does, a bruise may appear or profuse bleeding may occur. Take a piece of sterile cotton gauze, apply it to the wound to stop the bleeding, and get medical help without delay.

veins. Try these: Flex your feet in a pumping motion; rotate your feet clockwise, then counterclockwise; slide your heels back and forth.

Get up on your toes.

Here's a basic stretch that every varicose-vein sufferer should do several times a day to help squeeze pooling blood back toward the heart. Stand up straight with your weight on your toes. Rise up on your toes, lifting your heels off the floor. Lower yourself slowly and repeat ten times. It's that simple.

Keep the pounds off.

Excess pounds have negative effects on your varicose veins. For one thing, the more weight you carry around, the more strain you put on the veins in your legs. Second, when you are overweight your heart is overtaxed and not able to pump blood as efficiently as when you are at an appropriate weight.

Don't squeeze into your pants and panties.

A tight pair of pants, panties, panty hose or any other clothing that puts a lot of pressure on the groin, waist, or upper legs can prevent blood from flowing out of the legs and give rise to swelling in varicose veins.

Watch what you eat.

Good nutrition is not going to prevent you from developing varicose veins or make them go away once they develop. But certain foods can help varicose veins, and others can hurt them. A diet that's rich in protein, vitamin C (greens and citrus fruits are good sources), and vitamin A (found in fortified dairy products, dark leafy greens, and cantaloupe) will help you maintain healthy collagen, part of the support tissue in veins. On the other hand, salt and salty foods (canned goods and fast foods are often loaded with salt) may cause veins to swell.

Take an aspirin a day.

Not only will a daily dose help relieve the pain your varicose veins may trigger, but aspirin's blood-thinning activity may help prevent swelling by keeping the blood in your legs flowing. Check with your doctor before you begin regular aspirin therapy, however.●

WARTS

13 WAYS TO WAGE WAR AGAINST THEM

Don't worry, these days no one is going to think you got the warts you're sporting from hanging around with a frog. The truth is, if you have warts you're in good company—most of us get them at one time or another.

These ugly, persistent little bumps on the skin are simply viral infections that are extremely easy to pick up but very hard to get rid of. This is probably one of those facts of life you'd rather not think about, but the wart virus, medically known as the human papilloma virus (HPV), lurks everywhere: It likes warm, moist environments especially, and it's incredibly contagious. When HPV decides to hop aboard your body and settle in for a spell, it can manifest itself as one or several different kinds of warts.

Flat warts are smooth and small and usually show up on the hands and face. Plantar warts erupt on the soles of the feet and can make walking and wearing shoes darned uncomfortable. Periungual warts are stubborn little growths that form around and under your fingernails. Genital warts develop in the anal area as well as on the genitals and can be transmitted sexually.

Now, for the good news: In many cases warts will eventually disappear, though it may take a couple of years or even longer before you're rid of them. Medical treatments—such as burning, freezing, and zapping with a laser—can be effective (though once removed, warts have a way of popping up again) and may be in order for persistent warts or warts that are especially uncomfortable. There are also a lot of simple home remedies you can employ to hasten a wart's demise. You can also take measures to prevent yourself from getting warts and pursue schemes to avoid spreading them to other parts of your body as well as to other people.

Know when it's time to see a doctor.

In the elderly, whose immune systems may be flagging, or in others whose immune systems are suppressed because of illness or certain medications, warts can spread easily. People with diabetes and those suffering from circulatory problems are at risk of developing serious in-

---

IS IT A WART?

○ ○ ○

Sure, you know a wart when you see one…but do you? Don't be so certain. It's easy to mistake other skin growths for warts, and this could be a serious error. That persistent growth you think is a wart could be skin cancer, a precancerous mole, or something less dangerous like a corn. In general, a wart is pale, skin-colored, and dotted with little red capillaries. Warts usually have a fairly well-defined border. But don't take chances. If you have a growth and you're not sure that it's a wart, have your doctor check it out.

---

fections at the site of a wart. Any home remedy that irritates the wart and surrounding area can lead to further infection and skin ulcers. So, if you fall into any of these categories, put yourself in a doctor's care to keep a handle on the situation; don't try to self-treat the warts.

Keep it dry.

Warts are like plants—they flourish in damp and warm environments. Plantar warts, especially, will go to town in the sweaty confines of your shoes and socks. If you can, wear airy sandals and go sockless. If you have a plantar wart and must wear socks or stockings, change them several times a day and apply a medicated foot powder often—as often as once an hour.

Don't spread it around.

Remember, warts are caused by a virus, and viruses are contagious. This means you can give your warts to someone else, and you can also spread a wart from one part of your body to another. Therefore, anytime you touch a wart, wash your hands thoroughly. If you have a wart on your finger, say, and nick your face shaving, cover up the cut and try not to touch your face—that little gash is an open invitation for your wart to spread. And if you have a plantar wart, do yourself and your family a favor and wear shoes or slippers around the house—a wart sheds viral particles that love to lodge in carpeting. Consider wearing thongs while taking a shower, or at least rinse out the tub with a bleach solution after a shower.

Wrap it up.

Have a wart on your finger? Here's what many doctors consider to be one of the most effective—and definitely least expensive—ways to treat it. Wrap a piece of strong adhesive tape (duct tape works very well) lengthwise over the wart and extend it all the way over the tip of your finger. Then wrap a second piece of tape around your finger, covering the first piece. Wrap a third piece of tape lengthwise again, and a final piece around the finger. Make sure the wrap is snug but not too tight (you don't want to cut off circulation in the finger), and replace it whenever it becomes dirty. Keep your finger under wraps until the wart goes away, though it may take weeks or even months.

Go soak your feet.

Over time, repeated foot soaks may kill the virus and cause the plantar wart itself to shrivel up and die. In the meantime, soaking will soften up the wart, making it a little easier to slip into your shoes. Make sure the water is hot, as hot as you can stand, then soak for about 20 minutes or so. Replenish the water if necessary to keep it hot, but be careful not to burn yourself. The soak treatment also works well for warts on your hands and fingers.

Take your castor oil.

Mom was right—castor oil really does work wonders. Use a cotton swab to dab some onto a flat wart twice a day, then cover it up with tape.

Shop for an OTC.

Drugstore shelves are loaded with over-the-counter (OTC) wart remedies, but choose—and use—them with care. The most effective are the liquids, gels, ointments, and pads that contain salicylic acid in concentrations of 26 percent or higher. Keep in mind, though, that salicylic acid is an irritant that works by dissolving the wart, and it will irritate the skin around a wart, too. To protect your skin, you might want to apply a little petroleum jelly to the area around the wart before you apply a solution, and you should use just enough solution to cover the wart.

Pick a pad for plantar warts.

Medicated pads work well for plantar warts because they are easy to keep in place on the foot. If you're using a medicated pad, cut it to fit the size of the wart as closely as possible to avoid irritating the surrounding skin.

Soak before slathering.

Soak the wart in warm water before you apply an ointment, gel, or liquid. If you have plantar warts, you may want to apply pads after your foot soak. The moisture will increase penetration.

Get out a pumice stone.

If you're treating a wart with a solution or with warm water, occasionally—and ever so gently—pumice off any soft skin that forms on top of the wart. This will prevent calluses from forming and will speed up the healing process.

GO ON THE DEFENSIVE AGAINST WARTS

○ ○ ○

Don't let the wart virus get under your skin. Cuts and scrapes provide the perfect opening for the wart virus, which is highly contagious. So be on guard and take some preventive measures.

- Warts that grow around and under the fingernails are called periungual warts, and they're stubborn little devils that can hurt like heck and hang around forever. The virus just might be lurking on any surface you happen to touch. Therefore, if you tear a cuticle while cutting your nails, cover up the cut to keep a periungual wart from establishing a beachhead.

- Plantar warts easily take root in the little cracks on the bottom of your feet. This is a good reason to wear thongs or sandals when you're walking around the warm, moist environment of a swimming pool or locker room—great places to pick up one of these unwanted companions. Also change your shoes and socks frequently, since the moist environment around your feet is a favorite hangout for plantar warts.

- Get out the bleach. A good way to keep your tub, shower, and bathroom floor free of the wart virus is simply to douse these areas down frequently with a bleach solution. Be careful of the fumes.

Consider some vitamin therapy.

There is some anecdotal evidence that you can diminish warts by applying vitamins to them directly—by breaking open a vitamin A capsule and dribbling the liquid directly onto a wart or by making a paste of vitamin C and water and covering the wart with it. Well, it is known that both of these vitamins benefit the skin and help heal wounds (and the high acidity of vitamin C may help break down a wart). But bear in mind that there is no formal scientific evidence to support this treatment. Ask your doctor for an informed opinion before you attempt vitamin therapy. And do not take megadoses of these vitamins orally to rid yourself of warts: Eating or swallowing the vitamins won't have any effect on your warts, and you run the risk of toxic overdoses.

Put the power of suggestion to work.

Several studies have shown that it is actually possible to wish your warts away. In a study involving patients with multiple warts, for instance, one group was hypnotized and told that their warts were dissolving; another group was not hypnotized. The patients who were hypnotized lost as many as three quarters of their warts, while the other group showed no improvement. You might want to try this easy mind game at home: Sit quietly for about five minutes a day and imagine that your wart is tingling as it dissolves.

Use a condom to protect yourself against genital warts.

These are warts that no one wants to talk about, but genital warts constitute one of the most common sexually transmitted diseases (STDs). And don't think this is just a disease of the young and the reckless—anyone who has sex outside of a monogamous relationship is vulnerable. A condom is an effective way of protecting yourself from genital warts, which are extremely contagious, as well as from other STDs.●

WEIGHT GAIN

26 TIPS TO HELP DISLODGE EXCESS POUNDS

More than a third of all Americans are overweight. If excess pounds were an infectious disease, the nation would be in the throes of an epidemic, the likes of which have never been seen.

The problem seems likely to worsen before it gets better. Recent surveys indicate that the average American—man, woman, and child—weighs more than ever. In addition, the aging of the population may add to the problem: As people age, they tend to lose muscle mass and gain fat mass. Many older people find themselves eating less but weighing more.

All those extra pounds are not accumulating without a fight. Up to 40 percent of women and a fourth of men are trying to lose weight at any given time. Unfortunately, many of them lose the battle over the long term. On average, a person who loses weight regains about two-thirds of the pounds within a year. Within five years, virtually all the weight has been regained. For some people, women in particular, dieting becomes almost a way of life.

Health and nutrition experts agree that most weight loss programs are unsuccessful because they emphasize short-term results. In reality, successful weight control involves long-term changes in behavior and lifestyle.

If you want to make the changes necessary to keep your weight under control, consider the following suggestions.

Do you really need to lose weight?

Take a close look at your recent weight history. Have you gained weight? Do you or your family have a history of obesity-related health problems? Is your weight substantially out of proportion to your height? Has your doctor or other health authority recommended that you lose weight?

Start out by not gaining.

People who are truly obese may see normal weight as an insurmountable obstacle. In doing so, they set themselves up for failure before they've even started. Some never even take the first step because their circumstances seem so hopeless. Instead of focusing only on the desired end result, resolve first of all not to gain any more weight. For some people, halting the weight gain can be an encouraging first step.

Look at what, when, and where you eat.

Normal eating habits are a cornerstone of weight management. People who continually eat on the run or who alternately binge and starve themselves have no idea what or how much they are eating. Erratic eating patterns greatly reduce the chances of getting weight under control.

Commit your eating habits to writing.

A food diary is a simple but highly effective means of finding out just how much you eat. Equally important, you learn about the circumstances and emotions that surround and intermingle with your eating habits. Keep a diary for at least two weeks. If you decide to talk to a nu-

DUCK THE SCAMS

If a weight loss program sounds too good to be true, it almost certainly is. Weight loss has become big business in this country. With billions of dollars at stake, the potential for deception and fraud is great. Avoid companies, programs, products, or people who promise more than any reasonable individual should expect. Certain buzzwords, claims, and gimmicks should immediately tip you off to something that's too good to be true:

- Advertising or marketing materials that use terms such as "melt away," "painless," "effortless," or "no exercise"
- Promises of excessive weight loss, such as a pound or more daily
- Use of artificial foods or pills to achieve weight loss
- Claims that any single food or product can rid you of excess weight or possesses magical weight-loss properties
- Claims that a diet or gadget can cause weight loss from a specific part of the body, such as the hips or thighs

trition counselor or physician about losing weight, bring the diary along.

Plan for success.

Weight loss is no easy proposition. You can't just decide to lose weight and then expect it to happen. Develop a plan. Not just any plan, but one that's reasonable for you. A reasonable strategy might include meal plans and schedules, some form of physical activity, a time to do the physical activity, and a list of potential obstacles that need to be addressed to stick with your plan (such as a hectic work schedule or a social event that will tempt you to overeat). You might want to get professional advice from a physician, psychologist, registered dietitian, or exercise physiologist. Many hospitals, clinics, and medical centers now offer weight-control programs that involve a range of specialists, including physicians, dietitians, exercise specialists, and psychologists.

Don't be too ambitious.

People who succumb to the lure of rapid weight loss invariably regain the weight just as rapidly. Long-term weight loss comes from modest, gradual decreases that give your body time to adjust. Many experts recommend half a pound a week as an ideal weight-loss goal.

The timing should be right.

Make sure you're in the right frame of mind—personally, professionally, and socially. Embarking on a weight-loss plan before a big social event or right after you've lost your job may be too stressful. The additional stress can pressure you into a rapid-loss strategy that sets you up for almost certain failure.

Steady as she goes.

Don't try to change everything at once. Gradual changes are more likely to bring about steady weight loss that will be kept off for the long term. The habits that led to weight gain didn't come about overnight. Similarly, it is unrealistic to expect a 180-degree turnabout from one day to the next.

Lead me not into temptation.

It just makes sense: If you don't have chips, sweets, and snacks around the house, you're much less likely to eat them. Nip the temptation in the bud by keeping snacks and sweets off your grocery list and out of your cart. Instead, stock up on fruits and vegetables, which tend to be low in calories and fat and high in vitamins and other nutrients.

Look at how you cook.

The way you prepare food can have as much impact on weight gain as the food itself. Frying, especially deep frying, adds fat and calories. In general, baking, broiling, and grilling results in less fat and fewer calories. Other trouble areas include: cheese and cream sauces, gravies, mayonnaise and salad dressing, and marinades loaded with oil. Try to reduce the amount of oil, margarine, butter, and shortening that you use when cooking.

Bring out the measuring cups.

Thought admittedly a tedious chore for many people, measuring food portions for a few days can make you more aware of just how much you're eating. You also learn what a serving size truly is. After just a few days of practice, you probably can learn to serve accurate portions without measuring.

Don't obsess over calories.

Making smart food choices and limiting portion sizes probably will have more impact on your weight than will meticulous calorie-counting.

Don't ignore calories.

As a corollary to the previous tip, keep in mind that if you regularly consume more calories than you expend, you will gain weight.

Say no to alcohol.

Alcohol in any form is high in calories. Moreover, the calories are what nutrition authorities call "empty calories." They have no nutritional value. On average, Americans get ten percent of their calories from alcohol, so abstaining from alcohol completely can put a substantial dent in your total daily calorie count. And a reduction of 50 percent can make a worthwhile contribution to weight loss.

Don't skip meals.

Many people try to cut back on calories by skipping one or more meals. Breakfast is the most abused. People who skip meals tend to make up for the missed food at some time during the day. As often as not, skipping meals leads to binging, which will usually exceed the calories you would have gotten if you hadn't skipped a meal. Try to apportion your calories among regularly scheduled meals. Such a plan helps reduce the urge to snack.

Don't starve yourself.

Diets that are extremely low in calories may trigger the body into a starvation mode. The end result can be lower metabolism and a potentially harmful cycle of binging and starving.

Treat yourself occasionally.

Many people have a hard time with weight loss programs because they feel deprived. To avoid that feeling, allow yourself a treat every once in a while. The emergence of low-fat and nonfat desserts and snacks—such as frozen yogurt and cookies—means that you might even be able to reward yourself without exceeding your dietary goals for the day.

Give yourself a break.

An occasional slip-up is not the end of the world. A minor overindulgence once in a while does not mean you've lost the war, just that you've suffered defeat in one small battle. Keep the attitude that if you win far more than you lose, you'll come out ahead.

Don't cut nutrition corners.

Eat a balanced diet. That means two servings of meat or a meat substitute (eggs, dried beans and peas, and nuts); five to seven servings of fruit and vegetables; two servings of dairy products; and six to 11 servings of breads, cereals, and other grain products.

Consider the fat.

Fat makes the biggest contribution of calories to the diets of most people. The numbers tell the story simply and effectively: Each gram of dietary fat contains nine calories; each gram of carbohydrate or protein contains about four calories. Scaling back your consumption of high-fat foods not only helps you lose weight but reduces your risk of heart disease and some types of cancer.

The average American gets about 37 percent of daily calories from fat, down from 40 percent a few years ago, but still higher than many countries that, not surprisingly, have a lower incidence of obesity and heart disease. The American Heart Association recommends that no more than 30 percent of daily calories should come from fat. People who have other risk factors for heart disease should eat even less fat.

Pare down fat in meals.

A few simple steps can go a long way toward reducing the fat in your diet. As a bonus, most of these tips don't add to the cost of food and food preparation and may actually help save a little money as well.

- Cut back on meat and cheese, both of which are high in fat. Meat may be the biggest contributor of fat calories in a person's diet.

- When you buy meat, look for leaner cuts and trim all visible fat before cooking. Be sure to remove the skin from poultry before eating.

- Eat more fruits and vegetables. Government dietary guidelines recommend five to seven servings daily. Fruit and vegetables are low in calories and fat. Don't drown the benefits in butter or margarine.

- Avoid foods that contain the so-called tropical oils: palm oil, palm kernel oil, and coconut oil. Tropical oils are high in saturated fat, the type of fat that contributes most to heart disease risk.

- Use reduced-fat and nonfat foods and ingredients whenever possible. More and more foods come in low-fat and nonfat versions: dairy products, salad dressing, mayonnaise, even margarine.

Reduce fat in food preparation.

Don't squander the fat reductions achieved at the food store by using poor cooking methods.

- Use a nonstick vegetable spray instead of cooking oil.

- Roast, bake, broil, or braise your meat, poultry, and fish. Frying adds fat and calories. The most fat and calories come from deep frying.

- Use nonstick pans and skillets to eliminate much of the need for cooking oil, butter, and shortening.

- Learn to cook and season with spices as an alternative to butter or margarine.

Begin an exercise program.

Exercise has emerged as a key factor in successful weight loss and long-term weight control. As an added bonus, which should be of interest to food lovers everywhere, people who exercise

regularly can actually eat more. Exercise not only burns more calories but also may increase a person's metabolic rate. That means that exercise helps a person continue to burn calories even after the exercise ends.

Exercise by itself won't keep your weight under control. In fact, experts agree that you should develop and begin a plan to change your eating habits before you embark on an exercise program. If you need help developing a fitness plan, ask your physician for advice or consider hiring a fitness trainer.

The benefits of exercise, in terms of calorie expenditure, will depend on your current level of activity. If your physical activity consists of little more than lifting the TV remote control, you might be pleasantly surprised by how much a daily brisk walk will do for you. On the other hand, if you already get some physical activity, you might have to turn up the vigor level a notch with running, swimming, or cycling.

Change your routine.

Sometimes, just adding physical activity to your daily schedule can lead to surprising benefits.

- Whenever possible, use the stairs rather than the elevator or escalator.

- Park farther than usual from a destination and then walk the remaining distance.

- If weather and safety permit, give up riding or driving in favor of walking or riding a bike.

- If your schedule doesn't allow for one long walk, try several short ones.

Up the ante.

People who need higher levels of physical activity can improve their fitness and their chances of avoiding injuries with a few simple steps.

- Known as cross-training in fitness circles, variation gives exercised muscles a chance to recover and helps ensure that fitness and muscle development aren't too limited. Cross-training not only involves different activities and muscle groups but also includes giving yourself a day off.

- Alternating between hard and easy workouts helps reduce the risk of injury and gives your muscles a chance to recover. After a hard workout, muscle tissue may need up to 48 hours to replace cells that have been broken down by exercise. Variation also helps reduce the risk that you will grow tired or bored of exercise and drop out altogether.

Don't overlook strength training.

Muscle mass plays a key role in a person's overall metabolic rate. Lean mass (muscle) burns more calories than other types of tissue, especially fat. By adding the el-

ement of strength training to a physical fitness program, you can add to the weight-loss benefits of aerobic activity.●

FUTURE FAT

o o o

Obesity has become a problem for children, as well as adults, setting the stage for an increased health burden for future generations. Parents and grandparents can help head off the problem by following the guidelines below. However, getting specific advice from a pediatrician or physician is a good idea. Keep in mind that fat intake should not be restricted in children under two years of age.

- Encourage wise food choices. It's never too early to educate children about the value of limiting the intake of fat and calories. Encourage them at an early age to choose fruit over other snacks and to eat vegetables. Emphasize pasta, cereals, and whole-grain products over french fries and chips. Try pizza with vegetable toppings instead of meat. Eat nonfat frozen yogurt instead of ice cream. The possibilities are limitless.

- Do as I do, and as I say. Set a good example by following the same eating habits you're trying to encourage.

- Drink low-fat milk. Substituting low-fat and skim milk for whole milk can eliminate a major contributor of saturated fat in children's diets.

- Encourage exercise. Physical activity doesn't have to be structured or formal. Just encourage children to go outside and play. They'll burn calories whether they're riding a bike or playing ball.

- Don't go overboard. Children need some fat in their diet to promote proper development of nerves. Check with a pediatrician for specific recommendations.

WRINKLES

11 WAYS TO HANDLE THEM

Now that you're over the trauma of looking in the mirror and seeing your first wrinkle, you've probably accepted the fact that these lines and creases are an unavoidable part of getting older.

Yes, skin loses more and more of its elasticity with each passing year—and wrinkles form as a result. Wrinkles are also the telltale marks of some of the things you have and have not done in your lifetime. Lying out in the sun, not using sunscreen, and not bothering to wear sunglasses head the list, because the damage that exposure to the sun inflicts on your skin is, next to aging, a major cause of wrinkles. (If you lived under a toadstool all your life, you'd probably have some wrinkles, just not as many.) Smoking, frowning, smirking, squinting, scrubbing your face with hand soap—all these factors also contribute to wrinkles.

For what it's worth, we think wrinkles add character to your face—which is good, because short of running up a huge bill with a plastic surgeon, there's not much you can do to restore that baby-smooth skin of your youth. No matter how old you are or how many wrinkles you have, however, it's never too late to take some measures to prevent more wrinkles from forming and to make the ones you have a little less noticeable.

Shun the sun.

You'll be doing your skin a favor if you take some lessons from vampires, who sizzle and fry when they are exposed to the sun. The sun does similarly dreadful things to your skin—it destroys collagen and elastin (proteins that support skin and give it elasticity). As a result, the skin becomes less supple, and you wind up with wrinkles.

There's no need to sleep in a coffin all day, but a little protection against the sun will go a long way toward preventing wrinkles—along with other skin problems, including age spots and skin cancer. Apply a sunscreen with a sun protection factor (SPF) of 15 or greater at least 15 to 20 minutes before you go out (so the skin has time to absorb it); wear a hat; and try to stay out of the sun altogether when it is at full strength, from about 10 A.M. until about 2 P.M.

Start now.

Even if you've been a sun worshiper all your life, it's not too late to change your ways. Staying out of the sun will help prevent wrinkles you already have from deepening, and you may even notice a change in your complexion as damaged skin regains some of its pale luster.

Quit smoking.

You can't see the damage smoking does to your lungs and other internal organs, but you need only look in a mirror to see what it's doing to your face.

Don a pair of shades.

The sun makes you squint, right? And over time, that repeated action causes crow's feet and other wrinkles to form around your eyes. Sunglasses will make it a lot easier to see in the sun without squinting, and if the lenses provide protection against ultraviolet (UV) rays, your eyes will be better off as well.

Slather on the moisturizer.

Contrary to what some advertisements would have you believe, no moisture cream is going to make your wrinkles disappear. However, an application of moisturizer will temporarily plump up some wrinkles and make them less noticeable.

Go for cool and mild.

That's the antiwrinkle rule for cleansing your face. Use cool water and a gentle soap. This way you won't rob your skin of oils and nutrients.

Learn to relax your face.

Those frowns, grins, and scrunches that pass across your face repeatedly may be what give you character, but they can take their toll in the form of lines and creases. There's no need to stop expressing yourself, but look in the mirror and see if there aren't one or two facial expressions in your repertoire—such as frowning or creasing your forehead—that change the contour of your face excessively. By learning how to relax these movements a bit, you may prevent deep lines from forming.

THOSE MIRACLE ANTIWRINKLE CREAMS

○ ○ ○

When it comes to wrinkle cures, just remember that, in many cases, you may as well be buying snake oil. The creams just don't work. Collagen creams, for instance, often marketed as a means to restore elasticity to your face, are useless except for the moisturizing agents they might contain. As for the main and expensive ingredient, there's just no way to supply underlying tissue with collagen through the skin.

In recent years, the most-publicized wrinkle in the fountain-of-youth department has been the development of Retin-A, the synthetic wrinkle cream based on vitamin A. Studies show that it does help erase some very fine wrinkles—but not deep wrinkles, and what help it brings often comes at the price of severe skin inflammation, redness, and peeling. If you decide these drawbacks are worth the minor improvement you may see, be sure to have your physician monitor your treatments.

Skin creams based on alpha hydroxy acids, first released in 1993, have also become popular. They are used to treat wrinkles, discoloration, and dry skin by causing layers of skin to slough off, revealing newer skin underneath. Though they can be costly, such creams are said to carry minimal risk and to have fewer side effects than similar products based on Retin-A. Again, the safest course is to check potential wrinkle cures with your doctor.

Don't drown yourself.

There are a lot of antiwrinkle myths floating around: One of them is to drink as much water as you possibly can. While drinking a lot of water is beneficial in many ways, as far as wrinkles are concerned it won't do any good.

Eat right.

It's a fact: The right foods and the right vitamin supplements are not going to make your wrinkles disappear. Now that you understand that reality, you may find consolation in learning that a proper diet can help promote healthy-looking skin at any age. Vitamin A nourishes skin and underlying mucous membranes: fortified milk, carrots, fish, and cantaloupe are excellent sources. Vitamins B_3 and B_6 also promote healthy skin. They are found in bananas, poultry, whole-grain breads and cereals, and dairy products.

Don't bother with facial exercises.

The old "stretch your mouth and neck as taut as you can" routine just doesn't do a thing for wrinkles. In fact, it can promote wrinkling by making lines and creases in your face more pronounced. Facial massages may feel luxurious, but they won't help your wrinkles.

Deflate your bags.

The wrinkly bags under your eyes are caused by an accumulation of fluid. They become more pronounced with age because your skin loses elasticity and sags, increasing the puffiness. Short of surgery, there is no way to get rid of these bags, but there are some things you can do to make the puffiness a little less pronounced. Among them: Avoid, if possible, cortisone and other medications that promote fluid retention; avoid cigarette smoke and other pollutants that can aggravate the puffiness; and elevate your head on an extra pillow to allow the area to drain a bit overnight.●

YEAST INFECTIONS

15 HELPFUL HINTS

If you've turned to this page, you are probably a woman. Men can get yeast infections, too, but this is a trial ordinarily limited to the female side of the population. Here are the signs that alert you to the presence of a yeast infection, or candidiasis: You have a burning, intense itching in your genital area. Your vagina is red and perhaps a bit swollen. Skin on the inside of your thighs may be irritated and red. You notice that your discharge smells a bit like a loaf of bread baking. Yes, that's right: A yeast infection can make your discharge smell yeasty, like the critical ingredient in bread. But there is nothing amusing about this vaginal irritation. Many women suffer these yeast, or fungal, infections repeatedly. Now that you are over 50, the problem could even be compounded by the change in your hormones as you move through menopause.

What causes yeast infections? A combination of factors. The natural balance of normally occurring bacteria in the vagina can be upset when your immunity is low and especially when you are taking antibiotics for another health problem. Antibiotics can actually kill the "good" bacteria in the vagina that help to maintain a desirable acid/alkali (or pH) balance. A number of other culprits can be blamed for causing yeast infections, including physical or emotional stress, chemicals, diet, and hormonal ups and downs. Some women are more prone to infections around the time of their periods. Obesity, diabetes, and menopause can be factors.

Be careful about diagnosing yourself. You may have something besides an ordinary yeast infection. There are three common vaginal infections: 1) candidiasis, or the yeast infection described in the opening paragraph; 2) bacterial vaginosis, also known as nonspecific vaginitis; and 3) trichomoniasis, caused by a parasite. You could also have a sexually transmitted disease like chlamydia, gonorrhea, or syphilis. Don't take chances. These conditions are always annoying, could be embarrassing, and are possibly more dangerous than you think. The sooner you know exactly what you have, the sooner you can receive treatment and feel better. If you notice that any of your symptoms is unusual—your discharge smells fishy rather than yeasty, for instance—call your gynecologist and start off with the right diagnosis. In the meantime, if you're pretty certain about having a case of candidiasis, here are some suggestions to consider.

Don't douche.

Vinegar douches are often recommended as a way to correct the pH balance in your vagina. Most of the time, however, yeast can grow and thrive in a normal pH vaginal environment. Taking steps to correct what may be an imbalance in order to stop yeast growth makes no sense. Sometimes douching can actually irritate the delicate membranes of your genital tract.

Buy a nonprescription cream.

Pharmaceutical companies have produced several medications that effectively treat yeast infections. Look for products containing miconazole or clotrimazole. These drugs will work to eliminate the fungus—if you follow through on the entire course of treatment: Don't stop using the medication as soon as your symptoms disappear. Some doctors recommend that these antifungal medications be used before and after your period if you have recurrent yeast infections. Speak with your physician if you are considering this kind of routine. Meanwhile, if itching is driving you crazy, ask your pharmacist to recommend an anti-itch cream. If you've made an appointment to see the gynecologist, however, don't use these products before you go. They could mask your symptoms and make it difficult for your doctor to complete a proper examination. While it's unlikely that you are pregnant and over 50, if there is any chance you could be pregnant, do *not* self-medicate.

Don't overdress.

Yeast organisms thrive in the warm, damp circumstances so typical of your genital area, especially when there is little or no fresh oxygen. Don't wear tight clothing that restricts the flow of air. When you go to bed at night, take off your panties so air can more easily circulate in this area and make it less hospitable to the yeast organisms.

Go natural.

Weed out clothes made of synthetic materials from your wardrobe and wear only 100 percent cotton. Your underpants should be loose fitting and all cotton. Cotton fabric allows your skin to "breathe" easier, allowing oxygen near the infection site. If you need to wear pantyhose or stockings, be sure they have a cotton crotch. When you are at home and relaxing, exchange the pantyhose for cotton fabrics.

Bet on boric acid.

Research has demonstrated that boric acid can be a harmless and inexpensive remedy for yeast infections. Boric acid capsules can be used as suppositories, in-

Call the Doctor

○ ○ ○

Vaginal infections can be embarrassing. You may not want to share your bad news with anyone, not even your physician. Now that over-the-counter medication is available so readily, it's easy to consider skipping the important call to your gynecologist. It'll be gone in two weeks, you rationalize. If you recognize this thought process, then take the following warning signs very seriously. Call the doctor if:

- You are not noticeably improved in three days.

- You are experiencing severe pain in the abdominal area.

- Your discharge is bloody as well as yeasty during acute stages of the infection.

- Discharge persists after two weeks of self-treatment and smells fishy, not yeasty.

- You may have been exposed to a sexually transmitted disease, you have begun a new sexual relationship, or there is a possibility that your current partner has another sexual partner.

- Your yeast infections seem to be nonstop. This may indicate that a diabetic condition is contributing to your genital problems.

- Your discharge is thin, foamy, grayish, or yellow.

- You show any signs of pelvic inflammatory disease (PID), an infection of the uterus, fallopian tubes, or ovaries that can cause scarring and even death if it spreads to your circulatory system. Call immediately if you have fever, chills, lower abdominal pain or tenderness, back pain, spotting, pain during or after intercourse, and puslike vaginal discharge.

serted into the vagina once a day as directed. Be sure to discuss this remedy with your doctor: There are certain precautions regarding the use of boric acid that you should be aware of, such as avoiding contact with the eyes. You also need to know appropriate dosage recommendations.

Wash away discharge.

Yeast infections are certainly irritating, and the secretions produced during these flare-ups can actually add to the inflammation at your vaginal opening or on your inner thighs. You may need medication to clear up the internal infection, but you can ease your agony a bit by cleaning away any caked or dried discharge with water. Dry yourself thoroughly and change your underwear frequently.

Don't scratch.

Older women are more prone to a condition called pruritus vulvae, or itchy vagina. Initially brought on by a drop in estrogen or perhaps a yeast infection, the itchiness will only get worse if you keep scratching. You could end up in a very private battle with yourself, trying not to itch or scratch. Use only warm or even cool water to wash. Beware of anesthetic creams or sprays, which can cause allergic reactions.

Kick the perfume habit.

The chemicals in scented soaps, colognes, feminine hygiene sprays, and any product containing perfumes, including some toilet papers, can irritate the sensitive membranes of your genital area. Perfumes contain alcohol and so many scented ingredients that they can throw off your vagina's natural pH balance. Even bath bubbles, oils, and salts will rob your skin of its natural ability to fight off infections.

Keep scrupulously clean.

Before and after making love, you should bathe your genital area. Ask your partner to wash up as well, because yeast infections can be passed between partners. Uncircumcised men can carry yeast infections in the foreskins of their penises.

Don't make love.

When you are in an acute stage of the infection, postpone lovemaking. Intercourse will hurt, and you could be saving your special someone from the yeast hassle.

Consider condoms.

When you are feeling better and wish to use a contraceptive, have your partner use unribbed, unlubricated condoms, which offer the best protection from yeast infections for both of you. Avoid chemically irritating lubricants or jellies, however, and note that contraceptive sponges and birth control pills have been linked to a higher risk of yeast infections. If you are on hormone replacement therapy for menopause, discuss the situation with your gynecologist.

Urinate after lovemaking.

Urinating after sex helps flush out the germs in your urethra, protecting you from urinary tract infections. Your aim is to keep yourself free of any urinary or genital infections, including the ones caused by yeast.

Change toilet habits.

After using the toilet, wipe your genital area from front to back to make sure that you keep germs away from your vagina.

Take a sitz bath.

Sit in a tub of shallow warm water. Add some salt and a little vinegar. You don't need much—about half a cup of each will be fine.

Scrub your underwear.

Candida albicans, the organism responsible for your misery, can sometimes survive normal laundering, especially if you've been using mild detergents and warm or cold water in your machine. You need heat, and plenty of it, to kill these critters. Consider boiling the underwear in a pot on your stove if you've recently gone through a particularly acute infection. If you put them in the laundry, use bleach, put extra detergent on the crotches of your underpants, then run your clothes through the rinse cycle twice. Residual bleach on your underwear can cause significant irritation.●

INDEX